Heavenly Stories

DIVINATIONS: REREADING LATE ANCIENT RELIGION

Series Editors: Daniel Boyarin, Virginia Burrus, Derek Krueger

A complete list of books in the series is available from the publisher.

HEAVENLY STORIES

Tiered Salvation in the New Testament
and Ancient Christianity

ALEXANDER KOCAR

PENN

UNIVERSITY OF PENNSYLVANIA PRESS

PHILADELPHIA

Published by
University of Pennsylvania Press
Philadelphia, Pennsylvania 19104-4112
www.upenn.edu/pennpress

Printed in the United States of America on acid-free paper
10 9 8 7 6 5 4 3 2 1

A Cataloging-in-Publication record is available from the
Library of Congress
ISBN 978-0-8122-5326-9

Contents

Introduction

Differing Salvations, Differing Ethics

> The timequake of 2001 was a cosmic charley horse in the
> sinews of Destiny. At what was in New York City 2:27 P.M. on
> February 13th of that year, the Universe suffered a crisis in
> self-confidence. . . . It suddenly shrunk ten years. It zapped me
> and everybody else back to February 17th, 1991. . . . That the rerun
> lasted ten years, short a mere four days, some are saying now, is
> proof there is a God.
>
> —Kurt Vonnegut, *Timequake*

Heavenly Stories with Fixed Endings

The conceit of Kurt Vonnegut's *Timequake* is that the universe has suddenly
contracted instead of continuing to expand; the result of this is that we
must all repeat a ten-year chunk of time. Starting on February 13th in 2001,
everyone must go back to 1991 and do the last ten years over again. An
added wrinkle is that there is no free will. Everyone must repeat the last ten
years *exactly* how they happened before. We are bound to make the same
mistakes, suffer the same tragedies, and enjoy the same hollow triumphs.
Vonnegut has set up this apparent tragic loss of freedom to lambast the very
idea of free will.[1] We like to believe that we would do things differently, but
chances are, according to Vonnegut, we would have done the whole thing
the same way again anyways.[2]

By writing a story with a fixed ending—we know from the start of the
story about the rerun of the universe and the ending of the book at a writers'
retreat in Rhode Island—Vonnegut could fluctuate among various times

and topics in a way that both disorients and engages the reader. Ironically for a novel suffused with personal information, Vonnegut frequently castigates the reader for our predilection toward focusing on ourselves and our inner struggles instead of worrying about the world at large and society's issues.[3] In this way, Vonnegut created a story about a fantastical absence of free will to rebuke society's lack of will to improve itself. *Timequake*'s fixed ending and Vonnegut's spasmodic storytelling not only entertain the reader but help to convey and reinforce this central moral claim: we are complacent and thus complicit in quotidian hypocrisies and injustices.[4]

Implicit in the linearity of Vonnegut's *Timequake* as well as a number of his other works—for example, *The Sirens of Titan*, *Slaughterhouse-Five*, *Mother Night*—is that we play specific, inescapable roles in the story of the universe. Even should we come "unstuck in time," we would simply find ourselves at different points on the same track, destined for an ending that is and has always been fixed. What is remarkable about these novels—and likely explains their moral force—is that when you know how things *will* turn out, the narrative intrigue focuses instead on how we get there and what sort of characters and actions drive the narrative toward its inevitable end. Vonnegut uses the fixedness of his narratives not only to highlight the banal complacency and even depravity of everyday society but also to motivate his readers toward discrete moral values and practices.

The irony of stories with fixed endings, then, is that rather than undermining our agency or our sense of belonging to the world they can underscore our responsibility for and our role in making the world what we believe it should be. Yes, the narrative is predetermined, but it cannot end without us, the ones who matter, playing the roles we were destined to play.[5] This assurance of our own purpose and suitable end also helps to justify any suffering experienced along the way. This final observation builds upon anthropologist Michael Jackson's insights regarding the ability of storytelling to absorb, reinterpret, and integrate trauma into communal, therapeutic narratives.

> Though stories may concern events that seem to have singled a person out, isolated and privatized his or her experience, storytelling is, in the final analysis, a social act. Stories are composed and recounted, their meanings negotiated and renegotiated, within circles of kinsmen and friends. Like religions, they not only allow people to unburden themselves of private griefs in a context of

concerted activity; they bind people together in terms of meanings that are collectively hammered out. It is this sharing in the
reliving of a tragedy, this sense of communing in a common loss,
that gives stories their power, not to forgive or redeem the past
but to unite the living in the simple affirmation that they exist,
that they survived.[6]

Also, as Jackson demonstrates at length, stories are fundamentally "inter-
subjective" insofar as they can bridge the gap between the individual and her
community.[7] Reflecting a similar dynamic, the narratives explored in this
study—despite having fixed endings—are not static but interact dialectically with the circumstances of their authors as they attempted to navigate
their (perhaps putative) communities through various pitfalls along the
road by creatively course correcting and modifying how their stories end
accordingly.[8]

The texts that are the focus of this book—like so many of Vonnegut's
novels—are moralizing works with fixed endings. This study examines a
series of ancient Jewish and Christian authors who wrote teleological stories, or stories with fixed endings, to encourage their readers toward specific
ethical conduct. For each of the case studies examined in this book, the
fixed end point of their narratives is a divided heaven or multiple heavens,
where the saved enjoy greater or lesser rewards. Furthermore, just as there
was more than one heaven or salvific reward, there were multiple types of
ethical conduct, tailored to whether you were a Jew or a gentile, a saint or a
sinner, a spiritual (pneumatic) or merely soulish (psychic) person. A saint
will enjoy a higher level of salvation because she behaved differently than a
repentant sinner. Adding a soteriological element to Vonnegut, what sort of
character you were in the drama of salvation does not change at the end:
saints will remain saints, and sinners will remain sinners, and each class will
enjoy a different level of salvation.

To be clear: by a higher level of salvation, I do not always mean a higher
space in heaven.[9] There are myriad ways of describing equal and unequal
salvation. Consider an example of each from the Gospels of Matthew and
John, respectively. According to the parable of the workers in the vineyard,
a landowner pays all of his workers—despite great differences in how long
they each worked—the same wage (Matt. 20:1–15). "And on receiving [the
usual wage] they grumbled at the landowner saying, 'These last worked only
one hour, and you have made them equal to us who have borne the burden

of the day and the scorching heat.'"[10] This metaphor for equal salvation prompts complaints among the characters of the story who lament this apparent injustice. Their sentiment is echoed in John's inclusion of Jesus's words of comfort to his disciples in John 14:1–2. Just after Jesus reveals that Peter will deny him, his disciples become agitated. Jesus assures them, "Do not let your heart be troubled. Believe in God; believe also in me. In my Father's house are many dwelling places; if it were not so, would I have told you I go to prepare a place for you?" Despite Peter's less virtuous actions, Jesus consoles him that there is still a place for him among the saved. Nevertheless, this difference in rooms implies a hierarchy of salvation, and that one's heavenly reward is somehow tailored to one's conduct.[11] As we shall see throughout this book, these salvific hierarchies are often represented through metaphors, such as a tower, a tree, or a city.

In Part I (Chapters 1–2) I shall consider two Jewish followers of Jesus, the Apostle Paul and John of Patmos, as they envision and articulate God's plan for the salvation of Israel and the Nations. The crux for both authors was how to preserve and balance Israel's special status against the inclusion of gentiles qua gentiles. In Part II (Chapters 3–4), I examine the problem of saints and sinners living alongside each other in second-century Christian communities. Two early Christian texts, the "orthodox" *Shepherd of Hermas* and the "heretical" *Apocryphon of John*, constructed higher and lower levels of salvation to account for this ethical variance. And finally, in Part III (Chapters 5–6), I explicate the practice of an early Christian movement—most often called Valentinian—of dividing humanity into three types or natures. In particular, I focus on three texts: *The Excerpts of Theodotus*, the *Tripartite Tractate*, and Heracleon's *Commentary on the Gospel of John*. I argue that their tripartite division, typically seen as indicative of a determinist soteriology ("saved by nature"), was in fact a complex explanation of the missionizing successes and failures of this early Christian group.

Each of these authors solves specific social problems or ethical questions in light of how things will turn out in the end for whole groups of people.[12] That is, they all describe corporate salvation where salvific ends are tailored specifically to classes or types of persons, not individuals. They all present, with varying degrees of emphasis, teleological narratives that lay out different sorts of persons and the roles they play and will play—for good and evil—in the unfolding of salvation history. In order to be morally praiseworthy, a person must understand and play the role assigned to him or her. To put this another way and borrowing from an influential modern theologian and ethicist, the only freedom that truly matters is selecting the story we choose to believe in and our role in that story.[13] We can perhaps modify the narrative arc through revelation or reinterpretation, but we find meaning and purpose by situating ourselves in a story whose ending is fixed.[14]

The possible roles and the narratives themselves are particular to each author and products of specific, historical milieus. The portrayal of specific virtues and vices, differing ethical roles and standards, and various means to be saved all are indicative of the specific contexts and problems these authors were seeking to address. By examining the manner in which, for example, Paul or the *Shepherd of Hermas* has each constructed a cast of dramatis personae and located these characters in the drama of salvation history, we can understand better each author's ideological commitments and historical contexts.[15] Thus, in addition to elucidating the logic of these texts as narratives, we will also gain valuable insights into the social contexts and aims of their authors.

Finally, by organizing this book around the understudied typological feature of higher and lower levels of salvation, I hope to add nuance to a number of familiar questions and debates. To this end, we will compare odd or uncommon conversation partners (e.g., Paul and John or the *Shepherd of Hermas* and the *Apocryphon of John*) and break up texts and authors traditionally interpreted as saying the same things (e.g., the *Tripartite Tractate/ Excerpts of Theodotus* and Heracleon). This is all meant to complicate certain enduring dichotomies in the study of the New Testament and early Christianity—for example, universalism vs. particularism, orthodoxy vs. heresy, and free will vs. determinism. In what follows, I will outline how the chapters in this book offer paths past these misleading binaries.

The Anachronisms of Universalism and Particularism

In his thought-provoking book on the Apostle Paul, Daniel Boyarin asserts: "Paul was motivated by a Hellenistic desire for the One, which among other things produced an ideal of a universal human essence, beyond difference and hierarchy."[16] Due to his "Hellenizing" worldview, this Paul was a revolutionary thinker who sought to abolish all hierarchy and difference.[17] Similar characterizations of the Apostle Paul as an anthropological and soteriological universalist reappear throughout Pauline studies.[18] In this context, universalism connotes the radical equality or sameness of all humanity (Gal. 3:28:

"There is no longer Jew or Greek, no longer slave or free, no longer male and female; for all of you are one in Christ Jesus") and a uniform standard for salvation for all of humanity (1 Cor. 15:22: "For just as all die in Adam, so all will be made alive in Christ").[19] In other words, just as there is a single portrait of humanity, so too is there a singular source of salvation through Jesus Christ. Therefore, since every person is equal and saved by the same means, then, so it is argued, this entails a single set of criteria—variously conceived as exclusively soteriological or soteriological and ethical—according to which each person will be judged and thereby held morally accountable.[20] As a result, *this* Paul has rejected Judaism and its particularism in favor of a new and universal religion where salvation is available to every person on the same soteriological (and ethical) grounds.[21]

Although this perspective has no shortage of proponents, it does not make the best sense of our evidence. First, Paul could not reject "Judaism" in this sense because Paul's Judaism was not a reified and doctrinally bounded belief system that could be straightforwardly rejected in favor of another anachronistically formulated category, Christianity.[22] Second, although Paul does believe that Jews and gentiles are saved insofar as they become coheirs to the promise made to Abraham by participating in Christ (Abraham's seed) through baptism (Gal. 3:29), this does not entail a radical and totalizing universalism that eliminates social, ethical, or even eschatological difference.[23] For Paul, soteriology and ethics are related, but they do not have a strictly causal relationship where one (ethics) determines or earns the other (salvation). Nor does one (salvation) necessarily subsume or compress the other (ethics) into a uniform system wherein ethics is secondary and contingent insofar as they are only how one stays "in" the single saved people.[24] Third and finally, there is not a totalizing salvific path that transcends or subtracts all ethnic or eschatological difference in the service of a single soteriological and ethical system; instead, we find in Paul's letters—and John's Apocalypse—different timelines and different standards for appropriate conduct for Jews and gentiles, despite the fact that both share a single means, Jesus Christ, for salvation.[25]

With these points in mind, I will examine the complex soteriological and ethical views of Paul and the structurally similar views of his first-century Jewish compatriot John of Patmos as each described the eschatological salvation of the Nations and Israel. Both Paul the Apostle and John of Patmos differentiated between and prioritized the salvation of Israel over that of the Nations.[26] Paul programmatically underscored this priority at the onset of his Letter to the Romans (1:16; cf. 2:9–10; 9:24; 15:8–9) by noting that salvation (σωτηρία) comes first to the Jew and then to the Greek (Ἰουδαίῳ τε πρῶτον καὶ Ἕλληνι).[27] At the climax of his narrative of salvation history in Romans 11, Paul emphasized again Israel's salvific priority insofar as *all* of Israel will be saved while only the *full number* of gentiles (τὸ πλήρωμα τῶν ἐθνῶν) may be engrafted onto the metaphorical olive tree that represents the salvation reserved for Israel.[28]

John of Patmos similarly divided all of humanity into two groups—Jew and gentile—and maintained a salvific hierarchy between the two. Drawing upon the language of a holy war census in Revelation 7, John enumerated and thereby highlighted the 144,000 (12,000 from each of the restored twelve tribes of Israel) of the saved before describing the secondary and subordinate participation of the gentiles. In the eschatological vision of Revelation 21–22, John further described this hierarchical relationship by appealing to the concentric space of a new earth with a new Jerusalem as its center in order to accentuate how in the eschaton redeemed Jews and gentiles will play different roles: some Jews will serve as priests in the restored Temple, while saved gentiles, in accordance with Isaiah 60, will offer homage as repentant pilgrims.[29]

It was a given, according to Paul and John, that God has a special interest in the salvation of Israel over and above any who might be saved from the Nations. What remained to be elaborated were how all the puzzle pieces, culled from biblical prophecies, fit together, and what their final pictures meant.[30] What is God's plan to save Israel and the Nations, and what role(s) must each group play as the drama of salvation history enters its final stage(s)?

Clearly influencing their narratives, John and Paul interpreted the unfolding story of salvation history and the imminent end of the current age through the lens of Jewish scriptures and prophecies about the restoration of Israel and the ingathering of the Nations. Thus, Paul's and John's writings were not universal or timeless works. They each believed they were living in *the* special epoch in which God's promises to Israel had begun to be fulfilled (e.g., 1 Cor. 7:29–31; Rev. 1:3). Jesus Christ had initiated the eschaton, and the "firstfruits" of what would soon happen on a full scale have already begun to appear.[31]

Events, however, were not unfolding precisely as they expected. Jesus's parousia had not yet arrived, and God's enemies seemed to be prospering. Consequently, both John and Paul had to improvise and creatively adapt their exegetical expectations in an effort to reconcile them with their experiences.[32]

J. Christiaan Beker's hermeneutic of coherence and contingency is instructive.[33] Both Paul and John were committed to the truth of salvation history, the shape and content of which have been revealed throughout Jewish scriptures. Both authors, however, had to revise and adjust their expectations for salvation history dialectically in light of real world circumstances. Nonetheless, both John and Paul *know* that the final chapter of salvation history is unfolding all around, and what's more, they *know* how each member or group from the cast of characters is supposed to behave and what their end(s) will be.[34]

Despite sharing an organizing belief in higher and lower levels of salvation, John and Paul addressed themselves to different audiences.[35] As we shall see in Chapter 1, Revelation tells the ethical and soteriological story of several categories of people, ranging from heavenly priests to the eternally damned. John reconciled expectations for gentile salvific inclusion with complex spatial and temporal subordination while all the while underscoring that gentile salvation was not primarily about saving the Nations but was rather *part* of Israel's restoration. Where John devised an eschatological ethic aimed at his Jewish readers, Paul the Apostle wrote and thus formulated an ethic tailored for his gentile audience. In this way, we find a Jewish story about salvation that is intended for consumption by outsiders. Even though he was the Apostle to the gentiles, Paul, nonetheless, prioritized Israel's salvation over and above that of the Nations. There was not an ethnic transformation in Christ: Jews remained Jews and gentiles remained gentiles.[36] Paul creatively reshapes biblical precedent to claim that all—Jews and gentiles—are saved through the same means, namely baptism into Christ; yet, this singular means of salvation does not abrogate the differing ethical standards established for these two groups nor does it overthrow God's favoritism toward Israel.[37]

Over the course of Chapters 1 and 2, we shall investigate the problem of how, why, when, and to what degree gentiles could participate in Israel's impending eschatological redemption, and the social and ethical implications of such theoretical speculation. Although the Jesus movement became a predominantly gentile movement within a few generations after the death of Jesus of Nazareth, I will avoid as much as possible importing anachronistic assumptions shaped by this later development, in particular that the earliest Jesus followers imagined themselves as a "third race" existing alongside Jew and gentile.[38] Instead, by remaining sensitive to the binary between Jew and gentile undergirding the social and soteriological expectations of early Jewish authors such as Paul and John, I will argue that these two authors—the only two we confidently know by name from the whole of the New Testament—maintained differing ethical expectations for Jews and gentiles.

In the first two chapters then, we shall consider the similarities and differences between Paul and John as both wrestled with the theoretical and sociological difficulty of reconciling Israel's pride of place with various prophetic expectations about the eschatological redemption of gentiles. Although both authors similarly endorse what I call salvific hierarchy between Israel and the Nations, their rationales, boundary lines, ethical expectations, and eschatological narratives differ greatly. Much of their conceptual overlap arises because both Paul and John are drawing from and synthesizing many of the same divergent prophetic expectations regarding the salvific status of the gentiles. In this way, each author constructs a composite and "anthologizing" or "allusive" eschatological pastiche concatenating various biblical strands to illustrate and intertextually buttress his own vision for the salvation of gentiles.[39] Both agree, however, that there is a single, predetermined narrative—despite disagreeing about the specifics—and your apparent moral worth is based upon finding and playing your role correctly. There is not a universalizing or one-size-fits-all path toward salvation, but a complex and layered account that assigns different salvations and different ethics to differing groups of people.

Early Christianity Beyond "Orthodoxy" and "Heresy"

Scholarly attempts to explain the wide-ranging diversity of early (ca. second century) Christianity often rely on agonistic metaphors to concretize this amorphous period of competition and debate.[40] One such heuristic metaphor is that of a horse race, in which rival schools or "Christianities" vie for dominance, and one horse—"proto-orthodoxy"—ultimately wins the contest. According to this metaphor, race spectators (historians) observe the diversity of the field and document the relative fitness of each horse (type of Christianity) over the course of the race. This model, however, orients us in such a way that we base our interpretations upon the outcome of the contest—what did proto-orthodoxy do to win, and what did the other contenders (e.g., Marcionites, Valentinians, Sethians, etc.) do to lose? In this way, we infuse proto-orthodoxy's victory with a sense of inevitability, which simultaneously marginalizes the also-rans of early Christianity.[41]

This horse-race metaphor also artificially reifies these competing Christian groups, turning them into "discrete bounded entities that were clearly distinct from one another."[42] Thus, not only should we avoid a teleological perspective that privileges a certain group ("proto-orthodoxy") because it wins our horse race, but we should also question the apparent coherence of these "horses" themselves by highlighting the dynamic and fluid interactions of early Christian figures, groups, practices and ideas. Early Christian authors and groups were not hermetically sealed, but rather, practices, ideas, and texts circulated widely.[43] Many authors who are retrospectively included in the proto-orthodox camp were not in their own context socially or ideologically aligned with one another or unified against other camps; in fact, some figures claimed by later orthodoxy had more in common with their so-called heterodox peers (e.g., Clement of Alexandria and the Valentinians) than they did with each other (e.g., Clement of Alexandria with Ignatius or Irenaeus).[44] So, how do we even begin to describe this dynamic period of competition and growth?

One proposed way forward that has gained a great deal of traction among scholars has been dubbed "identity formation."[45] According to it, we must recognize that social categories previously assumed as static and bounded— such as orthodox and heterodox—are in fact rhetorically created and hotly contested.[46] We should instead concentrate on the discursive strategies— such as producing texts, practicing rituals, and constructing creeds and canons—that enabled ancient persons to devise, maintain, and/or subvert communal boundary lines.[47] Texts, therefore, do not provide unfiltered snapshots of the past, but are instead rhetorically constructed artifacts embedded in contests and debates.

Yet, in compensating for past historiographic errors, we ought not to swing the pendulum in the opposite direction so far as to make it impossible to speak of *any* ancient groups or communities.[48] While certainly rhetorical, such discursive strategies were contingent upon ancient practices (e.g., rituals of initiation or excommunication, catechetical instruction, the circulation or repression of certain texts, etc.), which in turn affected the social realities and communal life of early Christians.[49] Moreover, we may not know how successful our texts and authors were at forming like-minded communities, but we do know that this was important to them.[50] How, then, should we balance sensitivity to the fragmentary and messy evidence of ancient authors and thinkers—especially when so many bounded categories are misleading—with our role as modern historians committed to reconstructing, as much as possible, the interplay of values and behavior in the daily lives of our objects of study?[51]

There is no one-size-fits-all solution. Instead, the sorts of questions we want answered should determine how we use these fraught categories. In Chapters 3 and 4, I intentionally set such orienting categories aside to look at higher and lower levels of salvation as a rhetorical strategy among second-century Christian house-churches. In Chapters 5 and 6, I depend upon the category of Valentinian to explore possible causes for evident, internal diversity within this specific early Christian group. I have tailored my approach to the sorts of questions I—as the modern historian—want to pursue.

In the first case then, I will discuss the *Apocryphon of John* without connecting it to its broader "textual" or religious community, most often referred to as "Sethians."[52] I will study the rhetorical strategies of the *Apocryphon of John* and the *Shepherd of Hermas* as individual texts, setting out and enforcing mores and social boundaries in their congregations as they met together in house-churches in urban settings.[53] Despite similarities in imagined audience and social setting, the *Apocryphon of John* is still most often categorized as belonging to a fundamentally non-Christian social organization (e.g., an "audience cult," reclusive sect, or mystery cult), whereas the *Shepherd of Hermas* is said to belong to a house-church community.[54] This disparity in social setting is due more to presuppositions arising from the heterodoxy vs. orthodoxy divide than to evidence from the texts themselves. I will conclude instead that the *Shepherd of Hermas* and *Apocryphon of John*'s shared solution of higher and lower levels of salvation is a centralizing technology meant to address the problem of ethical variance, both within their tight-knit communities and theoretically around the world.[55]

In Chapters 5 and 6, I will take a different approach and situate the *Tripartite Tractate,* the *Excerpts of Theodotus*, and Heracleon's *Commentary on John* among a group of early Christian teachers, preachers, and prophets called "Valentinians." The name "Valentinians" is meant to indicate their alleged dependence upon a poetic and speculative second-century theologian named Valentinus.[56] "Valentinian," therefore, was not a self-designation, but rather an external and polemical label.[57] In fact, much of our information about the beliefs, practices, and social makeup of these early Christians is derived from hostile sources.[58] In addition to these heresiological sources, we have a half dozen Coptic texts from Nag Hammadi that a consensus of scholars categorize as Valentinian.[59]

This state of the sources raises two related methodological questions. First, what makes a text Valentinian?[60] Second, are some texts, such as the Coptic Nag Hammadi ones, more Valentinian than others or somehow more trustworthy?[61] Rather than settling these two questions, I intend to muddy the waters a bit more, by showing the diversity and contingency of views among Valentinian authors. As such, I will examine the social function of their tripartite anthropology, found among both patristic and non-patristic sources. Thus, I will consider texts often thought to say or mean the same thing, in order to demonstrate the situatedness and strategic use of the language of three natures.

Free Will vs. Determinism

While chastising one of his favorite opponents—the followers of Basilides—for incorrectly "regarding faith as a natural disposition, though also making it a matter of election,"[62] Clement of Alexandria also rebuked the Valentinians for similarly alleging that, due to their superior knowledge, they are "saved by nature."[63] According to Clement, however, if faith is predetermined as a natural disposition and not "the right action of a free choice," then there is no basis for salvific reward or condemnation, and thus there can be no ethical responsibility.

> In the [case of the Valentinians and Basilideans], faith is no longer the right action of a free choice, [but is instead] a natural superiority; the person without faith is not responsible and will not meet his just consequences; the person with faith is not responsible; the whole essential difference between faith and unfaith could not be a matter of praise or blame if you look at it rightly, being a foreordaining natural necessity determined by a universal power. We are like lifeless puppets controlled by natural forces. It is a predetermined necessity that forces the lack of willing.[64]

In this way, Clement skillfully deployed a stock polemic, namely the *argos logos*, to claim that the beliefs of his opponents are irreconcilable with basic modes of articulating ethical responsibility, such as praise and blame.[65]

Often marshaled against the Stoics, the *argos logos*, or lazy argument, was a potent and rhetorically effective critique of so-called deterministic cosmologies.[66] In short, the *argos logos* grounds ethical responsibility in autonomy and freedom of action and/or choice. If all events and actions are the necessary consequences of a preceding series of causes, then we are nothing more than Clement's "puppets" of fate.[67] Consequently, so the argument goes, it would be absurd to assess predetermined and ineluctable outcomes as either morally praiseworthy or blameworthy.[68] All events that have or will ever happen are simply the result of a preceding and inescapable series of causes; there is no human agency, and thus there is no moral responsibility.[69]

Too often "free will" is treated as the sine qua non of ethics: if I am not free to choose otherwise, how can I be responsible for what I do?[70] Putting aside whether the ability to choose otherwise is a sufficient placeholder for the idea of a free will, this formulation assumes that one mode of assigning praise or blame is the *only* way.[71] Yet, we hear about heroes who run into danger to save others later respond to questions about their remarkable conduct by claiming that they had no choice: they let their instincts or training take over, or they simply felt compelled do to the right thing. Should we withhold praise, since character and training took over, and their conduct was not the product of a completely autonomous free will? Of course not. What we should do is recognize is that there is more than one framework for talking about responsibility and ethics.[72]

There is an obvious tension between indeterminate freedom, especially the freedom to have chosen otherwise, and teleological narratives. Teleological narratives, like those of the Apostle Paul and John of Patmos, tell certain types of stories that answer specific questions—for example, What is God's plan for the world? How do the saved behave? How do the damned behave? Consequently, what is important for Paul and John is getting the script right and playing the correct role. They are extolling their readers to moral excellence and offering emotional consolation amid suffering; they are not interested in freedom for the sake of freedom, or how things could be otherwise. Their scripts, moreover, and the differing ethical frameworks undergirding them, privilege varying ideas or concepts, and these emphases often reflect the ideological contexts and aims of their authors.[73]

Much of the previous research and discussion about Valentinian ethics and soteriology has been influenced by the heresiological cliché that

Valentinians, without the capacity to choose otherwise, were determinists with no sense of moral accountability.[74] As a result, subsequent scholars have debated the veracity of this polemic, disputing whether it was a deliberate mischaracterization or an accurate description. Rather than playing a zero-sum game of right or wrong, I think it more advantageous to consider Valentinians and their opponents as espousing competing and at times incompatible ideologies. In other words, the Valentinians privileged different commitments, and even different rationales, than their opponents.[75] Once we uncover these underlying commitments and rationales, we can better understand the social position and ethical ideals of Valentinians and their opponents.

As we shall see in Chapters 5 and 6, the *Excerpts of Theodotus,* the *Tripartite Tractate*, and Heracleon's *Commentary on John* all distinguished between three types of humanity. Rather than preclude moral praise or blame, however, their tripartite division of humanity was a vital part of their ethics. Their tripartite anthropology privileged certain types of conduct (e.g., missionary work), and the overall linear progression of salvation history over and above other, *incompatible* ideological commitments (e.g., *voluntary* choices) held by some opponents of these Valentinians. As we shall see in Chapter 5, both the Valentinians and their heresiological opponents made rational arguments in support of competing ethical frameworks, thereby demonstrating the plurality of ethical frameworks in antiquity.

Furthermore, Chapter 6 shows that differing literary genres (e.g., cosmological or commentarial texts) also affected how these Valentinian texts and authors articulated their ethical and soteriological views. For example, the *Tripartite Tractate* is a totalizing narrative that begins with protology and concludes with the eschatological reunification of creation; in between it describes every successive benchmark on the linear path of salvation. As such, it is a teleological narrative that claims to show how things will turn out by explaining how they began and vice versa. Because the *Tripartite Tractate* narrates how things were, are, and will be, it is not interested in freedom for the sake of freedom, or how things could be otherwise.[76] Heracleon, in contrast, wrote a biblical commentary. Because of this difference in genre, Heracleon's views differ from the *Excerpts of Theodotus* and the *Tripartite Tractate* in distinctive ways. Thus, once we recognize that there was a multitude of frameworks and genres for writing texts meant to spur readers toward various kinds of ethical conduct, we must also jettison the simple binary of right or wrong, free will or determinism, in how we categorize ancient thinkers and their texts.

The Aesthetics and Ethics of Higher
and Lower Levels of Salvation

Robert Frost infamously compared writing in free verse to playing tennis without a net. True poetry, according to Frost, demanded a particular aesthetic that adhered to accepted norms, such as meter and rhyme schemes. As a prominent poet himself, Frost felt empowered to police and even enforce what constituted poetry. While I do not intend to wade into the deep and treacherous waters of poetry and its aesthetics, I find this brief anecdote illuminating for how I think about stories with higher and lower levels of salvation. It was fundamentally an aesthetic choice.[77] The authors I consider in this study—while some were certainly dependent upon others—do not represent a coherent historical movement or tradition.[78] Instead, and drawing out the analogy with Frost, they are a group of writers who employed a soteriological scheme—suited to their own tastes and contexts[79]—that was later suppressed and/or misunderstood by what became orthodox Christianity.[80]

Contrary to polemics later marshaled against them, stories with fixed endings of higher and lower levels of salvation could—paradoxically—provide their authors with the creative freedom to devise practical solutions, tailored to their specific ethical dilemmas. Has God radically transformed salvation history, reneging on his past promises and erasing prior ethical expectations? Is it really practical to expect everyone to be morally perfect? What happens when you fail or come up short at your divine calling? Rather than dismissing them as determinist, particularist, or heretical, we will examine these authors as they deployed malleable metaphors of salvation as a sophisticated and textured answer to these questions. Although this soteriological scheme or aesthetic fell out of favor with many early Christian arbiters of taste, this does not change that—for many ancient Jews and Christians—the afterlife was far more complicated than a simple binary between heaven and hell.

PART I

The Salvation of Jews
and Gentiles

Higher and Lower Levels of Salvation in the Letters of the
Apostle Paul and John of Patmos's Revelation

Chapter 1

John's Heavenly City

The Book of Revelation and Jewish Narratives
of Salvation

And I saw all the sheep that remained. And all the animals on the
earth and all the birds of heaven were falling down and worshipping the sheep and making petitions to them and obeying them in
everything. . . . And the Lord of the sheep rejoiced greatly because
they were good and returned to that house. . . . And I saw how a
white bull was born, and its horns were large. And all the wild
beasts and all the birds of heaven were afraid of it and made
petition to it continually. And I saw until all their species were
changed, and they all become white cattle. And the first one
became leader among them . . . and the Lord of the sheep rejoiced
over it and over all the cattle.

—1 Enoch 90:30–38

Judaism and Jewish Views of Gentile Salvation

There is scholarly disagreement over how best to interpret the above passage
from a section of 1 Enoch, conventionally referred to as the *Animal Apocalypse*.
Following the time of Jacob, according to the text, there was a persistent
difference between Israel, represented by sheep, and the Nations, often portrayed as wild animals.[1] The text's retelling of Israel's turbulent past culminates with the sudden and triumphant appearance of white cattle at 1 Enoch
90:37. Yet, what does this theriological and soteriological transformation

entail for ethnic identities? Are only the Jewish people transformed into these white cattle?[2] Did the *Animal Apocalypse* obliquely endorse a notion of universal salvation wherein all the saved—whether Jew or gentile—are uniformally transformed into white cattle and thereby recover Adam's lost glory?[3] Or did the *Animal Apocalypse*, despite acknowledging that some gentiles may be transformed into redeemable bovines, preserve the difference between Jews (sheep) and saved gentiles (cattle), even into the eschaton?[4] In this particular case, the second interpretation seems to be the most straightforward reading of this text.[5] What is important for our purposes here, however, is that all three of these options are present in ancient Jewish texts, and it is with this plurality of possible salvific narratives in mind that we shall consider the views of John of Patmos and Paul the Apostle.

Starting with John, we shall situate him within the context of first-century Judaism, consider his salvific hierarchies, and explicate his expectations for different standards of conduct as he tailored them to distinct groups. Although I shall endeavor to make sense of some of John's visions and their place in his overall narrative, I am not claiming to present here a systematic or comprehensive account of all the threads running throughout Revelation. John was not a systematic thinker, and there are any number of lacunae in the account I am offering.[6] As Helmut Koester rightly noted, John's narrative is propelled by images and metaphors, not "rational sequences, logical progression, and judicious conclusions."[7] As such, this chapter will attempt to make sense of John's image-based language of difference and priority. In particular, we shall consider not only how John, drawing upon but also redeploying biblical visions of the eschaton,[8] has constructed hierarchical images meant to console and consolidate his own community, but also how he was seeking to reinforce specific ethical ideals.

There was a wide range of overlapping and sometimes contradictory expectations for gentile involvement in Israel's eschatological redemption and celebration in ancient Judaism, ranging from complete transformation and entrance into the ranks of priests and Levites such as we find in Isaiah 66 to the utter annihilation of all gentiles found in the War Scroll (1QM 1:1–2) or 4 Ezra (12:33; 13:38). John and Paul are somewhere between these two extremes: John envisions gentile involvement, as gentiles, to be closest to the eschatological pilgrimage of Isaiah 60 and thus expects resurrected gentiles to turn to God and to be present at the eschatological celebration at Jerusalem as pilgrims offering veneration.[9] Although both authors expect that some gentiles will be saved insofar as they will participate in Israel's eschatological celebration, both Paul and John emphasize the temporal and spatial subordination of these saved gentiles to Israel. As we will see, Paul and John's soteriology is a continuation—with some modifications—of a strand in biblical and Second Temple Judaism of higher and lower levels of salvation for Jews and gentiles, respectively. To provide a context for their construction of higher and lower levels of salvation, we turn now to consider ancient Judaism and the diversity of fates for the Nations in ancient Jewish thought.

Ancient Judaism

Ancient Judaism was not monolithic.[10] Accordingly, there were several competing and often conflicting streams of traditions and opinions about the eschatological fate of gentiles. For the sake of brevity, I have typologically organized these varying opinions into three synthetic categories on the basis of how they represent the fate of gentiles: utter destruction; equal salvation of all the saved; and finally, higher and lower levels of salvation.[11] To illustrate the general features of each typological category, I will briefly consider a few paradigmatic examples. It is essential, however, to keep in mind that this overview is intended as a brief sketch of the diversity of Judaism in Paul and John's day and thus functions as prologue to my project of situating Paul and John within their broader context; I do not intend to be compendious nor will I be able to consider the numerous instances of texts and authors who transgress and problematize the artificially bounded categories I have created.

Before I consider these three specific typological groupings, a brief outline of what I mean by "Judaism" may be helpful. As numerous studies have shown, ancient Jewish identity is a complex amalgam of ethnic, cultural, and political factors that does not have a unifying objective or empirical criterion or series of criteria that can provide a single definition of what it means to be Jewish.[12] Nonetheless, although Judaism could mean different things to different authors depending on their social location and ideological commitments,[13] the very construction of such a category contributed to Jewish identity formation and boundary drawing.[14] In this way, Judaism or Jewishness could be fashioned and deployed not only to create social and theoretical distance from "outsiders," but also to reinforce and privilege various values and practices among "insiders."[15]

As part of an essentializing binary of us (Jews) and everyone else (gentiles/the Nations),[16] some ancient Jewish authors constructed Jewishness or Judaism on the model of Hellenism, in other words, as a totalizing way of life—encompassing beliefs, practices, and values—that could be learned.[17] "Even if 'Judean' always retained its ethnic meaning, in the Hasmonean period common mode of worship and common way of life became much more important in the new definition of Judean/Jew. Just as a barbarian could become a Hellene through speaking Greek and adopting a Greek way of life, a gentile could become a Jew through worshiping the God of Jerusalem (i.e., believing firmly in God) and/or adopting a Judean way of life (i.e., observing the ancestral laws of the Judeans)."[18] Epitomizing this notion of Judaism, the author of 2 Maccabees promotes a notion of Jewishness that privileges specific features of culture and practice: "[This is] the story of Judas Maccabeus and his brothers, and the purification of the great temple, and the dedication of the altar . . . of those *who fought bravely for Judaism* (τοῖς ὑπὲρ τοῦ Ιουδαϊσμοῦ φιλοτίμως ἀνδραγαθήσασιν), so that though few in number they seized the whole land and pursued the barbarian hoards, and regained the temple famous throughout the world, and liberated the city, and *re-established the laws* that were about to be abolished" (2 Macc. 2:19–22, emphasis added).[19] Nonetheless, despite privileging discrete cultural practices and values—in addition to or sometimes in place of ethnic heritage[20]—this notion of Judaism still aims to reinforce the fundamental binary of Jews and gentiles, thereby demarcating and distinguishing Jewish practice and identity, that is, a Jewish way of life, from that of the Nations.[21] It is with this functional notion of Judaism in mind, as a dynamic and high-stakes means to police boundaries and to privilege certain shared values and practices, that we can make better sense of John and Paul's distinctive views and their place in the broader context of Second Temple Judaism.[22]

Jewish Soteriologies and the Fate(s) of Gentiles

Turning to my first typological category, we note that some ancient Jewish authors affirmed the impending and inescapable eschatological destruction awaiting all gentiles. Emblematic of this perspective is the second-century BCE retelling of the book of Genesis, Jubilees, which recasts the story of Abraham and the significance of circumcision in order to detail the fate of the Nations as follows:

This law is for all the eternal generations and there is no circumcising of days and there is no passing a single day beyond eight days because it is an eternal ordinance ordained and written in the heavenly tablets. And anyone who is born whose own flesh is not circumcised on the eighth day is not from the sons of the covenant, which the Lord made for Abraham, since (he is) from the children of destruction. And there is therefore no sign upon him so that he might belong to the Lord because (he is destined) to be destroyed and annihilated from the earth and to be uprooted from the earth because he has broken the covenant of the Lord our God. (Jub. 15:25–26)[23]

Not only are all gentiles destined for destruction but even *former* gentiles,[24] according to the author of Jubilees, are doomed, since they too were not circumcised on the eighth day.[25] Echoing the "holy seed" ideology of the book of Ezra,[26] Jubilees features a genealogical model for inclusion among Israel.[27] The author of Jubilees goes even further than Ezra in fashioning Israel as a uniquely holy race by likening Israel and her priestly observances to angels and their temple practices in heaven.[28]

Adapting this binary of saved Israel and damned Nations, some texts argue that even some from among ethnic Israel will join the totality of the Nations in perdition. These texts contrast the holiness or piety of Israel (or at least the holy remnant) in order to condemn outsiders, who are portrayed as children of the demonic rulers of the world (the War Scroll 1QM 1:1–2; cf. the Community Rule 1QS 2:4–9) or as people who are sinfully disobedient of God's commandments (4 Ezra).[29] These texts, then, like Jubilees, deploy a salvific binary to help police boundaries and reinforce internal cohesion by emphasizing specific practices and values while forbidding activities that weaken these boundaries.[30]

According to my second typological category, the saved all appear to enjoy undifferentiated salvific rewards:

On this mountain the Lord of hosts will make for all peoples a feast of rich food, a feast of well-aged wines, of rich food filled with marrow, of well-aged wines strained clear. And he will destroy on his mountain the shroud that is cast over all peoples, the sheet that is spread over all nations; he will swallow up death forever. Then the Lord God will wipe away the tears from all

faces, and the disgrace of his people he will take away from all the
earth, for the Lord has spoken. It will be said on the day, "Lo,
this is our God; we have waited for him, so that he might save us.
This is the Lord for whom we have waited; let us be glad and
rejoice in his salvation. For the hand of the Lord will rest on this
mountain." (Isa. 25:6–10a; cf. Isa. 66:21–24)

Although this second typological grouping includes texts that may contain
additional passages more consonant with my third typological grouping,[31] one
apparent constant among these sections that emphasize the relative equality of
this shared salvation is that those saved from among the Nations must transform themselves. This transformation is variously described as a "conversion,"
or perhaps better "reorientation," to monotheism and worship of Israel's God.[32]

This transformation of the Nations appears frequently in contexts
where the authors are illustrating the oneness of God, his total supremacy,
and his universal rule of all creation: "In days to come the mountain of the
Lord's house shall be established as the highest of the mountains, and shall
be raised above the hills; all the Nations shall stream to it. Many people shall
come and say, 'Come let us go up to the mountain of the Lord, to the house
of the God of Jacob; that he may teach us his ways and that we may walk in
his paths.' For out of Zion shall go forth instruction, and the word of the
Lord from Jerusalem. He shall judge between the Nations, and shall arbi-
trate for many peoples" (Isa. 2:2–4; cf. Mic. 4:1–4). Thus, for Isaiah, as well
as a number of other Jewish prophets and writers, the radical inclusiveness
of all of humanity is not exclusively, over even predominantly, about minimizing or leveling out all differences distinguishing Israel from the Nations; rather, the more pressing concern is a theological claim about the
preeminence of Israel's God and the "ways of the Lord."

Isaiah 56 illustrates this theological promotion, stitching together
concern for the foreigner or alien (הַנֵּכָר-בֶּן; LXX: ἀλλογενής) as part of a
demonstration of the superiority of Israel's God and the proper worship of
him: "And the foreigners who join themselves to the Lord, to minister to
him, to love the name of the Lord, and to be his servants, all who keep the
Sabbath and do not profane it, and hold fast my covenant—these I will bring
to my holy mountain, and make them joyful in my house of prayer; their
burnt offerings and their sacrifices will be acceptable on my altar; for my
house shall be called a house of prayer for all Nations (πᾶσιν τοῖς ἔθνεσιν).
Thus says the Lord God, who gathers the outcasts of Israel, I will gather

others to them besides those already gathered" (Isa. 56:6–8). By extension, therefore, this inclusive yet inwardly focused rhetoric praises God's chosen people,[33] and extols them to persevere and withstand current oppression and difficulties until the world is set right again (e.g., Zech. 8:20–23).

Nevertheless, such radical inclusiveness was not unproblematic, nor was it without critique and disagreement.[34] Consequently, a number of texts differentiate and subordinate the salvific rewards meted out to gentiles, whether as proselytes or as gentiles, albeit usually these gentiles have at least become ethical monotheists. The Damascus Document, found in fragments among the Dead Sea Scrolls and the medieval Cairo Genizah, subdivides humanity into four usable but also hierarchical categories: priests, Levites, the whole assembly of Israel, and proselytes (CD XIV:4–5).[35] Although included among the saved, these proselytes are a "marginal group, like the poor and the biblical sojourner."[36] In this way, the Damascus Document maintained important conceptual boundaries among the saved, thereby preserving Israel's distinctiveness and elevated status.

Furthermore, a number of passages—often from authors who elsewhere seemingly endorse undifferentiated salvific rewards—indicate that gentiles may and could be saved as gentiles; yet, in these passages, gentile salvation was subordinate to Israel's and frequently required service to Israel. Although ritual conversion was not always required, it was expected that gentiles undergo some form of transformation or reorientation in order to be saved.[37] Thus, we have a number of texts that claim good gentiles could join in Israel's eschatological celebration, though only in a secondary and subordinate role.[38]

The narrative setting for these higher and lower levels of salvation is often expressed through the motif of eschatological pilgrimage, in which the Nations, after realizing their past errors, pay homage to God and bring reparations to Israel:[39] "Nations (גּוֹיִם; LXX: ἔθνη) shall come to your light and kings to the brightness of your dawn. . . . Foreigners (בְנֵי-נֵכָר; LXX: ἀλλογενεῖς) shall build up your walls, and their kings shall minister to you; for in my wrath I struck you down, but in my favor I have had mercy on you. Your gates shall always be open; day and night they shall not be shut, so that nations shall bring you their wealth, with their kings led in procession. For the nation and kingdom that will not serve you shall perish; those nations shall be utterly laid waste" (Isa. 60:3, 10–12).

A number of Second Temple texts similarly deploy the evocative imagery of this eschatological pilgrimage scene (e.g., 1 En. 10:21, 90:28–38; Pss. Sol. 17:26–34).[40] These eschatological scenes were meant to reassure Jewish readers not only that their current subjugation to and oppression by the Nations would be overcome, but that as part of the eschatological celebration the offending Nations—after they renounced their wickedness and paid for their crimes—would henceforth interact justly with Israel, since it would be Israel that would then have the upper hand (e.g., Philo, *De praemiis et poenis* 164–72). It is significant to note in these pilgrimage scenes that while the Nations play a role in the eschatological celebration of the restored Israel, they do not become Jews, instead remaining gentiles or at least some class of individuals that is fundamentally distinct from saved Jews.[41]

As even this cursory outline of Jewish views about gentile salvation shows, there was no consensus perspective. Furthermore, as I emphasized in each of my three typologies for the fate of gentiles (destruction, equal salvation, and higher and lower salvation), there were various situational and theoretical factors that could affect how these ancient authors devised and discussed gentile soteriology. To paraphrase Lévi-Strauss, gentiles are "good to think with."[42] Thus, we found not only that there was not a single Jewish perspective on whether, where, or how gentiles would be saved, but also that passages discussing gentile salvation were often part of larger or more pressing social and theological arguments, including issues of boundary drawing, demonstrating God's preeminence, or even offering consolation via hope for eschatological restoration and an era of fair dealing with the Nations of the world.[43] To put it another way, there was no foregone or inevitable view to which these Jewish authors *must* adhere.

Revelation and Ancient Judaism

Since a comprehensive study of John of Patmos's relationship to Second Temple Judaism would far exceed the scope of this chapter, I want to emphasize two key points. First, John, as a first-century Jew, saw the world as essentially dichotomous, divided between us (Jews) and them (gentiles). Second, John, like many other ancient Jewish authors, differentiated between the type or degree of salvation promised to Jews and gentiles. For John, certain good gentiles could enjoy salvation, if they repented and turned to the one true God; however, their salvation was secondary to the rewards promised to the elect from among Israel.

Neither of these two points is uncontroversial. Yet, David Frankfurter and John Marshall have laid out excellent cases for rejecting the anachronistic interpretation that John of Patmos was a "Christian" or even "Jewish Christian."[44] In a more recent study building on Frankfurter and Marshall, Martha Himmelfarb succinctly summarizes the issue thusly: "Altogether, it is clear that John continued to embrace many aspects of Jewish practice. There is no positive evidence that he rejected any aspect. Indeed, John addresses his readers as 'those who keep the commandments of God and the faith of Jesus' (Rev. 14:12)."[45] Additionally, Marshall and Frankfurter point also to the presence of ritual language and concerns over purity, the positive use of the label of Jew and Israel, and the absence of the term "Christian."[46]

Without repeating too much of Frankfurter's and Marshall's excellent studies, I would draw particular attention to the distortion that occurs when a third category (Christians, in addition to Jews and gentiles) is added to the text. Suddenly, the story of Israel's redemption has been overwritten and removed from this Jewish apocalyptic text. Now all positive references to Jews, the twelve tribes, and saints refer to the elect (i.e., Christians), thereby erasing Jewish presence from a text narrating the story of Jewish redemption, as predicted by Jewish prophets and enacted by the Jewish God and his Messiah for the benefit of Israel and secondarily for the Nations.[47]

For example, Revelation 7 is a relatively straightforward description (especially for John of Patmos) of the impending redemption of the elect of Israel and the subsequent salvation of gentiles:

> I saw another angel ascending from the rising sun, having the seal of the living God, and he called with a loud voice to the four angels who had been given power to damage the earth and sea, saying: "Do not damage the earth or sea or trees until we have marked the servants of our God with a seal on their foreheads." And I heard the number of those who were sealed, one hundred and forty-four thousand sealed out of every tribe of the people of Israel: From the tribe of Judah twelve thousand sealed; from the tribe of Reuben twelve thousand; from the tribe of Gad twelve thousand; from the tribe of Asher twelve thousand; from the tribe of Naphtali twelve thousand; from the tribe of Manasseh twelve thousand; from the tribe of Simeon twelve thousand; from the tribe of Levi twelve thousand; from the tribe of Issachar twelve thousand; from the tribe of Zebulun twelve thousand; from the tribe of Joseph twelve thousand; from the tribe of Benjamin twelve thousand sealed. After this I looked,

and there was a great multitude that no one could count, from
every nation, from all tribes and peoples and languages, standing
before the throne and before the Lamb, robed in white, with
palm branches in their hands. They cried out in a loud voice,
saying: "Salvation belongs to our God who is seated on the
throne, and to the Lamb!" (Rev. 7:2–10; cf. 14:1–7)

Nevertheless, certain scholars still struggle to insert Christians into this
bipartite story of salvation history:

Ultimately none of the three ways of interpreting the 144,000
survey above (i.e., the 144,000 as the remnant of Jews or Jewish
Christians, as all Christians, or as Christian martyrs) proves to be
entirely convincing . . . few scholars have drawn appropriate
conclusions in considering which Jewish eschatological traditions
provided a model for the author of Rev. 7:4–8 and 14:1–5. In my
view, *the 144,000 of Rev. 7:4–8 represent the particular group of
Christians (including all ages and both genders) who have been specifically protected by God from both divine plagues and human persecution
just before the final tribulation begins and who consequently survive
that tribulation and the great eschatological battle that is the culmina-
tion of that tribulation.*[48]

In this way, John's bipartite worldview is rewritten: Jews have faded from
the picture, and, instead, we have a false dichotomy between saved (Christians) and damned (gentiles and non-Christian Jews) that is anachronistic
and also obscures John's own expectation for social, ethical, and soteriological boundary lines between Jews and gentiles.

Ironically, this line of interpretation alters John's Jewish apocalypse so
much that the only living Jews John explicitly mentions are those whom he
castigates for *not* being true Jews, that is, Christians,[49] in Revelation 2:9 and
3:9.[50] As this argument goes, "the name 'Jews' is denied to the Jewish community in Smyrna. There is no good reason to think here of Judaizers
rather than actual Jews of the local synagogues. Jewish hostility to the early
Christian missionary effort is well attested for both the first and second
century. The name 'Jews' is denied them because the followers of Jesus are
held to be the true Jews."[51] Rather than an opaque, anachronistic, and supersessionist claim that *true* Jews are, in fact, Christians,[52] I am convinced by

the straightforward reasons put forth by Marshall and Frankfurter that, for John, Jews are Jews and non-Jews are non-Jews.[53]

In Revelation 2 and 3, John sees a dangerous group of outsiders purporting to be Jews and perhaps even claiming Jewish salvific priority without *really*—according to John—being Jews.[54] John responds by cleverly subverting his opponents' claims: you are wrong when you presume to be Jews; but if you want to be called Jews, then I shall call you a synagogue . . . a synagogue of Satan![55] Furthermore, John's description in Revelation 3:9 of the fate of "those who say they are Jews but are not" is strikingly similar to other Jewish accounts of the eschatological fate of the Nations: "I will make those who say they are Jews and are not, but are lying—I will make them come and bow before you and they will learn that I have loved you."[56] In so jealously policing who can authentically lay claim to Jewish identity, John, again, is quintessentially Jewish insofar as he maintains and reinforces this essentializing binary between us (Jews) and them (gentiles).[57]

John's salvific hierarchy reflects his personal situation as a first-century apocalyptic Jew and follower of Jesus who was writing in the aftermath of the destruction of Jerusalem in 70 CE. John's evocative images of judgment and salvation divided humans into fundamentally two camps: gentile and Jew; within these two camps, however, John acknowledged ethical and social difference.[58] Moreover, John's apocalyptic visions reflect and reinforce his own social and ethical ideals. Among the various visions of Revelation, John describes the heavenly throne room and the privileged few who worship and serve God therein. In this way, John rhetorically highlights specific values, practices, and people, most especially the sanctity of Jewish priests and their temple worship as well as the "purified" martyrs who were killed in the Jewish revolt against Rome.[59] To illuminate John's layered soteriological and ethical expectations, I will concentrate on his description of five specific groupings of persons: Jewish martyrs and the priestly elect; gentiles *selected* and transformed to serve as priests; the remedially saved from Israel; righteous gentiles; and finally the damned. Notably, none of these categories requires or is further clarified by the neologism of "Christian."

Different Dwellings and Different Tasks in the End Times

John of Patmos believed he was living in *the* special epoch in which God's promises to Israel had begun to be fulfilled (Rev. 1:3). The eschaton is imminent, and its "firstfruits" have already been identified (Rev. 14:1–5). God's enemies, however, still seemed to be prospering. Consequently, John improvised and dialectically reinterpreted prophetic expectations to account for this. Nonetheless, John *knows* that the final chapter of salvation history is unfolding all around, and what's more, he *knows* how each member or group from the cast of characters is supposed to behave and what their end(s) will be.[60]

Using elaborate, sensory-rich language, John subordinates gentile salvation to Israel's. The 144,000, 12,000 from each tribe of Israel, will be sealed and protected from the coming tribulations; afterward, they will reign with Christ for a thousand years; *only after all of this*, namely the tribulations and thousand-year reign, do gentiles qua gentiles appear to enjoy some modicum of salvation in the book of Revelation. Realizing their previous errors, these saved gentiles will penitently bring "the glory and honor" of the Nations to the heavenly and new Jerusalem (Rev. 21:26)[61] as part of Israel's eschatological celebration and restoration.[62] In doing this, John constructed a pastiche of biblical predictions regarding Israel's redemption and the role of gentiles.

In this section, we shall consider John's ethical expectations as he dialectically fashioned them in light of his biblically inspired visions for the eschaton and social circumstances. As we shall see, John used spatial and temporal hierarchies to distinguish between the different salvific ends of gentiles and Jews. Furthermore, and likely addressing himself only to Jews, John used the eschatological and imagined actions of gentiles as a foil to reinforce current social and ethical boundaries between his Jewish community and gentile outsiders.[63] In so doing, John tailored his ethical expectations so as to enact the eschatological pilgrimage motif, with special tasks allotted to saved Jews and gentiles.

Temporal and Spatial Hierarchies

John twice (Rev. 7 and 14) differentiated between the 144,000 who were sealed from Israel and the secondary ingathering of the Nations, both times emphasizing the primacy of the restored twelve tribes of Israel.[64] In so doing, John deliberately evoked Isaiah 56's account of the secondary ingathering of foreigners who will join those already gathered and take part in their worship of Israel's God.[65] Who, then, are John's gentiles who are stationed in the heavenly throne room and are worshipping the one true God (e.g., Rev. 7:9)? They are the priests and Levites drawn from among the Nations, who, according to Isaiah 66:21, will participate in the cultic worship of God.[66] Although the presence of these gentile priests might be read as encouraging gentile *conversion* to Judaism, it is more likely that they were meant to remind John's Jewish audience of the universal sovereignty of God and the importance of priestly virtues.[67]

These priests, however, are not the *only* saved gentiles in the book of Revelation. When we compare these liturgical scenes with other passages, such as Revelation 21–22, an interesting tension arises; namely there are *two* paths toward salvation for gentiles. There are those gentiles mentioned in these liturgical interludes who serve as priests,[68] thereby drawing upon and homogenizing Isaiah 56 and 66's expectations of the Nations; and there are those gentiles who, fulfilling Isaiah 60, will repent (but are not transformed into priests!) and will penitently bring the "glory and honor" of the Nations to Jerusalem (Rev. 21:24–27). John preserves both eschatological expectations but deploys them for *differing* purposes. In order to parse these varying roles and their rhetorical imports, we must first consider how John has fashioned a staggered account of salvation history through temporal and spatial hierarchies.[69]

Revelation's story of salvation history has multiple stages, including two resurrections; what stage(s) a person participates in and how depend upon the role he or she plays in the overall drama of salvation. In the first resurrection, those who had died for the witness of Jesus and the word of God are raised:[70] "Then I saw thrones and those seated on them were given authority to judge. I also saw the souls of those who have been beheaded for the testimony of Jesus and for the word of God, who had not worshipped the beast or its image and had not received its mark on their forehead or hands. They came to life and reigned with Christ a thousand years. (The rest of the dead did not come to life until the thousand years were ended.) This is the first resurrection" (Rev. 20:4–5). Throughout Revelation, martyrs enjoy salvific and temporal priority. In Revelation 11, John described two prophets, who, though killed, have already been raised and ascended to heaven (Rev. 11:3–12).[71] Here as elsewhere, John has underscored the soteriological and moral importance of martyrdom.[72]

After the thousand-year reign of the martyrs with Christ, there will be a general resurrection and judgment for those who were not worthy of the first resurrection: "Then I saw a great white throne and the one who sat on it; the earth and the heaven fled from his presence, and no place was found for them. And I saw the dead, great and small, standing before the throne, and books were opened. Also another book was opened, the book of life. And the dead were judged according to their works, as recorded in the books. . . . Then Death and Hades were thrown into the lake of fire; and anyone whose name was not found written in the book of life was thrown into the lake of fire" (Rev. 20:11–15). After this second resurrection, there is a general judgment of all, wherein those less praiseworthy than the martyrs but still deserving of a place in the book of life are saved; all others are thrown into the lake of fire. It is important to note that, apart from the idealistic expectation of gentile converts who become priests and Levites, gentiles qua gentiles do not appear again until after this secondary resurrection, that is, after the thousand-year reign of Christ with the 144,000 of restored Israel and the resurrected martyrs.

To paint the picture of *who* deserves the highest salvific rewards and *what* those rewards entail, John similarly deployed *spatial* distinctions to subdivide and hierarchically categorize the saved. For example, John has placed into the throne room and heavenly temple of God his saintly ethical exemplars, namely priests and martyrs.[73] John repeatedly portrayed the righteous as a "priesthood of the saved" and illustrated their priestly priority through spatial proximity to God and his holy places.[74] We glimpse an instantiation of this priestly priority during the heavenly liturgies unfolding before the throne of God in heaven. In addition to four living creatures, the twenty-four elders, and the Lamb, John explicitly described those present in attendance before the heavenly throne as "a kingdom of priests serving God the Father" (Rev. 5:9–10; 1:6).

Furthermore, in a passage reminiscent of 20:4, Revelation 6:9 grants priority seating to the martyrs, who reside near the altar of God.[75] In both cases, John has envisioned the spatial layout of the heavenly throne room and the accoutrements of the heavenly temple, respectively, to heighten the importance of the certain types of persons in each and their representative types of conduct. In this way, John has provided ethical exemplars for his fellow Jews to imitate.

Some of the most stunning and best-known images of the book of Revelation are the sudden appearances of the new spaces of a new heaven, new earth, and new Jerusalem in chapter 21: "Then I saw a new heaven and a new earth; for the first heaven and the first earth had passed away, and the sea was no more. And I saw the holy city, the new Jerusalem, coming down out of heaven from God, prepared as a bride adorned for her husband"

(Revelation 21:1–2). Scholars have rightly interpreted this passage as a synthesis of the poetic parallelism of Isaiah 65:17 (cf. 66:22), "For I am about to create new heavens and a new earth," with 65:18b's promise of the (re)creation of Jerusalem, "For I am about to create Jerusalem as a joy and its people as a delight."[76] Thus, the triad of the new heaven, new earth, and new Jerusalem is the hallmark of God's future promise to restore and redeem creation.[77] As such, this triad forms a coherent unit (and *not* discrete or individual spaces) and symbolizes the idealized community of the saints.[78]

This interpretation, however, homogenizes these distinctive places, especially the new earth and the new Jerusalem, and the types of people that will dwell within each space. This view assumes two questionable, interpretative moves. First, that John deployed the triad of new earth, heaven, and Jerusalem due to exegetical constraints, that is, due to their inclusion in Isaiah's prophetic vision; consequently, the new earth and heaven are treated as vestigial products of John's exegesis of Isaiah and, as such, are functionally superfluous to his narrative.[79] The saved, insofar as they *are* saved, will *all* dwell within the new Jerusalem.[80] Second, once the new Jerusalem becomes synonymous and/or coterminous with the new earth, the *physicality* of John's imagery is treated as *purely* metaphorical.[81] Thus, even though this triad and the context in which it appears uses the spatiality of the new Jerusalem's cityscape, this, so it has been argued, is a narrative convention that is actually meant "to convey a nonspatial notion."[82]

While it is certainly true that John has drawn upon a great deal of metaphorical language (e.g., a city adorned as a bride) to describe the new Jerusalem, this does not entail that the spatial contours of the new Jerusalem and the new earth be *merely* metaphorical. According to John, where certain people will end up and what they will do there matters.[83] I will show that by preserving the distinctiveness and the physicality of these places John has seized upon Isaiah's multitiered eschatological landscape and has used this hierarchical map to differentiate between specific eschatological roles and salvific privileges.

Consequently, when we examine this famous passage more closely, John—drawing upon and applying Isaiah's eschatological promises—has devised a hierarchical, sacred landscape of *two* levels of salvation that differentiates between the larger, less prestigious new earth and the center of this new earth, the new and heavenly Jerusalem. As a result, the new Jerusalem is the *axis mundi* of this new earth and is its point of contact with the new heaven.[84] Its sacrality and importance further enhanced, this new Jerusalem will not include a specific place for the Temple; instead, the whole city will serve as the dwelling place of God (Rev. 21:22; cf. 21:3).[85] As a result, the city radiates with the presence of God, shining "with God as its light and its lamp is the lamb" (21:23). Surrounding and separating this new Jerusalem from the new earth are its "great and high" city walls.[86] In his description of these walls, John has evoked Ezekiel's description of the Temple (Ezek. 40–42) and the walls of the city (48:30–35).[87] Finally, those meant to dwell within the heavenly city walls are "those who conquer" and are therefore counted among the "children of God" (Rev. 21:7). We will return shortly to flesh out who and what sort of conduct John has evoked here.

After describing the radiance of the heavenly city and its elaborate walls, John detailed the eschatological presence and role of gentiles qua gentiles: "The Nations will walk by its light [i.e., the glory of God], and the kings of the earth will bring their glory into it. Its gates will never be shut by day—and there will be no night there. People will bring into it the glory and the honor of the Nations. But nothing profane (κοινόν) will enter it, nor anyone who practices abomination or falsehood, but only those who are written in the Lamb's book of life" (Rev. 21:24–27). David Aune has shown that Revelation 21:24–27 is paraphrasing and expanding upon Isaiah's description of captive foreign kings led in procession to pay homage to Jerusalem in 60:3–5, 11.[88] Thus, according to Isaiah, *even* the kings of the earth shall penitently come to offer financial restitution to Israel and walk in her light as part of its eschatological celebration.

Yet, John has deftly modified Isaiah's account as well; unlike in Isaiah 60:5, 11, where the captive kings of the earth bring only financial restitution (e.g., 60:5's abundance or "wealth": πλοῦτος) to Jerusalem, John has employed the more wide-ranging terms "glory" (δόξα) and "honor" (τιμή). Elsewhere in Revelation (4:9, 11; 5:12–13; and 7:12), glory and honor are paired in liturgical scenes wherein the Nations praise and venerate the one true God of Israel. Moreover, δόξα is frequently used in the same manner throughout the LXX insofar as it appears in the context of non-Israelites recognizing and worshipping the one, true God of the whole universe.[89] Thus, John, although staying remarkably close to some elements of Isaiah's narrative, has shifted the tenor of the scene from financial restitution[90] to Israel to pious veneration of the God of Israel.[91]

John's complex pastiche of biblical prophecies, however, raises several interpretative difficulties. Do these gentiles, insofar as they finally recognize the sovereignty of God, also become Jews? If they remain gentiles, which I argue they do, do they ever physically enter into the new Jerusalem? What is the referent for πᾶν κοινόν? How should it best be translated? And finally, in what way, if at all, did John expect his description of the new earth and new Jerusalem to affect the behavior of his readers?

John has repurposed the spatial hierarchy of a new earth and new Jerusalem to differentiate and privilege different eschatological and ethical roles, namely Israel's priestly worship of God and the Nations' secondary support and imitation of this piety. We find a similar spatial hierarchy, with differing dwelling places and differing expectations for conduct, in the near-contemporary text of the Psalms of Solomon: "[The Lord] will distribute [the children of God] on the land according to their tribes; the alien and the foreigner will no longer live near them. . . . And [the Lord] will have gentile nations serving him under his yoke, and he will glorify the Lord in (a place) prominent (above) the whole earth. And he will purge Jerusalem (and make it) holy as it was even from the beginning, (for) nations to come from the ends of the earth to see his glory, to bring as gifts her children who had been driven out, and to see the glory of the Lord" (Pss. Sol. 17:28, 30–31).[92] In a similar vein, John has expanded and topographically reassigned the Temple's hierarchical, sacred spaces such that the whole city is now the sanctuary. and the new earth is the de facto courtyard for the Nations.[93]

Consequently, despite the dominant interpretation of this passage, according to which all the saved are Christians, this passage does *not* entail the total conversion of the Nations;[94] nor is it even addressed to them.[95] John has constructed an idealistic vision of how Israel, as a nation of priests, should comport itself. The inclusion of some saved gentiles on the new earth is a demonstration of God's universal sovereignty; it is not consolation for or exhortation to any gentile who might stumble upon and read John's text. Instead, John has used the eschatological role of some saved gentiles as a foil both to articulate and to impress upon his Jewish audience certain ethical ideals (e.g., priestly conduct and steadfast endurance).

Inclusion and Exclusion from the New Jerusalem

In order to clarify the ethical dimensions of John's salvific hierarchy, we must look specifically at both his *inclusive* (e.g., what are the ethical requirements to enter into the new Jerusalem?) and his *exclusive* language (e.g., who

and what sort of conduct is specifically forbidden from the new Jerusalem?).
When considering Revelation, as noted above, it is important to keep in
mind that John is an impressionistic and not a systematic author. Furthermore, although I shall offer an explanation for why John has employed certain language and images, this explanation can only skim the surface of
John's sensory-rich and exegetically thick portrait of the new Jerusalem.

   Who, according to John, is worthy to enter into the new Jerusalem?
"The one who conquers" (ὁ νικῶν) will be a child of God and thus among
his beneficiaries (Rev. 21:7), and "those who wash their robes" (οἱ πλύνοντες
τὰς στολὰς) will be able to enter the city by the gates (22:14).[96] What these
two phrases have in common is that John has associated both with steadfast endurance in the face of persecution and martyrdom.[97] Throughout the
book of Revelation, "those who conquer" are moral exemplars who were
able to withstand persecution and even endure bloody martyrdom (e.g., 2:7,
11, 26; 3:5, 11, 21; 11:7; 13:7; 15:2).[98] Thus, Christ is the paradigmatic example
of someone who "has conquered":[99] "See, the lion of the tribe of Judah, the
Root of David, has conquered (ἐνίκησεν), so that he can open the scroll and
its seven seals. Then I saw between the throne and the four living creatures
and among the elders a Lamb standing as if it had been slaughtered" (Rev.
5:5–6). Similarly, the phrase "those who wash their robes" evokes not only
successful endurance of "the great ordeal" but also the bloody sacrifice and
death of Christ:[100] "Then one of the elders addressed me, saying, 'Who are
those, robed in white, and where have they come from?' I said to him, 'Sir,
you are the one who knows.' Then he said to me, 'These are they who have
come out of the great ordeal; they have washed their robes and made them
white in the blood of the lamb'" (Rev. 7:13–14; cf. 3:4 and 9:14). In this way,
the martyrdom of Christ, according to John, was both the means and the
moral standard for those wishing to enter into the new Jerusalem.

   John's encouragement toward martyrdom raises a long-standing scholarly dispute about the social context of Revelation: Were John and his audience *really* experiencing persecution, or did John use this language for
psychological and social consolation and consolidation? In this way, the
general shape of the argument has become the following: since we have no
evidence apart from John of Romans systematically persecuting Christians
in the second half of the first century in Asia Minor, obviously there was
not any *actual* persecution; but perhaps there was a *perceived* crisis,[101] *or*
John has deployed the most powerful rhetoric available—persecution and
martyrdom—as part of his own boundary-drawing and solidarity-infusing

social program.[102] While some of these arguments are quite sophisticated, they start from a faulty assumption: that John and his audience were Christians, not Jews. Instead of searching for external, first-century evidence of Roman persecution of Christians in Asia Minor, we should ask: Was there a catastrophic event in the second half of the first century carried out by the Romans that created a large number of Jewish martyrs and left an indelible psychological scar and fear for personal safety?[103] Paula Fredriksen graphically underscores the precariousness and vulnerability of Jews living in "mixed cities" alongside gentiles in the aftermath of the First Jewish Revolt: "Consider . . . the casualty figures for mixed cites as a result of the outbreak of the First Revolt. In Caesarea, 20,000 Jews were killed; in Ptolemais, 2,000—the entire community; in . . . Damascus, variously 10,000 or 18,000 Jews were slain."[104]

Consequently, John's interest in martyrdom is best understood in light of the destruction of the Temple and sack of Jerusalem in 70 CE as well as the continual fear of renewed violence against Jews.[105] In much the same way, the sealing and protection of the 144,000 of the restored Israel against the impending eschatological travails and divine retaliation against hostile outsiders offers emotional consolation and social cohesion for John and his community. In short, God's retribution against the Romans is coming, and John and his community will be protected insofar as they successfully enact the role of the 144,000 sealed from Israel. Consequently, whether to encourage solidarity and resistance in the face of the future Roman persecution, or to provide a theological justification of greater salvific rewards after the fact, John of Patmos used his salvific hierarchy to differentiate among different types of Jews and privilege above all those who *have* steadfastly endured or *will*.[106]

In typical fashion for the author of Revelation, the righteous dwelling in the new Jerusalem are not simply those who have steadfastly endured; instead, John has woven together *several* ethical ideals for the righteous. Notably, John has synthesized three ethical ideals or profiles: (1) the heavenly martyrs; (2) the 144,000, with its echoes of a military census and requirements of celibacy;[107] and (3) the priestly elect.[108] Consequently, those who will dwell in the new Jerusalem are an army of the righteous, who have steadfastly endured, and who will also be the priestly elect living *in* the sanctuary of God itself (Rev. 21). As a result, John has fashioned an amalgam of heroic ethical actions (e.g., martyrdom, asceticism, and priestly worship) to describe those deserving to dwell in the new Jerusalem.[109]

Turning to John's *exclusive* language, we must resolve how best to interpret John's language of exclusion and difference from Revelation 21–22. As we saw above, Revelation 21:27 declares "nothing κοινόν shall enter [the new Jerusalem]; nor anyone who practices abominations or falsehood, but only those who are written in the Lamb's book of life." David Aune is emblematic of an apparent scholarly consensus on this passage: "The term *koinos,* used only here in Revelation, means 'profane' or 'ritually unclean'; a close synonym is *akathartos,* 'unclean, defiled,' which occurs in Revelation 16:13; 17:4; and 18:2. *Koinos* and *akathartos* denote ritual impurity, a central religious category in early Judaism [that was] carried over into early Christianity and transformed into an exclusively moral category."[110] Aune then connects the prohibition on anything *profane* (κοινόν) from Revelation 21:27 to a short list of those who are excluded from the new Jerusalem at Revelation 22:15 and argues that this list of excluded persons, namely "dogs, sorcerers, fornicators, murders, idolaters, and everyone who loves and practices falsehood,"[111] demonstrates that John has transformed the inherited notion of ritual impurity into a *Christian* concern about moral impurity.[112] According to Aune, Revelation 21:27 is a prohibition against morally impure persons and a blanket claim that they cannot enter into the new Jerusalem.

In contrast, however, to Aune's interpretation, I would caution against too readily conflating impurity and profaneness. What is more likely is that John has excluded both the profane and the morally impure from the new Jerusalem. When we consider John's ideological context as a first-century Jew writing for other Jews, the exclusion of the *profane* and the *morally impure* evokes different groups. Although these categories are not mutually exclusive—gentiles could become morally impure—I will suggest that John had two specific groups in mind: gentiles who *are* profane, and his fellow Jews whom he was concerned might *return* to moral impurity. In this way, John's caveat about profanity was meant to assure his fellow Jews of the sacrality of the new Jerusalem, whereas his prohibition against moral transgressions was meant to reinforce the high stakes required for inclusion among Israel as a nation of priests and entrance into the new Jerusalem as the new sanctuary of God.

In order to unpack these claims, we must consider the resonances of *profane* and *impure* among first-century Jews. Jonathan Klawans and Christine Hayes have shown that prior to the rabbis, biblical and Second Temple authors did not consider gentiles to be susceptible to the forms of ritual impurity detailed in Leviticus 12–15; instead, gentiles were best classified as being *inherently profane.*[113] In support of this claim, Klawans sets up *two* different dueling pairs: purity and impurity, and sacred and profane. Klawans cites Leviticus 10:10 to support these two different dichotomies: "You are to distinguish between the sacred and the profane; between the impure and the pure." According to Klawans's reading of the Torah, ritual impurity was a temporary state and could be transmitted; profaneness, in contrast, was nontransmittable and "referred to some violation of the sacred not connected to purity laws per se."[114]

Expanding upon Klawans, Hayes notes that profaneness and sacredness are not binaries, but rather opposite ends of a spectrum: "Within the Israelite community, a divinely ordained hierarchy extends from the most profane members to the most holy. Lay Israelites, being profane, have the least access to (and responsibility toward) the realm of the sacred; Levites have some access; holy priests have greater access; and the most holy high priest has the most complete and intimate access to the realm of the holy."[115] Gentiles, according to Hayes, stand even lower on this spectrum of relative sacredness, below lay Israelites, and thus cannot enter into the sacred precincts of the Temple because of their profane status. Josephus, John of Patmos's first-century contemporary, mapped out the relative hierarchy of various persons in terms of the ascending and concentric levels of sanctity in the Temple compound, with gentiles, due to their profane status, standing below ritually impure Jewish males: "[The temple] had four surrounding courts, each with its special restrictions. The outer court was open to all, foreigners included; women during their impurity were alone refused admission. To the second court all Jews were admitted and, when uncontaminated by any defilement, their wives; to the third, male Jews, if clean and purified; to the fourth the priests robed in their priestly vestments. The sanctuary was entered only by the high-priests, clad in the raiment particular to themselves" (*Against Apion* 2:103).[116] As I mentioned above, John has transformed and reapplied the spatial and sacred hierarchy of the Temple complex into a topographic dichotomy between the new Jerusalem as the inner sanctuary and the dwelling place of the priestly elect and martyrs in contrast to the new earth as the outer courtyard reserved for the Nations.[117]

Despite this spatial hierarchy, could saved gentiles, bearing the "glory and honor of the Nations," *enter* into the new Jerusalem? Could John prohibit profanity (i.e., gentiles) from the new Jerusalem while at the time emphatically and dramatically predicting the ingathering of nations and kings to eschatologically pay homage to Israel and her God? Perhaps John, similar to what we will see below with Paul, considered saved gentiles to be no longer inherently profane.[118] In other words, all saved gentiles *must* have been resurrected; and if they were resurrected, then their names were in the book of life because "anyone whose name was not found written in the book was thrown into the lake of fire" (Rev. 20:15).

Consequently, insofar as their names were written in the book of life, these saved gentiles would no longer be excluded from the sacred precincts of the new Jerusalem as profane: "They will bring into [the city] the glory and honor of the Nations. But nothing profane shall enter it, nor anyone who practices abomination or falsehood, but *only those who are written in the Lamb's book of life*" (Rev. 21:26–27, emphasis added). According to this argument, John has described the reality of the eschatological era through proscriptive language: in other words, since these gentiles no longer practice abomination or falsehood *and* they have been resurrected (thus included in the book of life),[119] they are no longer profane; therefore, they can enter into the new Jerusalem.[120]

While the entrance of gentiles into the new Jerusalem may appear feasible, I do not think it the best interpretation. John's eschatological scenario is an *idealistic* vision of how things should be; this idealistic picture is not, however, entirely discontinuous from the past or present. The content and shape of John's eschatological vision are determined by biblical expectations, which assume a binary of Jew and gentile. As a result, John, as we have seen, has no *tertium quid*; his saved gentiles are *still* gentiles.[121]

How does this affect John's narrative? In addition to building on Ezekiel's motif of measuring the eschatological temple, John's concern about the holiness of the Temple[122] echoed Ezekiel's language of gentile exclusion where no gentiles, even resident aliens, were allowed to cross into the sacred space of the Temple: "Say to the rebellious house, say to the house of Israel, Thus says the Lord God: O house of Israel, let there be an end to all your abominations in admitting foreigners (בְּנֵי־נֵכָר; LXX: ἀλλογενεῖς), uncircumcised in heart and flesh, to be in my sanctuary, *profaning* my temple when you offer to me my food, the fat, and the blood. . . . Thus says the Lord God: No foreigner, uncircumcised in heart and flesh, of all the foreigners who are among the people of Israel, shall enter my sanctuary" (Ezek., 44:6–7, 9, emphasis added; cf. Isa. 52:1). Epigraphic warning signs that survive from the Herodian period repeat Ezekiel's prohibitions against gentiles: "No alien (ἀλλογενῆ) may enter within the balustrade around the sanctuary and the enclosure. Whoever is caught, on himself shall he put the blame for the death which will ensue."[123] Yet John has not excluded *all* aliens; instead, he has forged a middle-ground position, accepting a homogenized reading of Isaiah 56 and 66 to include gentiles who have been transformed into eschatological priests and Levites, but still prohibiting *profanity* (i.e., gentiles qua gentiles) from entry into the sanctuary of the new Jerusalem.

Consequently, rather than evidencing a universalizing program of radical conversion, John's eschatological vision, in particular his prohibition against κοινόν, demonstrates his discomfort with Isaiah's expectation that the Nations will physically enter into the new Jerusalem.[124] As such, it will not be foreign kings led in procession to bring restitution, but the *honor* and *glory* of the Nations that will be brought into the new Jerusalem. As we noted above, this language evokes scenes from the LXX of non-Israelites offering praise and worshipping the one true God of Israel.[125] Thus, John's shift away from Isaiah's expectation of financial restitution signifies more than just a possible avoidance of the contamination of commercial activity;[126] rather, John has ingeniously fashioned an eschatological scenario that underscores the universal sovereignty of God but still subordinates the worship of the Nations and places it outside the new Jerusalem, where God's nation of priests will dwell.[127] It is not the Nations, therefore, who will enter into God's presence, but their prayers and offerings of glory.

What are the implications of this? In allowing gentile prayers but not their physical presence, John was able to reconcile certain prophetic expectations for the pilgrimage of the Nations while still preserving the sanctity of the new Jerusalem from their profanity. Furthermore, if we concentrate upon John's intended audience, there may be ethical implications as well. Foreshadowed in Revelation 15's Song of Moses, these saved gentiles will act as secondary and penitent pilgrims paying homage to God and offering worshipful glory and honor;[128] they will mirror what will be transpiring inside the new Jerusalem.[129] In this way, John has used the future role of saved gentiles as a foil to underscore again both the universal sovereignty of God and the importance of proper conduct (i.e., Jewish priestly practices and veneration of God). The impact of this subtle, rhetorical contrast may have been to remind his Jewish audience of what is expected of them. That is, as the elect, they should embrace and emulate righteous conduct—epitomized by Jewish priestly piety—because some from among the Nations *eventually*, inasmuch as they can, will imitate this righteous behavior.[130]

If Revelation 21:26–27 reflects John's discomfort over the possible entry of gentiles into the new Jerusalem, what is the rhetorical function of John's list of excluded and morally depraved individuals in Revelation 22:15 ("dogs, sorcerers, fornicators, murders, idolaters, and everyone who loves and practices falsehood")? As we have noted, this proscription is distinct from John's prohibition on the profane, namely gentiles.[131] Furthermore, it is nearly identical to the list of vices of those who will suffer the second death of the lake of fire (Rev. 21:8): "But for the cowardly, those practicing abominations, the murderers, the fornicators, the sorcerers, the idolaters, and all liars, their place will be in the lake that burns with fire and sulfur, which is the second death." Who are these sinners, and *why* do they still exist in the era of eschatological celebration and restoration?

Returning to the specifics of Revelation 21:27, John has excluded both the profane and those who may be morally impure, that is, members of his Jewish audience who may fall short of his high ethical standards. In this way, Revelation 21:27 is a paraphrase of Isaiah 52:1 (emphasis added): "Put on your beautiful garments, O Jerusalem, the holy (ἁγία) city; for the uncircumcised and the *impure* (ἀκάθαρτος) shall enter you no more." Isaiah is referring to two distinct sorts of people: the uncircumcised/profane and the impure/unclean.[132] Thus, like Isaiah, who has prohibited gentiles and the impure, John (Rev. 21:27) has also prohibited gentiles, but he has further elaborated what sources of impurity were especially illicit (i.e., blasphemy and lies). The rhetorical impact of this is that John has warned his Jewish brethren of some of the moral expectations for those who wish to dwell within the holy city of the new Jerusalem.

Consequently, although Revelation 22:14–15 introduces another list of excluded individuals through the disjunction of those "inside" and those "outside," I think it incorrect to deduce that John conceived of those "outside" to mean those *dwelling* on the new earth; instead, it appears that John was deploying the hortatory rhetoric of "two ways" (a way of life vs. a way of death) to reinforce ethical uprightness among his putative community of Jewish readers.[133] In this way, there is no remedial salvation for those Jews who might morally err from time to time. John has reminded his audience of the dire consequences awaiting those who might fall short of the moral uprightness required to belong "inside" the heavenly new Jerusalem: those

Jews who are outside John's community are destined for the lake of fire and the second death.[134]

Revelation's Ethics of Higher and Lower Levels of Salvation

Ultimately, Revelation tells the ethical and soteriological story of five groups of people: Jewish martyrs and the priestly elect, transformed gentiles, remedially saved Jews, gentile penitents, and all the rest who are destroyed. For John these groups were established characters in the drama of salvation history, with some (e.g., transformed gentiles) holding a more theoretical than practical place in John's conception of specific ethical tasks that were tailored to the end times. John reconciled expectations for gentile salvific inclusion with complex spatial and temporal subordination while all the while underscoring that gentile salvation is not primarily about saving the Nations but was rather part of Israel's restoration. In this way, according to John, salvation history will conclude with varying degrees of reward and different roles for the different types of saved.

Revelation, in particular its author's belief in different salvific statuses, was not an anomaly among first-century Jews. Paul the Apostle also hierarchically differentiated between gentile and Jewish salvation. Although he and John differed from each other in significant ways, both were early Jewish followers of Jesus who struggled to make sense of the inclusion of gentiles with God's specific and often greater promises to his beloved people. By studying these two figures as Jewish authors who allotted different levels of salvation and assigned different codes of conduct to Jews and gentiles, we gain insight not only into a formative period for what becomes early Christianity, but we also learn how early Jewish authors innovated within their tradition(s) to address the theoretical and practical problem of how God intends to save Israel and the Nations.

Chapter 2

Paul's Olive Tree

Saving Gentiles as Gentiles and Jews as Jews in Christ

> But if some of the branches were broken off, and you, a wild olive shoot, were grafted in their place to share the rich root of the olive tree, do not boast over the branches. . . . Do not become proud, but stand in awe. For if God did not spare the natural branches, perhaps he will not spare you. . . . For if you have been cut from what is by nature a wild olive tree and grafted, contrary to nature, into a cultivated olive tree, how much more will these natural branches be grafted back into their own olive tree.
>
> —Romans 11:17–18, 20–21, 24

The Jewish Paul: Called to Be the Apostle to the Gentiles

As he approached the climax of his rebuttal to arrogant gentile followers of Jesus who believed themselves to be now *superior* to Jews (Rom. 9–11), Paul slammed his fist down, at least rhetorically: it is not *you*, O Gentiles, who have done something incredible and praiseworthy, but God! He has en-grafted you, a wild olive-shoot (ἀγριέλαιος), into the metaphorical tree of Israel's redemption.[1] In so doing, God has offered you a *special* but also *limited* opportunity to be saved. It is his promise to *all* of Israel, that is, the natural branches, that is irrevocable; God has made no such promise to save *all* of you. Show some humility and appreciation for those Jews who have delayed in joining *in* Christ; but for this, you might never have been

saved! Perhaps surprisingly for the Apostle to gentiles, Paul fiercely preserves Israel's pride of place in God's plan for salvation.[2] In spite of this, the
Jewishness of the Apostle to the gentiles remains a hotly contested question
among scholars.

Gaining momentum in the second half of the last century, Pauline
scholarship has shifted away from depicting Paul as radically divorced and
separated from first-century Judaism and toward situating the Apostle to
the gentiles within the diverse strands of ancient Judaism.[3] This trend in
scholarship has come to be called the "New Perspective."[4] An important and
early voice at the epicenter of this tectonic shift in Pauline studies was Krister
Stendahl. In a seminal article demonstrating the utility of situating Paul
within Judaism, Stendahl argued that Paul's radical transformation in behavior and belief is best characterized as "called, not converted."[5] As Paul
himself declares at the beginning of his Letter to the Galatians, "Paul an
apostle—sent neither by human commission nor from human authorities,
but through Jesus Christ and God the Father, who raised him from the
dead. . . . When God, who had set me apart before I was born and called me
through his grace, was pleased to reveal his Son to me, so that I might pro-
claim him among the gentiles, I did not confer with any human being"
(Gal. 1:1, 15—16). Paul was *called* to a special task or vocation: the mission to
the gentiles; he did not cease being Jewish in order to become a Christian:[6]

> If anyone has reason to be confident in the flesh, I have more:
> circumcised on the eighth day, a member of the people of Israel,
> of the tribe of Benjamin, a Hebrew born of Hebrews. (Phil. 3:4–5)

> But whatever anyone dares to boast of—I am speaking as though
> a fool—I also dare to boast of that! Are they Hebrews? So am I!
> Are they Israelites? So am I! Are they descendants of Abraham?
> So am I! Are they ministers of Christ? Though I babble as a
> madman, I am a better minister! (2 Cor. 11:21–22)

Following Stendahl and noting Paul's deliberate invoking of Jeremiah in his
self-construction of Galatians 1:15,[7] we can avoid importing later and anachronistic categories, such as Christian, to describe Paul's self-representation
or motivation.[8] Moreover, we need not ascribe to Paul a supersessionist
ideology, which posits that a new, true religion, Christianity, has replaced
an old and failed one, Judaism.[9] Supersessionist readings of Paul inevitably

become untenable due to their inability to explain Paul's repeated emphasis on Israel's continued covenant and the benefit of the Law.[10]

By emphasizing Paul's self-understanding as called on a special mission but still within the boundaries of Jewish custom and belief, scholars may interpret more accurately Paul's seemingly conflicting opinions.[11] How can circumcision "count for nothing" yet still be of "great value in every way"?[12] Similarly, why are "those who rely on the Law under a curse" when "the Law is holy and the commandment is holy just and good"?[13] The short answer, always a risky proposition in Pauline studies, is that Paul devised and tailored different messages for different contexts and addresses, instead of a timeless or universal system applicable to all of humanity.

In 2 Corinthians 3, for example, Paul appears to reject the Law in favor of a new Spirit and covenant available through Christ.[14] In this specific context, however, Paul is not addressing the universal inadequacy of the Law;[15] instead, he is drawing a contrast between his personal *revelatory* authority and the authority of his rivals, which derives from letters of recommendation.[16] In the service of this dichotomy, Paul rhetorically sets up a contrast between his own recent and Moses's ancient revelations in order to further disparage his opponents who must rely solely on what others have said.[17] Thus, as he was wont to do, Paul turns a perceived weakness (his lack of letters of recommendation) into a strength: his authority, stemming from personal revelation, is *spiritual* whereas his opponents, who do so love their letters, are dependent on the writing or revelation of others for the content of their messages. The issue was not the Law itself but competing claims to authority.[18]

It is precisely when scholars introduce the category of Christian that Pauline scholarship is led astray, because the structural integrity of Paul's tailored messages to Israel and the gentiles about their related but distinct paths to salvation become homogenized and thereby acquire supersessionist overtones.[19] Instead, as part of his special vocation as a Jewish prophet, Paul self-consciously sought to become "all things to all people"—not as a rejection of Judaism—but in the service of spreading the gospel of Christ crucified to all peoples, and to each group in its own terms: "For though I am free with respect to all, I have made myself a slave to all in order to win more: to the Jews (*ioudaioi*), I became as a Jew (*ioudaios*) so that I could win Jews; to those under the Law, I became as one under the Law (although I myself am not under the Law) so that I might win those under the Law. . . . I have become all things to all people, that I might by all means save some. I do it all for the sake of the gospel, so that I may share in its blessings" (1 Cor. 9:19–23).[20]

Here, as in Romans 2:28–29, *ioudaioi* refers to Jews, distinguishing them from gentiles and thus not signifying a new category, Christian. Moreover, this passage reveals that different groups, according to Paul, demanded different approaches and not a one-size-fits-all—or "Christian"—message.[21]

As Paul's autobiographical recounting of his own Christ-like sufferings in 2 Corinthians 11 reveals, Paul was not an apostate who irrevocably separated himself from other Jews; instead, this passage shows that Paul, even as the Apostle to the gentiles, was still subject to Jewish authorities and punishment. This is made most clear when Paul recounts in 2 Corinthians 11:24 the sufferings he has undergone, including receiving from his fellow Jews "five times the forty lashings minus one." Paul submitted himself to the authority of those administering this punishment, continued to attend synagogue, and did not withdraw from Jewish society but remained within its conceptual and social boundaries.[22]

A second important point to keep in mind is that Paul expected the parousia, or return and reign of Christ, to occur in his lifetime:[23] "For this we declare to you by the word of the Lord, that *we who are alive*, who are left until the coming of the Lord, will by no means precede those who have died. For the Lord himself, with a cry of command, with the archangel's call and with the sound of God's trumpet, will descend from heaven, and the dead in Christ will rise first. Then *we who are alive*, who are left, will be caught up in the clouds together with them to meet the Lord in the air; and so we will be with the Lord forever" (1 Thess. 4:15–17, emphasis added).[24] I will return to this point below, but it is important to keep in mind that *time* is a central concept and motivation for Paul.[25] Paul considers himself and others all to be living in a *Sonderzeit* or "special epoch" wherein all persons and the world itself are on the very cusp of the eschaton.[26] The parousia is excruciatingly close, even if it is not quite here.[27] Paul extrapolates from this limited and ever-shrinking timeline to the conclusion that people ought to stay as they are.[28] This eschatological orientation is fundamental for understanding Paul.[29]

Seeking to bridge the chasm between the current age and the promised return of Christ, Paul sets forth two different sets of ethical expectations as well as higher and lower levels of salvation; uniting gentiles and Jews, however, is Paul's belief in a singular means for salvation, namely baptism *into* Christ. In this way, according to Paul, a single yet all-encompassing plan is *currently* coming to fruition for the salvation of Jews and gentiles, since God is the God of all (Rom. 3). All peoples, therefore, should remain and excel in the state in which they were called, since that is the state in which *God has called you* and the *Lord assigned you*.[30] In other words, who you *are* will determine the role you will play in the eschatological drama of the restoration of Israel and the secondary salvation of the Nations.

In this way, events are and *must* be proceeding according to God's plan. From the teleological perspective of salvation history, even the widespread rejection of Paul's message by his Jewish kinsmen is providential insofar as it delays the parousia, thereby giving Paul a limited time to evangelize among the Nations:[31] "Has [Israel] stumbled so as to fall? By no means! But through their stumbling salvation has come to the gentiles, so as to make Israel jealous. Now if their stumbling means riches for the world, and if their defeat means riches for gentiles, how much more will their full inclusion mean!" (Rom. 11:11–12). Thus, Paul describes *two* interrelated timelines—one for gentiles and one for Israel—each of which culminates in the image of shared salvation described in Romans 11.[32]

Of course, several questions remain: Why is Paul so critical of the Law—does this not represent a rejection of Judaism? Who or what is the "new creation" mentioned above in Galatians 6:15 (cf. 2 Cor. 5:17ff.)? How do we interpret Paul's language of radical equality in Galatians 3:28 ("There is no longer Jew or Greek, there is no longer slave or free, there is no longer male and female; for all of you are one in Christ Jesus")? And finally, what is the soteriological role of the Messiah, Jesus Christ?[33]

A number of scholars, often referred to as the "Radical New Perspective," have compellingly suggested that Paul's writings cannot be extracted from and understood outside of their situated context as ad hoc occasional letters written to a *specific* and, in almost all cases, gentile audience.[34] Thus, Paul does not describe the *universal* inadequacy of the Law for all humankind, only how it relates to *gentiles*. Thus, when Paul is critical about the Law or works, he is only critical vis-à-vis its application to his gentile audience: "For gentiles, who do not have the Torah as covenant, Torah as law functions in an exclusively negative way, to condemn."[35]

Moreover, in addition to its epistolary genre, Paul's intended message to his gentile audience was further obscured because of his deployment of sophisticated rhetorical devices.[36] For example, the ambiguous and challenging passage of Romans 2:17–29 can be made clearer by appealing to the ancient rhetorical convention of *prosōpopoiia* or impersonations of certain character types: "But if you call yourself a Jew and rely on the Law and boast of your relation to God and know his will and determine what is best because you are instructed in the Law, and if you are sure that you are a guide to the blind, a light to those who are in darkness, a corrector of the foolish, a teacher of children, having in the Law the embodiment of knowledge and truth, you, then, that teach others, will you not teach yourself? While you preach against stealing, do you steal?" (Rom. 2:17–21). Dripping with venomous sarcasm, Paul is not addressing a concrete or specific Jew. Instead, Paul is rhetorically constructing a "pretentious teacher" who is a hypocrite and arrogantly claims that he can *morally* transform gentiles into "righteous gentiles" in order to be saved, even though this pretentious teacher is himself terrible—so much so that he is undeserving of the name Jew.[37] Consequently, so the argument goes, we can reconstruct Paul's intended message by parsing his highly rhetorical gospel and considering exclusively how it relates to *gentiles only*.[38]

It is at this point that I depart from this interpretative approach to Paul.[39] Although I am convinced that Paul differentiated between the soteriological timelines and statuses of gentiles and Israel, I am not convinced that Paul thought Jesus Christ to be soteriologically effective and significant *only* for gentiles, as Lloyd Gaston so famously argued: "Had all of Israel followed Paul's example, it may be that we could have had a Gentile church loyal to the righteousness of God expressed in Jesus Christ and his fulfillment to the promise of Abraham, alongside an Israel loyal to the righteousness of God expressed in the Torah."[40] Although this is a compelling interpretation that explains a number of elusive problems, it cannot account for the whole of Paul's thought, and several cruxes remain.[41]

What could Paul mean, then, when he speaks of Peter's gospel to the Jews ("circumcised"; cf. Rom. 15:8), tantalizingly mentioned in Galatians 2?[42] What about Paul's own efforts among the circumcised (cf. 1 Cor. 9, cited above)? Moreover, why would Paul repeatedly emphasize (Rom. 9; 1 Cor. 15) that Jesus Christ is Lord over all? Elsewhere Paul similarly links God's oneness with the singular means of salvation: "faithfulness" (πίστις) through which God apparently delivers both Jew and gentile (Rom. 3:29–30).[43] Finally, when describing the final soteriological ends of both Israel and the Nations (Rom. 11), Paul speaks metaphorically of a *single* tree of salvation with, admittedly, multiple timelines and greater and lesser honors, but the *same* mechanism for inclusion, namely baptism into Christ.[44] This brings to light a deep tension in Paul's writings between some of his statements about radical equality in Christ (Gal. 3) and his seemingly conflicting claims about social (1 Cor. 7, 12; Rom. 12) and soteriological distinctions

(Rom. 11). Much of this confusion will dissipate, however, when we dissolve a simple one-to-one correspondence between ethics and soteriology.

In summary, I wish to reiterate the following points: (1) Paul was and continued to be a Jew; (2) he considered himself called, akin to the prophets of ages past, to a special mission; (3) he divided humanity into two major categories: Jew and gentile; (4) he wrote ad hoc letters that cannot be universalized or taken out of context; (5) he was an eschatological prophet who believed the world would imminently end; (6) he described two interrelated timelines of salvation; (7) the conduct of the majority of Jews was caused by God to allow Paul a limited window of time to spread his gospel among the gentiles; (8) thus, although Paul did address his message primarily to gentiles, he also expected his fellow Jews *at some point* to embrace a different style of conduct—not, I will argue, a rejection of Torah but instead baptism into Christ *in addition to* Torah observance; (9) the Messiah, therefore, is soteriologically effective for Jews as well as gentiles; (10) Paul's hierarchy of salvation, as we will see, castigates gentile initiates for believing they were now superior to Jews, even if these Jews *currently* were not members of the Jesus movement; (11) Paul's hierarchy is one of number and relative certainty: *all* of Israel will *surely* be saved, but only a *full* number of gentiles *may* be saved; and (12) Paul's portrait of salvation is unitary and shared—like the oneness of God; however, Israel will enjoy greater honors and possesses a more secure salvific status. In the sectarian and jargon-filled language of modern Pauline studies, I am advocating a modified two-path (but not two-covenant) approach with different ethical expectations for gentiles and Jews that, nonetheless, has a singular means for salvation (baptism into Christ) and greater honors for Israel.

Paul the Apostle: Ethics as This World Ends

Paul saw his mission to the gentiles as transpiring in the limited and ever-diminishing time left between the raising of Christ and his second coming. Oscar Cullmann famously characterized Paul's "between times" by analogue to the period between "D-Day" and "Victory Day" during World War II—in other words, the decisive battle has already been won and the imminent, final victory was a foregone conclusion.[45] Perplexingly for Paul, however, Christ's parousia *still* had not arrived. As time continued to elapse without the parousia, we see doubts began to grow within Pauline communities

(1 Thess. 4–5; 1 Cor. 15; Gal. 3).[46] Did this unexpected delay contradict Paul's preaching and therefore disprove his Christ-centric soteriology?

In response to these concerns, Paul, in typically Pauline fashion, adapted and modified his message to bring it into conformity with his deepest-held convictions.[47] This delay, likely a surprise to Paul himself, *must*, nonetheless, be providential.[48] What is important, therefore, according to Paul, is to understand God's reason for the delay. Paul concluded that this delay was to facilitate the "full" inclusion of the gentiles. As soon as this "full" number of gentiles was baptized into Christ, Christ would return (Rom. 11:25). Paul's successes in his mission to the Nations, consequently, would hasten Christ's return.[49]

What about the salvation of Israel? Were God's promises to redeem his own people still trustworthy? Of course they were—"the gifts and call of God are irrevocable!"[50] Despite the current fact that Israel has not en masse accepted Paul's Christ-centric gospel and soteriology, they *will* do so because otherwise God's promises would be broken; this, according to Paul, would be simply impossible. So, what was God's reason for making Israel delay?[51] Paul reasoned that this must also be so that a "full" number of gentiles might be saved. Further demonstrating his endearing egoism, Paul claimed that own his successes among the Nations would also spur his fellow Jews into joining in Christ out of jealousy.[52] In so doing, Paul has modified and reordered Isaiah's arc of salvation history.[53] What in Isaiah was an eschatological promise meant to follow Israel's deliverance—the ingathering of the Nations (Isa. 2:2–4; 60:1ff.)—was, according to Paul, occurring now and would help cause Israel's ultimate redemption.[54]

This shift in timelines coincided with Paul modifying traditional views of saved gentiles to describe how they were meant to behave in this *Sonderzeit*. Unlike John's shift away from financial restitution, Paul expected saved gentiles to offer reparations to Israel and her God.[55] As we shall see, Paul has fashioned an end-time ethic informed by biblical expectations for the conduct of saved gentiles, but has also tailored these expectations in response to problems that arose in his individual communities as they awaited the imminent parousia of Jesus Christ.

Similar to my discussion of John of Patmos, this is not a systematic or all-encompassing treatment. My focus here is specifically the phenomenon of salvific difference and its relationship with ethics. To this end, therefore, I will concentrate on the following five contentions regarding the Apostle to the gentiles: (1) Paul prioritized Israel's salvation over and above that of the

Nations;[56] (2) he affirmed the continued importance of Torah observance for Jews;[57] (3) he constructed *different* ethical standards for those gentiles who might be saved;[58] (4) he maintained that a gentile cannot become a Jew, but must stay as he or she is;[59] and (5) he claimed that all, both Jews and gentiles, who were saved were saved *in* Christ.[60]

Temporal, Quantitative, and Spatial Hierarchies

As 1 Thessalonians—likely Paul's earliest surviving letter—demonstrates, Paul could deploy the notion of time to address specific pastoral concerns and signal priority among members of the *ekklēsia* in response to situational concerns.[61] In 1 Thessalonians 4:13–5:11, Paul declared that on the day of the Lord those in Christ who have already died will rise first, prior to those who are still alive. Reading between the lines, it is probable that Paul had been preaching that the eschaton and Christ's parousia were so radically close that his gentile Jesus followers in Thessalonike were shocked when members of the community had died prior to Christ's return.[62] To alleviate these concerns Paul emphasized the temporal priority of those who have already died as well as the imminence of Christ's return.[63]

Similarly, in 1 Corinthians Paul again deployed temporal priority in response to another pastoral problem; in this case, Paul was addressing concerns over Christ's resurrection.[64] In defense of both the veracity and the salvific importance of Christ's resurrection, Paul outlines the chronology of resurrections: Christ first, and then all of humanity: "But in fact Christ has been raised from the dead, the first fruits of those who have died. For since death came through a human being, the resurrection of the dead has also come through a human being; for as all die in Adam, so all will be made alive in Christ. But each in his own order: Christ the first fruit, then at his coming those who belong to Christ. Then comes the end, when he will hand over the kingdom to God the Father, after he has destroyed every ruler and every authority and power. For he must reign until he has put all his enemies under his feet" (1 Cor. 15:20–26). Christ's *past* resurrection was not only the guarantee of the *future* resurrection of those in Christ, but it also signaled the *means* for this future resurrection, namely being *in* Christ. Furthermore, according to Paul, God has a plan, and it follows a deliberately sequential order.

We find another, albeit far less clear, instance of temporal priority when we consider the issue of when, that is, in what order, Jews and gentiles will be saved. Paul programmatically highlighted the priority of Israel over that of the Nations by stating salvation (σωτηρία) comes first to the Jew and then to the Greek (Rom. 1:16: "Ἰουδαίῳ τε πρῶτον καὶ Ἕλληνι"). During his account of salvation history in Romans 9–11, however, Paul has modified this sequence: "Lest you may claim to be wiser than you are, brothers and sisters, I want you to understand this mystery: a hardening has come upon part of Israel, until the full number of the gentiles has come in. And thus all of Israel will be saved, as it is written, 'Out of Zion will come the Deliverer; he will banish ungodliness from Jacob'" (Rom. 11:25–26). What prompted Paul to characterize salvation history in this way, and what are the implications?

Traditionally, scholars have taken Romans 9–11 to be evidence for Paul's Christian supersessionism.[65] Paul, so the argument goes, believed that non-Christian Jews have "forfeited" salvation.[66] As a result, Christians have now become the "true Israel," thereby replacing Jews (i.e., "carnal Israel") as God's chosen people.[67] According to this interpretation, salvation *did* first come to the Jews; however, because they rejected Christ they could no longer be considered God's elect.[68] This rejection of Christ, therefore, explains Paul's "grief over his kindred" (Rom. 9:2–3) and is the unstated source of "Israel's stumble" (Rom. 10:32–33; 11:11–12). Thus, the "all of Israel" who will be saved in Romans 11:26 is actually a cipher for all *Christian* believers, who are the "inwardly Jews" (Rom. 2:28–29) and the "Israel of God" (Gal. 6:16).

As a number of scholars have recognized, however, this supersessionist interpretation depends upon a facile reading of a number of passages, especially Romans 9 and its criticisms of Israel, Paul's "kindred according to the flesh" (Rom. 9:3–4):

It is not as though the word of God has failed; for not all those from Israel belong to Israel, nor is it that all children are Abraham's *seed* (σπέρμα). (Rom. 9:6–7, emphasis added)

And indeed, [God] says in Hosea, "Those who were not my people, I will call 'my people,' and her who was not beloved I will call 'beloved.'" (Rom. 9:25)

While Paul certainly has rebuked the conduct of his Jewish brethren here, this does not entail the presumed and radical rejection of Judaism and/or Israel; instead, Paul, again in the vein of a Jewish prophet, has censured incorrect behavior and belief.[69] For Paul, the Jewish prophet, Israel was behaving (or *mis*-behaving) as Israel has always behaved, but so will God insofar as he will steer Israel to redemption.[70] In short, I agree with the "broad consensus among contemporary exegetes" that Paul's "Israel" refers to the ethnic people of Israel.[71]

Rather than erasing or transferring God's promises away from Israel, Paul has reminded his *gentile* audience that it is God who is in charge and thus responsible for Israel's apparent stumble:[72]

> For the scripture says to Pharaoh, "I have raised you up for the
> very purpose of showing my power in you, so that my name may
> be proclaimed in all the earth." So then, [God] has mercy on
> whomever he chooses, and he hardens the heart of whomever he
> chooses. You will say to me, "Why, then, does he still find fault?
> For who can resist his will?" But who indeed are you, a human
> being, to argue with God? Will what is molded say to the one
> who molds it, "why have you made me like this?" Has the potter
> no right over the clay, to make out of the same clay one vessel for
> honor and another for dishonor? (Rom. 9:17–21)

Israel's stumble, therefore, does not and *cannot* eliminate God's promises. Israel *was, is,* and *will always be* God's chosen people to whom belong "the adoption, glory, the covenants, the giving of the Law, the worship, and the promises" (Rom. 9:4). It would be extremely presumptuous, according to Paul, to think that current Jewish obstinacy could somehow change God's plans.[73] Yet, just what was this obstinacy that led to Israel's stumble?

Although the traditional interpretation of Paul is certainly a misreading, we ought not swing our hermeneutical pendulum so far away from it that we lose sight of the fact that Paul was grieved over his Jewish compatriots and expressed concern about their salvation.[74] Lloyd Gaston's suggestion that Israel's stumble or "misstep" refers to the rejection by many Jews of Paul's message to gentiles, while ingenious and ecumenical, is not the most compelling solution.[75] Aside from its distortion of Paul's soteriology, it eliminates the rhetorical impact and obscures the logic of Paul's *inversion* of the expected temporal sequence of Jewish and gentile salvation: "So I ask, have they stumbled so as to fall? By no means! But through their stumbling salvation has come to the gentiles, so as to make them jealous. Now if their stumbling means riches for the world, and if their defeat means riches for gentiles, how much more will their inclusion mean!" (Rom. 11:11–12). The ingathering of the Nations, according to Paul, no longer follows Israel's redemption. Instead, Israel's providential stumble has delayed them and thereby made the salvation of the Nations possible; yet this stumble is only temporary, and Israel—all of Israel—will be saved.

In its most simple form, Israel's yes has turned to a no *so that* the no of the Nations (Rom. 1) can become a yes; this, in turn, will lead to Israel's future yes such that "all of Israel will be saved" (Rom. 11). Gaston's suggestion that Israel's no was in response to being a "light to the Nations" is unconvincing for historical and literary reasons. Not only does it disrupt the coherence of Romans 9–11 by importing a foreign idea, namely that Israel was (or was supposed to be) a missionizing nation.[76] This does not match the chronology that Paul has established. Put differently, why would Israel have to reject Paul's gospel to the gentiles *before* and *so that* Paul could spread his gospel among the gentiles?[77]

In addition to begging the question, Gaston's argument, as we shall see below, overlooks the participatory logic underlying Pauline soteriology. Instead, and to paraphrase Krister Stendahl's evocative "traffic pattern" metaphor,[78] what Paul has constructed is a staggered traffic pattern *on the same road*, namely baptism *in* Christ.[79] Currently, Israel has stopped to allow a "full number of gentiles" to merge; once this happens, however, this merge lane will be closed, and Israel—*all* of Israel—will again traverse this path and arrive at the final destination shared by all the saved.[80]

Despite Israel's temporary stumbling and current holding pattern, her special status (*Sonderplatz*), according to Paul, was never at risk. Romans 11:24–26 reasserts Israel's priority by demonstrating that (1) *all* of Israel will be saved as opposed to only a *full* number of gentiles (τὸ πλήρωμα τῶν ἐθνῶν), and (2) salvation history culminates with the full inclusion of Israel.[81] In this way, the inclusion of a full number of the gentiles, meaning a representative number of the various Nations of the world,[82] is instrumentalized and subordinated to the redemption of Israel, which is the climax of salvation history.[83] Elsewhere Paul similarly affirmed Israel's special status (e.g., Rom. 3:1; 9:4; 11:1) in God's eyes. Consequently, even if Israel's redemption is no longer temporally prior to that of the Nations, Paul, nonetheless, maintained the salvific hierarchy of Israel over the Nations.[84]

For further evidence of this point, we need look no further than a few verses prior to Romans 11:24–26 where Paul subordinated gentile salvation to Israel's via the spatial metaphor of a single olive tree (Rom. 11:16–24).[85] Capitalizing on the rich imagery of this metaphor, Paul emphasized the *spatial* priority of Israel and the dependence of gentiles upon Israel insofar as the wild shoots (gentiles) must depend upon the root (Israel) for support (Rom. 11:17–18). Scholars have long puzzled over Paul's inversion of ancient horticultural practices, as the common practice was to graft a domesticated shoot onto a wild tree rather than, as Paul describes, grafting a wild shoot onto a domesticated tree.[86] Yet through this rhetorical reversal, Paul has subverted expectations in order to emphasize Israel's elevated status and the dependence and subordination of the Nations.[87]

Therefore, Paul has not only castigated gentile Jesus followers for undeserved arrogance but also underscored Israel's *natural* (i.e., *privileged*) status in salvation history.[88] Despite the fact that the "natural branches" of Israel have been broken away to make room for the gentile "wild shoots," this is only temporary. In fact, the inclusion of these wild shoots was far more remarkable than the eventual *re*-inclusion of its natural branches will be:[89] "And even those [of Israel], if they do not persist in unbelief, will be grafted in, for God has the power to graft them in again. . . . For if you have been cut from what is by nature a wild olive tree and grafted, contrary to nature, into a cultivated olive tree, how much more will these natural branches be grafted back into their own olive tree" (Rom. 11: 23–24). Consequently, according to Paul, the "natural branches" of Israel will certainly be saved (i.e., "grafted in,") because "the gifts and the calling of God are irrevocable" (Rom. 11:29); in contrast, gentile salvation is precarious insofar as God has deviated from the *natural* course of things in order to include the "wild branches" of the Nations and attach them to Israel's well-cultivated root.[90] Thus, gentile salvation should prompt expressions of gratitude from the Nations, not boasting.[91]

Through the evocative imagery of this salvific olive tree, Paul has described the multiple but interdependent timelines for gentile and Jewish salvation, their differing natural affinities to this tree of salvation (natural vs. wild), the dependence of the new shoots of the gentiles on the root of Israel, and, ultimately, that they both share the same mechanism for inclusion or reinclusion into this salvific olive tree, that is, some sort of engrafting. In so doing, Paul has again underscored that (1) both Jews and gentiles are saved *as they are*: Jews qua Jews and gentiles qua gentiles;[92] (2) Jewish salvation holds a *Sonderplatz* or "special place" in God's plan for the redemption of Israel and the Nations; and (3) despite remaining distinct, Jews and gentiles are saved through the same means. What is this grafting technique? To answer this, we turn now to examine Paul's soteriology of baptism into Christ.

Pauline Soteriology: Salvation in Christ

The richness of Paul's olive tree, in addition to repudiating gentile arrogance, also embodies his complex and interrelated soteriological expectations for the Nations and Israel. Paul's metaphor of the olive tree facilitates expressions of difference and hierarchy (natural vs. wild branches) while still emphasizing that all of the saved are part of the same, single organism. Hierarchy among shared salvation epitomizes Paul's soteriology. Furthermore, as we shall see, not only was salvation shared, but Jews and gentiles were saved via the same means: by participating ritually in the seed of Abraham (Christ) and thus receiving the share of the promises made to Abraham.[93] This language of participation in Christ is not bland metaphor; it conveys the ontological reality that both Jews and gentiles are coheirs to Abraham insofar as they both share in the very same substance.[94]

Perhaps the best-known soteriological statement from all of Paul's letters is the "baptismal formula" from Galatians 3:26–29 in which all the saved, Jew or gentile, are saved in Christ: "For in Christ Jesus you are all children of God through faithfulness in Christ. For as many of you have been baptized, you have clothed yourself in Christ. There is neither Jew nor Greek, neither slave nor free, neither man nor woman; for all of you are one in Christ Jesus. And if you are of Christ, then you are the seed of Abraham, i.e., heirs according to the promise." Although this passage has often been and continues to be interpreted as Paul's great universalizing proclamation that all ethnic, social, and gender differences have been erased *in* Christ,[95] this is a mischaracterization of the scope and effect of Pauline soteriology.[96] Instead, Paul's global statement reflects two important implications of his monotheism, embodied best in programmatic claims such as what we find in Romans 3:29–31, where Paul has stated that God will justify all, the circumcised and uncircumcised, by means of the same faithfulness.[97] First, just as God is singular, so too is the means for saving both Jews and gentiles singular and the same (cf. Rom. 10:12). Second, since God is the God of both Jews and gentiles, they will not and should not change what they are in order to be saved.[98] God's plan of salvation assumes the continued existence of Jews and gentiles, and therefore they are both expected to stay as they are (1 Cor. 7).[99] If gentiles, in order to be saved, had to convert and become Torah-observant Jews, then God *would* be the God of Jews only and not of both Jews and gentiles (Rom. 3:29–31).

As the Apostle to the gentiles, Paul's attention was directed toward clarifying how gentiles could become heirs to Abraham. Thus, the crux and motivation for Galatians 3—and the letter as a whole—was to explain exactly why gentiles need not convert to some modified form of Jewish ritual practices in order to be considered heirs to Abraham. In her compelling monograph *If Sons, Then Heirs*, Caroline Johnson Hodge has outlined precisely how Paul was able to construct a new myth of ethnic descent in order to connect gentiles with Abraham so that they could become coheirs to promises made to him (e.g., Gal. 3; Rom. 4).[100] By reinterpreting a number of biblical passages, especially Genesis 12, 18, and 22, Paul retold the story of God's first covenant with Abraham.[101] According to Paul's version in Galatians, however, by participating in Abraham's seed, Christ, gentiles become heirs to Abraham and thus receive a share of the promises made to him and his offspring (Gal. 3:16). In order to participate in Christ and become the beneficiary of God's promises to Abraham, a gentile must be baptized and receive the Holy Spirit (*pneuma*) or Spirit of Christ.[102]

There are two consequences of Paul's participatory soteriology that deserve further attention, namely it sanctifies (makes holy) gentiles, and it transforms them into something Christ-like.[103] As we saw in Chapter 1, gentiles, according to most first-century Jews, were considered to be on the profane side of the sacred and profane spectrum; yet, following baptism, they were sanctified (1 Thess. 4:7) and thereby became a temple for God.[104] Unlike John of Patmos, therefore, gentiles who have been baptized into Christ, according to Paul, have been transformed by the infusion of Christ's *pneuma* so that they are no longer profane. This participation, moreover, was a two-way street so that just as people could enter into Christ (1 Cor. 12:12–13), so too would the Holy Spirit or Spirit of Christ enter into and dwell in that person.[105] In this way, those baptized into Christ became Christ-like. As a result, Christ's death and resurrection belong to a pattern that each person in Christ could now replicate, as we find in 1 Corinthians 15.

Yet, it is not just gentiles who were in Christ. As Galatians 3:26–29 makes clear, Jews also participated in Christ through baptism. Moreover, all, that is, both Jew and gentile, are "called through Christ," "made righteous through Christ," and baptized into the corporate "body of Christ."[106] Frustrating as it may be, however, we cannot settle exactly *why* Paul believed Jews must be baptized into Christ to receive the promises made to Abraham and his descendants.[107] Although he referred at times to a "gospel for the circumcised" (Gal. 2:7–9) and the differing strategies he adopted when preaching to Jews (1 Cor. 9:19–24), this version of a gospel addressed to the Jews does not survive. Reading between the lines, Paul did, nonetheless, expect some sort of benefit to be gained by his Jewish brethren from baptism into Christ. Based on what we have seen above regarding participation in Christ, a possible benefit that I tentatively suggest is that in order to participate in the resurrection, everyone, gentiles *and* Jews, need to participate in Christ's unique *pneuma*. In this way, a person will put on the imperishable and be transformed into something Christ-like because ordinary flesh and blood cannot inherit the kingdom (1 Cor. 15:50–57).

Furthermore, as I noted above, this shared participation in Christ parallels Paul's metaphor of the olive tree with its two distinct ethnicities belonging to the same organism. Although it was a foregone conclusion for Paul that all of Israel would be saved, this will occur only after they are engrafted again through "the power of God," a phrase we see elsewhere (1 Cor. 1:24) applied to Christ.[108] Finally, Paul concluded his overview of salvation history with the programmatic epitome, all people, Jews and gentiles, must be engrafted, in other words, baptized into Christ, so that "God may have mercy on all" (Rom. 11:32). Consequently, even if we do not know precisely why, we can conclude with relative certainty that both Jews qua Jews and gentiles qua gentiles are saved, according to Paul, by participating in Christ; ethical requirements specific to each ethnic group (e.g., Jewish Torah observance), therefore, were not the catalyst (i.e., principal cause) for salvation.[109]

This recognition cuts two ways. It entails that the rejection-replacement model, according to which Paul rejected salvation through works of the Torah for salvation through faith in Jesus, is patently false.[110] It also means that the two-covenant or *Sonderweg* approach to Paul cannot stand either.[111] As we read in Galatians 2:16, "A person (ἄνθρωπος) is not made righteous through the Law except (ἐὰν μὴ διά) through the faithfulness of Christ."[112] Paul's point here and throughout Galatians is that the Torah is not the means for salvation; rather, it is participating in Christ. Interpreters, however, who have translated ἐὰν μὴ διά as a strong disjunction—in other words, a person is not *saved* through the Law *but through* (ἐὰν μὴ διά) *faith*—have forcefully imported a rejection-replacement reading that obscures Paul's logic. For a Jew, Torah observance and participation in the faithfulness of Christ are not mutually exclusive. Although it is certainly a mystery when, how, and why all of Israel will en masse participate in Christ (Rom. 11:25–26), Paul has repeatedly stated that it is in Christ that both Jews and gentiles will be saved (e.g., Gal. 2–3). Despite advocating this single means to salvation, however, Paul did not preach an all-encompassing and universalizing ethical standard; rather, he constructed different ethical standards for Israel and the Nations.

Differing Codes of Conduct for Israel and the Nations

Therefore, since Jews are saved as Jews and gentiles saved as gentiles, Paul expects each to excel in the normative standards associated with being a gentile or a Jew:[113] "However that may be, let each of you lead the life that the Lord assigned, to which God called you. This is my rule in all the churches. Was anyone at the time of his call already circumcised? Let him not seek to remove the marks of circumcision. Was anyone at the time of his call uncircumcised? Let him not seek circumcision. Circumcision is nothing, and uncircumcision is nothing; but obeying the commandments of God is everything. Let each of you remain in the condition in which you were called" (1 Cor. 7:17–20). Consequently, if Paul, like John, expects people to play the role they were assigned in the drama of salvation history, what are the specific, normative duties that each of the dramatis personae must observe?[114] Insofar as Jews were supposed to stay as they are, they should continue to excel in what was expected of a good Jew, namely proper Torah observance.[115] As the Apostle to the gentiles, however, Paul wrote a great deal more about his expectations for gentiles. Let us conclude our analysis of Paul by examining just how his commitments to community-minded ethics,[116] and his eschatologically orienting belief that the current age is fading away,[117] affected his construction of an ethical standard tailored to the Nations.

Due to the ad hoc and pastoral nature of Paul's letter, we, unfortunately, never find a systematic or complete description of Paul's expectations for gentile ethics; however, we can piece together some important elements.[118] Paul enigmatically claimed that gentiles can "naturally do what is required of the Law without possessing the Law" (Rom. 2:14). What was required of gentiles included both negative and positive duties. In terms of negative duties, Paul frequently exhorted his gentile readers to avoid biblical vices such as idolatry, *porneia*, and other forms of immorality (e.g., 1 Cor. 6:9–11; Gal. 5:19–21). Furthermore, insofar as gentiles were meant to stay gentiles, according to Paul's vision of salvation history, they had the added negative duty of not ritually converting to Judaism or adopting Jewish Torah practices. In terms of positive duties, Paul expected his gentile readers to contribute to the saints in Jerusalem, thereby enacting the eschatological offering of the Nations.[119]

Although John of Patmos modified the motif of the eschatological pilgrimage of the Nations, Paul retained Isaiah 60's expectation of actual financial restitution.[120] As we see throughout his letters (Rom. 15; 1 Cor. 16; 2 Cor. 8–9; Gal. 2), a modus operandi for Paul was to take up a collection for "the saints" or "the poor" from his gentile congregations: "[James, Cephas, and John, i.e., the pillars of the Jerusalem church] asked only one thing, that we remember the poor, which was actually what I was eager to do" (Gal. 2:10). Writing on the biblical foundations undergirding Paul's gentile mission and collection, Roger Aus has argued that not only were biblical prophecies, such as Isaiah 60, motivating Paul to bring the wealth of the Nations to Jerusalem, but passages such as Isaiah 66:19–23 and Jeremiah 3:14 prompted Paul to travel to Spain in order to complete the eschatological ingathering of the Nations.[121]

Once he had completed his worldwide mission by baptizing and then collecting monies from *some* gentiles in Spain, Paul would have "brought in" the representative or "*full* number of the Nations" (cf. Rom. 11:25: τὸ πλήρωμα τῶν ἐθνῶν).[122] Thus, Paul believed he could cause Christ's parousia by gathering in the "full number of gentiles," defined not as the totality of all gentiles but rather a representative sampling of every variety or tribe from across the world.[123] Whether or not Paul himself would have viewed Spain as the only missing portion of a "full number of the Nations" is unclear. Aus's argument, however, rightly points to the fact Paul's ethical framework is eschatologically oriented; thus, Paul has tailored his expectations for a gentile financial collection on the basis of how the Nations ought to comport themselves in the eschaton.[124] As John Gager notes, "To ignore this [i.e., eschatological or 'end-time'] all-consuming orientation, or to downplay it, is to misread Paul at every turn. . . . This intense eschatological mentality underlies his every thought and action."[125]

Yet, another of Paul's commitments, his concern for continued harmony among the members of Christ, tempered the ethical rigor he could

demand of his gentile believers.[126] To illustrate this, let us consider a popular suggestion that has greatly influenced my own thinking on Pauline ethics, that is, Paul advocated that gentiles in Christ should follow the Noahide
Commandments (or something *very* similar), thereby becoming righteous
gentiles.[127] What is appealing about this argument is that it too differentiates between Jewish and gentile ethical conduct and even provides specifics
regarding what good gentiles are supposed to do or not to do. According to
this view, Paul adhered to a modified version of an ethic tailored to "righteous gentiles," that is, Luke's Apostolic Decree, "which set out the minimal ritual requirements for the 'stranger within your gates.'"[128] Thus, the
Apostolic Decree (Acts 15:19–35; 21:25) enabled righteous gentiles to live,
eat, and worship alongside Jewish followers of Jesus; due to the "pollution"
(ἀλίσγημα) they bring, gentiles, according to the Apostolic Decree (15:20,
29; 21:25), must avoid "things sacrificed to idols (εἰδώλων), blood (αἵματος),
things strangled (πνικτοῦ), and fornication (πορνείας)."[129]

There are at least two reasons, however, for why we ought to reject interpreting Paul's ethical expectations for gentiles as the implementation of a
concept such as the Noahide Commandments and/or Luke's Apostolic Decree.[130] First, Romans 2 shows that Paul opposed the contention that certain Judaizing teachers could make gentiles righteous through a modified
version of Torah practices.[131] Consequently, although Paul maintained that
his gentile believers ought, similar to the Apostolic Decree, to avoid *porneia*
and other vices, this was not so that these gentiles might become righteous.
Righteousness (or "justification," as it has traditionally been rendered)
comes from God through baptism into Christ.[132] Paul's participatory soteriology, then, provides a better, even if incomplete, explanation for some of
his concerns over holiness and his commitment to avoiding certain biblical
forms of impurity: you must keep your body holy, since it is now the dwelling place of the Lord (1 Cor. 3:16, 6:19; 2 Cor. 6:16).[133]

Second, when we consider the four prohibited elements of Luke's Apostolic Decree (i.e., things sacrificed to idols (εἰδώλων), blood (αἵματος),
things strangled (πνικτοῦ), and fornication (πορνείας), we see that Paul
never endorsed such a rigid standard. In fact, Paul allowed that some could
eat meat sacrificed to idols (τὰ εἰδωλόθυτα) so long as it did not upset anyone else (1 Cor. 8 and 10).[134] What was at issue for Paul was communal solidarity. Paul acknowledged that "no idol in the world really exists," and that
this should entail that eating meat sacrificed is licit (1 Cor. 8:4–13; cf. 1 Cor.

10:14–33). However, this was not the point, according to Paul. Yes, "all things are lawful, but not all things are beneficial" (1 Cor. 10:23).

Thus, what should determine the right action is how it might affect other members of the community. There may be some in the community who do not know that idols do not exist and are thus seriously disturbed and troubled when they see their brethren in Christ seemingly return to paganism by eating idol meat. Paul's solution: if it troubles your fellow members of Christ, you must avoid idol meat (1 Cor. 8:10–13). Paul's "ethic of accommodation," therefore, differs from Luke's Apostolic Decree insofar as it requires a different calculus of sin and the flexibility to address contextual problems.[135] To be sure, Paul's conception of what were gentile vices was likely determined by many of the same biblical precedents as the Apostolic Decree and parts of the Noahide Commandments (e.g., the Rules of the Sojourner); yet, Paul, for the sake of social solidarity, was willing to make accommodations so as to preserve the corporate body of Christ until Christ's impending parousia.[136]

Fundamentally, Paul's ethic was a balancing act between its eschatological focus and the everyday problems of his gentile believers. We should not import the later solutions that second-, third-, and fourth-generation followers of Jesus developed as their communities continued to develop and struggle with ethical questions; Paul never thought that far ahead. Nor should we, however tempting it may be, transform Paul into an advocate of modern, liberal values. Paul did not set out to establish a new world order free from all biases and completely harmonious, where there would no longer be Jews or gentiles, slaves or free, men or women. Paul's ethic was a frantic attempt to keep the body of Christ from bursting apart at the seams until Christ could return to set everything right. Paul was putting out fires, not establishing a systematic and timeless ethic.

When Universalism Becomes Triumphalism

"If there is truth in the claim of the Shema that God is one (Rom. iii.30), then God must judge all by the same standard and neither the ancestral possession of an air of superiority nor the possession of the Torah can make any difference. And is not this precisely the starting point of the argument of Romans? . . . It may turn out that [the book's] greatest contribution lies

in the conclusion which Sanders himself refrained from drawing."[137] So
George Caird criticized E. P. Sanders in his review of Sanders's seminal *Paul
and Palestinian Judaism*. For Caird, Paul got it right when the Apostle to the
gentiles erased Israel's special status; if he had not, God's judgments would
not be fair. This ill-defined but persistent concern about fairness or justice
permeates much of scholarship on ancient Judaism and Christianity. For
many still, it constitutes the raison d'être for Christianity because a truly
just God cannot have a favored people; he must instead treat all fairly without any concerns for preference and special dispensations. Thus, Christianity, a universalist religion, has replaced Judaism, a particularist religion.[138]
Unfortunately for these scholars, Paul and John of Patmos, their objects of
scholarly study, simply did not think this way.

The distinction between Israel and the Nations was operative for both
John and Paul. In light of the continued importance and existence of Israel
and the Nations, John and Paul hierarchically described salvation and the
ethical expectations enjoined on these different peoples. Neither John nor
Paul advocated a transcendent new race or religion; instead, both fashioned
elaborate teleological narratives wherein gentiles qua gentiles and Jews qua
Jews each had their own role to play in the drama of salvation history. It is
essential to bear in mind that both believed they were living on the cusp of
Israel's redemption; thus, the proximity of and activities expected in the eschaton provide both the motivation and the content for specific codes of
conduct.

In Parts II and III of this book, this recognition remains paramount.
As we shall see, texts and authors such as the *Shepherd of Hermas,* the *Apocryphon of John*, and some Valentinians similarly employed teleological or
fixed narratives containing higher and lower levels of salvation and different
profiles tailored to the roles that groups will play in the drama of salvation.
Like Paul and John, their approach to soteriology did not preclude concerns
for proper ethical conduct; on the contrary, by tailoring different ethical
standards to different sorts of people and constructing higher and lower
levels of salvation, these authors and texts could address the social difficulties posed by the coexistence of sinners and saints in the same community
(Part II) as well as provide justification for missionary successes and failures
(Part III).

PART II

Saints and Sinners in Early Christianity

Ethical Differences as Salvific Hierarchies in the *Shepherd of Hermas* and the *Apocryphon of John*

Chapter 3

In Heaven as It Is on Earth

Ethical and Salvific Differences in the *Shepherd
of Hermas* and the *Apocryphon of John*

The prayers and oblations of the faithful were not relevant to the
valde boni: for they could be assumed to have reached heaven with
no difficulty. Nor were they relevant to the *valde mali*: for they
could be assumed to be either *in* Hell or destined *for* Hell. The
"friction point" of early Christian eschatology, and of Early
Christian pastoral care, was the fate of the *non valdes*—the *non
valde mali,* the *non valde boni*: the "not altogether bad" and the
"not altogether good."

—Peter Brown, "Alms and the Afterlife"

The Problem of Suitable Deserts

As Peter Brown observes (albeit for a slightly later period of Christian history), a pastoral and theoretical "friction point" for many early Christians
was deciding what to do with those who were not so bad as to be excluded
from the community of the saved, but who, nonetheless, were not so good
as to deserve the same salvation as those who maintained the most righteous or saintly lives. This moral hierarchy, however, is at odds with the
fundamental binary of salvation–damnation. Can and should those who
are neither saints nor the damned be saved? If they could be saved, what
does this entail for their community's moral standards? Are there differing

standards within the same community: a saintly ideal and the merely acceptable life? What separates a minimally acceptable life from one deserving of damnation? And what impact do all these concerns have on the nature of both sin and salvation in early Christian discourse?

The *Shepherd of Hermas* (hereafter *Hermas*) and the *Apocryphon of John* (hereafter *Ap. John*) address these pastoral and theoretical concerns by constructing a salvific middle ground—below the saints but above the damned—for those who come up short of each text's highest ethical ideals. *Hermas* is a lengthy early Christian apocalypse from late first- to mid-second-century Rome, which contains a series of five visions, twelve mandates, and ten similitudes or parables.[1] The *Ap. John* is a second-century revelatory dialogue preserved in four Coptic manuscripts that date to the fourth or fifth century.[2] These Christian texts contain soteriological hierarchies that not only explain ethical shortcomings but also reinforce and justify social differentiation between insiders and outsiders. As part of their accounts of saints and sinners, each text provides diagnostic information for understanding the origins and ameliorating the dangers of sin. Thus, we find in *Hermas* and the *Ap. John* usable constructions of sinfulness and saintliness, fashioned in response to the social and theoretical problems posed by ethical variance within their communities.

Just as John of Patmos and Paul the Apostle devised different moral standards for different sorts of people, namely Jews and gentiles, *Hermas* and the *Ap. John* both subdivide the saved into different groups and similarly expect differing moral conduct from each. As opposed to Paul and John, however, who struggled to assign appropriate standards to classes of people that were divinely ordained and predated Paul and John themselves, the authors of *Hermas* and the *Ap. John* had to first devise categories of the saved in order to divide people into their appropriate groups. Rather than creative exegesis then, *Hermas* and the *Ap. John* reflect engagement with the practical concerns and even mundane moral disputes agitating their communities.[3]

For example, how could a saved person (and thus a member of the community) fall *back* into sin. To account for this relapse, *Hermas* and the *Ap. John* deploy sophisticated, demonological theories meant to explain how and why *good* persons might still sin.[4] To guard against potential moral degradation, *Hermas* and the *Ap. John* provide remedies and techniques designed to help people resist sin. In this and other ways, *Hermas* and the *Ap. John* provide modern readers with insight into how some socially minded early Christians developed explanations and practical solutions to the social and theoretical problem of ethical variance. Striking a balance, both adopted mediating positions, thereby maintaining ethical standards while remaining flexible enough to readmit penitent sinners.

Hermas and the *Ap. John*'s approach of higher and lower levels of salvation was just one among many solutions to the problem posed by the coexistence of sinners and saints in the first several centuries of the Common Era. There were a number of competing perspectives—reflecting a wide variety of contexts and agendas—on the dilemma of moral difference and the questions of whether and how to save sinners.[5] Some early Christians thought it was simply impossible to save sinners. Ethically rigorous authors, such as the author of the Letter to the Hebrews, maintained that anyone who falls back into sin after "enlightenment" is surely damned.[6] Tertullian, the cantankerous late second- and early third-century North African author, mockingly refers to the *Shepherd of Hermas* as "the shepherd of adulterers" because of its inclusive approach to sinners.[7] Sinners, according to Tertullian, should spend their remaining days groveling in prayer and penitential self-abnegation in hopes that God might forgive them after their deaths (e.g., *De pud.* 2, 4).

This rigorist opinion, however, was not universally accepted. Writing in the first half of the second century, Polycarp preached forgiveness and recommended active guidance of sinners toward repentance, and complete reintegration into the community.[8] A near contemporary of Polycarp, Ignatius of Antioch also advocated a less ethically rigorous and more socially inclusive approach, according to which sinners could—in the proper context—repent for their past sins and return to the community: "But where there is division and anger, God does not dwell. Thus the Lord forgives all who repent, if they return to the unity of God and the council of the bishop" (Ignatius, *Philadelphians* 8.1). By advocating that repentance must include "returning to the council of the bishop," Ignatius sought not only to curb social division but also to claim and consolidate authority solely in the hands of the bishops.[9] Disagreements over the inclusion or exclusion of sinners often intersected with concerns over proper sites and uses of authority.[10]

In addition to debating whether and in what contexts sinners could repent, many early Christians theorized about the very nature and source of sin. Sin, a moral category encompassing a wide range of referents, connoted disobedience and deviation from the will of God.[11] It was, however, a rather amorphous concept.[12] Thus, it could be constructed and reconstructed in a number of ways to address varying debates and questions. Why would someone sin? Is sin something internal or external to a person? How do you recognize sin and its effects on a member of the community? And are there methods or techniques to resist sinning? There are a number of competing answers to these questions. Some early Christians, echoing Paul (e.g., Rom. 5–8), regarded sin as a foreign and cosmic power; others internalized sin by locating the responsibility for wrongdoing solely in the volitions or choices of people.[13] *Hermas* and the *Ap. John* deployed a demonological construction of sinfulness; this specific permutation of sinfulness, reflecting their social circumstances, enabled both texts to diagnose the risk factors for sin and help save sinners from among their flocks.

In this same vein, many early Christians theorized about the practical and soteriological effects of sin. Were all sins the same? Could certain, less horrendous sins be forgiven, even if the worst offenses were unforgivable? If some sins were worse, were there different acts of penance or even posthumous punishments that were adjusted to correspond to a sin's relative wickedness? The second-century *Apocalypse of Peter*, containing perhaps the earliest Christian discussion of hell, takes up many of these issues.[14] This text colorfully tailors each sinner's postmortem punishment to his or her specific sins.[15] For example, those who were guilty of blaspheming were hanged by their tongues;[16] women who adorned their hair for adultery were hanged by their hair over a boiling mire;[17] and those men who similarly engaged in adultery were suspended by the offending organ over a boiling pit.[18] As opposed to speculating only about postmortem punishments, other early Christian authors sought to design remedies and penitential practices that could expunge one's sins, either in the here and now or to prepare a soul to receive God's forgiveness after death.[19] Yet just what those practices were, how long they were required, and whether they would be effective were all matters of much debate.

It is within this context—during which no one solution of whether, when, and how to save sinners had secured universal support—that *Hermas* and the *Ap. John* emerged. Reflecting its active engagement with rival thinkers and proposals, *Hermas* (*Man.* 4.3) addresses itself directly to these debates: "'I have heard, Lord,' I said, 'from some teachers that there is no other repentance except from the one when we went into the water and received forgiveness from our earlier sins.'" Yet, *Hermas* and the *Ap. John* were not only interested in the problem of saving sinners; both texts differentiate and explicate the content of a higher ethical standard reserved for saintly characters. Consequently, it is this dual function of *Hermas* and the *Ap. John*'s middle-ground salvific solution between total forgiveness/integration and uncompromising rejection/exclusion that we shall explore in detail.

Thus, we shall investigate the social and theoretical function of higher and lower levels of salvation for both *Hermas* and the *Ap. John* within the context of early (ca. second-century) Christianity, in particular as a strategy for dealing with communal difficulties posed by ethical variance. These two understudied texts present multitiered ethical and soteriological landscapes that are populated by more than simply good and bad people. Through their rhetorical constructions of higher and lower levels of salvation, *Hermas* and the *Ap. John* provide evidence of rich and sophisticated problem-solving and ethical reasoning that have been heretofore overlooked by scholars.[20] Despite describing what a saintly life would entail, both *Hermas* and the *Ap. John* pragmatically recognize the impossibility for large numbers to abide by this highest standard. Consequently, neither promulgates a zero-sum difference between right and wrong conduct.[21]

By examining what constitutes each text's highest ideals, minimum ethical requirements, notion(s) of sin, strategies for resisting deviant conduct, and means for reincorporating sinners, we gain insight into a formative period of Christian ethical discourse. In light of their shared concerns over communal stability, I will suggest that social location for the writers, readers, and perhaps even the first circulators of both *Hermas* and the *Ap. John* most likely resembled that of the small, tight-knit congregations meeting together in house-churches in urban settings.

An additional goal of Part II is to bring two texts that are normally studied in isolation from one another—*Hermas* and the *Ap. John*— into close conversation. Too often the labels modern scholars assign to texts are determinative of the sorts of questions and frameworks that will be employed.[22] This problem is perhaps best illustrated by the use of comparanda. So-called heterodox texts and authors are situated and compared almost exclusively to other heterodox, marginalized, or even non-Christian (e.g., Greco-Roman philosophical, mystery religious, or "auto-Orientalizing" and purposefully exotic) literature;[23] in contrast, so-called orthodox texts and authors are compared to biblical and other early Christian texts presumed to be normative or at least closer to the center of Christian discourse.[24] Consequently, even if we jettison the explicit use of problematic terms, such as "heresy" and "orthodoxy," we still reinscribe normative vs. nonnormative categories insofar as we will treat marginalized texts one way and retrospectively mainstream texts another way.[25] In what follows, I am seeking—inasmuch as is possible—to set aside terms and discourses that reinforce this dichotomy of mainstream orthodoxy and marginalized heresy.[26]

Higher and Lower Levels of Salvation

Shortly after the dawn of the second century of the Common Era, a distinctive and new religious movement, Christianity, had begun to emerge from its Jewish roots.[27] As time continued to elapse between the increasingly distant era of Christ and the present, these gentile converts or "ex-pagan pagans" were forced to confront a number of soteriological and ethical questions as they developed what became nascent Christianity.[28] Are all the saved—despite differences in moral quality—equal in the eyes of God? Is there (and/or should there be) a soteriological distinction of greater and lesser rewards between saints and merely average Christians? Furthermore, is there a reason why some people are saints, whereas most others come up short? How do we quantify and explain this apparent moral hierarchy? And perhaps most unsettling: What happens when the saved sin again? How is this possible? Can it be remedied? Are there different *types* of sinners? Are some worse than others? How should a community balance its standards for ethical uprightness with human moral frailty without either abandoning core values or eventually excluding all but ethical virtuosos?

Hermas and the *Ap. John* posit higher and lower levels of salvation to answer these questions. In what follows, I will introduce the texts of *Hermas* and the *Ap. John*, summarizing some of the key historiographic debates surrounding these texts and outlining their soteriologies of higher and lower levels of salvation. Both *Hermas* and the *Ap. John* employ utopian, salvific imagery to construct ethical ideals. In so doing, *Hermas* and the *Ap. John* create classes of people that are rhetorically useful both for elucidating the content of these higher and lower standards for ethical conduct and for justifying higher and lower levels of salvation.[29] In other words, saints, because they do saintly things, occupy a more prestigious heavenly residence than do repentant sinners.

Despite sharing these structural similarities of higher and lower ethical expectations and levels of salvation, *Hermas* and the *Ap. John* differ on the content of these ethical ideals. What makes a saint a saint in *Hermas* differs significantly from what makes a saint in the *Ap. John*. Furthermore, what sin and repentance signify differs as well. *Hermas* holds all of humanity account-able to the same, single moral code, namely the degree to which people obey and even suffer for the Law of God.[30] As a result, repentance, in *Hermas*, is a total and whole-minded turning back toward this single, moral code.[31] In contrast, the *Ap. John*, through its salvation-history narrative, outlines two avenues toward salvation and two repentances—one for its own putative community and one for those who live and die outside of it.[32] Nonetheless, both texts employ the soteriological technology of higher and lower levels of salvation to articulate ethical ideals and to address the social and theoretical difficulty of ethical variance—saints along with sinners—in their midst.

The Shepherd of Hermas: Making a Place for Both Sinners and Saints in the Church

Hermas was an extremely popular text and circulated widely among early Christians. From the Egyptian town of Oxyrhynchus alone, we have at least ten Greek and one Coptic late antique fragments of *Hermas*—significantly more than from any book from the New Testament, with the exceptions of the Gospels of John and Matthew,[33] from the same period at Oxyrhyn-chus.[34] Although not included among some of the best-known early Chris-tian canon lists, *Hermas was* included in some of the earliest Bibles, such as the fourth-century *Sinaiticus*.[35] *Hermas*, thereby, embodies the contested and overlapping categories that complicate straightforward accounts of the New Testament canonization process.[36] That is, even if *Hermas* was rele-gated to the secondary position of educationally useful in some canon lists (Athanasius; Muratorian Canon), it was still part of the *practical* canon for many early Christians, who read and used *Hermas* for theological reflec-tion.[37] As a result, *Hermas* was one of the most influential and oft-cited early Christian texts, surpassing many texts that were later included in the New Testament.[38]

Despite its ancient popularity, *Hermas* is notoriously difficult for schol-ars to categorize and date. It is not a straightforward tractate, epistle, or homily,[39] but is rather an eclectic collection of ethically minded dialogues concerned with reunifying rivalrous factions.[40] Compounding the enigma surrounding *Hermas* are questions related to its author: Who was this eponymous Hermas, and when and where did he compose his lengthy work?

Most scholars agree that the references to Rome (e.g., the Tiber in *Vis.* 1.1 and Via Campania in *Vis.* 4.1) provide plausible enough reason to place its author there.[41] Establishing a date for *Hermas*, however, is far more contentious. There are three "pegs" upon which all theories for dating *Hermas* hang: the reference to Hermas in Romans 16:14;[42] the mention of *a* Clement—who some scholars claim is *the* Clement of Rome[43]—in *Vision* 2.4.3; and the Muratorian Canon's claim that Hermas composed *Hermas* during the reign of his brother Pius, who was, according to Eusebius (*Hist. eccl.* 4.11), bishop of Rome in 140–154 CE.[44] On the basis of these, we are left with a possible time period stretching from the middle of the first century to the second third of the second century.[45]

Yet, even this cautious and broad range is not without controversy. Implicit in all three pegs is the belief that "Hermas" was not a literary fiction but a flesh-and-blood person. The opening scene of *Hermas*, however, where Hermas introduces himself—and is thus often interpreted as the most autobiographical section[46]—is largely a reworking of Greco-Roman literary motifs.[47] Adding further difficulty to our task: none of our three pegs is without serious methodological questions and concerns. Origen was the first author to connect *Hermas* with the Hermas mentioned in Romans 16:14 (*Comm. Rom.* 10.31), and he did so for the purpose of securing apostolic authority for the text.[48] The reference to a Clement in *Vision* 2.4.3 is tantalizingly sparse and does not provide enough information to securely identify this Clement with the author of 1 Clement.[49] And finally, the Muratorian Canon is an object of much debate, importantly with regard to both its date and the degree to which it reflects the realities of second-century Christianity;[50] but even if we put aside those serious caveats, the Muratorian Canon is still rather vague in its reference to Hermas, stating only that "Hermas wrote the Shepherd recently in our times (*nuperrime temporibus nostris*) while his brother Pius was sitting as bishop in the chair of the church of the city of Rome."[51]

Can we recover the historical Hermas (if there even was one!) and more precisely delimit his time period?[52] The best way forward, I contend, is to reject the extremes on either end of the possible time range and recognize that *Hermas* is neither exclusively autobiographical nor solely literary fiction but contains elements of both.[53] Therefore, *Hermas* is a complex narrative containing both semiautobiographical and stylized elements that was composed sometime between the very end of the first century and halfway through the second century in Rome. Thus, even if we cannot recover *the* historical Hermas, we can, nonetheless, examine *Hermas* as an artifact that can provide us with insight into this specific time and place.

The loose, often redundant, and seemingly disorganized style of the *Shepherd of Hermas* is off-putting to many modern readers. On account of *Hermas*'s disjointed style, some scholars have even maligned the intelligence of its author and speculated that *Hermas* may, in fact, be a piecemeal collection of various works by as many as six different authors that were hastily patched together.[54] These arguments are bolstered by the literary seams that appear throughout *Hermas* (e.g., *Vis.* 5 is distinct from *Vis.* 1–4 and introduces the *Mandates*; similarly *Sim.* 9.1 transitions to a different literary unit, as does *Sim.* 10.1).[55] Yet, careful analysis of *Hermas* has shown that its loose, repetitive, and "conversational" style is indicative of oral conventions for composition.[56] Thus, because of the elastic nature of the work, a single author could continue to add materials or ideas over an extended period of composition (*Sim.* 9).[57] It appears most likely, then, that *Hermas* was composed by a single author in the following four stages: *Visions* 1–4; *Vision* 5–*Similitude* 8; *Similitude* 9, and *Similitude* 10.[58]

In addition to its style and authorship, the genre of *Hermas* has also been the source of some debate. This disagreement can be summarized with the following question: Is the *Shepherd of Hermas* an apocalypse?[59] For some, although *Hermas* contains a number of apocalyptic conventions, it is not apocalyptic *enough* in content to truly warrant the label of an apocalypse.[60] According to this view, *Hermas* insufficiently employs typically apocalyptic features such as "detailed revelations about the world beyond and end-time catastrophes; historical speculations; pessimism about the outcome of this world; and pseudepigraphical nature."[61] As a result, these scholars characterize *Hermas* as an apocalypse in "form only" or as a "pseudo-apocalypse."[62] Other scholars have concluded that *Hermas* may be an apocalypse but of a special sort, adding clarifying modifiers such as "moral," "cooled-down," or "practical."[63] Yet, whatever modern modifier is affixed, *Hermas* is a revelatory text, and ancient readers recognized it as such.[64] The issue for these ancients was not just the degree to which *Hermas* corresponded to a series of genre traits but also the nature of the authority behind the text. Thus, *Hermas* and, as we shall see, the *Ap. John* are both revelatory dialogues that mediate and convey divine knowledge to humanity, thereby imbuing their literary content with heavenly authority.[65]

What is the content of the knowledge revealed in *Hermas*? Belying its "folksy" style, which is long on talk and short on action, *Hermas* is a subtly complex text that employs an array of sophisticated layering techniques.[66] For example, we find features such as dreams within dreams as well as the author's self-effacing, self-reflexive, and moralizing construction of "himself" as a hapless narrator, both of which help to convey *Hermas*'s overarching concerns and themes; central among these is the issue of repentance or conversion (*metanoia*).[67] Throughout the whole of the work, *Hermas* encourages repentance, at times even through the mouthpiece of the angel of repentance (*Vis.* 5.7; *Man.* 12.6.1). In so doing, *Hermas* describes the nature of sin and repentance (e.g., *Man.* 4) and also details how repentance affects one's salvific end (*Vis.* 8). Furthermore, often disappointing intellectual historians, *Hermas* is uninterested in theoretical or doctrinal theologizing about the nature of God, Christ, or creation;[68] instead, *Hermas* is concerned with seemingly mundane sins (e.g., unruly children, gossiping wives, sexual misconduct, and the improper use of wealth) and the social disharmony they cause.[69]

Hermas's interest in these everyday banalities has perplexed scholars and likely has contributed to the characterization of the text by some as intellectually inferior.[70] This negative appraisal overlooks some of the qualities that made *Hermas* so popular. *Hermas*'s preoccupation with everyday concerns, such as household management, was a "synecdoche" for concerns about church leadership.[71] Moreover, these were the types of problems that *Hermas*'s readers faced on a day-to-day basis; in other words, *Hermas* contains a mimetic strategy whereby its readers would identify with the troubles Hermas faced and thereby enter more fully into the narrative setting by adopting both his struggles and his solutions as their own.[72] Consequently, *Hermas*'s account of the fractionalization of his own household resembles the everyday difficulties of other Christians but is also a microcosm for the perils and rivalries threatening the unity of the "church" throughout the world.

As the text opens, *Hermas* introduces the reader to its complex and often conflicted eponymous protagonist. While traveling, Hermas comes across his former mistress, Rhoda, bathing in the Tiber; after helping her out from the river, he protests to no one and a bit too strongly that he did not have any untoward desires upon seeing her beauty (*Vis.*1.1.2). The reader's suspicions are confirmed when later Rhoda appears in a dream and confronts Hermas for the "evil desire" that arose in his heart (*Vis.* 1.1.8).[73] In response to Rhoda's accusation, Hermas laments: "If this sin is counted against me, how can I be saved?" (*Vis.* 1.2.1). Comforting Hermas and referring to him as the "self-restrained," the revelatory figure who appears, Lady Church, offers the following programmatic claim: even upright persons can sin (*Vis.* 1.2.4). Thus, whether they be his sins of desire or even his failures as a paterfamilias (*Vis.* 1.3), there is still hope that Hermas's sins—and by extension the cognate sins of the reader—can be expiated through repentance (*Vis.* 2.2.4). To borrow an excellent epitomization, "Hermas is not merely the messenger of *metanoia*, but the *exemplum*."[74]

Hermas, therefore, describes the activity and impact that repentance has upon a sinner. Over the course of three visions, the revelatory figure, Lady Church, alters her appearances, and these changes track Hermas's moral advancement.[75] As Hermas "rejuvenates his spirit," Lady Church becomes increasingly younger and more beautiful in appearance (*Vis.* 3.11–13).[76] Hermas progresses from being unable to translate even the syllables of Lady Church's book (*Vis.* 2.1.4) to being so full of faith that he courageously steps over a Leviathan he happens upon while traversing the Via Campania (*Vis.* 4.1). Fortified by the proper knowledge of repentance, Hermas provides guidance and encouragement for those seeking repentance.[77] Thus, *Hermas* constructs a character, Hermas, whose internal conflict and moral amelioration provide the blueprint for its practical advice for repentant sinners.[78]

In addition to its well-crafted and relatable protagonist,[79] *Hermas*'s compelling and evocative imagery may help explain its widespread popularity.[80] *Hermas* confronts and challenges the reader with a series of visually rich dreams and parables whose language is "mobile, many-faceted, [and] metaphoric."[81] Through this visual storytelling, *Hermas* not only externalizes and translates into commonplace but still vibrant images Hermas's emotional and moral struggles but also employs these images and imagined spaces to illuminate the social situations and ethical dilemmas faced by the Christian "church" all over the world.[82] In so doing, *Hermas* encourages idealized social relationships and ethical conduct through the creation of these imagined objects and spaces. In *Similitude* 2, for example, *Hermas* articulates the symbiotic (and idealized) relationship of the poor and the wealthy by analogy to the biological metaphor of the interdependent growth of the elm tree and its vines.[83] Similarly, *Similitude* 8 represents the relative moral quality of all Christians by analogy to different sorts of willow branches. Importantly for this book, *Hermas* routinely makes use of stylized visuals to describe and synthesize moral hierarchy (e.g., among saints, sinners, and the damned) with appropriate salvific statuses.

In the elaborate vision and lengthy clarifying dialogue of *Vision 3*, *Hermas* analogizes the moral and salvific hierarchy of humanity to a massive tower. During this exchange with Lady Church, Hermas is rebuked for his constant concern about sin and repentance. Lady Church interrupts Hermas as he confesses his sins and commands him to "ask also about righteousness" (Vis. 3.1.6). To illustrate what righteousness entails, *Hermas* describes a great tower made of different types of stone (Vis. 3.2.4–9). During the vision, Hermas sees thousands of men bringing stones from all over the world. Some stones, Lady Church explains, are accepted and seamlessly become part of the tower; others are rejected, broken, and tossed aside. As is clarified sometime later, this vision is the ideal church insofar as it is a composite structure comprised of different sorts of persons. Through this metaphor, *Hermas* characterizes different types of humanity by spatial analogy to how different types of stone relate to construction of the imagined space of the ideal church.

The engaging vision of the composite tower has a number of ethical functions. It underscores *Hermas*'s concern for social harmony among the different factions comprising the "church." By evoking the unity of the whole, *Hermas* reminds its readers that self-centered divisiveness damages everyone by weakening the corporate body of the church.[84] This imagery also prioritizes certain members over and above others on the basis of their apparent moral (i.e., spatial) utility for the building:

> "Hear now about the stones that go into the building. On the one
> hand, the squared and white stones that fit together at the joints
> are the apostles, bishops, teachers, and deacons who live reverently
> towards God and perform their duties as bishops, teachers, and
> deacons for the chosen ones of God in a holy and respectful
> way. . . ." "But who are the ones drawn from the depths of the
> sea? . . ." "These are those who have suffered on account of the
> name of the Lord." ". . . But who are those who were tossed aside
> and cast out?" "These are those who have sinned, but wish to
> repent . . . they will be useful for the building if they repent . . . if
> they repent while the tower is still under construction." (Vis. 3.5.1–5)

For *Hermas,* there are certain moral *exempla* whose place in the tower is more secure and useful than others; these *exempla*, moreover, and their distinctive tasks form the content of *Hermas*'s highest ethical standard.

Yet, this spatial metaphor does more than valorize apostles, bishops, teachers, deacons, and martyrs; to highlight their exemplary nature, *Hermas* also delineates an inferior subsection of the "church." In contrast, then, to the extraordinary are the ordinary, namely repentant sinners, who fall short of the highest moral standard. Their secondary status is introduced by emphasizing the uncertain and diminishing time available for them to repent (*Vis.* 2:2.5; 3:5.5). Furthermore, *Hermas* spatially subordinates these repentant sinners by noting that although they can be saved, they will be fit into a "greatly inferior place," which they will enter only after suffering expiating torments (*Vis.* 3.7.5–6).

At the start of *Similitude* 8, *Hermas* again describes the unequal moral standing of different types of Christians and their different salvific rankings. Recalling the totalizing dichotomies of the *Mandates*, *Similitude* 8 divides all of humanity into either the virtuous or the vicious.[85] As we will see below, the vicious are further subdivided on the basis of both their sins and the likelihood and speed at which they will repent. Similarly, the virtuous, although they all will "enter into the tower" and thus be saved (*Sim.* 8.2), are also subdivided, with some enjoying even greater honors. The virtuous are all saved due to their steadfast obedience to the "Laws of God" (*Sim.* 8.3); some, however, go further and uphold the divine law even in the face of persecution. These martyrs, according to the Shepherd, receive crowns that set them apart and above others (*Sim.* 8.3.6–7).

Other early Christians also attributed higher salvific rewards to those who endured suffering on account of their faith. In both *De Anima* (55) and *Scorpiace* (12), Tertullian ascribes greater salvific rewards to those who have suffered and died for the sake of their faith.[86] Like Tertullian,[87] *Hermas* deploys these saintly characters in the service of its ideological agenda.[88] *Hermas,* therefore, is an important and early instance of a Christian text domesticating the authority of the martyrs.[89] In this way, *Hermas* exploits the social capital of martyrs to authenticate its ethical ideals and social injunctions—for example, in *Mandate* 8.

In addition to extolling and authorizing specific ethical ideals by appealing to higher and lower levels of salvation, *Hermas* employs a different salvific hierarchy, one of only sinners, in order to console those who may have sinned and to distinguish between those who might still return to the fold—both eagerly repentant and recalcitrant sinners—and those who never will, who are apostates. As Hermas himself illustrates (*Vis.* 3.4.3; cf. *Sim.* 7.1), not everyone is a saint, and many have fallen short of the highest of ethical ideals. It is to this group that *Hermas* addresses the bulk of its paranetic material, and in so doing provides a nuanced and layered account of those sinners who may yet repent.

In the second half of *Similitude* 8, *Hermas* deploys a spatial metaphor similar to *Vision* 3 to differentiate among different types of persons; in this case, however, *Hermas* distinguishes among types of sinners and allocating higher and lower levels of salvation based on the swiftness of one's repentance: "All those who have repented have a dwelling place in the tower. All those who repent more slowly will still dwell within the walls. But those who do not repent but remain in their deeds will surely die" (*Sim.* 8.7.3).[90] In this passage, relative proximity to or distance from the center of the structure conveys the salvific status of the class of person. This spatial hierarchy, unlike in *Vision* 3, is not about representing the ethical hierarchy of the whole church, comprised of sinners and saints alike. Instead, *Hermas* assigns different salvific rewards on the basis of how quickly or easily the sinner repents. In so doing, *Hermas* devises a corresponding hierarchy of *three* types of sinners that plays upon its earlier hierarchy of saints, sinners, and the damned; those sinners who excel at repentance are structurally analogous to saintly figures such as apostles or martyrs. Repentance itself, in contrast to what we will see in the *Ap. John*, remains constant (i.e., it is a return to obeying the laws of God), and is thus the same for both the eagerly repentant and the recalcitrant sinner.

Furthermore, *Hermas*'s three types of sinners in *Similitude* 8 appear to be all postbaptismal sinners, namely those who have "received the seal (of baptism) but have broken it": "Lord, now explain to me what kind of person each one is . . . so that those who have believed and received the seal, but broken it and not kept it intact, may hear and recognize their own deeds, and so repent, receive a seal from you, and glorify the Lord, because he showed them mercy and sent you [the angel of repentance] to renew their spirits" (*Sim.* 8.6.3). This is one of the earliest references to the "seal" of baptism.[91] Baptism, according to *Hermas*, is the only means of salvation (*Vis.* 3.3.3, 5; cf. *Sim.* 9.16). Moreover, *Hermas* warns those who undergo baptism about both the rigorous standards for purity of postbaptismal life (*Vis.* 3.7.3) and the potentially dire consequences awaiting those who violate this seal with postbaptismal sins (*Man.* 4.3).

Hermas, therefore, must explain not only why someone might sin after baptism but also why someone would delay before repenting for these postbaptismal sins. To account for the possibility of postbaptismal sins, *Hermas* draws upon the demonological discourse of rival angels, one good and one evil (*Man.* 6).[92] Furthermore, *Hermas* constructs an innovative category of postbaptismal sinners, those who are "double-minded," in order to account for prolonged sinfulness. Importantly, however, these sinners are still distinct from apostates because although they delay they will eventually repent: "Many of them were double-minded (ἐδιψύχησαν). These still have a chance to repent, if they do so quickly; and they dwell in the tower. But if they repent more slowly, they will dwell only within the walls. And if they do not repent, they too have destroyed their lives" (*Sim.* 8.8.3). In this way, *Hermas* uses spatial metaphors to differentiate and subdivide postbaptismal sinners into distinct and usable categories of persons—for example, recalcitrant sinners who are not apostates. In so doing, Hermas is crafting a hierarchy of human behavior and dispositions that is suited for his own pastoral concerns: he can reintegrate different types of sinful community members—even those who may have strayed more seriously and for longer periods of time—but still, ultimately, insulate his community from (the idea of?) dangerous apostates. By means of this new category of postbaptismal sinners, Hermas can encourage these postbaptismal sinners to return and participate in the shared salvation of the unified church, even if, because of their double-mindedness, these sinners are ultimately sequestered in a lower level of salvation.

Before turning to the *Ap. John*, I wish to reiterate a few key points. First, *Hermas* deploys a salvific hierarchy that tailors salvific rewards according to the degree persons satisfy an ethical ideal epitomized by saintly figures. In addition to a highest level of salvation for saintly figures, there is also a middle class of salvation for those who fall short of this ideal. Second, *Hermas* devises a second hierarchy structurally similar to the first (i.e., of saints, repentant sinners, and damned sinners) that consists only of sinners. Thus, the position of saint is occupied by virtuosos at repenting, that is, those who do so immediately and wholeheartedly. By creating a hierarchy of repentant sinners, *Hermas* can encourage immediate repentance by warning of the impending day of the Lord but still has the theoretical flexibility to address the problem of those sinners who have not *yet* repented.[93] Third, *Hermas* curbs the impulse to police social boundaries too absolutely. *Hermas* warns steadfast community members against maintaining too rigid boundaries between themselves and apparent apostate sinners.

From an eschatological vantage point of knowing how everything will turn out, it is possible to distinguish between apostates and those sinners who will eventually repent; but from the point in time in which Hermas and his readers are currently living, however, apostates and future repentant sinners resemble one another. Consequently, though there may—at some point in the future—be true apostates, it is unclear which postbaptismal sinners will ultimately return or remain in mired in sin. Thus, *Hermas's* middle class of salvation and their delayed repentance blur the boundary between repentant sinner and apostate in order to facilitate the reintegration of sinners.

The Apocryphon of John: Narrativizing Sin and Salvation

A revelatory dialogue between John the son of Zebedee and the risen Christ, the *Apocryphon of John* is likely the earliest Christian text to present a unified and totalizing narrative of the nature of God, the source of sin, the origin of the world, the creation of humanity, and the plan for salvation.[94] In the four manuscripts in which it survives, the *Ap. John* was placed in the first position or directly following the *Gospel of Mary* in the Berlin Codex (NHC II, 1; III, 1; IV, 1; BG 8502, 2), thereby reflecting the *Ap. John's* perceived role as an overview of Christian theology and cosmology.[95] The *Ap. John* is a remarkably rich text that blends cosmogonic ideas drawn from Platonic (*Timaeus* and *Parmenides*) and Jewish (Genesis) sources, presents a similarly synthetic account of human psychology and behavior, and retells the story of salvation history by interacting, correcting, and expanding on the accounts of Genesis and the Gospel of John.[96]

Although the *Apocryphon of John* survives only in four fourth- or fifth-century Coptic manuscripts,[97] most scholars agree that it was likely composed in Greek and that this Greek *Vorlage* comes from approximately the second century.[98] Two external witnesses appear to support this approximate date for the composition of the *Ap. John*. In his late second-century (ca. 180) work *Against Heresies* (1.29), Irenaeus cites something very much like the cosmogonic myth found at the beginning of the *Ap. John*. Furthermore, in the mid-third century, Porphyry criticizes a group affiliated with the study circle of his teacher Plotinus that read books similar to the *Ap. John* (*Life of Plotinus* 16); one such book title ("the Book of Zoroaster") appears in the *Ap. John* itself (NHC II, 19.10).[99]

Among the four manuscripts, there are two different recensions: a shorter version (BG and NHC III) and a longer version (NHC II and IV). Some of the major differences between the shorter and longer recensions are that the shorter lacks the concluding *Pronoia* hymn (NHC II, 30.11–31.25) and the lengthy *melothesia* section describing the archontic construction of the various parts of Adam's body (NHC II, 15.29–19.10). Although it is difficult to establish a clear stemma among the four manuscripts, there are some general tendencies.[100] The longer recension (NHC II and IV), especially when compared to the shorter recension (BG and NHC III), appears more internally consistent and to have fewer "contradictions and ambiguities."[101] It has been plausibly suggested, therefore, that the longer recension underwent editorial redaction to bring the whole of the text into agreement with the addition of the concluding *Pronoia* hymn.[102] Fortunately for my purposes, both the shorter and the longer recension contain the hierarchical description of the four luminaries (BG 35.6–36.16; NHC II, 8.35–9.24) and the dialogue concerning various salvific fates of different types of souls (BG 64.14–71.2; NHC II, 25.16–27.30). Thus, although I will not appeal to any manuscript as containing the *original* reading, I will note differences among the manuscripts and offer explanations where I can of the probable cause for some variants.[103]

In terms of content and form, the *Ap. John* clearly draws upon conventions from the revelatory dialogues of the "traditions of Jewish apocalyptic."[104] For example, the *Ap. John*'s format of a dialogue between the distressed John and his heavenly interlocutor echoes a well-established trope in apocalyptic literature.[105] Furthermore, as we saw with *Hermas*, the *Ap. John*'s genre as a revelatory dialogue enabled a degree of textual elasticity, wherein certain ideas could be expanded upon or inserted over the course of the *Ap. John*'s transmission history while still preserving the relative stability of the work as a whole.[106] Moreover, the *Ap. John*, as a textual vehicle for revelation, plays the role of the revealer figure.[107] In this way, the reader identifies with John, whose questions aim to anticipate and reflect the reader's concerns; primary among them, as we will see, are the following: What is the source and nature of evil? How can people be saved? Are all people saved, and if not what happens to sinners? Through its dialogue format, the *Ap. John* answers these pressing questions with responses imbued with the authority of the Savior.

As the *Ap. John* opens, John, the brother of James and the son of Zebedee,[108] is accosted by a Pharisee named Arimanios.[109] Since this conversation takes place after the Savior's ascent, Arimanios asks John where his master has gone, and then ridicules John for his response that his master has returned to "the place from which he came."[110] Distressed by Arimanios's accusation that he has "abandoned the traditions of your fathers," John vacates the temple for a deserted mountain (BG 20.4–6).[111] There, John becomes emotionally distressed and pleads for answers to his questions: "How was the savior appointed? Why was he sent into the world by his Father? Who is his Father who sent him? And what sort is that aeon to which we shall go?" In answer, the heavens open up, the earth shakes, and a revelatory figure, having the appearance of a child, an old man, and a servant, appears. This figure, who identifies himself as the "Father, Mother, and Son," promises to reveal to John "what is, what was, and what will come to pass . . . the things concerning the immovable race of the perfect man" so that John can reveal these things to "your fellow spirits."[112] So begins the revelatory dialogue of the *Ap. John* (NHC II, 1.1–2.25; BG 19.6–22.16).

In what follows, this enigmatic figure—later identified with the Savior (NHC II, 22.10, 12) or Christ (BG 58.2)—reveals to John the nature of the true and highest God (the "Father" or "Invisible Spirit") and the most perfect levels of reality, as well as why the material world was created and what humanity's role is in this sweeping narrative spanning all time (i.e., present, primordial past, and eschatological conclusion). Engaging with but also qualifying contemporary Middle Platonic theological and epistemological speculation, the *Ap. John* employs both *apophatic* and *kataphatic* strategies in its revelatory description of the highest God.[113] In this way, the Savior reveals the nature of the Father to John through a complex mix of strategies (e.g., *via negationis*, *via eminentiae*, and *via analogiae* claims).

It is plausible that the *Ap. John* is disputing the apparent claims of Middle Platonists, in particular Alcinous, that human rationality can comprehend the reality of the highest divinity;[114] instead, and underscoring the transcendence of the highest God, the *Ap. John* maintains that it is only through revelation that one can *know* about him (NHC II, 4.10–5.4; BG 26.1–27.19).[115] Nonetheless, it is important to note that negative (apophatic) theologies could be deployed in support of a variety of claims.[116] Thus, in addition to addressing epistemological concerns, the *Ap. John*, through its pious reflection on the transcendence of the highest God, also establishes a vertical orientation and hierarchy of values that foreground the remainder of the text's ontological, ethical, and soteriological discussions.

The importance of this hierarchy is further underscored during the *Ap. John*'s account of the emergence of the remaining two members of the divine triad (the "Mother" or "Barbelo" and the "Son" or "Autogenes"), the four Lights or Luminaries, and the twelve aeons.[117] The *Ap. John* recounts the gradual emergence of the divine realms in a "metaphysical fiction that reenacts the stages of God in a folktale sequence."[118] These stages imbue the mythic narrative with a value-laden hierarchy of stations and ranks. For example, the four Lights or Luminaries (NHC III and BG: ΟΥΟΕΙΝ; NHC II and IV: ⲪⲰⲤⲦⲎⲢ), which also house the twelve aeons, are introduced in descending, hierarchical order: "Grace is with the first light, Harmozel, who is the angel of light in the first aeon, with him there are three aeons: Grace, Truth, and Form. The Second light is [Oro]iael, the one He placed over the second aeon, with him are three aeons: Providence, Perception, and Memory. The third light is Daveithe, the one He placed over the third aeon, with him are three aeons: Understanding, Love, and [Idea].[119] And the fourth light is [Ele]leth, the one He placed over the fourth aeon, with him are three aeons: Perfection, Peace, and Wisdom (*Sophia*)" (BG 33.7–34.7). Further accentuating its utopian but also hierarchical portrait of the divine realm, the aeons operate analogously to a well-regulated household, with the paterfamilias at its head.[120] In this way, the unfolding of the heavenly realms occurs only with the consent of the Father. Thus, the heavenly realms are an idealized collection of aeons, organized in a spatial and temporal hierarchy, all of which came to be with the consent of the Father.[121]

This ordered and harmonious congress of heavenly realms is ruptured by the deviant behavior of its lowest (last mentioned) aeon, Sophia (NHC II, 9.25–13.7; BG 36.16–45.4). Sophia's unruly conduct (namely desiring "to manifest a likeness of herself" [NHC II, 9.28–29: ⲞⲨⲰⲚϨ ⲈⲂⲞⲖ Ⲛ̄ⲞⲨⲈⲒⲚⲈ Ⲛ̄ϨⲎⲦⲤ̄] without the consent of the Father or her consort) upsets the pattern of deference and single-minded obedience to the governance of the Father that had previously epitomized the organization of the divine realms.[122] Sophia's deviant conduct produces the "problem child" Ialdabaoth, who is a deformed monstrosity but also steals a portion of his Mother, Sophia's power.[123] In her shame, Sophia hides Ialdabaoth from her aeonic colleagues in a bright cloud.

Ignorant of his own origins, Ialdabaoth creates—according to the divine pattern (BG 39.9: ⲦⲨⲠⲞⲤ) and by means of the great power (NHC II, 10.21: ⲆⲨⲚⲀⲘⲒⲤ) he stole from Sophia (cf. NHC II, 12.5–8)—his own, lower world order consisting of inferior aeons and authorities.[124] Because he has this stolen power in him, Ialdabaoth is able to fashion the lower world "according to the model of the first aeon" (ⲕⲀⲦⲀ ⲠⲒⲚⲈ Ⲛ̄Ⲛ(ϣ)ⲞⲢⲠ [Ⲛ]ⲀⲒⲰⲚ) and "the pattern of the indestructible ones" (Ⲙ̄ⲠⲤⲘⲀⲦ Ⲛ̄ⲀⲦⲦⲈⲔⲞ).[125] After surveying his creation, Ialdabaoth boasts: "I am a jealous God; there is no other God beside me" (BG 44.14–15; NHC II, 13.8–9). Although Ialdabaoth's boast resonates with biblical authority (Isa. 45:5–6; cf. 46:9), it is patently false;

the narrative voice of the Savior even peevishly asks: "If there are no other gods of whom could he be jealous?" (BG 44.17–18; NHC II, 13.12–13). And so, by reinterpreting and synthesizing Jewish and Platonic creation accounts, the *Ap. John* recounts how the world—a mixture of good and evil—came to be: through an ignorant and rebellious (BG 43.4: ⲈϤⲞ ⲚⲚⲀⲦⲠⲒⲐⲈ) creator who, nonetheless, employed a divine and superior power and model.[126]

In what follows, the *Ap. John* narrates the story of Sophia's repentance and redemption, which leads to the ultimate restoration of the divine harmony; of special importance to the *Ap. John* is the role of humanity in this cosmological drama of salvation history. Upon seeing the wickedness of her offspring and grasping the depth of her error, Sophia becomes distressed. Sophia's agitated state, according to the *Ap. John*, explains why Moses said (Gen. 1:2) that God's Spirit "moved to and fro" over the waters.[127] Seeing the wickedness of Ialdabaoth, Sophia becomes ashamed and "repented and wept with much weeping."[128] Upon hearing Sophia's prayers of contrition, her aeonic colleagues[129] intercede on her behalf before the Invisible Spirit (BG 46.15–47.3; NHC II, 14.1–9).[130] In response, the Great Spirit devises a plan through Pronoia (BG 47.6) to restore Sophia's deficiency, placing Sophia into the ninth heaven until her deficiency is corrected (BG 46.19–47.13; NHC II, 14.4–13).

In a series of moves and countermoves, Sophia and various agents of the Invisible Spirit[131] attempt to recover the power Ialdabaoth stole while Ialdabaoth and his authorities jealously seek to retain it.[132] These contestations help explain, according to the *Ap. John*, the strange bricolage of divine power and psychic and material parts that is the human person.[133] Ialdabaoth and his cronies are tricked into creating humans. They hear a voice from on high declare, "The Human/Man (ⲠⲢⲰⲘⲈ) exists and the Son of Man (ⲠϢⲎⲢⲈ ⲘⲠⲢⲰⲘⲈ)," followed by his image appearing reflected in water (BG 47.14–48.9; NHC II, 14.14–34). Seeking to possess this great light as well, Ialdabaoth exhorts his authorities: "Come let us create a man according to the image of God and according to our likeness (ⲔⲀⲦⲀ ⲠⲚⲈⲒⲚⲈ) so that his image may become a light for us" (NHC II, 15.1–4).

The *Ap. John* then recounts the individual efforts of the rulers and authorities as they each construct a specific part of the composite body of Adam (BG 48.14–50.11; NHC II, 15.5–28); the longer recensions provide a lengthy excursus on the names of "365 angels" (NHC II, 19.2–3) and the specific zones for which each was responsible (NHC II, 15.29–19.10).[134] In the end, however, this psychic and material human body remained inert.

Prompted by Autogenes and the Four Luminaries, Ialdabaoth breathed his spirit into the body (cf. Gen. 2:7), thereby passing the power he stole from Sophia into Adam (BG 51.12–20; NHC II, 19.21–32). Infuriated at his loss of his mother's power, Ialdabaoth and the authorities attempt to reclaim this power in a series of tactics (e.g., the trees of paradise; the extraction of Eve; the rape of Eve); however, they are routinely frustrated and outmaneuvered in their attempts (BG 52.2–64.13; NHC II, 19.34–25.16).

In light of this series of moves and countermoves, significant events from the biblical narrative—including the expulsion from the Garden of Eden and the Great Flood—all take on a different meaning as they turn out to be evidence of Ialdabaoth's failed attempts to extract Sophia's divine power from humanity.[135] Yet, humanity is not simply a passive victim caught between these warring factions.[136] As the introduction and function throughout of the Counterfeit Spirit (ⲀⲚⲦⲒⲘⲒⲘⲞⲚ ⲘⲠⲚⲀ̅) make clear (BG 56.14–15),[137] the *Ap. John* expects active participation and moral effort by persons to resist Ialdabaoth's efforts and help restore Sophia's stolen power. Thus, the *Ap. John* invites its readers to self-identify as "agents of Providence" and locate themselves and their attendant ethical roles as they appear in the *Ap. John*'s unfolding story of salvation history.[138] For example, those who have received the Spirit of Life, likely a reference to baptism, are able to save other souls and free them from the cycle of metempsychosis.[139]

Reinforcing this appeal to ethical conduct, the *Ap. John*, like *Hermas*, links ethical achievement with greater salvific rewards. An important theoretical and rhetorical feature of the *Apocryphon of John* is that there is symmetry between its cosmogony and eschatology. Much of the drama of salvation history revolves around explaining the effects of the primordial rupture that created sin/deficiency and the human contribution toward restoring the primordial harmony. Emblematic of its overall symmetry, the *Ap. John*'s hierarchy of cosmic realms corresponds to different sorts or classes of humanity.[140] Thus, there are four aeonic luminaries, and each corresponds to a class or type of humanity. Employing its vertical, cosmic hierarchy, the *Ap. John* conveys the relative merits of each class of humanity eschatologically on the basis of which aeonic luminary or level of heaven a soul will inhabit:

> The perfect man (came forth) . . . and he placed him, Adam (BG 35.5)/Pigeradamas (NHC II, 8.35), over the first aeon . . . by the first light Armozel. . . . And he placed his son Seth over the

second aeon in the presence of the second light Oroiel. And in the
third aeon was placed the seed of Seth, over the third light of
Daveithai. And the souls of the saints were placed (there). And
in the fourth aeon were placed the souls of those who do know
the Pleroma and did not repent (ⲘⲈⲦⲀⲚⲞⲈⲒ) at once, but who
persisted for a while and repented (ⲘⲈⲦⲀⲚⲞⲈⲒ) afterwards; they
are by the fourth light Eleleth. (NHC II, 8.32–9.23)

Analogous to what we saw in *Hermas*, the *Ap. John* differentiates between
higher and lower levels of salvation spatially, through different ranks of the
heavenly realms.[141] Further echoing what we saw in *Hermas*, the "saints"
will enjoy a higher level of salvation (Daveithai, the third Luminary) than
those "who persisted for a while and repented afterwards" (Eleleth, the
fourth Luminary).

In contrast, David Brakke has recently argued that the first three of
these four classes represent historical stages from the biblical narrative.
Drawing upon two other texts with close mythological affinities with the
Ap. John (the *Hypostasis of the Archons* and *the Holy Book of the Great and Invisible Spirit*), Brakke concludes that *all* those who are saved in the present
today (of the author) will reside in Eleleth: "All of these passages (drawn
explicitly from *Apocryphon of John, Hypostasis of the Archons,* and *the Holy
Book of the Great and Invisible Spirit*) suggest the Eleleth is the luminary of
the archetypes of the contemporary Gnostics and other saved human beings.
And so there are four divine archetypes of humanity: Adam (Harmozel),
Seth (Oraoiael), the primeval descendants of Seth (Daveithai), and the contemporary Gnostics, the present-day seed of Seth (Eleleth)."[142] While
Brakke's interpretation *may* be correct for the *Holy Book* (NHC III, 65.17–
22; IV, 77.16–20),[143] there is no compelling reason to read the *Ap. John* in
this way.[144] The hierarchical relationship of the saints or seed of Seth and
those who repent/convert more slowly maps onto the divide found later in the
text between the "immovable race" (BG 65.2–3; NHC II, 25.23) and "those
who have not known the All (ⲠⲦⲎⲢϤ̅)" (BG 68.14–15).[145] Moreover, the immovable race is described analogously to Seth and the seed[146] insofar as they
are all formed by the infusion of the Spirit (Seth and the seed: BG 63.14–64.13;
immovable race: BG 65:3–8), which is likely a reference to baptism.

Despite this hierarchical ranking of classes of humanity and heavenly
stations, which is indebted to its eclectic blending of Jewish biblical history

and Platonic metaphysics, the *Ap. John* is concerned with the salvation of *all* of humanity and the importance of ΜΕΤΑΝΟΕΙ.[147] In fact, the *Ap. John* is universalist in scope insofar as it expects that almost all of humanity eventually will be saved, so long as people eventually realize their error and repent.[148] Giving voice to this overarching concern, John asks whether all souls will be saved (BG 64.14–16; NHC II, 25.17–18). In response, the Savior assures John that all who are of "immovable race" will be saved and become perfect; the souls of sinners, into whom the *Counterfeit* Spirit enters—even those who may not "have known the All" (BG 68.14–15)—will still be saved but only after extensive purgation; apostates, however, are utterly damned: "Those who did know and turned away, where will their souls go?" Then he said to me, "To that place where the angels of poverty go—[that] is where they will be taken. And they will be kept on the day on which those who have blasphemed the spirit [and] will be tortured and punished with eternal punishment" (NHC II, 27.21–29). Consequently, the *Ap. John*—similar to what we saw in *Hermas*—has a tripartite salvific scheme of highest salvation (the seed of Seth or immovable race), middle ground (repentant sinners), and the damned (apostates). In this way, both *Hermas* and the *Ap. John* have tailored higher and lower salvific rewards to reflect the ethical achievements of different sorts of persons. Unlike *Hermas*, however, for the *Ap. John* this tripartite scheme comprises the whole of humanity and not just insiders or baptized members of the community.

Michael Williams and Karen King have rightly marshaled the above passage (NHC II, 27.21–29) and others to overturn the tired cliché of "Gnostic" ethical indifference. Those who are saved, in fact, *deserve* to be saved because of either the merit of their conduct while alive (BG 65.3–66.12; NHC II, 25.23–26.7) or redemptive, postmortem purgation (BG 68.13–69.13; NHC II, 26.32–27.11).[149] Emphasizing the universality of salvation for all (except apostates), Williams suggests that the difference between the seed of Seth and others saved may be provisional.[150] Instead of genetic determinism, so the argument goes, all have the capacity to be counted among the seed of Seth or the immovable race. This latent but potential identity is available to everyone but requires moral effort to activate. Yet, even those who are unable to activate this latent identity in life, still have access to salvation, albeit only through postmortem cycles of reincarnation and purgation.[151] Thus, as both Williams and King conclude, the *Ap. John* is *not* representative of "salvific elitism" but is rather engaged in ethical paraenesis that encourages all—whether in this life or after death—to progress and become part of the immovable race.[152]

Expanding upon the significant insights of Williams and King, I, however, argue for preserving and even highlighting the soteriological distinction between the seed of Seth or immovable race and penitent sinners.[153] By concentrating on the *Ap. John*'s use of salvific difference, we can focus on the text's multitiered ethical framework and sophisticated problem-solving. Through its rhetorical construction of higher and lower levels of salvation, the *Ap. John* can deploy a sophisticated ethical map that is not only a binary between good and bad conduct. The *Ap. John*, like *Hermas*, privileges a certain class of saintly figures who, strengthened by the infusion of the Spirit of Life, are paradigms for Stoic virtue, living the life of the sage free from the passions (anger, envy, fear, and desire) and indifferent to any problems they might experience.[154] Nonetheless, as we will see further in the following chapter, the *Ap. John* also makes pragmatic accommodations for community members who fall short of this rigorist standard as well as establishes a secondary path for the salvation of outsiders, namely postmortem purgation.[155] In short, the *Ap. John* does not reduce the salvation of humanity to a single ethical standard of good vs. evil, but offers *three* possible ways for a person to be saved.

To summarize, the *Ap. John*'s revelatory account of the highest echelons of reality is not only speculative philosophy about ontology and epistemology; nor is its discussion of the angelic construction of the body evidence of world-hating asceticism.[156] Instead, the *Ap. John* is an exegetically and ethically engaged text concerned with the redemption of different types of persons. The *Ap. John* provides a sophisticated narrative that explains the origins as well as practical solutions for how to save different kinds of people. Thus, unlike *Hermas* and its exhortation toward repentance as a return to a single, ethical code, the *Ap. John* lays out different paths for how to be saved, namely baptism or postmortem purgation, as well as different strategies to assist persons on each path, namely demonic adjuration and spiritual assistance given by a baptized member.

Ultimately, although very different in terms of content, both *Hermas* and the *Ap. John* differentiate among different types of people and different levels of salvation. Both employ utopian, heavenly imagery to articulate the highest of ethical ideals—for example, the martyr or the Stoic sage. Additionally, both texts are concerned with the rigors and difficulties of remaining morally upright and construct secondary levels of salvation for those who fall short of these highest ideals. And finally, both texts employ revelatory authority to sanction this two-tiered ethical framework. As we shall see in the next chapter, by investigating and categorizing different types of persons, especially vis-à-vis their sinfulness, both *Hermas* and the *Ap. John* can develop and deploy strategies to resist and overcome sin as well as repair the social damage caused by sinning members of their communities.

Chapter 4

Diagnosing Sin and Saving Sinners
Early Christian Ethical and Soteriological Problem-Solving

Finally, be strong in the Lord and in the strength of his power. Put on the whole armor of God, so that you may be able to withstand the wiles of the devil. For our struggle is not against enemies of blood and flesh, but against the rulers, against the authorities, against the cosmic powers of the present darkness, against the spiritual forces of evil in the heavenly place.

—Ephesians 6:10–12

Dealing with Sin and Sinners

In the previous chapter we considered the two-tiered ethical and soteriological frameworks of *Hermas* and the *Ap. John*. In particular, we demonstrated how these hierarchies tell an inclusive story of salvation insofar as it is not only the saints who will be saved. In so doing, we also examined the content of each text's ethical ideals by asking: What made a saint a saint? How are they different from other, morally average Christians? And how do these ethical ideals help them to make sense of and locate themselves in the world and the unfolding narrative of salvation history? In this chapter we consider the flip side of higher and lower levels of salvation: Who are the sinners who can be saved? What is sinfulness, and how can or should someone resist it? And what are the practical implications of diagnosing and proposing solutions to human sinfulness?

As we shall see, *Hermas* and the *Ap. John* share a demonological etiology of human sin or wrongdoing. This, I suggest, may reflect their analogous social contexts and comparable ideological aims. Both texts deploy higher and lower levels of salvation to justify ethical difference within their communities. This entails that just as some Christians are better than others, then some must also be worse. Through both *Hermas* and the *Ap. John*, we can investigate ancient Christians as they struggled with the ongoing sins of some of their members. Both *Hermas* and the *Ap. John*, therefore, construct a notion of human sinfulness tailored to these circumstances—in other words, it not only seeks to explain how it is that some members have fallen back into sin but it also facilitates the creation of practical techniques to protect against the dangers of future relapses. Thus, just as higher and lower levels of salvation enabled the privileging of certain ethical ideals without anticipating that every member could achieve all of them, so too did this soteriological technology provide the flexibility to handle the social and theoretical difficulties of reintegrating sinners into these ethically mixed communities.[1]

To these ends, I will open this chapter with an overview of human sinfulness in *Hermas* and the *Ap. John*. The closest parallels for both *Hermas* and the *Ap. John* are Jewish texts that ascribe human wrongdoing to demonic influences.[2] In each case, externalizing the source of human sinfulness has important consequences for how each text assesses moral responsibility; importantly for our purposes, this externalization of responsibility does not cohere with our modern conception of a "free will" or the Cartesian distinction between body and mind. Finally, I will situate *Hermas* and the *Ap. John* within the dynamic context of circa second-century Christianity.

Demons as a Source of Human Sinfulness

In his monograph on the *yetzer* (evil) inclination in rabbinic literature, Ishay Rosen-Zvi points to *Hermas* as one of the closest parallels to his object of study.[3] In particular, *Hermas's* description of two competing angels—one good and one evil (*Man.* 6)[4]—appears structurally analogous to some contemporary rabbinic discussions of the good and evil *yetzarim* (e.g., m. Ber. 9:5).[5] Rosen-Zvi rightly contends that *Hermas*, like the rabbis, explains moral evil and ascribes the source of sinfulness to the influence of external entities, be they demons or angels. Rosen-Zvi emphasizes demonology as part of a corrective he is offering to a hyper-Foucauldian and Hellenizing trend in scholarship.[6] According to Rosen-Zvi, this trend has psychologized evil and uncritically employed Foucauldian concepts with the result that "the rabbinic concept of *yetzer hara* has been incorrectly contextualized, as part of the ancient discourse of *self-control* and *self-fashioning*. It should be understood as part of the biblical and post-biblical search for the sources of human sinfulness. Rabbinic *yetzer* should therefore not be read in the tradition of the Hellenistic quest for control over the lower parts of the psyche, but rather in the tradition of Jewish and Christian demonology."[7] Thus, according to Rosen-Zvi, we ought to avoid psychologizing sin into the desires or appetites arising from a *natural*, if lower, part of the soul.

To concretize this point, Rosen-Zvi sets up a strong contrast between demonology and psychology.[8] In so doing, Rosen-Zvi is responding also to a particular application of the burgeoning field of scholarship into "whole and divided selves."[9] In contrast to partitioning the soul,[10] the rabbinic *yetzer* is an external *intruder*; in other words, it is fundamentally *foreign* to the human person and the layers of his or her psyche.[11] Yet *Hermas*'s enigmatic term for a sinner, someone who is *dipsyche* or "two/divided souled,"[12] poses some difficulty for such a radical divide between demonology and psychology.[13] Rosen-Zvi, however, contends that this term and similar expressions are evidence of a "wider *koine* in late antiquity, in which cosmic multiplicity was transferred into the human mind, creating a 'multiplicity of the self.'"[14] Although the particulars of Rosen-Zvi's argument are at times elusive, especially as regards his construction of a "self," his distinction between demonology and psychology is, nevertheless, instructive for how *Hermas* and the *Ap. John* conceive of sinfulness and, in particular, for how each constructs remedies to it and thereby assesses moral responsibility.[15]

Both *Hermas* and the *Ap. John* ascribe the origins of human sinfulness to demons. They each contain characters (angels and demons) who tempt and compel people to sin. Accordingly, both texts depict the moral struggle to resist sin as a battle against an external, invading force.[16] To overcome sinfulness, both contain strategies tailored to conquer demonic compulsion, rather than to control a lower yet natural part of one's own soul. Thus, Rosen-Zvi's model is especially useful for highlighting the difference between self-mastery and fighting off an external threat.

Yet, both texts blur this boundary between internal (psychological) and external (demonic) in a number of ways; most notably, the way in which each diagnoses different affinities or vulnerabilities to sin. Though each text's remedy treats sinful inclinations as an invasive threat, both *Hermas* and *Ap. John* must account for why some people are more vulnerable to demonic compulsion than others.[17] Moreover, the differing perils facing certain persons or practices further illustrate and help to explain the texts' ethical and soteriological hierarchies. To address these risks, both *Hermas* and the *Ap. John* encourage self-reflection to recognize one's own specific and differing vulnerabilities to demonic influence.[18] As a result, *Hermas* and the *Ap. John*'s discussions of the origins of sin supply both theoretical explanation and practical guidance for dealing with the problem of human wrongdoing.

The Shepherd of Hermas: The Dangers of Evil Angels and Permeable Persons

As we saw in the preceding chapter, there is an enduring preoccupation throughout *Hermas* with general human sinfulness, especially the moral failings of "good" persons. Even Hermas the self-controlled (Ἑρμᾶς ὁ ἐγκρατής) can be overcome by a wicked thought (πονηρὰ βουλὴ) and led into sin (*Vis.* 1.2.4; cf. *Sim.* 7). Why, however, would a person, especially a *good* person like Hermas, sin? What could compel him, or any of the other "saints," to sin? (*Vis.* 2.2.4) And what can an upright person do to stand fast and not fall into sin (again)? *Hermas* claims that the source of human sinfulness is an external and hostile force, variously described as an angel or, in some cases, specifically as the devil (e.g., *Man.* 12.5). Furthermore, although everyone is at risk, certain persons are even more prone to falling back into sin under this demonic compulsion. This is due to their competing and conflicted commitments, which, according to *Hermas*, mark them as *dipsychoi*. Resisting sin, then, requires a two-directional defense: an external one aimed at preempting the pernicious efforts of this hostile angel, but also an internal and self-reflective process whereby a person acknowledges the elements of his or her own character and social position that may make a person more likely to become *dipsychos* and thus dangerously vulnerable to the temptation to sin (*Sim.* 8.8–11; *Man.* 10.1; cf. *Vis.* 3.6, 9).

Throughout the *Mandates* and the *Similitudes*, the angel of repentance explains to Hermas what the nature of sin is and why it is so difficult for Christians to resist falling back into sinfulness. Most prominently in *Mandates* 6, *Hermas* maintains that there are two, opposing angels who can enter into the heart of every person: an angel of righteousness (δικαιοσύνης) and one of wickedness (πονηρίας).[19] Since both are angels, a person can recognize and distinguish between them only on account of their differing activities and effects. The angel of righteousness is associated with a series of beneficial traits and works. As such, when the angel of righteousness rises up, "he straightaway speaks with you about righteousness, purity (ἁγνείας), reverence (σεμνότητος), self-sufficiency/contentment (αὐταρκείας),[20] and every righteous deed and every glorious virtue" (*Man.* 6.2.3). In contrast, the angel of wickedness is linked to a list of negative characteristics and actions. Thus, when this angel enters into a person, he provokes a person toward "irascibility or bitterness. . . . Desire of extravagant foods (πολυτέλειαι ἐδεσμάτων), drinking bouts (μεθυσμάτων), carousing (κραιπαλῶν), fancy delicacies (ποικίλων τρυφῶν), desire for women (ἐπιθυμίαι γυναικῶν), greed (πλεονεξία), arrogance (ὑπερηφανία), pretentiousness (ἀλαζονεία), and everything that is closely aligned to these" (*Man.* 6.2.5).

Although this picture superficially resembles the "two ways tradition" of the Didache (1–6), in which there are two types of conduct (good vs. evil) that a person must choose between, *Hermas* does not ascribe to people the volitional freedom to select between these two angels.[21] Instead, a person is subject to the compulsions of whichever angel may, at that time, exert control over his or her heart:[22] "For even if someone is a most faithful (πιστότατος) man, should the thought (ἐνθύμησις) of the [wicked] angel rise up in his heart, then that man or woman *must* (δεῖ) commit a sin (ἐξαμαρτῆσαί τι). On the other hand, even if someone is a most wicked (πονηρότατός) man or woman, should the works of the angel of righteousness rise up in the heart of that one, then he or she *necessarily must* (ἐξ ἀνάγκης δεῖ) do something good (ἀγαθόν τι ποιῆσαι)" (*Man.* 6.2.7–8, emphasis added). Character, whether praiseworthy or blameworthy, is no stable indicator of future conduct.[23] According to *Hermas*, people are exceedingly permeable[24] and thus susceptible to external, angelic compulsion.[25] Although there are precautions and strategies for resisting such angelic puppetry, it is *not* something that is up to an internal, deliberative choice between alternatives. Thus, according to *Hermas*, sinfulness (as well as righteousness) can arise as a result of external forces and not through a person's conscious choice.[26]

These two opposing angels, therefore, are not stylized or literary representations of lower and higher parts of the agent's very own soul between which a third and governing part of a person must select.[27] The *person* is the *container* for these two forces, which can be expelled and removed from the person. To further illustrate the specific contours of this conception of a person, let us consider two parallels that may seem structurally analogous yet differ in significant and illuminating ways. 4 Ezra's use of the opposition between an evil heart and the Torah within a person appears markedly similar to *Hermas's* opposing angels, although its author suggests that the evil heart is not (or no longer) foreign but natural to all descendants of Adam (4 Ezra 3:20–22, 26; cf. 4:30; 7:118).[28] Through its figural language, especially the metaphor of seeds, 4 Ezra emphasizes the natural and inborn status of this evil heart. By contrast, the erudite and eclectic Christian teacher Clement of Alexandria (*Strom.* 2.20.110–11) *did* conceive of evil impulses as foreign entities; however, he also ascribed to people the volitional power to either assent to or reject these impulses on their own.[29] Unlike 4 Ezra or Clement then, *Hermas* portrays the demonic origins of human sinfulness as something both foreign and overpowering.

Despite this demonological explanation of good and evil conduct, *Hermas* does not absolve individuals from responsibility for their behavior. On the contrary, *Hermas* employs this demonic source of evil to exhort its readers toward moral preparedness. Employing a series of spatial metaphors of various containers, *Hermas* argues that the best defense against demonic invasion is to ensure that there is no *room* in a person's heart for a wicked entity to enter and inhabit. Analogizing people to wine jugs, *Mandate* 12 claims that so long as a person is full of "wine," there is no room for the devil to enter; however, if he or she is only half full, "[the devil] comes to those who are partially empty (ἀποκένους), and because there is room, he enters them; he does whatever he wishes, and they become his obedient slaves (ὑπόδουλοι)" (*Man.* 12.5.4). As the passage continues, the Shepherd explains that the "wine" a person ought to fill him-/herself with are the habituated and habituating practices of obeying the commandments (*Man.* 12.6).[30] This has a striking parallel to a passage from rabbinic literature where Torah observance is portrayed as a bandage defending against demonic attack, and this bandage must be constantly worn and maintained in order to be effective:

> *Therefore impress these My words upon your heart* (Deut. 11:18)—this tells us that the words of the Torah are like an elixir of life. This is comparable to a king who was angry with his son, struck him a violent blow, and placed a bandage on the wound. He told him: My son, as long as this bandage remains on your wound, you may

eat whatever you please and drink whatever you please, and bathe either in hot or cold water, and you will come to no harm.[31] But if you remove it, it will immediately fester. . . . Be occupied with the words of Torah and [the evil *yetzer*] will not reign over you, as it is said (Gen 4:7): *sin crouches at the door, its urge is toward you*.[32]

Thus, the bandages and the wine were physical representations of persistent and daily practices—practices meant to keep a person protected from demonic compulsion, that is, from the *spatial intrusion* of such a demonic force. For both this rabbinic example and *Hermas*, the ongoing contests against demonic compulsion are portrayed through physical imagery and metaphor.

By contrast, those who fill their hearts with wickedness increase their predilection for immoral conduct. Just as filling up one's heart with "wine" reduces demonic access due to spatial constraints, so too does filling a heart with wickedness make it less habitable for the Holy Spirit. When a heart become polluted by wickedness, the Holy Spirit, who is also imagined as an occupant of the heart, may find that such a person's heart feels "cramped," and will thus vacate, increasing the person's susceptibility to compulsion by evil angels (*Man.* 5; cf. 10.2). For *Hermas*, therefore, the struggle to resist demonic compulsion does not come down to the proper, volitional response (e.g., assenting to the correct angel) at a decisive moment of temptation and choice; rather, *Hermas* encourages moral preparedness.[33] If a person has not prophylactically filled him- or herself with the proper stuff prior to an attack by an evil angel, it is already too late.

What might stop a person from preparing for and defending against compulsion by an evil angel? *Hermas* is remarkably sensitive to the competing interests and divided loyalties of many within its community. In particular, *Hermas* highlights the dangers that certain circumstances present to wholeheartedly obeying the commandments (e.g., *Man.* 8), in particular tragedy and financial success. These circumstances could lead to improper emotional responses (e.g., λύπη or "grief") in the first case or in the latter case holding onto incongruous loyalties, thereby becoming a double-minded (*dipsychos*) person.[34] As a result, these circumstances—when unrecognized for their potential dangers—could increase a person's likelihood of falling under demonic compulsion and sinning again.

Thus, *Hermas* encouraged self-scrutiny and increased self-awareness by describing the risks these conditions could pose. Grief, according to *Hermas* (*Man.* 10.2–3), renders the prayers of a person ineffective "'because,' [the

Shepherd] said, 'when grief lounges in his heart, grief is thereby mixed with the petition and does not allow it to rise pure onto the altar. For just as vinegar mixed with wine does not produce the same pleasure, so too does grief mixed with the Holy Spirit not produce the same petition'" (*Man.* 10.3.3). Grief here is described as a physical entity *distinct* from the person. As a physical entity that dwells *within* a person, it cannot cohabitate with the Holy Spirit or Spirit of God (τὸ πνεῦμα τοῦ θεοῦ), who, since it too occupies space, cannot stand to be mixed with the polluting vinegar of grief.[35]

As in the case of grief, *Hermas* describes the malady of *dipsychia* (e.g., *Man.* 9) and its impact (e.g., *Man.* 11) through spatial analogies that portray the person as a vessel or container.[36] *Dipsychia* has a special prominence in *Hermas*.[37] It refers to a person who has divided, and in *Hermas*'s view, incompatible commitments; often these divided loyalties include financial concerns or status among outsiders.[38] Attracting like to like, when a person holds opposing commitments, *dipsychia* enters into him or her (*Man.* 9). Through this rhetorical portrayal of *dipsychia* as an invading force, *Hermas* also echoes the Hellenistic sensibility that emotions, the soul, and the human mind are all physical, insofar as they are comprised of bodies that occupy space and thus can act and be acted upon.[39] *Hermas*, however, characterizes emotional states as invasive and personified forces that dwell within the heart of a person.[40] By demonizing emotions as well as sin, *Hermas* can offer distinctive strategies tailored for its materialist constructions of demonic compulsion and persons.

Whether *Hermas* intended the physicality of these emotions or demons to be merely metaphors or to be an accurate portrait of their actual nature is besides the point here. What is important for our purposes is that by representing the problem posed by a physical threat of a demon or emotion against a person, represented as physical space, *Hermas* could offer solutions similarly couched in spatial rhetoric. Put simply, we must fill up on what is right to resist the intrusive compulsions of what is wrong. Furthermore, to prophylactically defend ourselves, as a symbolic space, from this demonic invasion we need to exercise self-scrutiny to prepare against circumstances and commitments that might increase our vulnerability of falling back into sin.

To summarize, human sinfulness and wrongdoing are not something wholly external or internal to a person; instead, they are a confluence of differing circumstances and causes. Nevertheless, because of their permeability, people are constantly at risk of demonic invasion and compulsion. This permeability of persons makes sense of why even good people can still fall back into sin. Furthermore, by offering this explanation of moral hierarchy, *Hermas* reinforces and justifies its soteriological hierarchy. And finally, although never systematically elaborated,[41] *Hermas*'s treatment of sinfulness provides a multilayered answer to the question "Why would the saved sin again?" that makes use of real-world examples and circumstances. Furthermore, *Hermas*'s practical recommendations for preparing against demonic compulsion rhetorically highlight the physicality of both human persons (including mind or soul) and demonic influence so that it can offer pragmatic techniques designed to insulate the human person, as a physical phenomenon, against foreign, demonic contamination.

The Apocryphon of John: Warring Against the Counterfeit Spirit

Like *Hermas*, the *Ap. John* attributes human sinfulness to demonic causes. Although the *Ap. John*'s account of moral struggles cannot be understood apart from its layered and interrelated narrative of the fall of Sophia, the archontic creation of the world and humanity, and the agonistic series of moves and countermoves propelling salvation history, I will focus on the role of the Counterfeit Spirit in human wrongdoing.[42] In contrast to modern conceptions of personhood and morality, a person does not commit wrongs simply because of volitional mistakes; instead, her choices are influenced by the ongoing, physical contest between competing external forces.

While the archontic creation of the body is significant, it does not, however, entail that the body be *the* source for evil or evil itself; rather this composite creation is a battleground.[43] The body may be a rich target for demonic compulsion, but it also encompasses the means for resisting such demonic influence. Thus, like the temporal world itself, the body is simultaneously a mix of possible pitfalls and dangers as well as the locus for redemption, especially for those requiring remedial metempsychosis (BG 68.13–70.8; NHC II, 26.32–27.21). In contrast, the Counterfeit Spirit—one of the greatest strategies of Ialdabaoth and his archontic colleagues to recapture Sophia's lost power—serves no other purpose than to lead humanity astray.[44] This Counterfeit Spirit is able to push seemingly stalwart Christians into sin and eventually apostasy; thus, it is against the demonic Counterfeit Spirit that the *Ap. John* offers strategies for overcoming human sinfulness.

After Ialdabaoth and his demonic colleagues are deceived into creating humanity and thereby lose Sophia's captured power, they respond with a series of failed attempts to reclaim this power. Every attempt—for example, casting Adam into lowest material realm (BG 52.15–54.9; NHC II, 20.7–31), introducing human mortality (BG 54.9–55.18; NHC II, 20.32–29.16) and the deception and temptation in the garden (BG 56.18–58.10; NHC II, 21.30–22.18)—was foiled by divine intervention.[45] Although Adam's freedom was diminished as a result of these archontic attempts, he remains superior to these demonic rulers and does not fall victim to their efforts to make him forget his own origins and "perfection" (ΠϤϪШК; BG 56.16–17; cf. 54.5–1; 55.17–18; 58.8–10).[46] In other words, these early attempts do not result in human sinfulness; rather they explain the origins of the limited and mixed (both salutary and pernicious) facets of the embodied person.[47] Patricia Cox Miller's inimitable assessment of the late antique ascetic view of the body is apropos here: "The body was perceived to be problematic, not because it was a body, but it was not a body of plenitude."[48] Similarly, when compared to the highest echelons of reality, the human body is remarkably inferior and limited; yet it is not evil, nor is it even the source of evil.[49]

It is not until the separation of Eve from Adam and her subsequent rape by Ialdabaoth that the *Ap. John* introduces human wrongdoing or sinfulness (BG 58.6–64.13; NHC II, 22.15–25.16). Frustrated by the failure of their previous attempts, Ialdabaoth and his colleagues place Adam into a "trance" in order to extract the divinely infused "power" (BG 58.11: ΤϬΟΜ) and "reflection of light" (BG 59.10: ЄΠЄΙΝΟΙΔ ΜΠΟΥΟΙΝ) that had thus far enabled Adam to resist the demonic machinations.[50] Yet, despite his efforts to capture her, the Chief Ruler could not grasp ЄΠЄΙΝΟΙΔ (BG 59.8–12; NHC II, 22.29–32).[51] Instead and continuing its exegetical expansion and adaptation of Genesis 2, the *Ap. John* narrates how Ialdabaoth constructed a form in the shape of a woman, namely Eve, by means of the essence (ΤЄϤΟΥϹΙΔ) of Adam (BG 59.12–60.19).[52]

Upon seeing Eve, Adam is "awakened" from the trance that had dulled his senses (BG 59.20–60. 2; NHC II, 23.4–8). In contrast to Adam's virtuous response, Ialdabaoth immediately rapes Eve upon seeing her (BG 62.8–20; NHC II, 24.15–25). As a product of their illicit union, she begets Eloim and Yave, who are later called Abel and Cain, thereby blending exegesis of Genesis 2–3 with 6:1–4. An additional by-product of Ialdabaoth's rape of Eve is sexual procreation through marriage (BG 63.3: ΠϹΥΝΟΥϹΙΔ ΜΠΓΔΜΟϹ).[53]

Sexual congress transmits the Counterfeit Spirit, previously mentioned as a feature of Adam's bodily tomb or prison, to subsequent generations without transmitting the divine infusion of power that enabled Adam himself to resist this demonic character.[54]

The *Ap. John*'s sexualized, demonological etiology of sin resembles some elements of the motif of the fallen angels of Genesis 6 who raped women and introduced evil to humanity.[55] In fact, *Ap. John* provides a *second* etiology for human sinfulness, which much more closely resembles the Enochic story of fallen angels (1 En. 6–16) who rape the daughters of men and produce unnatural offspring but also bring illicit products and knowledge to corrupt humanity (BG 73.19–75.14; NHC II, 29.16–30.11).[56] In this second version, the *Ap. John* alters the chronology of the biblical account so that it is Noah's daughters who were raped by Ialdabaoth's fallen angels. Through the Counterfeit Spirit,[57] these fallen angels assume the appearance of their husbands and seduce Noah's daughters as well as corrupt them with the temptations of fine goods (e.g., gold and silver) and metallurgy (iron and copper). As a result, their offspring—and thus all of humanity (NHC II, 30.4–7)—are doubly burdened with sinful inclinations, since we are both the products of the sexual congress of this Counterfeit Spirit "mixed with darkness and evil" (BG 74.13–16; cf. NHC II, 29.28–29) and continue to be tempted by these illicit technologies and gifts (BG 74.16–75.3; NHC II, 29.30–30.2).

Although this second account of the Counterfeit Spirit differs from the first, the importance of this elaborate and agonistic prehistory is that it explains the situation that humanity finds itself in now.[58] The Counterfeit Spirit, linked to Adam's fleshly body or "prison" (BG 55.9–13; cf. 56.14–15), is no longer kept at bay by divine intervention (BG 63.18–64.13; NHC II, 25.2–16); instead, operating analogously to *Hermas*'s materialistic evil angels, it is portrayed as a physical entity that dwells in the flesh and seeks to lead people astray. In either version, therefore, these demonic characters are members of an alternative–but ultimately suppressed[59]–narrative for the origins of human sin that differs from the anthropocentric idea that Adam's disobedience in the Garden was the source of human wrongdoing.[60]

On this point, the *Ap. John* and its near contemporary Justin Martyr (2 *Apology* 5) agree: the origins of human sinfulness may lie outside of the human mind or heart insofar as it was either fallen angels or demons who were first responsible.[61] Justin claims:[62] "The angels, having transgressed (παραβάντες) their appointment (i.e., care of humanity), were captivated by the love of women and begat children who are those that are called demons;

and afterwards they enslaved (ἐδούλωσαν) humanity to themselves, partly through magical writings (μαγικῶν γραφῶν), partly through the fear and punishments (τιμωριῶν) they inflict, and partly by teaching them to offer sacrifices, incense, and libations of the sorts of things they (the angels) needed after they were enslaved to lustful passion" (*2 Apol.* 5.3–4).[63] Justin and the *Ap. John* differ, however, in how they envision these external forces interacting with and fostering human wrongdoing. For Justin, these fallen angels are responsible for human sinfulness insofar as they revealed forbidden and dangerous knowledge to humanity. Once the angels had corrupted humanity by revealing illicit knowledge and irreligious practices (i.e., paganism), they could sow (ἔσπειραν) pernicious societal ills such as murder, wars, adultery, and licentiousness (ἀκολασίας) into the hearts of humankind with seeming impunity (*2 Apol.* 5.4).[64]

In addition to sharing with Justin the Enochic etiology of human sin as illicit, angel-bestowed technology, the *Ap. John* ascribes a more active role to the Counterfeit Spirit that is comparable to what we saw above in *Hermas*. As the *Ap. John*'s soteriological catalogue makes clear, it is the relative influence of the Counterfeit Spirit upon a person that determines his or her degree of sinfulness. The saints who are from the immovable race (BG 65.2–3; NHC II, 25.23: ΤΓΕΝΕΑ ΝΑΤΚΙΜ) are infused with the Spirit of Life[65] and thus use (BG 66.1: ΧΡΑϹΘΑΙ; NHC II, 25.35: ϮΟΡΕΙ) the flesh (ϹΑΡϨ) but are not affected or "ruled" (ΑΜΑϨΤΕ) by it (BG 64.17–66.12; NHC II, 25.18–26.7). In contrast to those who are infused with the Spirit of Life, and thus will surely be saved (BG 67.1–14; NHC II, 26.10–19), are those into whom the Counterfeit Spirit enters and leads astray (BG 67.14–71.2; NHC II, 26.20–27.30). Echoing similar rhetorical strategies found among Second Temple Jewish texts, such as the Treatise of the Two Spirits (1QS 3:13–4:26), the *Ap. John* deploys the contrast between the Spirit of Truth[66] and the Counterfeit Spirit to establish a boundary between its Christian insiders and all others.[67]

The *Ap. John*, however, complicates this totalizing binary between insiders/saved and outsiders/damned by exploring the gray areas of sinful insiders and savable outsiders. Like *Hermas* (*Vis.* 3 and *Sim.* 8), the *Ap. John* further subdivides and hierarchically describes sinners. There are those in whom the power (likely of the Spirit of Life) overcomes the Counterfeit Spirit; despite their sinfulness; these members of the community will be saved and taken up to "the repose of the aeons" (ΤΑΝΑΠΑΥϹΙϹ ΝΑΙΩΝ; BG 67.18–68.12; NHC II, 26.22–26.32). Outsiders, who do not know the All (BG

68.14–15) and over whom the Counterfeit Spirit has greater control, require postmortem punishments and metempsychosis before they are ultimately saved (BG 68.13–70.8; NHC II, 26.32–27.21). And finally, there are those who were insiders (BG 70.9–10; cf. 68.14: "did know [the All]") who still blasphemed the Spirit of Life and turned away;[68] these sinners are punished eternally (BG 70.8–71.3; NHC II, 27.21–30).

If sinfulness does not arise from human disobedience or exclusively from illicit technology, where else does it arise? To put it more simply, how does the Counterfeit Spirit affect a person? The Counterfeit Spirit, like *Hermas's* angels, is represented as a physical entity, insofar as it inhabits the space of the "fleshly prison" of a person, the lowest part of humanity's composite body. This bodily hierarchy is comparable to other texts, such as *Timaeus* 90, the Thanksgiving Scroll,[69] and Paul (e.g., 1 Cor. 15; cf. Gal. 5), which similarly feature physiological or anthropological hierarchies as analogues to psychological or mental hierarchies and/or cosmic or soteriological hierarchies. Dwelling within the lowest parts of a person, the Counterfeit Spirit "burdens the soul" and draws it down into "works of evil and casts it down into forgetfulness."[70] As a result, the *Ap. John's* etiology of sin not only explains the demonological origins of human sinfulness; it also provides a diagnostic tool for recognizing when a person is under attack. Uncontrollable passions and illicit practices are, in fact, evidence that a person is in the throes of a battle (and losing) against the Counterfeit Spirit.[71]

The means, therefore, to resist the Counterfeit Spirit was to expunge its presence from the body. The most explicit technique for overcoming the Counterfeit Spirit was to receive, as Adam did, an infusion of the Spirit of Life (BG 52.17–53.10; NHC II, 20.9–19). Echoing Pauline baptismal language of rebirth (e.g., Rom. 6), the *Ap. John* later represents this entry of the Spirit of the Life as the (re)birth of the soul: "Those into whom the Spirit enters will surely live and come away from evil. For the power enters into every person, for without it they could not stand. After it (the soul) is born then the Spirit of Life comes into it. Thus, when this mighty Spirit of Life has come, it makes strong the power that is the soul, and it (the soul) does not stray into evil" (BG 67.1–14; NHC II, 26.10–19). The *Ap. John* encourages and expects its readers to become like Adam and Seth, both of whom were insulated from the influence of the Counterfeit Spirit due to divine intervention and spiritual infusion (BG 63.12–64.13; NHC II, 24.25–25.16).[72]

But what happens if this infusion of the Spirit is not enough? The example of those Christians who required providential assistance (BG 68.8–10) indicates that some members of the *Ap. John*'s community may have continued to struggle with sin. What recourse do these Christians, who have regrettably sinned again, have? The *Ap. John*, in particular its passages on the archontic/demonic construction of the human body, may provide additional resources for resisting demonic compulsion. This list, in particular the longer recension's extensive *melothesia* section,[73] specifies the name of the demon responsible for the construction of individual body parts (e.g., NHC II, 15.32–33: "Asterechmen [created] the right eye; Thaspomocham [created] the left eye") and even sinful impulses like the passions (e.g., NHC II, 18.15–18: "Ephememphi who is pleasure; Yoko who is desire; Nenentophni who is grief; Blaomen who is fear").[74] It may have been possible, as Origen of Alexandria claims, to use these lists to adjure and command a specific demon by name to cease its activities, if it was assumed to be causing illness or inflaming particular passions.[75]

If the *Ap. John*'s list of demonic names could be used in this way, then this list belies easy classification as a collection of "amoral magical" incantations consisting simply of *voces magicae*.[76] Instead, this list of demonic names is embedded in a narrative that is, as we have seen, clearly invested in ethical and theological concerns.[77] Moreover, knowledge of these names provides the reader with both an explanation of evils and tactics to deal with various moral struggles. Why has someone sinned again or worse become an apostate? Perhaps, as we saw with *Hermas*, they let their guard down and did not practice the correct, persistent, and self-reflective analysis meant to recognize when a demonic force was acting against them. If it was recognized in time, a person could cure bodily dysfunction, however it might be manifested, through proper ritual incantations.

Despite some distinctive and important differences, both *Hermas* and the *Ap. John* view the source of human evil as demonic insofar as it is an external, invasive, and personalized force acting upon persons. This externalization of the source for human sinfulness, however, does not mean that *Hermas* or the *Ap. John* absolves people from moral responsibility. As we have seen, both texts were not only committed to ethical ideals but also developed elaborate theories and strategies for dealing with those who come up short. In so doing, *Hermas* and the *Ap. John* crafted compelling but also useful constructions of human sin as part of their broader strategies of addressing ethical variance through higher and lower levels of salvation. As we shall see in the next section, *Hermas* and the *Ap. John*'s demonological construction of sin has important implications for how we discuss important moral concepts and questions.

The Internalization of Demonology and the Externalization of Moral Accountability

As we saw above, sin is an invasive and overpowering demonic force; with proper preparations, however, people could—with moral effort—avoid such demonic compulsion. How should we characterize this moral effort and the decision-making behind it? Neither *Hermas* nor the *Ap. John* ascribes to humans the volitional power to choose against demonic compulsions. Instead of an idealized moment of ethical choice during which a person stands in the breach between moral improvement and degradation and has the mental autonomy to choose between, demons, according to *Hermas* and the *Ap. John*, are far too powerful for the human heart to resist without assistance.[78] In other words, *Hermas* and the *Ap. John* do not contain a modernist idea of a will free to elect any course of action.[79] Thus, it is anachronistic to speak of the presence of a "free will" in either text.[80] By moving away from this problematic and later concept, I do not mean to claim that these texts *lack* ethics or moral responsibility; rather, I am attempting to shift the focus toward a more precise but also thicker description of the moral choices and habituated practices imagined by these texts.[81] This more theoretical discussion foregrounds a consideration of the practical implications of ethical and soteriological hierarchies in the small, tight-knit Christian communities of the second century.

Although neither the *Ap. John* nor *Hermas* adhere to strict terminological distinctions, we can, in light of what we have seen, make the following claims: both texts attempt to encompass the complex nature of persons, especially their conflicting desires. For *Hermas*, a person is a great mixing bowl of competing impulses that one needs to either fill up on or purge.[82] For the *Ap. John*, people are comprised of higher and lower parts as a result of their demonic construction. In recognizing this limited capacity of persons, both *Hermas* and the *Ap. John* are pragmatic texts insofar as each makes accommodations to people as they struggle to live a moral life. Responding to the tension that arises between enforcing ethical standards but still reintegrating at least some sinners, both texts correlate superior ethical conduct with superior salvific rewards. And finally, each text connects moral achievement and security from demonic compulsion with habituated practices and not singular or isolated cognitive events, namely giving/withholding assent or voluntarily willing/choosing a course of action. In this way, the goal is to encourage constant moral preparation; without this a person is not (and could not be!) free to not sin.

Yet, if apostates "knowingly do wrong" do they not also thereby demonstrate the presence of something like a free will?[83] Once we recognize that sinfulness in *Hermas* and the *Ap. John* is demonic, we must then alter some of the presuppositions undergirding this question. Rather than placing the onus for sinfulness on a single cognitive event—knowingly doing wrong—the rabbinic metaphor of maintaining a bandage against demonic infection illustrates the types of practices and choices that could lead to apostasy more precisely. In short, a person will sin when demonic influence seeps into that unwary person; an apostate is someone who *ought* to have been conscientiously and carefully maintaining his or her bandage—correct moral choices and practices—as a ward against such demonic influence. The apostate did not knowingly rip off the bandage for the purpose of letting the demon in; rather, he or she did not carefully and continually observe the practices and self-reflective analysis meant to keep these pernicious forces at bay.

Consequently, everyone is still responsible for his or her sins. This externalization shifts the focus of ethical metrics from an anachronistic interest in internal or cognitive activities toward external and visible practices.[84] As Peter Brown noted, there was a crowded and nearly claustrophobic atmosphere in antiquity, according to which there was little privacy and everyone knew each other, perhaps too well.[85] Heretofore our focus on internal or cognitive questions has meant that we have paid too little attention to *Hermas* and the *Ap. John*'s interest in ethical diagnostics and therapies, and how these fit into their communal setting.

What this interpretation also alerts us to is that *Hermas* and the *Ap. John* use demonology for different purposes than did many of their Christian peers.[86] In his survey of "superstition" in antiquity, Dale Martin finds that Christian authors often deployed demonology to explain the illicit practices and beliefs of outsiders, especially the errors of paganism.[87] In contrast to some of their fellow Christians, *Hermas* and the *Ap. John* are concerned with the sinfulness of their own community members. Foreshadowing the monastic battles against demons, *Hermas* and the *Ap. John* articulate the ongoing moral struggle to resist sin as one against demonic opponents. Demons, therefore, are not something outside the confines of the community but are an intimate threat already ravaging through individuals and thus affecting whole Christian congregations, even leading to the apostasy of some members.

On Earth as It Is in Heavens: Soteriology as Script in *Hermas* and the *Ap. John*

Hermas and the *Ap. John*'s concern about apostates further attests to the communal setting of both texts.[88] The social location for the second-century Christian writers, readers, and perhaps the first circulators of both *Hermas* and the *Ap. John* most likely resembled that of the small, tight-knit congregations meeting together in house-churches, probably in urban settings.[89] As such, both texts are attempts to accommodate and make sense of the social complexity of a morally mixed community, comprised of saints living alongside sinners. Put somewhat differently, the soteriology of higher and lower levels of salvation was one among a host of experimental, rhetorical strategies meant to encourage virtuous conduct, rehabilitate savable sinners, and exclude deviant apostates among second-century Christians.[90]

A recent and excellent example of a study that situates ancient rhetorical strategies in their likeliest social context is Einar Thomassen's "Orthodoxy and Heresy in Second-Century Rome."[91] Thomassen's specific interest is the forms and scope of ecclesiastical authority in second-century Rome. His point of entry is the apparent paradox that Valentinus and Marcion, figures considered to be the two marquee heretics of second-century Rome, were never excommunicated by a bishop, a council of elders, or any other form of ecclesiastical authority.[92] What does this tell us about the structures and notions of authority in second-century Roman Christianity? Conversely, what does this tell us about the rhetorical aims, social context, and practical impact of someone like a Justin Martyr, who as a Christian denizen of second-century Rome wrote a condemnation of so-called heretics, including his near contemporaries the Valentinians (*Dial.* 35.4) and Marcion (*1 Apol.* 26)?[93]

Building on the work of earlier scholars,[94] Thomassen recognizes that there was no "unitary church" in second-century Rome; instead, there were a number of small and semi-independent congregations. Each congregation most likely met in a house-church or place of business, thereby entailing the relatively small size but also tight-knit mentality of each group.[95] In this context, prestigious teachers such as Valentinus or Justin would be the pride of their congregation. Yet these small congregations were not ignorant or unconcerned with their Christian brothers and sisters spread throughout the city (or even across the world), but imagined themselves as members of a much larger community than the one confined by the spatial limits of their house-churches.[96] Exemplifying this conception of broader unity, *Hermas* (*Vis.* 2.4.3) describes the roles that certain officers play on behalf of the whole of the Roman *ekklēsia*, such as education, foreign correspondence, and charity.

Thomassen characterizes the inward and outward orientations of these groups as decentralizing and centralizing forces, respectively, and uses this dichotomy heuristically to reinterpret authors and texts such as Marcion, Valentinus, and the *Shepherd of Hermas*. As Thomassen demonstrates, there are several decentralizing forces, such as the small, private setting for gatherings, the diversity of congregations (further exacerbated by the influx of immigrants with varying beliefs and customs), social and economic inequality among and within the congregations, and the established norm that religious *collegia* were autonomous and thus independent from centralized authority, that would work against unifying or centralizing efforts.[97] Nonetheless, Marcion, Valentinus, and *Hermas*, despite holding very different theological views, each sought to enact centralizing reforms. In other words, although disagreeing over what constituted the core or theological center of early Christian discourse, and thereby demonstrating the very lack of such a core, each author strenuously preached a message of unification and eradication of diversity. Thus, Thomassen rightly destabilizes the assumption that ideological commitment to unity was the sole possession of certain, retrospectively orthodox authors; instead, just as Justin sought to restore and unify his beloved Christian commonwealth spread throughout the world, so too did Marcion.[98]

Similarly, *Hermas*'s and the *Ap. John*'s efforts to navigate the complexity of morally mixed communities through a layered soteriology were two instances of early Christians seeking to restore social harmony, both in their proximate social circumstances and in their imagined, global communities. In both texts we find salvific ends represented by spatial metaphors— whether a tower or gradated heavens—used to encourage moral excellence, reintegrate savable sinners, and exclude unsavable sinners. Furthermore, rather than individuals actors each text constructs corporate characters or types, for example, the immovable race or the building blocks of a heavenly tower.[99] The rhetorical force here is rather straightforward: once you find your part, you find you are part of something greater than yourself. As anthropologist Michael Jackson notes, this realization provides a clear sense of identity: "In other words, one thinks of one's self not as an autonomous unit with distinctive internal character and external appearance, but as a part of a collectivity; a member of a family, lineage, or community in which there are many other members. Re-membering therefore evokes the image of a person's life and identity as an association or a club."[100] Through this sense of corporate identity and their metaphors of unequal salvation, *Hermas* and the *Ap. John* account for the diverse topography of the moral landscape, pinpoint each person's address, and detail what path you—and others like you—must follow to reach your appropriate destination. Thus, *Hermas* and the *Ap. John*'s hierarchies of salvation are innovative instances of what Thomassen called centralizing tendencies insofar as they address the social and theoretical difficulties of ethical variance at home and abroad.[101]

Saints and Sinners in Early Christianity

Throughout Part II, we have considered another instance of higher and lower levels of salvation, one rather different from what we saw in Paul and John. Both the *Hermas* and the *Ap. John*, I have argued, devised soteriological hierarchies to address the social and theoretical problem of ethical variance. In so doing, these texts extolled their highest ethical principles, accommodated those who could not abide by this highest standard, and crafted a concept of sinfulness that allowed for the reintegration of sinful yet penitent community members. This hierarchy of saints, sinners, and the damned, moreover, is an understudied branch of the early Christian soteriology that cuts across later divides of orthodoxy and heresy. In Part III, we will consider another instance of higher and lower levels of salvation: the hierarchy of salvation connected to the tripartite division of humanity (pneumatic, psychic, and hylic) promulgated by some Valentinian Christians. Just as we have seen in Parts I and II, the Valentinian construction of higher and lower levels of salvation is not a continuation of a stable and static soteriological technology, but is rather an innovative solution meant to address a specific social and theoretical concern, namely the problem of missionary successes and failures.

PART III

The Threefold Division of Humanity

Identity, Soteriology, and Moral Responsibility in the *Excerpts of Theodotus,* the *Tripartite Tractate,* and Heracleon's *Commentary on John*

Chapter 5

Mapping the Heavens

The Missionizing Ethics and Soteriology
of Valentinians

If, on the other hand, some are by nature good and others are by
nature bad, then neither the former ones are worthy of praise on
account of their goodness, since they were created like this; nor
the latter ones are worthy of blame, since they, too, were created
like this.

—Irenaeus, *Adversus haereses* 4.37.2

Valentinians and Valentinian Anthropogony

Irenaeus of Lyons, in his five-volume second-century heresy finding and
fighting work *Adversus haereses* (hereafter *Haer.*),[1] claimed that Valentinian
soteriology entails ethical indifference because merit is not required to be
saved: a person is either made to be saved or made to be destroyed. Especially dangerous, Irenaeus warns, is that these Valentinians justified their
soteriology by constructing a threefold division of humanity that insidi-
ously draws upon the writings and authority of scripture, in particular the
Apostle Paul: "They conceive, then, of three kinds of people: pneumatic,
psychic, and hylic, represented by Cain, Abel, and Seth. . . . Paul, too, very
plainly set forth the hylic, psychic, and pneumatic, saying in one place: 'As
is the earthy, such as they also who are earthy' (1 Cor. 15:48) and in another
place: 'But the pneumatic judges all things' (1 Cor. 2:15) and 'the psychic
does not receive pneumatic things' (1 Cor. 2:14)" (*Haer.* 1.7.5; 1.8.3). Perhaps

most offensive of all for the bishop of Lyons was that according to the soteriology of this tripartite division of humanity Irenaeus and the majority of
his Christian flock, as the less advanced or psychics, were destined for a
lower level of salvation: "On this account, they tell us that it is necessary for
us whom they call psychics . . . to practice continence and good works, that
by this we might attain at length to the intermediate habitation. . . . The
pneumatic seed, having been divested of their souls, and having become
intellectual spirits . . . shall enter into the Pleroma and be bestowed as
brides to those angels who wait upon the Savior. . . . In the intermediate
place [outside the Pleroma] shall be the souls of the righteous [i.e., good
psychics], but nothing of these psychics shall find entrance into the Pleroma" (*Haer.* 1.6.4; 1.7.1). Thus, according to Irenaeus, these dangerous
rival preachers were misappropriating scriptures to bolster an offensive system (*hypothesis*) that was especially pernicious because it entailed soteriological determinism and would thus undermine the ethical basis of salvific
deserts.

Obviously Irenaeus, as a hostile interpreter of Valentinian soteriology
and anthropogony, recasts Valentinian beliefs and practices in a negative
light; however, as he himself admits, these "Valentinians" were also members of his own congregations. So concerned was Irenaeus with these supposed wolves in sheep's clothing that he "performed interviews" and "read
their commentaries (ὑπομνήματα)" in order to provide clear and convincing
demonstration that their views were both foreign and dangerous: "A clever imitation in glass casts contempt, as it were, on the precious jewel the emerald . . .
unless it might come under the eye of someone able to test and expose the
counterfeit. Or, again, what inexperienced person can with ease detect the
presence of brass when it has been mixed with silver? To prevent, therefore,
through my neglect, that some should be carried off, even as sheep are by
wolves when they do not perceive their true character because they dress in
sheep's clothing. . . . I will show how absurd and inconsistent with truth
their opinions are." (*Haer.* Preface 1.2). In other words, these were not distant outsiders about whom Irenaeus could invent polemics without concern
about their plausibility; instead, they were mixed among and throughout
Irenaeus's own communities. One of the primary tasks of *Adversus haereses*,
as Irenaeus himself outlines it in his preface, was to expose what he thought
were counterfeit Christians in his midst. Thus a constraint upon his polemical representations was that his descriptions, hostile though they might

be, must also still be usable for the purpose of recognizing a contemporary subgroup of early Christians.

As we shall see, three Valentinian texts, the *Excerpts of Theodotus,* the *Tripartite Tractate,* and Heracleon's *Commentary on John,* each employ a threefold division of hylic (or choic), psychic, and pneumatic. What, if anything, was the relationship between this tripartite anthropology and soteriology? And was Irenaeus correct that this tripartite division of humanity precludes ethics?

Concluding our survey of higher and lower levels of salvation, in Part III we shall investigate this anthropogony of three classes and its association with a soteriology of higher and lower levels of salvation. As in the case of what we found previously wherein a social problem (the inclusion of gentiles or sin after baptism) sparked theoretical speculation and soteriological innovation, I will argue that this soteriology and anthropology were meant to accommodate the successes but also account for a lack thereof experienced by a group of missionizing ancient Christians. Similar to the Apostle Paul, these early Christians viewed themselves as having received a special calling and revelatory knowledge.[2] Moreover, Paul and his language of different types of persons supplied the terminology needed to describe and justify why some people might immediately accept, delay before being persuaded, or categorically and resolutely reject the proselytizing efforts of these spiritually elected individuals. Although, as we will see, they had limited social coherence due to rituals of initiation and perhaps even specialized training, these pneumatics, as they sometimes called themselves, were immersed within and part of larger Christian communities. Indeed, their social proximity likely fueled Irenaeus's alarm and his eagerness to label them unethical, soteriological determinists.

Yet, when we consider Valentinian texts, we find that they *are* concerned with ethical conduct and merit. In his groundbreaking work, *Sin in Valentinianism,* Michel Desjardins challenged the then-dominant scholarly view of a Valentinian movement that was indifferent to ethical concerns. Desjardins demonstrated that Valentinian literature contains a consistent interest in ethical conduct, and that this interest was often expressed by redirecting the attention of the audience toward obedience to the "will of the Father." Desjardins observed that "these Christians—all of them—are intent on 'doing the Father's Will.' They are definitely not gnostics for whom actions have no significance and sin is of no concern whatsoever. Sin for them is an action not in keeping with the heavenly Father's will. They are worried about their salvation . . . and struggle to remain sinless in the hope that this will make the difference when they die."[3] Frequently in these Valentinian texts, this injunction to do the "will of the Father" is connected with ethical directives. The *Gospel of Truth*, for instance, presents an extensive list of ethically minded imperatives motivated by doing the "will of the Father":

> Make firm the feet of those who stumbled and stretch out your
> hands to those who are ill. Feed those who are hungry and give
> repose to those who are weary, and raise up those who wish to
> rise and awaken those who sleep, for you are the understanding
> that is drawn forth. If strength acts thus, it becomes even stron-
> ger. Be concerned with yourselves; do not be concerned with other
> things which you have rejected from yourselves. Do not return to
> what you have vomited to eat it. Do not be moths. Do not be
> worms, for you have already cast it off. Do not be a (dwelling)
> place for the devil, for you have already destroyed him. Do not
> strengthen (those who are) obstacles to you who are collapsing, as
> though (you were) a support (for them). For the lawless one is
> someone to treat ill rather than the just one. For the former does
> his works as a lawless person; the latter as a righteous person does
> his works among others. So you do the Will of the Father, for you
> are from him. (*Gos. Truth* 33.1–32)[4]

These injunctions to do the will of the Father were possibly grounded in an exegesis of Matthew 7:21: "Not everyone who says to me, 'Lord, Lord,' shall enter the Kingdom of Heaven, but he who does the Will of my Father who is in Heaven."[5] As we will see, these Christians felt that doing the will of the Father meant accepting their special role to proselytize and give assistance to the less advanced.

This, however, leads us to a persistent scholarly impasse: Is Irenaeus's testimony of Valentinian belief in higher and lower levels of salvation and three classes of humanity reconcilable with Valentinian interest in ethical conduct? Often scholars have said no: some have claimed that Irenaeus polemically altered and distorted the views of the Valentinians;[6] others, that those Valentinian texts concerned with ethical conduct were either reacting or accommodating to heresiological critics, like Irenaeus.[7] Still others have claimed that Irenaeus's account is fundamentally accurate, and that scholars have been misreading Valentinian texts by finding ethical concerns where, obviously, they could not be.[8] It should be a given that Irenaeus's writings reflect his background and commitments, that Valentinian literature did not exist in a vacuum, and that Valentinian texts were not sui generis aberrations or unique among ancient texts insofar as they had no concern for ethics.

To help move beyond this impasse, we will consider the ethics and soteriology of the *Excerpts of Theodotus*'s and the *Tripartite Tractate*'s threefold division of humanity for the remainder of this chapter. I will argue that through this threefold division and soteriology of higher and lower levels of salvation, both the *Excerpts of Theodotus* and the *Tripartite Tractate* promote an ethical ideal in which the more advanced were responsible for the less advanced. In Chapter 6, I will compare our findings on the *Excerpts of Theodotus* and the *Tripartite Tractate* with Heracleon's views on the threefold division of humanity.[9] Ultimately, despite theoretical differences among these three texts, I will conclude that each deploys the threefold division of humanity to encourage committed individuals (pneumatics) toward their ethical ideal of missionizing and saving others. In this way, these three texts and their tripartite anthropology offer evidence of an underappreciated strand of early Christian ethical discourse.

Ethics and Salvation in the *Excerpts of Theodotus* and the *Tripartite Tractate*

Scholars continue to debate how best to interpret the language of soteriological and anthropological difference espoused in a few Valentinian sources: some have argued that the language of hylics, psychics, and pneumatics referred to ritual categories and fixed eschatological ends that emerged from theoretical speculation about the composition of the cosmos and the derivation of matter; others have argued that these three classes were pedagogical stages of moral development through which a person advanced.[10] The crux of this disagreement is the following: these Valentinians either believed a person was "saved by nature," and thus salvation had little to do with ethical merit; or these Valentinians were just like many other early Christian authors who connected ethical growth and salvation, and they differed from their peers only insofar as they used Pauline terminology to describe benchmarks along this pedagogical path.[11] Drawing upon insights from both camps,

I will carve out a middle position that affirms that some Valentinians deployed a soteriology with multiple and fixed levels of salvation, but that they also maintained standards for ethical conduct and moral responsibility by means of this soteriology.

To this end, I will consider two Valentinian texts: the *Excerpts of Theodotus* and the *Tripartite Tractate*. I agree with the first camp that in the case of these two texts the three classes are ritually differentiated categories of people with fixed salvific ends. As such, both texts use compelling visual and spatial metaphors drawn from biblical sources to articulate these soteriological distinctions. Their tripartite anthropogony and its apparent devaluation of choice does not, however, preclude ethical responsibility and practice.[12] Instead, both the *Excerpts of Theodotus* and the *Tripartite Tractate* deploy a version of moral responsibility that privileges *causal* moral responsibility. According to causal moral responsibility, an agent is morally responsible if there is a causal relationship between the agent and his or her actions; in other words, it is the agent and not something else that brought about the action.[13] As we will see, the *Excerpts of Theodotus* and the *Tripartite Tractate* tailored their notion of moral responsibility to balance their commitments to a teleological and predetermined narrative of salvation history with ongoing expectations of proper conduct. By interpreting their notion of moral responsibility as motivated by their ideological commitments and a specific social context, I contend that the *Excerpts of Theodotus* and the *Tripartite Tractate* rhetorically highlight their self-identity as a subgroup of Christians called to special missionary practices.

I will first introduce passages pointing to belief in higher and lower salvation in the *Excerpts of Theodotus* and the *Tripartite Tractate*.[14] Then, I will briefly summarize how scholars have interpreted these passages differently, that is, as either final eschatological ends or progressive stages of advancement. Moving beyond the false binary that Valentinian anthropology is either indifferent to ethical merit or refers only to transient stages of moral development, I will conclude instead that both the *Excerpts of Theodotus* and the *Tripartite Tractate* privilege a different framework, causal responsibility, for ascribing moral praise and blame. As we will see, both the *Excerpts of Theodotus* and the *Tripartite Tractate* appeal to higher and lower levels of salvation to justify and motivate committed readers toward their ethical ideal of proselytizing and saving others.

The Texts of the Excerpts of Theodotus *and the* Tripartite Tractate

As we shall see—due to genre, transmission history, and state of preservation—each text presents distinct interpretative challenges. The *Excerpts of Theodotus*, for example, are preserved among the writings of Clement of Alexandria in two codices, one of which is directly dependent upon the other.[15] The titular Theodotus is something of a mystery; although he is named in the *Excerpts*, we have no other patristic reports about him.[16] Furthermore, despite their attribution to "Theodotus and the so-called Eastern School,"[17] the so-called *Excerpts of Theodotus* appear to be a composite work from at least four different sources, with the excerpts breaking down into the following sections according to source: (1) 1–28; (2) 29–43.1; (3) 43.2–65; (4) 66–86.[18] Robert Casey, one of the modern editors, claims that Theodotus himself was the source of only the following: 1.1–2; 2; 3; 17.1; 21; 22; 23; 24.1; 25; 26; 28; 29; 30.1; 31; 32; 33.1, 3–4; 34; 35; 36.1; 37–41.[19] Furthermore, throughout the *Excerpts of Theodotus*, Clement of Alexandria interjects his own opinions or excurses.[20] Based on the at times haphazard nature of the *Excerpts of Theodotus*, scholars have described its genre as an "author's notebook" or "fragmentary counter-commentary."[21]

My focus will be the third major section (43.2–65), which appears to share a common source with Irenaeus's description of the followers of Ptolemy in book 1 of *Haer.*[22] As we shall see, this section contains a sweeping narrative that begins with the Pleroma, alludes to the fall of Sophia, and continues to describe the origins of matter, the creation of humanity, the advent of the Savior, and finally the eschatological restoration of the saved. Most importantly for my purposes, it contains a fully articulated division of humanity into three types and a soteriology of higher and lower levels of salvation: "Now the pneumatic is saved by nature, but the psychic, having power over itself, is suited for faith and incorruptibility as well as for unbelief and corruption according to its particular choice, but the hylic is by nature destroyed. . . . The psychics are raised and saved, but the pneumatics, having believed, have a superior salvation to theirs" (*Exc.* 56.3; 61.8).[23] This soteriology of higher and lower levels of salvation draws extensively upon Pauline ideas and language that were presumably useful for mobilizing committed and like-minded Christians toward missionary work.

The *Tripartite Tractate* is one of the longest tractates of the Nag Hammadi Codices, occupying the final eighty-eight pages of Codex I.[24] Similar

to *Excerpts of Theodotus* 43.2–65, it contains a totalizing narrative that begins
with protology, cosmology, and anthropogony and continues by describing
the eschatological judgment and redemption for deserving humans, angels,
and even aeonic powers. According to its soteriology, the Father providentially withheld perfection, and thus began the pedagogically driven fall and
ultimate restoration of the whole of creation:

> The whole structure of the aeons, then, is yearning and seeking to
> find the Father perfectly and completely, and this is their irre-
> proachable union. Although the Father does reveal himself, he did
> not want them to know him from eternity, but he presented
> himself as something to be reflected upon and sought after, while
> keeping for himself that by which he is inscrutably preexistent.
> For the Father gave the aeons as a starting point and a root, so
> that they are stations on the calm road leading to him, as to a
> school of good conduct; for he spread out faith and prayer for
> what they do not see, a firm hope in what they do not compre-
> hend, a fertile love longing for what they do not behold, an
> eternally receptive understanding of the mind, a blessing that it is
> richness and freedom, and, for their thoughts, the wisdom of one
> whose desire is the glory of the Father. (*Tri. Trac.* 71.7–35)

Similarly, the expulsion of humanity from the Garden of Eden and the contingent emergence of death were providentially orchestrated as part of the
Father's *oikonomia* or salvific ordering of the cosmos.[25] Thus, there is an
emphasis on the deliberateness and providential guidance of all cosmic levels and all episodic periods of salvation history.[26]

As a tractate found among the Nag Hammadi Codices, the *Tripartite
Tractate* presents unique issues regarding the circumstances of its composition and transmission. Einar Thomassen has persuasively suggested that
the *Tripartite Tractate* originated as a mid-third-century text composed in
Greek.[27] Its current form, however, is that of a fourth- or fifth-century
Coptic translation; as such, it reflects the exigencies of this transmission
process. Nonetheless, without additional copies of the *Tripartite Tractate* it
cannot be anything more than pure speculation to engage in redaction criticism aimed at isolating the interpolations of so-called later or foreign ideological content. Although some ideas may be conducive to later theological
debates (thus explaining their preservation), we cannot persuasively isolate

scribal interventions into the text without additional copies or textual seams. Thus, we shall avoid the perils of speculating as to whether these ideas may have been present at the earliest stage of the *Tripartite Tractate* or may have been added later. Treating the *Tripartite Tractate* as a coherent whole, however, does not mean that we can use the text *uncritically* as evidence of second- or third-century Christianity, despite close parallels with the *Excerpts of Theodotus* and Irenaeus, *Haer.* 1. As a result, while I advocate treating the text as a whole, I am also aware that the text itself poses distinct difficulties, such as garbled or corrupted translations, which need to be addressed on an ad hoc basis.

Higher and Lower Salvation

According to the *Excerpts of Theodotus* and the *Tripartite Tractate*, there are three classes of people (choic or hylic, psychic, and pneumatic), and each has a distinct salvific end. Both the *Excerpts of Theodotus* and the *Tripartite Tractate* contain the classic formulation of this tripartite division, which adopts and synthesizes into a single hierarchical anthropology Paul's rhetorical classification of pneumatic, psychic, and earthly types of people, thereby combining chapters 2 and 15 from Paul's First Letter to the Corinthians.[28] Furthermore, each of the three classes has a different salvific profile: "The pneumatic race will receive complete salvation in every respect. The hylic race will perish in every respect, as happens to an enemy. The psychic race, however, since it is in the middle by virtue of the way it was brought forth as well as by virtue of its creation, is double according to its assignment to good as well as to evil" (*Tri. Trac.* 119.16–24). As we saw above, the *Excerpts of Theodotus* also contains a threefold division of humanity and ascribes different soteriological profiles to the pneumatic, psychic, and hylic: "Now the pneumatic (τὸ πνευματικόν) is saved by nature, but the psychic (τὸ ψυχικόν), having power over itself, is suited for faith and incorruptibility as well as for unbelief and corruption according to its particular choice, but the hylic (τὸ ὑλικόν) is by nature destroyed" (*Exc.* 56.3).

Elsewhere, this hierarchical stratification of hylic, psychic, and pneumatic is further accentuated by descriptions of the higher and lower levels of salvific reward enjoyed by pneumatics and psychics, respectively, as well as by the different roles they play over the course of salvation history. One of the Valentinian authors preserved in the *Excerpts of Theodotus* appeals to a sophisticated scriptural metaphor to illustrate the compatibility of greater and lesser rewards within shared salvation. *Excerpts of Theodotus* 56–58 deploys Paul's metaphor of the olive tree from Romans 11 to describe the dynamic process through which two groups—the gentiles, representing the psychics, and Israel, representing the pneumatics—are both saved: "When, therefore, the psychic ones (τὰ ψυχικά) 'are engrafted on the olive tree' (Rom.11:24) into faith and incorruptibility and share 'the richness of the olive tree' (Rom. 11:17) and 'when the gentiles come in,' then 'thus shall all Israel' (Rom. 11:25–26)" (*Exc.* 56.4).[29] Yet, although both are saved, hierarchy persists in this olive tree, as our Valentinian author refers to the elect, or pneumatics, as the root and the called, or psychics, as the shoots (*Exc.* 58.1–2). In this way, our author imports Paul's hierarchy of the sure salvation of all of Israel and the secondary salvation of gentiles to underscore the superior status of the pneumatic over and above that of the psychic.[30] Therefore, according to our Valentinian author, different salvific statuses await psychic and pneumatic types: "For when the body died and death was lord over it, the Savior sent forth the ray of power which had come upon him and destroyed death and raised up the mortal body which had put off passion. In this way, therefore, the psychic ones (τὰ ψυχικά) are raised and saved, but the pneumatic ones (τὰ πνευματικά), having believed, have a superior salvation to theirs, because they received their souls as 'wedding garments'" (*Exc.* 61.7–8).

In addition to containing the same tripartite division of humanity, the *Tripartite Tractate* posits two separate but interrelated eschatological timelines: on the one hand, a realized eschatology enacted ritually through baptism for the pneumatics, and on the other, a final day of judgment for hylics and psychics.[31] In this vision of salvation history, the church, consisting of pneumatics (*Tri. Trac.* 123.3–12),[32] is set apart from the rest of humanity by ritually participating in the body of the Savior as a "preliminary" unification prior to the final restoration that will occur only after the reunification of the Pleromatic realms.[33] This preliminary unification of the pneumatics is described in symbolic language emerging from the use of Pauline baptismal formulae in ritual practice: "The Election is consubstantial with the Savior and of one body with him. Because of its oneness and union with him, it is like a bridal chamber" (*Tri. Trac.* 122.12–17). Following this initial or preliminary unification, the pneumatics, according to the *Tripartite Tractate*, will escape beyond the powers of the hylic (those on the left) and psychic (those on the right) by receiving the complete redemption, which "was not only the release from the domination of the left ones, nor was it only [escape][34] from the powers of those of the right . . . but the redemption is also an ascent [to] degrees which are in the Pleroma and [to] those who have named themselves according to the power of each of the aeons, and an entrance into what is silent, where there is no need for voice . . . but where all things are light, while not needing to be illumined" (*Tri. Trac.* 124.3–25).

While it is clear that these Valentinians used biblically inspired categories to differentiate among types or natures—hylic, psychic, and pneumatic— the social and salvific implications of these different classes are still hotly contested. As we have seen, the pneumatics are unquestionably saved; the hylics are unquestionably damned; but the fate of the psychics is uncertain (*Tri. Trac.* 119.16–24; *Exc.* 56; cf. Irenaeus, *Haer.* 1.7.5). Will psychics be saved, and if they are, is it to the same degree as pneumatics? In other words, are psychics in a preliminary stage, like catechists, and will they ultimately become pneumatics, or are they permanently differentiated from pneumatics and thus cannot enjoy the highest level of salvation?

A microcosm of the contours of the debate surrounding Valentinian soteriology are the contrasting views of Elaine Pagels and James McCue, who clashed over how best to interpret the accounts of Valentinian soteriology preserved by two early Christian polemicists, Irenaeus of Lyons and Clement of Alexandria.[35] According to Pagels, Irenaeus polemically altered his summary of Valentinian soteriology in order to claim that Valentinians excluded ordinary ("psychic") Christians from full inclusion and coequal celebration alongside the Savior at the eschatological celebration.[36] In contrast, McCue argued that Irenaeus's account, while certainly polemical, is nonetheless reliable.[37] Moreover, while there may be an "equalization" among pneumatic and ordinary (psychic) Christians at the penultimate eschatological stage of the wedding feast, it is clear, according to McCue, that both Irenaeus's and the *Excerpts of Theodotus*'s versions of Valentinian soteriology agree that ordinary ("psychic") Christians do not participate in the highest eschatological reward, symbolized by the bridal chamber.[38]

Undergirding much of Pagels's and McCue's disagreement were their opposing responses to the question of whether, according to the Valentinians, a person could change his or her "nature" in order to earn a different salvific desert. Central to their debate is the account of the eschatological celebration beginning at *Excerpts of Theodotus* 63:

Now the repose of the pneumatics (τῶν πνευματικῶν) on the
Lord's Day is in the Ogdoad, which is called the Lord's Day, and

is with the Mother who keeps the souls, the wedding garments, until the end; but the other faithful souls are with the Creator, but at the end they also go up into the Ogdoad. Then comes the marriage feast that is common to all of those who are saved until all might be made equal (ἀπισωθῇ) and know each other. Afterwards, the pneumatic ones (τὰ πνευματικά), having put aside the souls, are led by the Mother, who is guiding the bridegroom, and these same ones [lead] bridegrooms, i.e., their own angels, and go into the bridal chamber beyond the Limit and go towards the vision of the spirit/*pneuma*, having become intellectual aeons through the intellectual and eternal marriages of the syzygy. (*Exc.* 63–64)

On the basis of *Excerpts of Theodotus* 63–64, Pagels proposed that psychics could and would be saved in the end, claiming that the difference between ordinary ("psychic") and Valentinian ("pneumatic") Christians is only "provisional," since it will be "obliterated" during the eschatological celebration, wherein psychics and pneumatics receive the same salvific reward.[39] In response McCue contended that the wedding feast of *Excerpts of Theodotus* 63–64 refers only to a preliminary eschatological reward. The logic of Valentinian soteriology, McCue argued, is such that the composition of one's nature indicates how high one can climb on the eschatological ladder of rewards; in other words, pneumatics, who possess pneumatic, psychic, and hylic elements, can, once stripped of the lower two elements, ascend to the rewards of pneumatic elements.[40] In contrast, psychics, who lack the pneumatic elements, simply cannot ascend into the final bridal chamber described in *Haer.* 1.7.1, 5 and *Exc.* 64–65:[41] "Afterwards, the pneumatic ones (τὰ πνευματικά), having put aside the souls (τὰς ψυχάς) . . . go into the bridal chamber beyond the Limit . . . having become intellectual aeons through the intellectual and eternal marriages of the syzygy. And the 'master' of the feast who is the 'best-man' for the ceremony, 'and the friend of the bridegroom, standing in front of the bridal chamber and hearing the voice of the bridegroom, rejoices greatly' (John 3:29). This is 'fullness of his joy' and his repose (John 3:29)" (*Exc.* 64–65). From this, McCue concluded that the difference between psychics and pneumatics is not provisional, but is a fundamental distinction that continues to separate Valentinians from ordinary Christians forever.[42]

To adjudicate between these two competing interpretations, we must explain the presence of both masculine and neuter categories (e.g., οἱ

πνευματικοί vs. τὰ πνευματικά), determine who is present at the final
stage of the bridal chamber, and decide whether and to what degree Valentinian soteriology preferred radical equality or salvific hierarchy. As we shall
see, both the *Excerpts of Theodotus* and the *Tripartite Tractate* express ideological commitments to eschatological unity; this does not mean, however,
that salvation in either text is a simple binary between the saved and the
damned. Nor, as we have seen throughout this book, are the *Excerpts of
Theodotus* and the *Tripartite Tractate* the only ancient texts that attempt to
simultaneously maintain equality and hierarchy. One need look no further
than the Apostle Paul to find the uneasy tension of extolling equality
among ritual initiates while simultaneously maintaining hierarchical relationships among members.[43] Moreover, the phenomenon of higher and
lower rewards within shared salvation is not unique to the *Excerpts of Theodotus* or the *Tripartite Tractate*. In addition to the texts already considered
in this book, noted heresiologists, such as Clement of Alexandria[44] and even
Irenaeus,[45] all describe higher and lower levels of reward within shared salvation. For all of these authors, as well as for the *Excerpts of Theodotus* and
the *Tripartite Tractate*, the phenomenon of higher and lower levels of salvation was a useful technology that could help maintain expectations for ethical conduct, but could also help account for moral shortcomings.

An important point of contention remains: Is the distinction between
psychic and pneumatic a permanent division, or is it merely provisional? In
support of her view that all difference between pneumatics and psychics will
be obliterated, Pagels argued that natures or elements, in the neuter (e.g.,
τὸ πνευματικόν/τὰ πνευματικά), were fundamentally distinct from classes
of people, in the masculine (e.g., ὁ πνευματικός/οἱ πνευματικοί): "According to Theodotus, it is not the 'pneumatics' (οἱ πνευματικοί) who 'leave off
their souls' and enter into the Pleroma, but the pneumatic elements (τὰ
πνευματικά). Since after the equalization 'psychics' and 'pneumatics' no
longer exist as distinct species, the πνευματικά can only be the pneumatic
seed or τὰ ἀγγελικά of both those who previously were pneumatic and psychic (cf. *Exc.* 21 and 39)."[46] Thus, in *Excerpts of Theodotus* 56 and following,
the road map of salvation outlined above describes the salvific fate of different "elements" or "seeds," but not classes of people.[47] As I will show below,
however, both the "pneumatic elements" and "seeds" are uniquely and exclusively connected with pneumatic persons and the salvation of pneumatics
as a corporate class.[48]

Similarly supporting the view that Valentinian soteriology is concerned with saving certain elements or parts of a person but not classes of people, Ismo Dunderberg observed that *Excerpts of Theodotus* 50–57 is building on an extended exegesis of Genesis 1–2 and the composite creation of Adam:[49] "'Taking a clump from the earth' (Gen. 2:7) not of dust but from a portion of matter of various parts and colors, he fashioned an earthly and hylic (ὑλικήν) soul, irrational and consubstantial with the one (i.e., the soul) of the beasts. This is the human being 'according to the image' (Gen.1:26). But the one 'according to the likeness' is the one that the Demiurge himself 'breathed into' (Gen. 1:26; 2:7) and in which he sowed and placed something consubstantial with himself through angels" (*Exc.* 50.1–2). After differentiating between two types of souls (the hylic or earthly and the psychic or divine soul),[50] *Excerpts of Theodotus* 53–54 describes a third soul, the logical or heavenly soul, that comes to be after Wisdom sows the spiritual seed into Adam.[51] After listing the three (hylic, psychic, and pneumatic) souls, the *Excerpts of Theodotus* mentions an additional component, a leathery cloak of earthly material, which surrounds Adam (*Exc.* 55.1–2). In summary, Adam's anthropology is an elaborate dualism between earthly flesh and immaterial soul, wherein there are three types of soul (hylic, psychic, and pneumatic). Extrapolating from this narrative of the composite creation of Adam, Dunderberg claims that at the eschatological celebration a person would be separated again into these component parts. In other words, these "elements," in the neuter, are distinct from classes of persons, in the masculine, and it is these "elements" that receive different salvific rewards.[52]

This is a significant observation and an important distinction; however, this rigid dichotomy between elements and classes of people overlooks the Pauline exegetical intertexts motivating and undergirding this portion of the *Excerpts of Theodotus*.[53] Thus, in order to clarify the overlapping referents of the neuter singular and plural forms of pneumatic, psychic, and hylic and their eponymous anthropological classes, it is necessary to uncover and explain their underlying exegetical framework, in particular Pauline metaphors of sowing and the corporate body of the Savior. As we will see, our Valentinian author composed a complex and exegetically driven narrative. In this way, the *Excerpts of Theodotus* accounts for how different people emerge by analogy to the sowing of disparate seeds, and it illustrates their corresponding salvific deserts via the body of the Savior and its internal hierarchy. It is not a coincidence that the three types of souls have the same names as the three classes of humanity. The physiological hierarchy of the paradigmatic and first human (Adam) is a blueprint of the salvific hierarchy of the three classes of humanity, and the salvific destinies of each class are illustrated by their eponymous level in the corporate body of the Savior, which is modeled after Adam.

Let us look more closely at this Pauline exegesis, beginning with the metaphor of sowing. Expanding upon its exegesis of Genesis, *Excerpts of Theodotus* 53 also claims that the sowing of different seeds (σπέρμα, a neuter noun) accounts for the differences among Adam's three sons: Cain, Abel, and Seth: "From Adam three natures were begotten: first the irrational, which was Cain's, the second the rational and just, which was Abel's, and third the pneumatic, which was Seth's. And the one that is earthly is 'according to an image,' and the psychic 'according to a likeness' with God, and the pneumatic according to [God's] own property" (*Exc.* 54.1–2). The *Excerpts of Theodotus* exegetically blends the story of Adam and his progeny with Paul's metaphor of sowing and his terminological distinction between psychic and pneumatic from 1 Corinthians 2–3.[54] This metaphor of sowing seeds illustrates how difference arose and was obliquely transmitted.

> Therefore, Adam sows neither from the pneumatic nor from "that which was breathed into [him]" (Gen. 2:7). For both are divine and both sprout through him but not by him. But his hylic is energetic towards seed and generation, as though blended with its seed and unable to separate from this merging in life. . . . And if Adam had sown from the psychic and the pneumatic just as he had from the hylic, everyone would have been equal and righteous and everyone would have the teaching. Therefore, many are the hylics (οἱ ὑλικοί), not a lot are the psychics (οἱ ψυχικοί), and a few are the pneumatics (οἱ πνευματικοί). (*Exc.* 55.1–56.2)

In the same way that we do not interpret Paul's seeds as autonomous or separate entities from their current manifestation as his congregation members, so too we should not obscure the meaning of the narrative in the *Excerpts of Theodotus* by creating an absolute distinction between these seeds and their manifestation.

This sowing metaphor has several important interpretative implications: first, there is a causal relationship between these seeds and the emergence of different types of people. Importantly, this relationship is not strictly biological or predictable; instead, the differences represented by these

seeds are transmitted obliquely.[55] The imagery of a seed, which disappears
and whose contents (i.e., its future maturation and actualization) are unknown before it reappears, is particularly useful because it can convey both
theoretical fixity as well as sociological fluidity.[56] In theory, Valentinian soteriology has fixed, or predetermined, salvific classes; yet in practice there is
sociological fluidity in how persons might discover their true identities and
accept the codes of conduct attendant to their roles in the ongoing drama of
salvation history. Thus in practice, the imagery of a seed, the true nature of
which is only later revealed, places the emphasis on the actualization of these
seeds because it is only after a person is identified as one of the three classes
that the cause, his or her seminal nature, is retrospectively realized.[57] In this
way, these seeds function as Aristotelian-like causes insofar as they are ex-
planatory; that is, with hindsight they can be appealed to in order to explain
the actualization of different sorts of people.[58] Finally, the metaphor of a
seed works only in one direction: it describes how certain people emerge as
a result of their seeds. It does not, however, work in the opposite direction
such that a person can change or transform his or her seed; such an interpretation would destroy the power and clarity of the metaphor.

In addition to this metaphor of sowing, the *Excerpts of Theodotus* is also
drawing upon the Pauline imagery of the corporate body of the Savior. *Excerpts of Theodotus* 63–65 describes the higher level of salvific reward awaiting the pneumatic (τὰ πνευματικά) in the bridal chamber; and so, some
scholars have similarly interpreted this passage as indicating that the highest level of salvation is rewarded not to pneumatic people, but to pneumatic
elements. This interpretation, however, overlooks the Pauline metaphor of a
corporate, ecclesial body constructed from differing members.[59] At *Excerpts
of Theodotus* 58.1, "the Great Champion, Jesus Christ" "takes up" the church,
consisting of the pneumatic elect (τὸ ἐκλεκτόν) and the psychic called (τὸ
κλητόν), and saves them according to the logic of participation.[60] According to this salvation by participation, the "Great Champion, Jesus Christ,"
becomes a composite whole made of differing parts, and will save the different classes of humanity by redeeming that respective and consubstantial
part of himself manifested by each class: "Jesus Christ took up through his
own power the Church, the elect and the called; the former is the pneumatic (τὸ πνευματικόν) from the Mother, and the latter is the psychic (τὸ
ψυχικόν) through the salvific organization (ἐκ τῆς οἰκονομίας). He saved
and bore up what he had taken up and through them also what was consubstantial. 'For if the first fruit is holy, the dough will be also; and if the root

is holy, the branches will be also' (Romans 11:16)" (*Exc.* 58.1–2). As at 56.4, *Excerpts of Theodotus* 58.2 mines Romans 11 for imagery that conveys hierarchy within shared salvation.

Moreover, our Valentinian author appeals to the composite nature of the Savior in order to explain that apparently incongruent sayings of the Lord emerged from these different parts of his corporate body (*Exc.* 61:1–8; cf. Irenaeus, *Haer.* 1.7.3). Drawing upon several scriptural intertexts, these parts of the composite Savior are personified differently, referencing the hierarchy of bodily members and the corresponding hierarchy among its eponymous classes of people: "Now the psychic Christ sits at the right hand of the creator, just as David said: 'Sit at my right hand' (Ps. 110.1), and so on. And he sits until the completion, 'in order that they may see whom they pierced' (John 19:37). But they pierced the appearance, which was the flesh of the psychic. For it says 'not a bone of his shall be broken' (John 19:36). Just as in the case of Adam, the prophecy allegorizes bone as the soul (Gen. 2:23). For the soul deposited itself into the hands of the father while the body of Christ suffered, but the pneumatic in the bone is not yet deposited, but he preserves it" (*Exc.* 62.1–3). By the time we arrive at the eschatological celebration, our Valentinian author is juggling several scriptural intertexts; most importantly for our current purposes are Adam's composite creation and Paul's ecclesial body with multiple members. We have a description of a single, paradigmatic person composed of various parts; but we also have a corporate body, which is made up of different members, and each represents a whole class of people. The soteriology of this blended exegesis maintains that corporate salvation works analogously to the hierarchy of the single, paradigmatic human being and vice versa.[61] Therefore, τὰ πνευματικά does not exclusively refer to either the highest part of an individual or to a corporate class of people, but rather to both.

Moreover, this interpretation, which highlights that people and not just elements are saved, makes better sense of the descriptions of the higher salvific award reserved for the bridal chamber: "Afterwards, the pneumatic ones, having put aside the souls, are led by the mother, who is guiding the bridegroom, and these same ones [lead] bridegrooms, i.e., their own angels, and go into the bridal chamber beyond the Limit and go towards the vision of the spirit/*pneuma*, having become intellectual aeons through the intellectual and eternal marriages of the syzygy" (*Exc.* 64). Though some scholars have interpreted the "equalization" that occurs at the dinner celebration as a radical transformation of all guests into a single substance or element (τὰ πνευματικά), this does not account for other passages that emphasize the varying statuses of the wedding attendees.[62] Foreshadowing this eschatological scene where "the pneumatic ones put aside the souls," these souls are referred to as the "wedding garments" for the pneumatic ones (*Exc.* 61.8; 63.1). Thus, although the marriage festival is celebrated coequally by the participants—psychics and pneumatics alike—this coequal marriage feast does not entail a complete merging between the dinner guests (psychics) and the bridal party (pneumatics). Instead, it is quite the opposite: because of what happens in the bridal chamber, there is a stripping off of the wedding garments (souls), and thus the celebration therein consists exclusively of the pneumatics (and their syzygies) without the garments of their souls.[63] The exclusiveness of this reward is further underscored by the spatial metaphor in play; namely the highest salvation is limited because a bedroom is a private place and is not spacious enough to accommodate the entire dinner party of the saved.

In addition to the passages outlined above, the specific terms deployed in this eschatological scene to demarcate higher and lower levels of salvation may provide additional evidence of the soteriological hierarchy between psychics and pneumatics in the *Excerpts of Theodotus*. For example, the higher and lower salvific levels are characterized by different and gradated sensory experiences: the pneumatics in the bridal chamber see, whereas those standing outside the bridal chamber only hear the sounds of celebration (*Exc.* 64–65). We find this same sensory hierarchy between pneumatics and psychics in the *Tripartite Tractate* (118–19), where pneumatics receive knowledge through revelation, and the psychics are instructed by means of voice.[64]

Moreover, at this final eschatological phase, only the pneumatics pass beyond the Limit and become pure aeons through "the marriage of the syzygy." Though from another part of the *Excerpts of Theodotus* and likely from a different author/source,[65] *Excerpts of Theodotus* 21–22 and 35–36 state that the angelic syzygies required to cross the Limit and enter into the Pleroma are available only to pneumatics.[66] This unifying syzygy, *Excerpts of Theodotus* 35–36 declares, not only redeems the pneumatics themselves, but also restores angels to the Pleroma through their reenactment and participation in the Savior's baptism.[67] Consequently, through these ritualized unions, pneumatics play a different and much more active role than psychics in the ongoing drama and salvation history—one intimately involved with the restoration of the cosmos and the salvation of others, including even angels:[68] "For, as they [angels] are bound for the sake of a part [of themselves] and, though being restrained in their desire to enter on account of us, they plead and beg remission for us in order that we might enter together with them. For it is almost as if they need us in order to enter, since without us they are not permitted (on account of this not even the mother has entered without us, they say), probably because they are bound for our sake" (*Exc.* 35.3–4). In summary, although it consists of several Valentinian sources, the *Excerpts of Theodotus* repeatedly maintains that pneumatics and psychics are distinct and play different roles in the drama of salvation history. This does not mean that psychics cannot be saved, but rather within the shared salvation of pneumatics and psychics, pneumatics enjoy greater rewards and honors: "The psychic ones are in this way raised and saved, then, but the pneumatic ones, having believed, receive a higher salvation" (*Exc.* 61.8).[69]

We find a similar soteriology of higher and lower rewards within shared salvation in the *Tripartite Tractate.* Drawing on the radical equality of the Pauline baptismal formula found in Galatians 3, the author claims that there will be a return to the primordial unity such that all differences shall be abolished: "For if we confess the kingdom that is in Christ it is an abolishment from all multiplicity, inequality, and change. For the end will receive a unitary existence just as the beginning is unitary—the place where there is neither male nor female nor slave nor free, nor circumcised nor uncircumcised neither angel nor man, but all in all is Christ" (*Tri. Trac.* 132.16–28; cf. 127.19–25). Nonetheless, the *Tripartite Tractate* goes on to clarify that, while all the saved—angels and humans—will obtain the kingdom, the confirmation, and salvation, "some are exalted because of the *oikonomia,* having been set up as causes for the things that happened" (*Tri. Trac.* 133.8–10).[70] Consequently, although the *Tripartite Tractate* imagines a final apokatastatic return to unity (133; 135–36), there are still persistent indications of difference.[71] Moreover, this original unity to which the saved will return is the Pleromatic union, and that unity is comprised of the concord of aeons of various stations and powers. It is likely, therefore, that this imagined eschatological ideal will resemble the hymning aeons of the Pleroma who form a "union, a mutual intermingling, and oneness" through their hymns despite individually remaining different and having different powers: "But every name that is thought or is spoken about him is brought forth in glorification as a trace of him according to the power of each of those who glorify him" (*Tri. Trac.* 65.39–66.5; cf. 68.20–28; 70.8–19). Consequently, although differing from the *Excerpts of Theodotus,* the *Tripartite Tractate,* nonetheless, similarly expresses a belief in soteriological hierarchy.

Ultimately then, if the *Excerpts of Theodotus* and the *Tripartite Tractate* did devise a soteriology consisting of predetermined levels of salvation and different classes of humanity, were they indifferent, as some heresiologists claimed, to ethics and moral responsibility? As we will see, such allegations presuppose a model of ethical responsibility that privileges voluntariness and the choice between alternatives. This model, however, was not the only notion of moral responsibility deployed in antiquity. Instead and similar to earlier Stoic philosophers, the Valentinians employed a model of causal moral responsibility. This observation makes two contributions to the study of Valentinianism. First, it enables us once and for all to put aside the heresiological cliché that Valentinians were unethical determinists.[72] Second, by extrapolating from what practices Valentinians privileged through their model of causal responsibility, we can reconstruct the ethics of higher and lower salvation, namely the idealized portrait of what a pneumatic ought to do.

Responsibility and Ethics

To provide context for the conflict between moral frameworks, let us now consider two types of moral responsibility: causal and two-sided. Both are heuristic categories designed to illustrate that ancient thinkers could privilege different theoretical and social commitments while still retaining moral accountability. Following this overview, I will argue that the *Excerpts of Theodotus* and the *Tripartite Tractate*'s fixed anthropogony and eschatology preserve moral responsibility insofar as agents, because of either their essence or nature, are still the cause of their moral or immoral actions. Finally, I will examine what discrete ethical practices the *Excerpts of Theodotus* and the *Tripartite Tractate* expect pneumatics to enact. I will conclude that, according to the *Excerpts of Theodotus* and the *Tripartite Tractate*, a pneumatic is morally responsible for missionizing to and saving others.

Over the past two decades, Susanne Bobzien, an expert on determinism and freedom in ancient philosophy, has persuasively demonstrated that there were different modes or ways of articulating moral responsibility in antiquity.[73] An agent is morally responsible when moral praise or blame can be assigned to the agent on the basis of his or her moral choices and actions.[74] Too often we have reduced moral responsibility to the question "Did an agent use his or her free will for good or for evil?" However, as numerous studies have shown, a "free will" as an autonomous, governing psychological faculty, distinct from reason, was (and still is) a complex and often elusive concept; moreover, it did not coalesce until rather late in antiquity, and even then it was not consistently formulated.[75] A better question for determining moral responsibility is to ask: "What is up to or dependent upon us?" Based upon their differing interests and presuppositions, however, ancient theorists disagreed about what precisely *is* up to us, and for what, therefore, we are morally responsible as agents.

In light of those disagreements, Bobzien delineates two types of moral responsibility.[76] In the first case, described as causal moral responsibility, an agent is morally responsible when the agent is causally the source for an action or choice; that is, it is the agent and not something else that brought about the action. In this first case, the primary concern is that the agent be autonomous and free from external compulsions. As we see in Cicero's *De fato*, causal moral responsibility is associated with the views of Stoics, in particular Chrysippus, who was attempting to balance universal causation with moral accountability. Chrysippus's solution was to claim that events are codetermined by external and internal causes, and that even if external or auxiliary causes are fated, an agent is still responsible for the internal or principal cause:[77] "'Some causes,' [Chrysippus] says, 'are perfect and principal, others auxiliary and proximate. Thus, when we say that everything happens by fate owing to antecedent causes, what we wish to be understood is not perfect and principal causes, but auxiliary and proximate causes'" (Cicero, *De fato* 41). As we will see below, causal moral responsibility posits an agent (or "self") that is foreign to many modern readers because it does not subdivide him or her into competing, internal faculties; rather, an agent is causally responsible when he or she, treated as a whole, is the source of an action or decision.[78]

In Bobzien's second type of moral responsibility, an agent can be praised or blamed only if he or she could have done otherwise; in other words, there is not a strong belief in universal causation, and thus there is an element of indeterminateness to our choices and actions. In this second case then, autonomy from external compulsion is not the primary concern; instead, to be morally accountable, we must have made a voluntary and deliberate choice between the alternatives of x and not x.[79] Emblematic of this second type of moral responsibility, the second- to third-century Peripatetic Alexander of Aphrodisias describes *prohairesis* as a choice between alternatives that is not predetermined by preceding causes: "For we assume that we have this power in actions, i.e., we can choose the opposite, and not that everything which

we choose has causes laid down beforehand on account of which it is not
possible for us not to choose it" (Alexander of Aphrodisias, *De fato* 180.26–
28). In this way, Bobzien sets out two competing notions of moral responsibility by asking: "What is up to us?" In the first case, an action depends upon
us if the cause for the action originated in us and not elsewhere;[80] in the
second case, we are responsible for an action only if we voluntarily chose it
and could have chosen otherwise. These two models privilege different concerns and construct moral agents differently.

Accordingly, there are also different formulations for what constitutes
the "us" in the programmatic question "What is up to us?" Causal responsibility often depends upon a notion of self that Bobzien refers to as "the
whole person" model; on the opposite end of the spectrum is a notion of the
self that is divided into parts or mental faculties in conflict with one another.[81] According to "the whole person" model, a person's choices and actions result from his or her disposition and character and are entwined with
his or her past experiences and memories. The "divided self," on the other
hand, frequently portrays decision-making as a contest of rival parts or separate faculties, wherein the "I" that decides is distinguishable from beliefs,
experiences, and character. For our purposes here, it is important to keep in
mind that an agent is causally responsible when he or she, treated as an ag-
gregate whole, is the source of a decision or action. Because any decision or
choice is contingent upon the type of person I am, I could not have done
otherwise because there is no additional faculty or "I" separable from the
type of person I am.[82] As we will see, the Valentinian soteriology of higher
and lower levels of salvation has striking parallels with both Bobzien's two
models of responsibility and different types of selves.

In what follows, I will appeal to Bobzien's heuristic categories in order
to describe with greater clarity the ethics and moral psychology underlying
the Valentinian soteriology of higher and lower levels of salvation. We must
set aside the heresiological cliché that without the ability to choose otherwise Valentinians (as well as a number of other teleological storytellers)
were determinists with no sense of moral accountability (e.g., Irenaeus,
Haer. 4.37.2); there were, instead, a multitude of ways for encouraging moral
action in antiquity. Differences in moral framework and assumptions, rather
than representing correct vs. incorrect ideas or rational vs. irrational arguments, reflect differing social positions, agendas, and ideals among these
ancient Christian authors.[83]

For example, Clement of Alexandria was an influential promoter of the claim that Valentinians, due to their absence of voluntary choice, were unethical determinists. In book 2 of the *Stromata*, Clement characterizes the Valentinians as soteriological determinists who believe they are saved by nature and concludes, therefore, that they have no regard for ethical accountability. Without the ability to assent to or reject God voluntarily, Clement asserts, we are simply "lifeless puppets controlled by natural forces and led involuntarily by predetermined impulse . . . and moved by external cause" (*Strom.* 2.11.1–2). Clement's critique mirrors anti-Stoic polemics that claimed that if an action was the exclusive result of external causes, then there could be no room for moral accountability.[84] Moreover, although Clement himself does not endorse a completely voluntary portrait of moral psychology, he, nonetheless, strategically deploys Peripatetic terminology to privilege the voluntariness of the choice between obedience and disobedience as part of his polemic against Valentinian soteriology.[85] Choice, as Clement uses the term, does not possess the indeterminate sense of a deliberative choice from all possible sets of alternatives; instead, it is functionally synonymous with a single choice between the alternatives of offering or withholding *sugkatathesis* or assent to God.[86]

As result, "what is up to us," according to Clement, is often described as the moral choice between obedience or disobedience to the commandments of God and the instruction of the Logos: "What is in our power is readiness for education and obedience to the commandments" (*Strom.* 2.15.62; cf. *Prot.* 11.115.1; *Paed.* 1.12.100.2; *Strom.* 2.20.115). This emphasis on a person's preparedness and willingness for instruction makes sense in the case of an individual, such as Clement, who made his living as a teacher.[87] In this way, Clement's construction of moral psychology is an expression of his own ideological commitments, including his social position as a professional instructor.[88]

For their part, the *Excerpts of Theodotus* and the *Tripartite Tractate* deploy a soteriology that privileges naturalist (physical) explanations of ethical difference and a causal model for ethical responsibility. Moreover, this soteriology not only encourages correct behavior, as we will see below, but also can help explain moral shortcomings. For example, *Excerpts of Theodotus* 56.3, which I introduced above as evidence of Valentinian belief in higher and lower levels of salvation, also provides a tantalizing psychological portrait of psychics: "Now the pneumatic is saved by nature, but the psychic, having power over itself,[89] is suited for faith and incorruptibility as well as for unbelief and corruption according to its particular choice, but the hylic is by nature destroyed" (*Exc* 56.3). According to *Excerpts of Theodotus* 56.3, psychics have a limited range of choice: they can select between the alternatives of "faith and incorruptibility as well as unbelief and corruption."[90] Merging several disparate scriptural passages, *Excerpts of Theodotus* 51–52 describes in detail the inner turmoil and psychological struggles of these divided persons:

> This is the meaning of "this is now bone of my bones." (Gen.
> 2:23): it hints at the divine soul which is hidden in the flesh,
> solid, impassive, and very powerful. And "flesh from my flesh"
> [hints] at the material soul (τὴν ὑλικὴν ψυχὴν), which is a body
> for the divine soul. (Gen. 2:23) Concerning these two [the
> material and divine souls], the Savior says: "one must fear the one
> able to destroy that soul and that psychic body in Hell." (Mt.
> 10:28) For the Savior calls the flesh an "adversary" (Mt. 5:25), and
> Paul calls it a "law warring against the law of my mind," and the
> Savior urges us "to bind" and "to plunder the property as of a
> rich man," (Mt. 12:29) who was warring against the heavenly
> soul. (*Exc.* 51. 2–52.1)[91]

Taken together, *Excerpts of Theodotus* 51–52 and 56 portray the psychics as internally divided and struggling between the alternatives of faith and unbelief. This is a useful caricature, underscoring the capriciousness of psychics, and thus can account for good and bad psychic conduct vis-à-vis pneumatics.[92] Moreover, as we will see, the contrast in the *Excerpts of Theodotus* between the internal instability of the psychics and the ethical consistency of pneumatics helps justify their soteriological hierarchy as well as remind pneumatics of ethical expectations.

In contrast to those psychics who are internally conflicted about whether to choose faith or unbelief, certain Valentinian sources, in particular the *Tripartite Tractate*, portray pneumatics as holistic agents who are causally responsible, due to their nature or essence, for their correct conduct. As I outlined above, someone is causally responsible if it is through the agent and not something else that an action is brought about. In the case of the early Stoic Chrysippus, the primary concern was reconciling universal causation or "fatalism" with his belief that a person can still be held morally responsible. To accomplish this, Chrysippus distinguished between two types of causes—internal or *perfect* and external or *auxiliary*—and argued that, though events might be fated to happen, they are nonetheless also codetermined by internal responses to external causes. Therefore, "what is up to us" is how we respond, either giving or withholding assent, to external impressions.

The *Tripartite Tractate* presents an instance of this codeterminism that is strikingly similar to the Stoic account of internal and external causes:[93] "Now, humanity came to be according to three essential types—pneumatic, psychic, and hylic—reproducing the pattern of the three kinds of dispositions of the Logos, from which sprung hylic, psychic, and pneumatic beings. The essences of the three kinds can each be known by its fruit. They were nevertheless not known at first, but only when the Savior came to them, shedding light upon the saints and revealing what each one was" (*Tri. Trac.* 118.14–29). According to the *Tripartite Tractate*, how people reacted to the advent of the Savior is causally linked to their "essence" and thus indicates to which class of humanity they belong, that is, whether they are pneumatic, psychic, or hylic. In this way, the anthropogonic section has structural parallels with Stoic compatibilism and causal moral responsibility. The advent of the Savior acts like an impression to which people respond, and the manner in which each individual responds reflects his or her moral quality:

> The pneumatic race is like light from light and like spirit from spirit. When its head appeared, it immediately rushed to it. At once it became a body for its head. It received knowledge straightaway from the revelation. The psychic race, however, being light from fire, tarried before recognizing the one who had appeared to it, and still more before rushing to him in faith. And it was instructed only by means of voice. . . . The hylic race, however, is alien in every respect: it is like darkness that avoids the shining light because it is dissolved by its manifestation. (*Tri. Trac.* 118.29–119.13)

Consequently, each race's essence is identified with the appropriate *diathesis* of the Word, and their essences are shorthand for the types of actions and agency each race will display.[94] In addition to emphasizing the *causal* relationship between an agent's essence and action, the *Tripartite Tractate* also represents agents holistically; that is, an agent's past experiences and present dispositions are not separable.[95] In the *Tripartite Tractate*, how an agent responds to the Savior is not determined by an autonomous decision-making faculty, but rather is the product of the whole person and is indicative of his or her soteriological class. To summarize its anthropogonic section, the *Tripartite Tractate* assigns ethical praise or censure on the basis of whether an agent gave or withheld assent to a deserving external cause, in this case, the advent of the Savior. Thus, from the point of view of causal responsibility the pneumatic is morally praiseworthy because it is through and on the basis of his or her essence and its *diathesis* that he or she responded favorably to the Savior.

In what sense, then, is a person morally responsible for his or her nature or essence? Although less explicit than the *Tripartite Tractate* about the moral psychology of pneumatics, the *Excerpts of Theodotus*, as we have seen, provocatively claims that they are "saved by nature" (*Exc.* 56.3). In his recent article, Einar Thomassen observed that Valentinian texts deploy naturalistic language to unify disparate topics, such as the composition of the world, the emotional discharges of the *Logos/Sophia*, the gradated parts of a person, and whole types of humanity, into a single physical discourse.[96] In addition to the Pauline exegetical interests outlined above, the Valentinians also devised their naturalistic cosmogony and anthropogony in order to economically provide the same explanation for material difference as for ethical difference. Consequently, the *Excerpts of Theodotus*, like the *Tripartite Tractate*, employs these multifaceted terms to denote a person's constitution, ethical profile, and even his or her eschatological destiny. As *Excerpts of Theodotus* 53–54 states, pneumatic conduct comes about because of one's nature. Thus, pneumatics are causally responsible for their conduct because it originates in them and not elsewhere. Also, as we will see, since pneumatic nature qua agency is entirely rational, pneumatics can be held morally accountable for their conduct, even if they could not choose otherwise, that is, act against their nature.[97]

As the *Excerpts of Theodotus* describes them, pneumatics do not appear to have an "I" separable from their rational, pneumatic nature. As a result, a pneumatic's agency and self are synonymous with his or her eponymous nature. Furthermore, the rational marrow of the pneumatic seed and pneumatic soul operating throughout his or her body is structurally reminiscent of the Stoic *hegemonikon* or "control center" of the person, which is infused into and dispersed throughout the pneumatic's body (*Exc.* 53):[98]

Therefore the soul is found to be natural breath (*naturalis igitur spiritus anima esse invenitur*) . . . the soul's parts flow from their seat in the heart, as if from the source of a spring, and spread throughout the whole body. They continually fill all the limbs with vital breath, and rule and control them with countless different powers—nutrition, growth, locomotion, sensation, impulse to action. The soul as a whole dispatches the senses (which are its proper functions) like branches from the trunk-like commanding-faculty to be reporters of what they sense, while itself like a monarch passes judgment on their reports. (Calcidius 220 [*SVF* 2.879])[99]

The *Excerpts of Theodotus* employs an eclectic, exegetically motivated, and naturalistic narrative of salvation history committed to a recurrent hierarchy of terms, which are thus strained to encompass all material, anthropological, psychological, and ethical difference. From the perspective of the *Excerpts of Theodotus* and its teleological narrative, pneumatics, on the basis of their pneumatic nature, are both destined to and responsible for a specific soteriological role and will, accordingly, receive their appropriate salvific reward.[100] It is not necessary for a pneumatic to have been able to act otherwise in order to be worthy of praise.[101]

Therefore, that the *Excerpts of Theodotus* and the *Tripartite Tractate* could reasonably assign moral praise or blame despite privileging such naturalistic explanations for difference is now clear.[102] But just what sort of conduct should a pneumatic embrace? Both the *Excerpts of Theodotus* and the *Tripartite Tractate* describe the *types* of characters who play specific roles in the drama of salvation history in the past, present, and future. Although these are, of course, highly imaginative and idealistic descriptions, pneumatics *could* be held accountable for whether or not they embodied the ethical ideals expressed in these texts.[103] For example, the *Tripartite Tractate* represents pneumatics as perpetuating the Savior's saving actions by caring for the fallen, preaching the good news, and teaching those who need instruction: "They have been appointed to care for those who have fallen. These are the apostles and the evangelists. They are the disciples of the Savior and are the teachers for those who need instruction" (*Tri. Trac.* 116.15–20). Moreover, and based on the importance of typology in the logic of salvation throughout the *Tripartite Tractate*, it is likely that conduct expected of pneumatics was patterned in part after analogous types that appear at other cosmic levels. For example, the aeon of the images, which is analogous to pneumatics in the tripartite division of the aeons and is similarly designated as a church comprised of pneumatic powers (*Tri. Trac.* 97.5–27), may represent ethical expectations for an ideal community that is "filled with everything agreeable—brotherly love and great generosity" (*Tri. Trac.* 96.35–97.3). Consequently, the pneumatics who emerged alongside the incarnation of the Savior (*Tri. Trac.* 116.1–5) were expected to care for the fallen, teach those who needed instruction, and preach the special revelation that leads to the redemptive unity of the cosmos (*Tri. Trac.* 116.7–117.23).[104]

Similarly, a Valentinian author preserved in *Excerpts of Theodotus* 76 deploys the missionizing language of Matthew 28:19 to encourage adherents to actively save others through proselytizing and baptism: "For the one baptized into God, advanced towards God, and has received 'authority to tread on scorpions and snakes,' (Luke 10:19) [who are] from the powers of the evil ones. And he commanded his Apostles, 'Go and preach, and baptize those who believe in the name of the Father, and the Son, and the Holy Spirit,' (Mt. 28:19) in whom we have been born again, having come to above all the other powers" (*Exc.* 76.2–4).[105] Moreover, prior to these missionary activities, *Excerpts of Theodotus* 83–84 enumerates the lengthy training, culminating in baptism, that is required in order to ensure "that only one who is pure goes down into the water. There are fasts, supplications, prayers, laying on of hands, genuflections because a soul is saved from the world and 'mouths of lions' (Ps. 22:21)." Once the initiate has proven his or her commitment and, as *Excerpts of Theodotus* 78.2 indicates, has undergone the proper instruction, he or she is baptized.[106] *Tripartite Tractate* 127–29 also may provide evidence of a similar process of catechetical training in which an initiate must "come to believe what has been said to them is real," before receiving baptism (*Tri. Trac.* 128.1–2). Everett Ferguson links this passage and its apparent recitation of previous instruction and profession of faith with Tertullian's claim in *Against Valentinians* 1 that "the perfect disciples" of the Valentinians required five years of training and instruction.[107] As a result, these initiates were highly trained and committed to the Valentinian view of the cosmos; moreover, by accepting their roles as missionaries they fulfilled the part they had discovered they were meant to play.

Consequently, ethics and soteriology were intimately linked and mutually reinforcing in the *Excerpts of Theodotus* and the *Tripartite Tractate*. Although the *Excerpts of Theodotus* and the *Tripartite Tractate* do claim that pneumatics are saved by nature or essence and that their salvific rewards are superior to psychics, this does not entail ethical indifference; rather the *Excerpts of Theodotus* and the *Tripartite Tractate* expect pneumatics to be actively engaged in saving others. As a result, these specialized and highly committed ritual initiates are charged with a special and salvifically important task. To a hostile observer like Irenaeus, in contrast, such self-important missionaries resemble pompous, preening roosters: "For this is the subterfuge of false persons, evil seducers, and hypocrites, as they act who are from Valentinus. . . . Such a one is puffed up to such an extent that he thinks he is neither in heaven nor on earth, but that he has passed within the Pleroma; and having already embraced his angel, he walks with a strutting gait and a supercilious countenance, possessing all the pompous air of a cock" (Irenaeus, *Haer.* 3.15.2). But from the perspective of the *Excerpts of Theodotus* and the *Tripartite Tractate*, these soteriological distinctions would motivate ongoing missionary practices and explain the difficulties and resistance these pneumatic missionaries might encounter. Thus, through a soteriology of higher and lower levels of salvation, both the *Excerpts of Theodotus* and the *Tripartite Tractate* promote an ethical ideal in which the more advanced were responsible for the less advanced.

Chapter 6

The Threefold Division and Exegesis

Ethics in Heracleon's *Commentary on John*

At first people are led to believe in the Savior by other people, but
when they read his words, they no longer [believe] on account of
human testimony alone, but believe on account of the truth itself.
—Frag. 39; Heracleon's *Commentary on John* 13.53.363

Putting the Pieces of Heracleon Back Together

In this final chapter, we shall examine the language of difference from a
third Valentinian text, Heracleon's *Commentary on John*.[1] Heracleon's surviving fragments are notoriously ambiguous, so much so that various scholars have cited him as both a supporter and a detractor of the tripartite
anthropology and higher and lower levels of salvation outlined in the preceding chapter.[2] While there is evidence of both the tripartite division of
humanity and the ethical expectation that the more advanced pneumatics
are responsible for and obligated to help save psychics, there is no evidence in
Heracleon of higher and lower levels of salvation.[3] Moreover, Heracleon employs an alternative emphasis in his naturalistic explanations for conduct that
highlights ideas of birth and genealogical descent. As a result, Heracleon
both complements and complicates what we know about Valentinians.

In contrast to Theodotus, Heracleon is mentioned by a number of ancient authors. Origen refers to him as a pupil of Valentinus (*Commentary on
John* 2.100); Clement of Alexandria calls him the most famous of all the
branches of the Valentinian school (*Strom.* 4.9.71); other heresiologists, like

Irenaeus (*Haer.* 2. 4.1), Tertullian (*Val.* 4.2), and Hippolytus (*Haer.* 6.30), say little about Heracleon except to mention him as a prominent Valentinian teacher alongside Ptolemy. His major surviving work is a *Commentary on the Gospel of John*, one of the earliest, if not *the* earliest, Christian commentary on a New Testament text (Origen, *Commentary on John* 6.92).[4] Heracleon's commentary survives only in fragments preserved in Origen's own fragmentary *Commentary on the Gospel of John* (hereafter *Comm. Jo.*).[5] Even though a hostile tradent, Origen grudgingly acknowledges that some of Heracleon's exegetical solutions are "ingenious" (*Comm. Jo.* 6.199). Forty-eight fragments survive of Heracleon's *Commentary*[6] as part of Origen's *Comm. Jo.*: three on John 1:3–18 (the Prologue), seven on John 1:21–29 (John the Baptist), six on John 2:12–20 (Jesus's travels to the Temple), twenty-four on John 4:12–53 (the Samaritan woman and the healing of the petty king's son), and eight on John 8:21–50 (hostility to Jews as children of the devil).[7]

Although Heracleon imports the tripartite anthropology that we saw in the preceding chapter, he presents a different notion of the fixedness of these classes. Moreover, in what survives, he does not describe higher and lower salvific rewards. Regardless, Heracleon agrees with both the *Excerpts of Theodotus* and the *Tripartite Tractate* about what constitutes good ethical conduct: the more advanced (pneumatics) are obligated to lend assistance and imitate the saving actions of the Savior toward less advanced, but likely receptive individuals (psychics). In this way, these three texts and their tripartite anthropology offer evidence of an underappreciated strand of early Christian missionary activity and soteriology.

Heracleon uses this hierarchical language to describe allegorically different characters and regions in John's Gospel; he does not, however, at least in what survives, use it to elucidate protological, Christological, or anthropological origins or soteriological ends as the *Excerpts of Theodotus* and the *Tripartite Tractate* do. Like the *Excerpts of Theodotus* and the *Tripartite Tractate*, Heracleon does describe different ethical profiles by means of these three classes, in particular their different reactions to the advent of the Savior; in contrast to the *Excerpts of Theodotus* and the *Tripartite Tractate*, however, there appears to be greater sociological fluidity—despite allusions to ritualized practices such as angelic syzygies (frag. 12)—among these types or categories in Heracleon. On the basis of Matthew 10:28, Heracleon also concludes that souls can be destroyed (frag. 40). This provocative claim has led some scholars to interpret Heracleon as promoting a soteriology in which psychics, if saved, *become* pneumatics.[8]

In what follows, I will consider Heracleon's tripartite division of humanity and the social and theoretical implications of his construction of three different types of persons. To this end, I will first introduce Heracleon's commentarial genre and the interpretative difficulties it presents. Next, I will consider Heracleon's views, insofar as they are preserved, on the issue of these three classes, especially how each class responds differently to the advent of the Savior. After this focused survey of the threefold division of humanity, I will examine the appearance of *physis* (nature) and *ousia* (substance) in the fragments of Heracleon, as well as his enigmatic claim that souls could be destroyed. I will suggest that although Heracleon differs from his Valentinian peers on the issue of anthropological difference, it is unclear whether his views may have resulted from deliberate intra-Valentinian debate or from his choice of intertexts and literary genre.[9]

Heracleon's *Commentary on John*

What do scholars mean when they say that Heracleon was perhaps the first Christian author to write a commentary (ὑπόμνημα) on a New Testament text (cf. *Comm. Jo.* 6.15.92)? The term ὑπομνήματα has a wide range of possible meanings from medical or scientific treatises to biblical commentaries to classroom notebooks.[10] It appears that Heracleon's ὑπόμνημα was a commentary of biblical *lemmata;* in other words, it is a collection of exegetical statements on individual phrases or words from the Gospel of John. As such, each fragment is based upon a selected text from the Gospel of John, to which Heracleon affixes an exegetical discussion of the meaning and significance of specific terms or the passage as a whole.

In addition to glossing unfamiliar terms and providing supplementary information, Heracleon's commentary often offers allegorical interpretations and thus explores deeper levels of meaning lurking beneath the surface of John's Gospel. For example, in fragment 18, which is based upon John 4:16 ("Go and call your husband"), Heracleon directs our attention to a referent beyond the literal text: "For [the Savior] was not speaking about a worldly husband (ἀνδρὸς κοσμικοῦ), when he told her to call [her husband] because he was not ignorant that she did not have a lawful husband. . . . [When] the Savior said: 'Call your husband and come here,' it refers to her syzygy [spouse] from the Pleroma" (frag. 18; *Comm. Jo.* 13.11.67–68). Unfortunately, Heracleon's allegorical interpretations are frequently brief and enigmatic; as such, they are difficult to satisfactorily explicate.

Moreover, it is unclear how large a work Heracleon's *Commentary on John* was. Based upon Origen's comments, we can infer that Heracleon did not compose an exhaustive commentary on every single line of John's text.[11] After concluding his treatment of John 4:32 ("But he said to them, 'I have food to eat you do not know about'"), Origen complains that Heracleon did not address this passage at all (frag. 29; *Comm. Jo.* 13.34.225). Despite these apparent gaps, Heracleon's *Commentary on John*, as Ansgar Wucherpfennig has argued in great detail, was a detailed, scholarly work.[12] As such, and analogous to contemporary commentaries on Homer, it engaged rigorous philological issues, such as determining semantic divisions, historical referents, and rhetorical constructions.[13]

Heracleon's *Commentary on John* survives only in selected fragments preserved in Origen's own incomplete *Commentary on John*.[14] Adding a further degree of difficulty, Origen's commentary is often hostile toward the "impious" Heracleon (*Comm. Jo.* 6.199). If the fourth-century historian Eusebius's report is accurate, Origen's patron, Ambrose, was formerly an admirer of or perhaps even one of these Valentinians himself before Origen "illuminated" him, and Ambrose "declared allegiance to the teachings of the orthodox church" (Eusebius, *Hist. eccl.* 6.18.1). Based on this background, scholars have speculated that Ambrose may have commissioned and "zealously encouraged" Origen to compose a commentary on John in part to refute his own former beliefs (*Hist. eccl.* 6.23.1–2). Origen himself sporadically alludes to Ambrose goading him into writing his *Comm. Jo.* When, for example, having already completed four volumes of his *Commentary* but not yet finished with his treatment of John's prologue, Origen comically lamented that because Ambrose has pressured him into writing on these "divine matters," Origen had fallen victim to the danger Solomon (Eccl. 12:12) warned about: once you begin writing too much, you cannot stop (*Comm. Jo.* 5.1.1). In any case, Origen's *Commentary on John* often engages with portions of Heracleon's commentary; however, it is not always clear where Heracleon's fragmentary commentary ends and Origen's (hostile) interaction with it begins.

A significant instance of this phenomenon is fragment 13, long interpreted as evidence that Heracleon endorsed a doctrine of higher and lower levels of salvation (*Comm. Jo.* 10.33.210–15). Yet, this is likely a misreading of the fragment insofar as it conflates Origen's citation of Heracleon with Origen's own epexegetical comments. While interpreting John 2:13–16,

Heracleon applies the spatial hierarchy of the temple to make the soteriological claim that both psychics and pneumatics require the Savior to be saved: "He found them in the temple (ἱερῷ), not in the inner sanctuary (ναῷ),[15] so that it might not be supposed that simple 'calling,' apart from the Spirit, is assisted by the Lord" (*Comm. Jo.* 10.33.211). In other words, the saving actions of the Savior, described later in this fragment as the cleansing of the Temple, apply both to the psychic "called" and the pneumatic elect. In the spatial terms of the temple, the Savior did not come just to the sanctuary (the pneumatics) but to the temple as a whole (pneumatics and psychics).[16]

The passage, however, continues: "For the temple (τὸ ἱερόν) is the Holy of Holies, into which only the High Priest enters (Heb. 9:7), where the pneumatics come. But the area of the forecourt (τὰ δὲ τοῦ προνάου) of the temple, where the Levites also are, is a symbol of the psychics outside of the Pleroma who are found to be in salvation" (*Comm. Jo.* 10.33.211). Wucherpfennig contends that important sections from this passage do *not* come from Heracleon, but instead were inserted by Origen, who is supplying the references to higher and lower levels of salvation.[17] Thus, according to Wucherpfennig, it is Origen, not Heracleon, who reads higher and lower levels of salvation into the description of the temple space. Applying Wucherpfennig's argument, Einar Thomassen distinguishes between Heracleon's comments (marked in bold) and those of Origen: "**'The temple' is, on the one hand, the Holy of Holies, where only the High Priest enters**—that is where the spirituals end up, I think he is saying—**and on the other hand, the area of the forecourt, where the Levites are as well**, is a symbol of the psychics, who will attain a salvation outside of the Pleroma."[18] Consequently, according to Wucherpfennig and Thomassen, once we identify and isolate Origen's editorial comments, we find that Heracleon does not describe higher and lower levels of salvation in this passage or anywhere else in what survives from his *Commentary on John*.

Tripartite Anthropology

If we accept Wucherpfennig and Thomassen's division of the text, it appears that unlike what we saw in the *Excerpts of Theodotus* and the *Tripartite Tractate*, Heracleon, at least in what survives of his *Comm. Jo.*, does not explicitly link the threefold division of humanity with three different salvific profiles. Heracleon, nonetheless, does employ this threefold division to characterize three types of worship, distinguishing among the Greeks, Jews, and pneumatics on the basis of John 4:21 ("Woman believe me, the hour is coming when you will worship the Father neither on this mountain nor in Jerusalem"):[19]

> The mountain means the devil or this world (κόσμος), since the
> devil is one part of the whole of matter (τῆς ὕλης), but the world
> (κόσμος) is on the whole a mountain of evil, a desert dwelling
> of beasts, which all prior to the Law and the gentiles worship;
> Jerusalem is the creation of the creator, whom the Jews worship.
> In a second sense the mountain is the creation, which the gentiles
> worship; and Jerusalem the creator, whom the Jews serve. You,
> therefore, as pneumatics (οἱ πνευματικοί), will worship neither
> creation nor the demiurge, but the Father of truth. (*Comm. Jo.*
> 13.16.95–97)

In this way, Heracleon uses the threefold division to describe three types of conduct in the world. As we will see, this threefold division is particularly important for Heracleon insofar as it corresponds to humanity's three different responses to the Savior.[20]

Moreover, although Heracleon outlines the corresponding conduct of each class, he does not appeal—in contrast to the *Excerpts of Theodotus* and the *Tripartite Tractate*—to sweeping cosmological and mythical narratives about the origins of matter or the creation of humanity. In fact, whether out of deliberate disagreement with other Valentinian teachers or due to the constraints or fragmentary preservation of his Gospel commentary, Heracleon lacks a number of Valentinian staples—for example, he does not explicitly refer to the fall of a Sophia/Logos figure, and he uses the term *choic* only once in his surviving fragments (frag. 46).[21] Heracleon was much more interested in rhetorically classifying typological characters according to a threefold scheme of conduct, epitomized by their reactions to the Savior and subsequent roles in proselytizing efforts.

Our first typological character is the Samaritan woman from John 4 who is a type of the pneumatic. As such, she reacts to the Savior with immediate faith (τὴν ἀδιάκριτον πίστιν) and receives from above "[water] gushing forth, which leads to eternal life for others" (frag. 17; *Comm. Jo.* 13.10.62–63). Following her interaction with the Savior, the Samaritan woman goes forth to proselytize to the "calling," namely psychics: "She left [the water jug; cf. John 4:28] with [the Savior] . . . and she turned back to the world (τὸν κόσμον), proclaiming the good news (εὐαγγελιζομένη) to 'the calling' (τῇ κλήσει) of the *parousia* of Christ. For the soul is led to the Savior through the spirit (διὰ τοῦ πνεύματος) and by the spirit (ὑπὸ τοῦ πνεύματος)" (frag. 27; *Comm. Jo.* 13.31.187). For Heracleon, pneumatics are those who immediately accept the Savior and then go forth to preach the good news of his coming to the psychics.

Heracleon further underscores and encourages this proselytizing ethic through his allegorical interpretation of John 4:39 ("Many Samaritans from that city believed because of the testimony of that woman"): "Heracleon takes 'out of the city' to mean 'out of the world,' and 'because of the testimony of the woman' to mean 'because of the pneumatic church.' And 'many' signals that there are many psychics; but he says there is one imperishable nature for the elect that is uniform and single" (frag. 37; *Comm. Jo.* 13. 51.341). In this way, Heracleon interprets the preaching of the Samaritan woman as a type of the corporate activity of the whole pneumatic church and its proselytizing mission to psychics.

Psychics, according to Heracleon, are those to whom pneumatics proselytize and are symbolically represented by the petty king, who is also a type for the demiurge, and his ill son, who, as a psychic, belongs to the Demiurge (ὁ ἴδιος αὐτοῦ ἄνθρωπος; frag. 40; *Comm. Jo.* 13.60.416):[22] "Heracleon says the royal officer (βασιλικός) represents the demiurge, since he rules over those beneath him. Because his kingdom is small and temporary, Heracleon says, he was named a 'royal officer' as though he was some petty king having been set over a small kingdom by a universal king. His son in Capernaum is described as being in the lower part of the middle area beside the sea, that is, in the part joined together with matter" (frag. 40; *Comm. Jo.* 13.60.416). In contrast to the Samaritan woman who believes immediately and with uncritical faith, Heracleon contends that John 4:48 ("Jesus said to him, 'Unless you see signs and wonders you will not believe'") characterizes the psychics, who, in contrast to pneumatics, must be persuaded to believe through works and sense perception (frag. 40; *Comm. Jo.* 13.60.419).[23]

As Einar Thomassen convincingly argues, an important distinction between pneumatics and psychics, according to Heracleon, is that they come to believe through different means.[24] Sociologically, we can imagine these two terms may have applied to community members involved in different activities and possessing disparate levels of prestige as a result.[25] Drawing upon Pauline studies, the difference between pneumatics and psychics might resemble the distinction among Paul's churches between certain elite preachers and teachers and their less advanced community members.[26] In scholastic terms, this may refer to the difference between an inner circle of followers and the more amorphous crowd of auditors who might attend the public lectures of a renowned teacher.[27]

Finally, Heracleon speaks of the children of the devil (frag. 44; *Comm. Jo.* 20.20.168), who are functionally synonymous with choics or hylics[28] (as well as damned psychics) and are typologically represented by the hostile Jews in John 8:44 ("You are from your father the devil, and you choose to do your father's desires [καὶ τὰς ἐπιθυμίας τοῦ πατρὸς ὑμῶν θέλετε ποιεῖν]. He was a murderer from the beginning and does not stand in the truth, because there is no truth in him. When he lies, he speaks according to his own property [ἐκ τῶν ἰδίων λαλεῖ], for he is a liar and the father of lies"):

> Heracleon, for his part, replies that the reason they are unable to listen to Jesus or understand his speech is explained by the line "you are from your father the devil." He says in these very words: "And why can you not hear my word, except that you are from your father the devil?" This means "from the substance of the devil" (ἐκ τῆς οὐσίας τοῦ διαβόλου), thus revealing the nature (τὴν φύσιν) of those ones. And he had rebuked them because neither were they the children of Abraham—for they would not have hated him—nor were they children of God—for they did not love him. (frag. 44; *Comm. Jo.* 20.20.168)

In contrast to the immediate faith of the pneumatics and the delayed acceptance by good psychics, the hostile Jews are the children of the devil insofar as they resolutely reject the Savior. Thus, as in other Valentinian texts, we have a tripartite division of humanity that emphasizes three typological responses to the Savior: immediate acceptance, delayed belief, and resolute rejection.[29]

Nature and Substance

Immediately following his citation of Heracleon (frag. 44), Origen elucidates what he finds objectionable about his interpretation of John 8:44:

"Now if the line 'you are from your father the devil' was taken as we explained above, and he said 'because you are *still* from the devil you are unable to listen to my word,' we would have accepted his interpretation. But it is clear now that he is saying that some people have the same substance (ὁμοουσίους) as the devil and, as those who follow him believe, they have different substances from those whom they call psychic or pneumatic" (*Comm. Jo.* 20.20.169–70).[30] Furthermore, Origen claims that if people's actions are exclusively the result of substance, then there is no moral culpability, since his or her actions would be predetermined; consequently, actions are neither praiseworthy nor blameworthy, since they are the result of the relative quality of one's substance, and do not depend upon choices and moral growth: "[Heracleon's claim] appears to be similar to those that state there is a different substance (ἑτέραν οὐσίαν) for an eye that overlooks [something] and another that sees, and also a different substance for an ear that mishears and [another substance for ears that] hear soundly" (*Comm. Jo.* 20.23.199). Origen clearly believes that he has cleverly boxed Heracleon into a corner. By suggesting that Heracleon's use of *ousia* precludes voluntary choice or action, Origen can conclude that Heracleon's beliefs are incompatible with assigning praise or blame and thus cannot hold anyone ethically accountable. When we consider Heracleon's own views, however, it appears that Origen is accusing him of commitments that he simply does not hold.[31]

What, then, does Heracleon think about nature (*physis*) and substance (*ousia*), and what is their relationship with his threefold division of conduct? Does Heracleon's usage, as Origen maintains, entail some notion of a-ethical predeterminism?[32] And finally, do these two terms relate in any way to the perennial question: Are the three classes of pneumatic, psychic, and hylic fixed or mutable/transitory? To answer these questions, let us consider how Heracleon actually uses the terms *ousia* and *physis*.[33]

After citing Heracleon's interpretations of the hostile Jews from John 8 as children who "share the substance of the devil" (frag. 44; *Comm. Jo.* 20.20.168), Origen, as we just noted, lambasts what he considers to be the determinist implications of attributing a specific substance to the devil and, by extension, to his children: "Often we have said that if this impossibility be allowed—I mean that the devil possesses another substance incapable of experiencing better things—we will devise a defense for him from all responsibility for wickedness, and we will saddle the one who gave substance to and created him with the charge of wrongdoing, which is most absurd of all" (*Comm. Jo.* 20.24.202). Upon closer examination, however, the meaning and implications of Heracleon's use of both nature (*physis*) and substance (*ousia*) are quite different from Origen's polemical representation. Unlike the author(s) of the *Excerpts*, Heracleon does not use *physis* to mean the material origins or first principles that are causally responsible for subsequent action; rather, Heracleon's particular conceptions of *physis* and *ousia* expand on John 3's themes of birth and genealogy.

Physis appears in the fragments of Heracleon for the first time when the Samaritan woman responds with immediate faith "in accordance with her *nature*" (κατάλληλον τῇ φύσει ἑαυτῆς; frag. 17; *Comm. Jo.* 13.10.63, emphasis added).[34] In the narrative setting of the Gospel of John, Jesus's encounter with the Samaritan woman follows two episodes—the first, a brief dialogue with a Pharisee called Nicodemus (3:1–21), and the second, a monologue by John the Baptist (3:23–36)—that distinguish between two types of people through a series of binaries: spirit and flesh; light and darkness; and heaven and earth. The salvific and ethical import of these binaries is highlighted by Jesus's programmatic yet enigmatic statement (John 3:3): "Amen, amen I say to you, if someone is not born from above/again (ἄνωθεν), he is unable to see the Kingdom of God."[35] Nicodemus, understandably confused, queries Jesus (John 3:4–5): "How is it possible for a person to be born after having grown old? Can someone enter into his mother's womb a second time?" In response, Jesus explains this type of (re)birth occurs when a person is a descendant of water and spirit (John 3:5): "Amen, amen I say to you, if someone is not born from water and spirit (ἐξ ὕδατος καὶ πνεύματος), he is unable to enter the Kingdom of God."[36]

Soon afterward (John 3:10–15), Jesus and Nicodemus's dialogue shifts gears, and Jesus distinguishes between earthly (τὰ ἐπίγεια) and heavenly affairs (τὰ ἐπουράνια), while criticizing Nicodemus (and others apparently like him) for their lack of belief in "our testimony" (καὶ τὴν μαρτυρίαν ἡμῶν οὐ λαμβάνετε). This spatial binary of heaven and earth leads into the contrast between light and darkness as Jesus proclaims that all who believe are saved and those who do not have already been judged (John 3:18, 21): "The one who believes in him is not condemned (κρίνεται); but the one who does not believe is already condemned (ἤδη κέκριται) because he has not believed (πεπίστευκεν) in the name of the only Son of God . . . but the one who does what is true comes to the light so that it may clearly be seen that his deeds have been done in God (αὐτοῦ τὰ ἔργα ὅτι ἐν θεῷ ἐστιν εἰργασμένα)." Following a sudden shift, we find John the Baptist picking up on similar themes in his instructions to his own students (John 3:31–36), beginning with his description of the paradigmatic teacher who comes from above (ἄνωθεν).[37] Anyone who believes in the testimony of this teacher, according to John, receives eternal life; anyone who is not convinced, however, must endure God's wrath.

The term ἄνωθεν is ambiguous, and Heracleon deftly deploys its polyvalence to help incorporate the themes of ethics, birth, and genealogical descent from John 3 into the stories of the Samaritan woman from John 4 and the Jews from John 8.[38] As we will see, Heracleon is puzzling through the implications of what it means to be born from above *and* again in his use of *physis* and *ousia*. On the one hand, Heracleon is similar to the *Excerpts of Theodotus* and the *Tripartite Tractate* insofar as he enlists naturalistic explanations to account for differences of conduct; on the other hand, he is distinct in terms of how he parses the nuances of these terms in light of their relationship with biological descent. Thus, while there is no evidence of fixed endings in Heracleon, there is an explicit rhetorical appeal to fixed origins.[39]

In acknowledging and reacting favorably to the Savor, the Samaritan woman acts as suits her nature (frag. 19; *Comm. Jo.* 13.15.92: ὡς πρεπόντως τῇ αὐτῆς φύσει). The actions that suit or epitomize this nature appear to be twofold: an immediate response of faith (τὴν ἀδιάκριτον πίστιν) in the Savior and proselytizing efforts to save others.[40] Is the pneumatic *physis* the cause for the Samaritan's behavior, or does she behave this way because she possesses this *physis*? At first glance, these might seem to say the same thing; however, when we recall that in order to "see the Kingdom of God" we must be "born from above/again" (ἄνωθεν), the contrast becomes clearer. Heracleon makes this point evident by contrasting the Samaritan's previous life, epitomized by the deficient water of Jacob's well, with her new life, signified by the water of the Savior, which comes from his Spirit (τοῦ πνεύματος) and Power.[41] Heracleon makes the connection between John 3 and the story of the Samaritan woman even clearer with the following (*Comm. Jo.* 13.10.62): "['Water gushing up to eternal life'; see John 4:14] refers to those who richly receive [a new life] from above/anew (ἄνωθεν) and pour out eternal life (ζωὴν αἰώνιον) to others").[42] It is directly following this epexegetical claim that Heracleon then states that the Samaritan woman responded with immediate faith "in accordance with her nature" (κατάλληλον τῇ φύσει ἑαυτῆς; frag. 17; *Comm. Jo.* 13.10.63). Thus, her nature was not the *archē* or source of her actions; instead, the Samaritan woman has been born again and through her rebirth and subsequent proselytizing demonstrates her pneumatic *physis*.[43]

Once the paradigmatic pneumatic is born again, Heracleon's use of *physis* shifts to feature more its association with genealogical descent in order to address the question of how other pneumatics might be born now, if the Savior is no longer among us. This is most clear in Heracleon's schematizing statement of generation and kinship (frag. 46; *Comm. Jo.* 20.24.215); here Heracleon notes that someone can be called a "child" of someone for various reasons, but *physis* refers to the specific scenario in which a child is the biological descendant of a parent. In this way, Heracleon uses *physis* comparably to how Paul uses the term in Romans 11:21–24: "For if God did not spare the natural branches (τῶν κατὰ φύσιν κλάδων), neither will he spare you. . . . For if you have been cut from what is by nature (κατὰ φύσιν) a wild olive tree and grafted, against nature (παρὰ φύσιν), into a cultivated olive tree how much more will these natural branches be grafted back into their own olive tree (οὗτοι οἱ κατὰ φύσιν ἐγκεντρισθήσονται τῇ ἰδίᾳ ἐλαίᾳ)."[44] Like Paul, Heracleon uses *physis* to refer to certain genealogical categories that each has its own profile of defining characteristics and transmittable traits. Heracleon's near contemporary Plotinus further attests to this association of *physis* with genealogical descent: "But, in fact, all individual things come into being according to their own natures (κατὰ τὰς αὐτῶν φύσιν), a horse because it came from a horse, and a man from a man, and a being of a particular kind because it comes from a particular kind."[45]

Through this resonance of *physis*, in particular its association with generation and descent, Heracleon clarifies how someone could not only be born again but also become a member of a distinctive genealogy, capable of making descendants of their own. Recalling Jesus's response in John 3:5, the catalyst for this rebirth is to become a descendant of water and spirit (γεννηθῇ ἐξ ὕδατος καὶ πνεύματος). John 3:5's specific language here would have evoked for his readers, Heracleon included, concepts of kinship and race. In her seminal study on the language of kinship and ethnicity in the Letters of Paul, Caroline Johnson Hodge demonstrated that the preposition *ek*, even when paired with abstract concepts, can indicate the origin of a line of descent: "Thus *hoi ek pisteôs* might be translated as something like 'those whose line of descent springs from faithfulness.' More concretely, this phrase might be rendered, 'those who descended from Abraham's [or Christ's] faithfulness to God.'"[46] For Heracleon, pneumatics are those who have the great privilege and responsibility of sharing kinship with the Savior.

Once a pneumatic was reborn he or she exchanged the inferior water of Jacob for the spiritual water of the Savior (frag. 17; *Comm. Jo.* 13.10). It is through this rebirth that a pneumatic enters into the Savior's line of descendants. Interpreting John 1:4 ("That which came to be in him was life"), Heracleon claims that what was "in him" (ἐν αὐτῷ) refers to the pneumatics because the Word/Savior was responsible for their generation: "Heracleon interprets 'in him' to refer to the pneumatic people ... [and says that] he (the Savior/Word) provided them their first form, according to generation."[47] Heracleon may be influenced here by Paul's frequent use of cognate expressions (e.g., "in Christ" or "in Isaac")[48] to delineate specific claims of lineage and ethnic descent, in which descendants share defining traits with their ancestor.[49] Thus, the *physis* of the pneumatics is encapsulated by their kinship with the Savior, which they demonstrate by generating like him: " [The Samaritan woman] left [the water-jug; cf. John 4:28] with [the Savior] ... and she turned back to the world (τὸν κόσμον), proclaiming the good news (εὐαγγελιζομένη) to 'the calling' (τῇ κλήσει) of the *parousia* of Christ. For the soul is led to the Savior through the spirit (διὰ τοῦ πνεύματος) and by the spirit (ὑπὸ τοῦ πνεύματος)" (frag. 27; *Comm. Jo.* 13.31.187).[50] In this way, Heracleon has answered Nicodemus's question from John 3 ("How can someone be born again/from above?") by appealing to the paradigmatic example of the Samaritan woman and her generation of new pneumatics.

Since a person is born again and acquires a new origin story, Heracleon's usage of *physis* suggests sociological flexibility that belies the predeterminist register of naturalistic causes. This flexibility, however, is in tension with the notion of fixity that once you acquire your second birth and your new genealogical profile, your descendants do, necessarily, resemble you.[51] Like previous authors discussed in this book, Heracleon encodes ethical expectations in light of corporate identity and the construction of certain roles or profiles.[52] In this way, *physis* is not concerned with particular *individuals*, but encompasses the characteristics shared by a whole class.[53] This may lead some to wonder: Since Heracleon claims that a person can be reborn with a new genealogical profile, does this mean a person transforms his or her nature? To use a turn of phrase, what is the nature of Heracleon's *physis*? To help answer this question, let us consider more closely the pivotal moment in salvation history, the Savior's advent.

Analogously to what we saw in Chapter 5 on the moral psychology of the *Tripartite Tractate*, a pneumatic (the Samaritan woman) responds immediately and favorably to the advent of the Savior; in this way, moral responsibility depends upon how one reacts to the external impression of the Savior.[54] After this decisive moment, the Samaritan woman's conduct is characterized by the traits and dispositions of the pneumatic nature, which prior to the advent of the Savior did not and could not have had any living members.[55] *Physis*, as a set of actions and transmittable traits, is not what is transformed; people can be reborn and become members of a different classification, *physis*. In practice then, the full range of three types of people did not come into existence *until* the advent of the Savior.[56]

After the Savior's arrival, however, Heracleon depicts the three natures as static categories and indicative of the three specific social positions and traits—for example, missionaries, receptive targets and learners, and finally steadfast opponents. A person, in contrast, can be reborn, and thus different labels might be applicable to a person at various stages over his or her life:[57] "At first people are led to believe in the Savior by other people, but when they read his words, they no longer [believe] on account of human testimony alone, but believe on account of the truth itself" (frag. 39; *Comm. Jo.* 13.53.363). Here, Heracleon may be describing the transition of an individual from a missionized person (psychic) to a committed missionary (pneumatic). In any case, this emphasis of the threefold division of humanity on the various responses to the Savior supports our portrayal of Heracleon as invested in missionizing practices, just as we saw in the *Excerpts of Theodotus* and the *Tripartite Tractate*.

From the point of view of boundary drawing, then, those characterized as children of the devil are those who resist these ongoing proselytizing efforts. Thus, this category of damned individuals encompasses both what other texts would call choics/hylics and bad psychics, insofar as the defining trait for both is their persistent rejection of the message of someone like Heracleon.[58] An interpretative puzzle, however, is the sudden intrusion of the term *ousia*.[59] "'And why can you not hear my word, except that you are from your father the devil?' (John 8:44) This means 'from the substance of the devil,' (ἐκ τῆς οὐσίας τοῦ διαβόλου)" (frag. 44; *Comm. Jo.* 20.20.168). At first glance, *ousia* appears to be synonymous with *physis* insofar as both are associated with the distinctive traits of a group of people and their genealogical transmission. This, however, is incorrect.

While the sudden inclusion of *ousia* as well as its absence from the remainder of Heracleon's *Commentary on John* might raise the suspicion that this term may have been inserted by Origen, we are not justified in ejecting the term as merely an interpolation.[60] *Ousia* appears exclusively during Heracleon's exegesis of John 8:44, that is, his discussion of the children of the devil (frags. 43, 44, 45, and 46).[61] In two instances (frags. 44 and 46), Heracleon includes the term while repeating: "'You are from your father the Devil' means 'you are from the substance of the Devil.'"[62] The other two instances (frags. 43 and 45) may be epexegetical insertions by Origen clarifying what Origen accuses Heracleon of meaning, although this is far from certain.[63] In either case, whether written by Origen with polemical intent or by Heracleon himself, a careful reading of fragment 43—in light of fragment 46— can still assist us in making sense of what Heracleon might actually have meant by his use of *ousia*.

Two preliminary observations, however, may help us to determine the meaning of this term in Heracleon's *Commentary*. First, it is only in the context of the devil that Heracleon employs the term *ousia*; thus, it is not a positive or even neutral term but possesses a negative valence for him.[64] Second, these children of the devil, who are associated with his *ousia*, become like the devil by doing his works (frag. 46; *Comm. Jo.* 20.24.218: τὰ ἔργα τοῦ διαβόλου ποιοῦντες ὡμοιώθησαν αὐτῷ). Perhaps reminiscent of the mechanics of Pauline participation, Heracleon draws upon the materiality of a term like *ousia* in order to claim that those who do wicked acts participate in and become the same substance as the devil.[65] Many scholars— following Origen's polemic remarks—have argued that Heracleon used *ousia* to indicate a specific and deterministic relationship wherein those who possess the substance of the devil do his works necessarily; what we find is the inverse of this.[66] Sharing in the substance of the devil is the consequence of wicked conduct, not the cause of it.[67]

Returning to our discussion of John 3 and remembering its importance for Heracleon's interpretation of John 4, we can more effectively puzzle through Heracleon's interpretation of the children of the devil in John 8 by posing the following rhetorical question: "How is one born again in order to become a descendant of the Devil?" According to Heracleon (frag. 46; *Comm. Jo.* 20.24.215), there are two ways: the first is by decision or choice (γνώμη), and the second by merit (ἀξίᾳ). In the first instance, Heracleon is referencing susceptible psychics who can become descendants of the devil "by doing someone else's will," or being convinced that the message of pneumatics is wrong.[68] These "bad" psychics have been persuaded by hylics, who are, from the point of view of pneumatics, antimissionaries of truth and are persuading psychics of lies. It is through these antimissionizing efforts that these hylics have earned (ἀξίᾳ) the title of "children of the devil." In this way, these hylics have, like the devil, been born from error and lies and generate others like themselves through the very same means of error and lies.[69]

Yet, it is clear that for Heracleon *ousia* and *physis* are not the same. These antimissionizing hylics are the children of the devil—replicating his conduct (*physis*)—and are from his *ousia*. In light of *ousia*'s function in other Valentinian texts, what likely prompts Heracleon's specific inclusion of *ousia* here is John 8:44's mention of "the desires (τὰς ἐπιθυμίας) of your father the devil." *Ousia* is associated elsewhere with the passions and errant emotions of the fallen Sophia or Logos during the cosmological drama that leads to the creation of the material world.[70] In *Excerpts of Theodotus* 45–46, for example, *ousia* was the by-product of the Savior's healing of Sophia's passions; elsewhere in the *Excerpts* (33.4), the inferior Ruler was said to have come to be "from the passion of desire."[71] Similarly, in *Tripartite Tractate* 118.14–15, the three effluences of the Logos (spirit, soul, and matter)—stemming from his "presumptuous love" (76.13–23)—are ΟΥϹΙΑ, and are the sources for the three types of humanity.[72] Irenaeus (*Haer.* 1.2–4), Tertullian (*Val.* 10), and Hippolytus (*Haer.* 6.27ff.) all connect Sophia's desire with the mistaken creation of the deficient, material world.[73] Contrary to Origen's presentation of it, then, *ousia* in Heracleon is not a generic philosophical term denoting the distinctive essence of each person; rather, it is likely part of an esoteric polemic against rival teachers: you are not only children of the devil, but you share in his very desires/passions.[74] Thus, fragment 43 warns that "bad" psychics can become the children of the devil not only through an erroneous choice but also as a result of their devil-like desires.

As we shall see in the following section, the interpretations of *physis* and *ousia* I have advocated have implications for how we will answer the question of whether psychics could transform and become pneumatics. Unlike the *Excerpts of Theodotus* or the *Tripartite Tractate*, Heracleon does not deploy *physis* or *ousia* as part of sweeping cosmological narratives where natures or substances are represented as causally responsible for material and moral difference. Instead, Heracleon's exegetical project is best understood as part of his activities as an early Christian teacher who encouraged his students to emulate the proselytizing activities of the earliest followers of Jesus.

"The Death of the Soul": Ethics Not Soteriology

Finally, we return to the question: Do saved psychics become pneumatics? It does not appear so. If a person remains "converted" but never becomes a missionary, that person is a good psychic; if a person is reborn and thus becomes a missionary, that person is a pneumatic. A passage that has been raised as complicating this socially determined classification scheme is fragment 40, which describes the death of the soul of the son of the petty king:

> His son in Capernaum is described as being in the lower part of the middle area beside the sea, that is, in the part joined together with matter. He says the man belonging to [the petty king] was sick, that is, not by nature but in ignorance and sins. . . . From the statement "he is about to die" he thinks the teachings (τὰ δόγματα) of those who suppose the soul to be immortal are overturned. . . . He says that the soul is the corruptible clothed in incorruption and mortality [clothed] in immortality when "its death is swallowed up in victory" (1 Cor. 15:53–54). (frag. 40; *Comm. Jo.* 13.60.416–18)

Einar Thomassen has interpreted this passage soteriologically as indicating that psychics qua psychics are not saved but instead are transformed, likely into spirit: "This view seems logically to preclude any notion that the psychic will attain an enduring salvation qua psychics. Instead, therefore, he quotes Paul, who speaks about how the perishable will put on imperishability and the mortal will put on immortality, death being swallowed up in victory (1 Cor. 15:53–54). Heracleon thus envisages a total transformation of the psychics into a new state of being. Once again, he does not explicitly state that they will become spiritual, though the context of 1 Cor. 15:44–49 makes that a natural assumption."[75] So the argument goes: because souls are said to be perishable and not immortal, they must be transformed when saved.[76]

On the basis of close parallels with Philo of Alexandria, it is more likely that Heracleon deploys this evocative image of the death of the soul to illustrate the stakes of the psychological conflict raging within psychics. Consequently, Heracleon's warning about the death of the soul is not exclusively (or even primarily) a soteriological claim, but rather a warning against the risks of moral depravity. Philo of Alexandria uses exactly the same imagery to describe the double death that God warns Adam and Eve about if they eat from the tree of life: "That death is of two kinds, one that of the man in general, the other that of the soul in particular. The death of the man is the separation of the soul from the body, but the *death of the soul is the decay of virtue and the bringing in of wickedness.* . . . The one is the separation of combatants that have been pitted against one another, i.e., body and soul. The [death of the soul], on the other hand, is a meeting of the two in conflict. And in this conflict the worse, the body, overcomes the better, the soul" (*Leg.* 1.105–7). In her *Death of the Soul in Romans 7*, Emma Wasserman situates Philo's description of the death of the soul against its Platonic background.[77] To this end, Wasserman catalogues the various metaphors Philo deploys to describe this "moral-psychological drama," observing that "the basic model is consistent in depicting an ongoing struggle between the good mind and the evil passions."[78] Drawing upon Platonic language, Philo depicts extreme moral depravity as the death of the soul in which it dies "to the life of virtue and is alive only to the life of wickedness" (*Leg.* 1.107).

This link between a "death of the soul" and moral depravity, I suggest, may illuminate the portrayal of the son of the petty king who was sick because of his ignorance and sins. Consequently, although it obviously has soteriological implications, the main force of Heracleon's rhetorical appeal to the death of the soul is to encourage the psychic to resist a life of sin and be saved through belief in the Savior:

> [When the Savior says] to them the following: "unless you see signs and wonders, you will not believe," it was said to such a person having a nature (φύσιν) to be persuaded through works and perception, and who does not believe only [because of] a word. He believes the phrase "descend before my child dies" was said because death is the goal/end (τέλος) of the law that destroys through sins. Therefore, he says, the Father needs the only Savior to help [the petty king's] son, that is, to one belonging to such a nature (τουτέστιν τῇ τοιᾷδε φύσει), before he is finally put to death, on account of his sins. He has interpreted [When the Savior says] to them the following: "your son lives" (John 4:40), to have been said by the Savior with modesty, since he did not say, "let him live," nor did he show that he himself provided the life. But [Heracleon] says that after [the Savior] descended to the sick son and healed him from his illness, that is, from his sins, and have given him life through forgiveness, he said "Your son lives." (frag. 40; *Comm. Jo.* 13.60.419–21)

The psychic is internally divided, drawn to both redemption and perdition (frags. 40 and 46). This internal division, when unchecked, could lead to moral depravity and sin, epitomized by the illness of the petty king's son;

but when the Savior heals the petty king's son, he redeems him from the death of his soul by cleansing him of ignorance and sin.[79]

Similarly drawing upon Matthew 10:28, *Excerpts of Theodotus* 51–53 also describes the internal battle raging within a psychic: "Concerning these two [the material and divine souls], the Savior says: 'one must fear the one able to destroy that soul and that psychic body in Hell.' (Mt. 10:28) For the Savior calls the flesh an 'adversary' (Mt. 5:25), and Paul calls it a 'law warring against the law of my mind,' and the Savior urges us 'to bind' and 'to plunder the property as of a rich man,' (Mt. 12:29) who was warring against the heavenly soul" (*Exc.* 51.2–52.1). The *Excerpts of Theodotus* encourages psychics to subdue these lower and warring passions and "put them to death" so that the heavenly soul might defeat the material soul (*Exc.* 52.1). Consequently, fragment 40 and its appeal to the death of the soul does not entail that psychics, when saved, be transformed into pneumatics; instead, it demonstrates that psychics, due to their divided selves, are at great risk of turning away from the Savior and falling into soul-destroying moral depravity.

Modes of Writing and Modes of Responsibility

In many ways, comparing Heracleon with the *Excerpts of Theodotus* and the *Tripartite Tractate* is like comparing apples and oranges. Having examined the threefold division of humanity found in these three Valentinian texts, however, we conclude that while each text deploys this tripartite division differently, in every instance it reflects Pauline exegetical tradition and an ethical ideal of bringing others to salvation. This anthropological speculation arose among a group of second-century Christians who, similar to Paul, viewed themselves as having received a special calling and revelatory knowledge: "In the same fashion as the Paraclete, Paul became the apostle of the resurrection. He was also sent to preach immediately after the Lord's passion. Therefore, he preached the Savior in these two ways: as begotten and passible for the sake of those on the left, because being able to recognize him in this position they have become afraid of him, and in the spiritual/pneumatic manner stemming from the Holy Spirit and a virgin, as the angels on the right know him. For each one knows the Lord after his own fashion, and not all in the same way" (*Exc.* 23.2–4). We have seen that Paul's language of different types of persons supplied the terminology used to describe and justify why some people might immediately accept the gospel message, delay before being persuaded, or categorically and resolutely reject what these spiritually elected individuals were offering.

Despite sharing this contention that there are three types of persons detectable by their responses to the Savior and his message, Heracleon differs from the *Excerpts* and the *Tripartite Tractate* insofar as—at least in what survives—there are no fixed endings.[80] Furthermore, the naturalistic explanations of conduct are connected to questions of kinship and descent rather than puzzling through the creation of material and moral difference at every level of the cosmos. This important distinction, I suggest, may be due to a difference in genre or mode of writing. The contours of Heracleon's *Commentary* depend on the Gospel of John; thus, the onus of his work was to explicate the Fourth Gospel's correct meaning. In contrast, the *Excerpts of Theodotus* and especially the *Tripartite Tractate* are constrained as teleological narratives that were meant to justify the origins and ends of all material and moral difference. Despite the *Excerpts of Theodotus* and the *Tripartite Tractate*'s fixed endings and the rhetoric of kinship or fixed origins in Heracleon, each promotes a clearly ethical worldview: the elect are obligated to help save others.

In arguing that this threefold division and—in the case of the *Excerpts of Theodotus* and the *Tripartite Tractate*—higher and lower levels of salvation do not preclude ethics, I have also sought to bridge a divide in current Valentinian studies. As previously mentioned, this divide is between two viewpoints: the Valentinians either (1) envisioned three natures, higher and lower levels of salvation, and thus did not consider ethics to be the cause of salvation; or (2) envisioned only temporary categories through which one advances, equal salvation, and an ethical system that resembled their peers. Each side of this dichotomy homogenizes the diverse views of the ancient authors and texts, and thus each interpretive camp sacrifices an important facet of the soteriology and ethics of this missionizing movement.

Therefore, I find the first account to be inadequate because it undervalues the centrality of ethics in this missionizing movement. Without this foundation, why would someone adhere to a Valentinian view of the world, and how would these beliefs have motivational force and affect the lives of adherents? I suggest that we should not treat ethical practices as peripheral consequences of theoretical speculation, but instead consider them as part of an ongoing and dialectical relationship through which cosmological and eschatological beliefs were embodied and mutually reinforced. Thus, ethical values and practices, far from being secondary to theoretical speculation, were, to paraphrase Catherine Bell, an inseparable part of the structured and structuring ideological commitments and practices of these authors and their putative communities.[81]

Scholars from the latter camp—while arguing *for* the centrality of ethics—have done so by transforming the soteriologies and anthropologies of the *Excerpts of Theodotus* and the *Tripartite Tractate* in order to bring them more closely in line with other early Christian thinkers, such as Irenaeus, Clement, or Origen. Such a homogenization has led to scholars discounting or overlooking the logic of kinship and generation in Heracleon's *Commentary*. In minimizing the theoretical distance between, for example, the *Excerpts of Theodotus* and Origen, these scholars have implicitly reinscribed the traditional divide between orthodoxy and heterodoxy. In order for a heretical group to be ethical, they must resemble more orthodox thinkers, who are *really* ethical.[82] The *Excerpts of Theodotus,* the *Tripartite Tractate*, and to a lesser degree Heracleon's *Commentary on John* employ models of ethical responsibility that differ in important ways from the models of ethical responsibility employed by their early Christian rivals, such as Clement and Origen.[83] Thus, we should not construct and judge "Valentinian" ethics in light of *our* inherited notions, such as a free will. We should instead attempt to understand the *Excerpts of Theodotus*, the *Tripartite Tractate*, and Heracleon on their own terms and in their own historical context.

By removing a false binary of either free choice or determinism, we can recognize that ancient authors could, for a variety of reasons, privilege different, even sometimes incompatible, models for moral responsibility. Thus, both the *Excerpts of Theodotus* and the *Tripartite Tractate* deploy a tripartite division of humanity and a soteriology with higher and lower levels of salvation in order to motivate and reinforce expectations that a pneumatic ought to be engaged in proselytizing, and other practices meant to save others. Similarly, Heracleon's *Commentary on John* deploys its threefold division of humanity to justify and encourage his readers toward missionizing psychics. Although these missionaries (pneumatics) ultimately disappeared into the fog of time, their tripartite division of humanity is a lasting artifact of an important and highly influential movement—if heresiological accounts are any indication—that spanned the whole of the ancient Mediterranean world.

Conclusion

Moral Imagination and Ancient Christianity

A central thesis begins to emerge: man is in his actions and practice, as well as in his fictions, essentially a story-telling animal.

—Alasdair MacIntyre, *After Virtue*

That is to say, the incongruity of myth is not an error, it is the very essence of its power. Or (to borrow Kenneth Burke's definition of the proverb) a myth is a "strategy for dealing with a situation."

—J. Z. Smith, *Map Is Not Territory*

Comparing Heavenly Stories

The stories of higher and lower levels of salvation examined in this book are far from the only instances we find of tiered afterlives in antiquity. Just as the authors we have considered assigned gradations of salvation to differing persons, so too did a number of other ancient writers in order to encode their own specific ethical values and political agendas. Writing in the first century before the Common Era, Cicero navigated the contentious political climate of his day, describing—when politically expedient—the elevated, celestial awards awaiting prominent Roman statesmen after death:[1] "Accordingly we find in those men of old whom Ennius styled the 'ancient' the fixed belief that there is sensation in the state of death, and in quitting life man is not annihilated so as to perish utterly . . . but [it is] a kind of shifting and changing of life which often served as a guide to heaven for illustrious men and women, while for all others the ghostly life was kept underground, yet all the same survived."[2] As in his *Dream of Scipio*, Cicero has adapted Plato's description of the immortality of the soul and its postmortem journey.[3] What sets Cicero's higher and lower levels of salvation apart from the corporate salvation we have explored is that Cicero emphasized the individual fate of the saved. Roman elites, according to Cicero, could immortalize themselves and their memories through their services to the state. Elite power players, such as Cicero himself, earned divine honors in the here and now, and afterward their divinized souls could ascend to the highest realms of the cosmos to dwell among the gods.

Nearly half a millennium later, Pelagius, a contemporary and heresiological target of Augustine of Hippo, wrote that exemplary lives earn stellar afterlives:

A life corresponds to its reward. Thus those who will receive the splendor of the sun then should already radiate a like justice, their holy deeds should illumine the blindness of unbelievers. This connects with the same Apostle's idea in writing to the Corinthians: "The splendor of the sun differs from the splendor of the moon, and from the splendor of the stars. Moreover, each star differs in splendor from the others. So it will be in the resurrection of the dead." The many mansions in the kingdom differ according to the merits of individuals. As good works differ, so do their rewards. Thus a person will shine there in glory as he has shone here in holiness.[4]

Multiplying John 14's expansive mansion and linking these paradisiacal palaces with 1 Corinthians 15's heavenly hierarchy, Pelagius urged his readers to exceptional feats of moral excellence in order to earn ever greater salvific rewards. Unlike Augustine, who viewed human nature as deficient and requiring an infusion of God's grace to compel us toward good choices and actions, Pelagius contended that human nature afforded us the freedom to elect evil as well as good, and thus we could and should strive toward moral excellence and even perfection. To help achieve this moral perfection, Pelagius encouraged his wealthy patrons toward "heroic" acts of almsgiving whereby they would donate most or even all of their wealth in grand and highly public acts.[5]

In contrast to the narratives we have explored, we find in Pelagius's as well as Augustine's responses a pronounced focus on each person's soul and its individual destiny. As Peter Brown observed, this focus on the individual included a biography for each soul, whose narrative extended long after death: "Every soul had a specific destiny—one might say a biography of its own—in the other world that was directly related to the aspirations and failures of their former selves."[6] There is a different sort of freedom at stake here: it is not the freedom to play a role in a story whose ends are fixed; rather, it is a question of whether each individual is free to choose to commit righteous or evil acts. Am I part of a larger drama of salvation, or am I the author of my own, tailored fate, free to earn my own heavenly rewards or hellish punishments?

Comparisons, implicit and explicit, have been a persistent organizing principle for this book. When done effectively, comparisons can help highlight not just points of similarity but also points of difference. As J. Z. Smith has masterfully shown, comparisons are complex mental operations that examine "relations and aspects" with respect to a specific trait or characteristic.[7] As a result, comparisons do not have ontological reality or "tell us how things are"; instead, they depend upon the mind of the scholar to circumscribe a set of phenomena as well as to select the primary characteristic or aspect for comparison: "Comparison does not deal with phenomenon *in toto* or in the round, but only with an aspectual characteristic of them. Analytical control over the framework of comparison involves theoretically focused selection of significant aspects of the phenomena and a bracketing of the endeavor by strategic *ceteris paribus* assumptions."[8] To borrow Smith's apt description, a comparison is a "disciplined exaggeration in the service of knowledge."[9] In other words, comparisons are subjective, intellectualist creations that provide a scholar the imaginative space to explore possible relationships and investigate hypotheses.

Over the course of this book, we have considered a number of instances of higher and lower levels of salvation. Unlike what we saw in Cicero or Pelagius, the emphasis herein was on corporate classes of people who play specific roles in narratives whose endings are fixed. Yet, just as we can find commonalities across our texts, so too can we point out significant differences. Although John of Patmos and Paul the Apostle both described the hierarchy of salvation awaiting Jews and gentiles, they wrote for different audiences. Paul tailored his message for a predominantly gentile audience; John wrote for a Jewish audience. Both the *Apocryphon of John* and the *Shepherd of Hermas* confront the problem of sinners and saints existing alongside each other in tight-knit communities; yet, the Platonic assumptions of the *Ap. John* lead to a different postmortem biography of souls. Finally, both the *Excerpts of Theodotus* and the *Tripartite Tractate* divide humanity into three races on the basis of their roles in ongoing evangelization of the world, and adopt the Pauline metaphor of the corporate body of Christ as a reflection of the church; they differ, however, on who belongs (pneumatics or pneumatics and psychics) in the body of the church. Selecting this phenomenon for comparison enabled us to examine both the usefulness and the flexibility of tiered afterlives as scripts for the drama of salvation history.

The Ethics of Stories with Fixed Endings

When I first began working on the dissertation that became this book, one of the first comments I received was that I was wrong in seeing in the *Tripartite Tractate* or *Apocryphon of John*'s narratives any evidence of even a slight concern over ethics. If the authors behind these texts had cared about ethics, this notable expert had told me at the time, they would have just said so. Ancient authors writing to encourage ethical conduct had clear sections of *paraenesis* and/or lists enumerating positive and negative duties; the *Tripartite Tractate* and the *Apocryphon of John*, so the argument goes, did not have such sections because they lacked such prosaic concerns. Instead, they were stories about the salvation and damnation of different types of people; there is no choice here, and without a choice there can be no moral responsibility. What was important was that you properly understood how the universe works. If you possessed this correct knowledge (*gnosis*), then you were among the elect who would be saved—not because of anything you did, but because of what you knew.

Similarly, by arguing that Paul the Apostle and John Patmos believed in unequal salvation wherein Jews were saved as Jews and gentiles as gentiles, *but* that the catalyst for salvation for both groups was Jesus Christ, I disagreed with two prominent, modern, and morally minded hermeneutics.[10] Many believe that God should not play favorites; thus, any indication of favoritism should be explained away in the interest of preserving divine impartiality and justice. Their solution: God judges all people fairly (that is, without regard to ethnicity), and so Christians qua Christians transcend old ethnic distinctions. In contrast, the second, modern hermeneutical approach maintained that Jews were saved as Jews and gentiles as gentiles, *but* Jesus is salvifically effective only for gentiles. In this way, God's preference for Israel is preserved, and there is no danger of sliding into supersessionist claims that Jews need to become "Christians" in order to be saved.

What I have tried to show over the course of this book is that we have approached these narratives with incorrect expectations of what a morality tale must look like. Stories with fixed endings, like the *Tripartite Tractate* or the *Apocryphon of John*, do not preclude moral responsibility because of the absence of choosing otherwise. Instead, they can provide convincing and multi-layered explanations of the world and our place in it and can orient us toward discrete moral practices as we learn to find our appropriate role in the story of salvation. Furthermore, just because the ancient authors we studied did not share our modern values (e.g., impartiality or ecumenicalism) does not mean they did not have any values themselves. John and Paul wrote a script for how Jews and gentiles ought to comport themselves in the near-to-end times. Although both agreed the Messiah plays a role in God's plan, this shared soteriological feature did not erase for either author the biblical framework of prophecies tailored to the Nations and Israel, respectively. Their teleological tales of salvation history require the continued existence and activities of Israel and the Nations. If we erase this distinction, we lose sight of how each author was creatively implementing these biblical prophecies in rhetoric and practice.

To interpret these stories apart from their embeddedness in the moral concerns of their authors and their putative communities is to misread them. These stories are narratives insofar as they provide structure, meaning, and the resources to navigate through various rough spots as their authors and readers quest after their particular *teloi* or goals:

> Two key features of the medieval conception of a quest need to be recalled. The first is that without some at least partly determinate conception of the final *telos* there could not be any beginning to a quest. Some conception of the good for man is required. . . . But secondly it is clear the medieval conception of a quest is not at all that of a search for something already adequately characterized, as miners search for gold or geologists for oil. It is in the course of the quest and only through encountering and coping with the various particular harms, dangers, temptations and distractions which provide any quest with its episodes and incidents that the goal of the quest is finally to be understood.[11]

Put differently and merging Alasdair MacIntyre's work on narrative with J. Z. Smith's discussion of the dialectical nature of myth, these narratives were malleable, moral maps for their readers.[12] Transforming narrative into spatial terms, you know where you are (i.e., who you are), where you want to go (i.e., your *telos*), and how to get there (i.e., how to live ethically *and also* compensate for unexpected turbulence) because of these maps. If stories with fixed endings or higher and lower levels of salvation do not fit our expectations for moral stories, we, too, must adjust and perhaps reject problematic assumptions so that our expectations better encompass the diverse forms of moral imagination in antiquity.

Higher and Lower Levels of Salvation and the Study of Ancient Christianity

Although this book is organized around a single typological feature, it was never my intention to trace a single idea—higher and lower levels of salvation—from its prehistory through its various permutations or forms. Instead, I have used the broad typological grouping around which this book is organized both to broaden our notions of ancient morality tales and to offer my own answers to several different questions that continue to be debated by scholars (e.g., What was Paul's view of Jewish and gentile salvation? Were the "Gnostics" ethical determinists?). Rather than rehearsing past debates and/or championing an established position, my use of this understudied organizing principle has enabled me to navigate as best I could away from well-trod paths, and to create odd or uncommon conversation partners (e.g., Paul and John or *Hermas* and the *Ap. John*),[13] as well as to nuance texts and authors traditionally interpreted as saying the same things (e.g., *Exc., Tri. Trac.,* and Heracleon).[14]

In this approach, I have attempted to apply the maxim that "incongruity gives rise to thought."[15] If higher and lower levels of salvation are a proposed solution to a theoretical and/or practical difficulty or inconsistency, then by using it as my organizational principle I could investigate the social situations and conceptual commitments that prompted its invention and/or implementation. Moreover, by manufacturing my own incongruity through odd conversation partners or by estranging traditional partners, I hoped to provide some new answers to old questions.

What I have found is that ancient morality and soteriology cannot be explained by appealing to a one-size-fits-all model. Modifying the title of a well-known and still highly valuable introduction to ancient Christian morality, it is better to speak of the origins of Christian moralities than a singular morality.[16] Whether deliberately or not, investigations into ancient ethics often assume a right/wrong or normative/aberrant binary. This helps explain some of the most enduring dichotomies we find in the study of the New Testament and early Christianity—for example, universal vs. particular (Part I), orthodoxy vs. heresy (Part II), or free will vs. determinist (Part III). In every case, the first term of each pairing connotes authors or texts committed to ethical concerns, while its opposing term is shorthand for a lack of concern over ethics, typically held by an outside (i.e., not authentically "Christian") group. Yet, upon closer scrutiny, we discover that these binaries—and the narrow moral frameworks they reinscribe—do not accurately encompass the diverse forms of ancient ethics.

By examining stories with fixed endings of higher and lower levels of salvation, I have sought to accomplish three things. First, I have expanded our canon of usual suspects for research into ancient ethics to include teleological narratives with differing levels of salvation.[17] Second, I have contributed to the continuing trend in scholarship to revisit our disciplinary binders and problematic historiographic binaries. And finally, I have offered new and plausible interpretations of the social contexts and aims of specific ancient authors. In so doing, I hope that we can better appreciate the diversity of ancient, ethically minded stories and the moral force with which they were written.

Notes

1. This is certainly not the first time Vonnegut has done so. Consider this exchange from his 1969 novel *Slaughterhouse-Five*: "'You sound to me as though you don't believe in free will,' said Billy Pilgrim. 'If I hadn't spent so much time studying Earthlings,' said the Tralfamadorian, 'I wouldn't have any idea what was meant by 'free will.' I've visited thirty-one inhabited planets in the universe, and I have studied reports on one hundred more. Only on Earth is there any talk of free will'" (86). Cf. Vonnegut, *Timequake*, 194: "'You know what you can do with free will?' asked Prince. 'No,' said Trout. 'You can stuff it up your ass,' said Prince."

2. Vonnegut, *Timequake*, 161.

3. See, for example, Dr. Schadenfreude's rage at any of his patients who used "I," "me," "my," "myself," or "mine," in Vonnegut's *Timequake*, 70.

4. On the connection between moral content and literary form, see further Nussbaum's *Love's Knowledge*.

5. In contrast to Vonnegut's self-depreciating humor and criticism of peoples' inflated sense of their own self-worth, the authors we will explore in this book (e.g., Paul, the Valentinians, etc.) were quite confident they were playing the starring roles in the drama of salvation.

6. Jackson, *Politics*, 112.

7. Jackson, *Politics*, 40.

8. Jackson's study is far more wide-ranging than my own and does not focus on stories with fixed endings. Jackson, in places, even eschews the traditional structures of narrative (e.g., beginning, middle, and end). Nonetheless, his findings on the social dimensions of storytelling are apropos here.

9. "Salvation" itself can be a fraught term, especially when it is subsumed into a particularly modern notion of "religion" that is individualistic and private; see further Nongbri's *Before Religion*. As we shall see in the Conclusion to this book, the shift toward individualizing salvation—superseding in importance the redemptive narrative of history—becomes increasing entrenched in late antique and medieval Christianity.

10. All biblical translations are NRSV; however, I frequently adapt and modify these translations in order to highlight possible interpretations that may go overlooked in conventional renderings.

11. Clement of Alexandria (e.g., *Strom.* 7.2.9) alludes to John 14:2 to argue for higher and lower levels of salvation.

12. As we shall see in Chapter 6, Heracleon is a partial exception to this claim.

13. My thinking on the role of narrative and its impact on ethics has been influenced by Stanley Hauerwas; see further Hauerwas, *Peaceable Kingdom,* chapters 2 and 3 especially.

14. On the importance of such a "narrative quest," see Alasdair MacIntyre (*After Virtue,* 219). For more on meaning-making and narrative in general, see further Paul Ricoeur's three-volume work *Time and Narrative.*

15. I do not use "ideology" to connote a *false* consciousness; rather, I employ the term to refer to various beliefs and dispositions—as well as their instantiations in practice—that people may subscribe to without formal or conscious choice. See Martin's similar parsing of ideology in his *Corinthian Body,* xiv–xv.

16. Boyarin, *Radical Jew,* 7.

17. Critics of Boyarin's Paul have pointed out that his Paul resembles that of Ferdinand Christian Baur. For a clear historiographic survey and contextualizing critique of Baur's Paul and similar formulations, see Martin, "Paul." See also Himmelfarb's 1996 review of Boyarin's *Radical Jew* in *Association for Jewish Studies.*

18. For competing notions of "universalism" in Paul, see the excellent but also eclectic collection of papers exploring the historical appropriateness and philosophical usefulness of (re)framing Paul's writings in light of "universalism" in Caputo and Alcoff's *St. Paul Among the Philosophers*; for a study making use of ethnic reasoning and discourse to critique alleged Pauline universalism, see further Johnson Hodge's seminal *If Sons.*

19. Some interpreters might also add to this series universalism *in scope,* i.e., including all of humanity; this theoretical development, however, makes better sense in the ideological context of someone like Origen and his cosmological and theodicean concerns than in the letters of Paul, who was constrained by an ever-dwindling timeline and motivated by several pressing pastoral concerns specific to his addressed communities. For a concise and contextualizing treatment of Origen's universalism, see Fredriksen, "Historical Integrity."

20. Although most modern scholars would not subscribe to Luther's radical interpretation that every person is saved by faith and faith alone, a number of scholars have proposed a lowest common denominator of ethical and soteriological criteria. Although with some notable variation, this lowest common denominator option often takes one of two forms: the *subtraction* of all Jewish practices that might distinguish or separate Jewish Jesus followers from gentile converts; or the *addition* of some ethical and purity requirements to gentiles in order to facilitate the creation of a unified community of Jews and gentiles where certain Jewish practices and/or scruples can still be observed. Representing this second view are Mark Nanos and Terence Donaldson, who have incorporated Jewish justifications for righteous gentiles, e.g., the Noahide Commandments and the Rules for the Sojourner. See Nanos, *Mystery*; and Donaldson, *Paul.* See also Alan Segal's enlightening discussion of the difference between the Rules for the Sojourner and the Noahide Commandments; particularly helpful is Segal's careful attention to the possible power disparities in play; e.g., the Rules for the Sojourner might be more prevalent in a context in which Jews are the majority in power, whereas the Noahide Commandments may fit better within the context of Diaspora Judaism. See Segal, *Paul*; and Segal, "Universalism." Drawing upon Nanos, Donaldson, Segal, and others, I will return to the Jewish construction of ethical expectations tailored specifically to gentiles in the following two chapters.

21. Thus, Paul supposedly rejects the "works of the law," since they are the parochial and nationalist practices of the Jews through which they socially differentiate themselves

from the Nations; consequently, insofar as the works of the law do not contribute to salvation but instead only create dissent and disparity between Jews and gentiles, Paul, so the argument goes, has embraced a new, universal religion, Christianity, that is free from this source of nationalistic boasting. See the influential article by Dunn, "Works."

22. *Pace* E. P. Sanders's (*Paul and Palestinian Judaism*, 552) oft-quoted claim: "In short, this is what Paul finds wrong in Judaism: it is not Christianity." See Chapter 1 for my discussion of the historically contingent and nonessentialist nature of "Judaism" and my own functional definition of it.

23. There are a number of excellent studies that examine the dynamic between Paul's continued Jewish identity and his preaching to gentiles; in addition to Johnson Hodge's *If Sons*, see also Pamela Eisenbaum, *Paul Was Not a Christian*; Matthew Thiessen, *Paul and the Gentile Problem;* and Paula Fredriksen, *Paul: The Pagans' Apostle.*

24. This language of staying "in" is an obvious reference to E. P. Sanders's famous construction of covenantal nomism; see, for example, Sanders, *Paul and Palestinian Judaism*, 419–28 and 511–23. It is not that I think Sanders is categorically wrong. In fact, I think Sanders's explanation is admirably economical for the vast number of sources it seeks to encompass; however, as we will see, I am interested in parsing the situatedness of Paul—especially his pastoral concerns and the impact of his eschatological beliefs—and this situatedness tends to be minimized when we try to fit Paul into a one-size-fits-all idea of Jewish soteriology.

25. Thiessen, *Paul*, 9: "Paul's statement that neither circumcision nor uncircumcision matters now makes better sense. Paul does not contrast the rite of circumcision to the commandments of God; rather he claims that being Jewish (circumcision) or being gentile (uncircumcision) does not matter—only keeping the commandments that God requires of each group of people."

26. Many scholars have transformed this dichotomy of Israel vs. Nations to mean Christians vs. all others. As we shall see, this is untenable for John and Paul. On the issue of *who* was included by the title Israel, see further Graham Harvey's *True Israel* and Peter Richardson's *Israel*.

27. Although Luke's (Acts 17:1–2) description of a two-step program, wherein Paul first preached in the synagogue of each city, is provocative, caution dictates that we must treat Luke's reconstruction of Paul with a healthy degree of skepticism (*pace* Mark Nanos, *Mystery*).

28. See Dale Martin's recasting of *extra ecclesiam nulla salus* to *extra Israel nulla salus* in his "Promise," 101.

29. As we will see, these saved gentiles likely played a more theoretical rather than practical role in John's thought. See further Fredriksen, *Paul*, especially chapter 3.

30. For two excellent studies that deal effectively with the subtlety while still stressing the paramount importance of exegesis in Paul and John, see further Richard B. Hays's *Echoes* and Richard Bauckham's *Climax*.

31. 1 Corinthians 15:20–23; Revelation 14:1–5. Although fascinating, it is unfortunately beyond the scope of my current project to examine just how Paul and John construct the function and significance of Jesus as their Messiah. For an excellent survey of the relevant issues and texts relating especially to Paul's deployment of the title "Christ," see Novenson's *Christ*; on Christology generally in the book of Revelation, see further Stuckenbruck's *Angel Veneration*.

32. See Fredriksen's ("Judaism," citation from 562) poignant phrasing of this in relation to Paul: "Ingeniously, tortuously, Paul integrates biblical history and his religious convictions as a Jew with precisely those discouraging facts of the Christian movement mid-century—too many Gentiles, too few Jews, and no End in sight—to formulate a solution to both dilemmas." Thus, we should not force Paul—or John—into the bind of being a *systematic* thinker, building from the ground up (or from creation to the eschaton); instead, Paul is a dialectic and dynamic thinker creatively improvising for rhetorical emphasis and situational need.

33. Beker, *Paul*; cf. Donaldson, who, in his *Paul* (37), argues against Beker that *three* levels (convictional core, theological explication, and contingent hermeneutic) are required.

34. I use "know" here for rhetorical emphasis to highlight the certainty of John and Paul's beliefs; John and Paul *know* they are right, and, if pressed, both could offer rational (to their minds and in light of their commitments) defenses and justifications for these beliefs. In addition to Jeffrey Stout and Alasdair MacIntyre on situated rationality (see below, note 75), see also the statements by Richard Hays (*Echoes*, 171) and Richard Bauckham (*Theology*, 7), who note that Paul and John have prophetic authority and certainty insofar as they *know* how things will turn out.

35. On the importance of the difference among empirical, encoded explicit, and encoded implicit readers, see Stanley Stowers, *Rereading*, chapter 1.

36. In addition to Thiessen's *Paul*, see his earlier book *Contesting Conversion*.

37. On God's preference and "Jewishness," see further Fredriksen, "How Jewish."

38. See Denise Kimber Buell's *New Race* and Philippa Townsend's "Another Race." On how early Christian studies have continued to be "haunted" by faulty, anachronistic assumptions about the rhetoric of race and ethnicity, see further Cavan Concannon's *Gentiles*.

39. See Michael Fishbane's (*Biblical Interpretation*, 515) description of Daniel's similar practices of anthologizing old prophetic announcements in Daniel 9–12: "Several factors give this clustering its particular cultural and exegetical value. First, Dan. 9–12 does not simply contain the *ad hoc* explication, reapplication, or (re)specification of the then ancient Jeremian oracle (Jer. 25:9–12), but is a coherent formulation of an apocalyptic programme out of many earlier prophetic pronouncements." See also John Collins's (*Apocalyptic Imagination*, 18) germane comments on the allusive use of prophecy in apocalyptic texts and the capacity of these prophetic patchworks to engender rich and layered levels of meaning.

40. For a recent introduction and representative collection of topics relating to Christianity in the second century, see the excellent volume edited by Paget and Lieu, *Christianity in the Second Century*. Of particular interest is the metaphor of a laboratory to characterize and clarify second-century Christianity; I shall return briefly to this metaphor in Chapter 4. For more on the metaphor of a laboratory, see from the same volume Löhr, "Modelling," and Lieu, "Modelling."

41. In other words, this teleological retelling is interested primarily or even exclusively in reconstructing proto-orthodoxy's refutation of its rivals' shortcomings or searching for those nascent kernels among proto-orthodox figures of what will develop into normative or "orthodox" Christianity (especially canon, liturgies, creeds, or doctrines) in the fourth century and beyond. In so doing, we either bypass large amounts of evidence that does not cohere with later creeds and doctrines ("heretics") or propose contorted and anachronistic interpretations to bring the allegedly authentic ("proto-orthodox") texts into line with the post-Constantinian views we are so certain they would adopt, if only they had lived a few centuries later. For the metaphor of a horse race, see further Rousseau, *Pachomius*, 19.

42. Brakke, *Gnostics*, 9.

43. On the sociology of reading networks, in particular how ancient texts circulated through interpersonal and informal friendship networks, see further Starr, "Circulation"; Gamble, *Books*; Haines-Eitzen, *Guardians*; Johnson, "Sociology"; and Johnson, *Readers*.

44. Brakke, *Gnostics*, 10.

45. For an accessible essay laying out this approach, see Karen King, "Which Early Christianity."

46. This facet of heresiological discourse was influentially noted by Le Boulluec in his *Notion*.

47. Karen King, "Which Early Christianity," 73; see also Lieu's *Christian Identity* and Boyarin's *Borderlines*.

48. Brakke, *Gnostics*, 15ff.

49. Brakke, *Gnostics*, 14–15.

50. Stanley Stowers ("Concept") rightly argues that—similar to the horse-race metaphor—"community" is too often deployed to reify disparate beliefs, practices, and peoples into coherent wholes. It is incorrect to assume that texts convey—in a one-to-one relationship—the attitudes and practices of a coherent, unified community; instead, they are skillfully produced and highly rhetorical portraits of what a certain author or authors believed the community ought to be. By acknowledging the idealistic nature of these texts, we can, nonetheless, gain insight into the tensions bubbling beneath the surface as these authors responded to and were forced to adapt their utopian visions. Each author examined in this study wrote to resolve the social concerns of his intended audience. Thus, I use "community" here not to signal absolute social cohesion and consolidation of beliefs and practice, but to demarcate the social scope and agenda of these authors. They wrote about the particular social concerns affecting their putative communities, and—based on the transmission of these texts—at least some in their audience valued what they had to say. A recurrent focus in this monograph will be the tensions, adaptations, and dissolutions of various Jewish and Christian communities as authors within them struggled to form like-minded and morally coherent wholes. Any interpretation of these texts without their social dimensions—imagined or realized—dismisses their authors' efforts at and commitment to forming ethically focused communities.

51. See, for example, the influential studies of Michael Williams's *Rethinking* and Karen King's *Gnosticism*.

52. I use the term "textual community" to refer to the social phenomenon whereby the production, interpretation, and circulation of particular texts has such a high level of ideological importance that it could help create shared identity and thus communal solidarity. See, for example, Brian Stock's definition of a textual community: "We can think of a textual community as a group that arises somewhere in the interstices between the imposition of the written word and the articulation of a certain type of social organization. It is an interpretative community, but it is also a social entity" (Stock, *Listening*, 150). On the category of "Sethian," see Schenke, "Das sethianische System"; Schenke, "Phenomenon"; Turner, *Sethian Gnosticism*; and Michael Williams, "Sethianism." Cf. Rasimus, *Paradise*.

53. For *Hermas*'s origins in Rome, see Chapter 3. For the urban setting of the *Apocryphon of John*, see Karen King, *Secret Revelation*, 9–17; I am not as confident as King, however, that we can securely place the *Ap. John* in Alexandria.

54. In an article examining the social organization of the producers of a corpus of literature (including the *Ap. John*) called Sethian by most scholars, Alan Scott ("Churches or

Books?") concludes that these Sethians did not organize themselves into communities like early Christian house-churches or congregations. Instead, according to Scott, these Sethians, *if* they displayed *any* interest in communal organizations, resembled "audience cults," a model borrowed from Rodney Stark and William Sims Bainbridge's *Future of Religion*. In support of the contention that Sethians were not a coherent group, Scott cites their wide-ranging diversity of beliefs, their apparent parasitic relationship to other communities, and a dearth of external witnesses to their social organization. In this way, Scott's argument depends upon Fredrik Wisse's seminal article "Stalking Those Elusive Sethians." For a thorough dismantling of arguments like Scott's, see Michael Williams, "Sethianism"; Williams, *Rethinking,* chapters 4 and 5; and Williams, "Plotinus' 'Friends.'"

Hermas's fundamental social structure, i.e., a late first- or early second-century house-church, is not disputed. There are a number of excellent studies that consider the social circumstances (assumed to be house-church) of *Hermas*: see Osiek, *Rich*; Osiek, *Shepherd*; Maier, *Social Setting*; and Lampe, *Paul to Valentinus*.

55. My use of "centralizing technology" is indebted to Thomassen's "Orthodoxy and Heresy."

56. Christoph Markschies has argued against linking later Valentinianism (in particular the system of Ptolemy's followers) with Valentinus because of, in his mind, its unbridgeable difference and distance from the fragments of Valentinus. In contrast, Einar Thomassen's extensive study of Valentinianism concludes that the fragments of Valentinus, though not fully elaborated and obviously fragmentary, nonetheless contain many of the elements of these later systems in inchoate form. See Markschies, *Valentinus Gnosticus*; and Thomassen, *Spiritual Seed*.

57. In addition to patristic sources, the Nag Hammadi tractate the *Testimony of Truth* also uses this label polemically. See further Geoffrey Smith, *Guilt*.

58. For example, at least eight "fragments" from their putative founder, Valentinus, survive, preserved by Clement of Alexandria and Hippolytus. (Six fragments are preserved by Clement and two by Hippolytus; there is an additional but likely "spurious" fragment listed as fragment 9 in Völker's *Quellen*.) We also have reports of and citations from alleged students of Valentinus, such as Ptolemy, Heracleon, and Theodotus, preserved by Irenaeus, Hippolytus, Tertullian, Clement of Alexandria, Origen, and Epiphanius. While most of these citations are rather short, a few are extensive reports on Valentinian teachings and practices. Most notable of these are Irenaeus's account of the followers of Ptolemy, various other Valentinian teachers, and the so-called Marcosians (*Haer.* 1. 1–21), Ptolemy's Letter to Flora (Epiphanius, *Panarion* 33.3.1–10), Heracleon's *Commentary on John* (preserved primarily in Origen's *Commentary on John*), and Clement of Alexandria's *Excerpts of Theodotus*. In addition to these more famous Valentinian figures, Ismo Dunderberg (*Beyond Gnosticism*, 2) lists some of the lesser-known ones, such as Florinus, Secundus, Axionicus, Ardeisanes, Theotimus, and Alexander. For a helpful summary of Valentinian prosopography, see Thomassen, *Spiritual Seed*, 493–502.

59. Namely the *Gospel of Truth* (I,3), the *Treatise on the Resurrection* (I,4), the *Tripartite Tractate* (I,5), the *Gospel of Philip* (II,3), the *Interpretation of Knowledge* (XI,1), and the *Valentinian Exposition* (XI,2). See Einar Thomassen, "Notes," 243–45; Thomassen had previously included the *1 Apocalypse of James* but has since changed his mind and now considers it a non-Valentinian text preserving Valentinian ritual dicta. See Thomassen, "Valentinian Materials."

60. On this question, see Thomassen's *Spiritual Seed* and "Notes."

61. Desjardins's response to this question ("Sources") is a deft reminder that we must evaluate each text individually, assuming neither that the patristic sources are a priori less trustworthy nor that the Nag Hammadi sources are more trustworthy.

62. *Stromata* 2.3.10.1.

63. *Stromata* 2.3.10.2.

64. *Stromata* 2.3.11.1.

65. Löhr, "Gnostic Determinism."

66. On Stoic determinism generally, see Long, "Freedom and Determinism"; Stough, "Stoic Determinism"; Bobzien, *Determinism*; and Dorothea Frede, "Stoic Determinism."

67. In varying degrees of complexity, the Stoics developed a psychological solution to refute claims, such as the *argos logos*, that their view of physics was incompatible with ethical responsibility. In short, though external events may not be in our control, how we respond to external impressions—even if our responses are entirely internal or psychological—is still within our control and "up to us." Thus, Stoics trained themselves to make better use of assent (*sunkatathesis*) and choice (*prohairesis*) free from external or inappropriate influence as part of cultivating a virtuous disposition or character (*diathesis*; *habitus*).

68. Cicero (*Fat.* 40, quoted in Bobzien, *Determinism*, 245) polemically summarizes this line of reasoning as follows: "If everything happens by fate, everything happens by way of an antecedent cause. And, if desire, so too those items which follow desire, hence also assents. And if the cause of desire does not lie with us, neither does desire depend on us. But if this is so, those items, too, that are the effect of desire do not lie with us; therefore neither assents nor actions depend on us. From which it follows that neither praise nor blame, nor honors, nor punishments are just."

69. For more on the Stoic emphasis on causation, see Long, "Freedom and Determinism," 173–80. For more on "harmonizing" or teleological determinism, see Bobzien, *Determinism*, 28–33; and Dorothea Frede, "Stoic Determinism," 201: "According to Stoic theory, not only do people act the same way in the same situation and do so necessarily, but . . . this causal sequence is also supposed to be preordained teleologically." See also Cleanthes's didactic *Hymn to Zeus:* "Most majestic of immortals, many-titled, ever omnipotent Zeus, prime mover of nature, who with your law steer all things, hail to you. . . . All this cosmos, as it spins around the earth, obeys you, whichever way you lead, and willingly submits to your sway. Such is the double-edged fiery ever-living thunderbolt, which you hold at the ready in your unvanquished hands. For under its strokes all the works of nature are accomplished. With it you direct the universal reason which runs through all things and intermingles with the lights of heaven both great and small" (Long and Sedley, *Hellenistic Philosophers*, 1:541).

70. Just what constitutes "free will" is not agreed upon by scholars. As such, diachronic surveys of free will often attribute the invention of the idea to differing authors or contexts. See, for example, Dihle's *Theory*, Kahn's "Discovering," and Michael Frede's *Free Will*.

71. Conventionally speaking, being able to have done otherwise appears to be an essential feature or outcome in how many scholars treat the idea of "free will." I will refrain here from pursuing the precise nuances of "free will" and what it has meant to various thinkers over millennia. For an excellent discussion of the historical context in which this contrafactual notion of free will, i.e., the ability to have done otherwise, arises, see further Bobzien, "Inadvertent Conception."

72. For a discussion of the problem of competing and seeming incompatible ethical systems in modern moral philosophy, see MacIntyre's *After Virtue*.

73. For a paradigmatic example of this sort of an approach to Stoicism and the social/ideological context of its propagators, see Brent Shaw's "Divine Economy."

74. Cf. Irenaeus, *Haer.* 4.37.2: "If, on the other hand, some are by nature good and others are by nature bad, then neither the former ones are worthy of praise on account of their goodness, since they were created like this; nor the latter ones are worthy of blame, since they, too, were created like this."

75. In making this claim, I depend upon the discussions of embedded or situated rationality in Stout, *Flight*, 149–76; and MacIntyre, *Whose Reason*.

76. Irenaeus, Clement, and Origen, in part because of their opposition to Valentinian texts and their apparent language of fixed classes, privileged a limited sense of voluntariness in choice. Thus, it is important, Clement claims, that a person be able to voluntarily assent or reject the teaching of the *logos*; otherwise, his or her actions could be neither praiseworthy nor blameworthy (*Stromata* 2.11.1–2; 5.1.3). See further Clark, *Clement's*.

77. This is not to say that such an aesthetic choice is an ahistorical phenomenon disconnected from the milieu from which it emerges or that the ethical or soteriological claims of these authors were *merely* aesthetic choices. Rather, I want to avoid inserting inevitability into these narratives—i.e., "Of course, John of Patmos wrote a teleological narrative—he wrote an apocalypse!" These authors were certainly bound by certain genre conventions and their own ideological commitments, but they also possessed the agency to creatively play within their own traditions. On the constraints on moral improvisation in literature, see Nussbaum, *Love's Knowledge*, 155–56.

78. Drawing on J. Z. Smith, I will approach this soteriological technology analogically, not genealogically. See Smith, *Drudgery Divine*. My approach also agrees with Bruce Lincoln's contention that similar narratives can reflect similar social and ethical concerns rather than indicate textual dependence; see further Lincoln, *Apples*, 40, 49, 113, 121, and 128.

79. On the "practical" importance of aesthetics, see Nussbaum, *Love's Knowledge*, 16: "Art was thought to be practical, aesthetic interest a practical interest—an interest in the good life and in communal self-understanding."

80. See the three sections above; Chapters 2, 4, and 5; and the Conclusion.

1. JOHN'S HEAVENLY CITY

Note to epigraph: Translation from Nickelsburg and VanderKam, *1 Enoch*.

1. See also Ezekiel 34.

2. Collins, *Apocalyptic Imagination*, 70.

3. Olson, *New Rereading*.

4. Thiessen, *Paul*, 22 and 25; Thiessen, "Paul," 68–71.

5. As we will see below, however, this "universality" should not be misinterpreted as a call to proselytize; rather, as in similar passages in Revelation, this passage is meant for internal consumption and confirms the universality and total supremacy of Israel's God, over and against the gods of the Nations.

6. For an admirably succinct and accessible overview and commentary of the whole of John's Revelation, see Barr, *Tales*.

7. Koester, *Introduction*, 2:257.

8. In contrast to scholars who, in discussions of John's use of the Hebrew Bible, focus only on verbatim citation or his ("Christian") repurposing of specific imagery, I wholeheartedly agree and follow Richard Bauckham's approach to John's exegesis, which seeks to recover how John's visions are shaped by and subtly allude to his biblical precedents but also are best interpreted within the context of ancient Jewish exegesis; see Bauckham, *Climax*, 297–98.

9. Paul, for his part, constructs a biblical pastiche to explain both the unexpected delay in the parousia and Israel's apparent "stumbling" and to reconcile these apparent difficulties with God's guarantee that *all* of Israel will be saved. Consequently, Paul devises a complex narrative of salvation history with differing and staggered timelines for gentile and Jewish baptism into Christ (Rom. 9–11). See further Chapter 2.

10. There are a number of first-rate studies emphasizing the diversity and historical contingency of various elements and strands of ancient Jewishness/Judaism: see especially Cohen, *Beginnings*; and Seth Schwartz, *Imperialism*. On the issues of continuity, rupture, and change in ancient Judaism, see further Ra'anan Boustan's helpful historiographic outline of competing perspectives: those highlighting rupture through top-down or global shifts and those concentrating on continuity, especially in localized practices such as synagogue observances; Boustan, "Augustine," especially 75–78.

11. My three typological categories are formulated to suit the needs of this chapter and are thus in some ways idiosyncratic; nonetheless, I found a number of scholarly overviews of the general diversity of Jewish views on the salvation of gentiles to be illuminating, even if I differ from their conclusions. See especially Sanders, *Jesus*, 212–21; Donaldson, *Paul*, 51–78; Donaldson, *Judaism*; and Nanos, *Mystery*, 57–64.

12. Cohen, *Beginnings*.

13. Clearly, however, not every ancient Jewish author was actively constructing or even concerned about the category of Judaism or what it means to be a proper Jew; but for those who were, e.g., Ezra or Paul the Apostle, it played an important role in group identity and formation.

14. Significant categories of identity will have elements of theoretical fixity and social fluidity. See Buell, *New Race*.

15. Matthew Novenson ("Paul's") has recently argued along similar lines, claiming that Paul's use of *Ioudaismos* in Galatians 1 shows that this term refers to a sectarian effort among Jewish insiders toward more zealous adherence to (or "activism" for) particular Jewish practices and policies.

16. This is not to say that *all* Jews organized the world through a straightforward and all-encompassing dichotomy between us (Jews) and them (gentiles), or that Judaism as a concept functioned only to articulate difference and mutual exclusivity. John, however, *did* assume these things. For a recent study examining the complex formation and fluid nature of the opposite side of this binary (i.e., gentiles), see further Rosen-Zvi and Ophir, "Paul."

17. Cohen, *Beginnings*, 109–39, especially 132–39; Himmelfarb, "Judaism."

18. Cohen, *Beginnings*, 133.

19. See 2 Maccabees 4:9–17 for the author's opposing definition for Hellenism.

20. See Himmelfarb's *Kingdom* for her excellent, diachronic survey of this tension between ancestry and merit.

21. Cohen (*Beginnings*, 136) shows how the Hasmoneans modeled their expectations for membership (or "citizenship") after the Greek concept of *politeia* and were thus able to enact the politically advantageous "enfranchisement" of outside peoples, such as the Idumaeans and Ituraeans.

22. I use "Second Temple Judaism" as an imperfect placeholder for the period of time between the era of Ezra and Nehemiah (sixth–fifth c. BCE) to the composition and consolidation of the Mishnah (second–third c. CE).

23. Jubilees 15:25–26, translated by O. S. Wintermute in Charlesworth's *Old Testament Pseudepigrapha*, vol. 2.

24. On not calling these former gentiles "converts," see Himmelfarb (*Kingdom*, 74–84), who notes the conceptual impossibility, according to Jubilees, for anyone *not* born of Israel to convert and *become* a Jew.

25. Elsewhere, Jubilees (7:20–21) supplies a moral rationale for this universal condemnation of gentiles via the story of Noah and his commands to his sons to honor parents, love neighbors, do justice, and to avoid fornication, pollution, and injustice. Although this story is similar to what in later and rabbinic texts becomes called the Noahide Commandments (e.g., t. Sand. 13.2; t. AZ 8.4), Jubilees, as Alan Segal notes, uses this narrative to justify the categorical exclusion and salvific unworthiness of gentiles because they do not obey these commands (Segal, "Universalism," 10–11). In rabbinic interpretation, however, the Noahide Commandments function *inclusively* and entail that some (perhaps very few) gentiles *could* be righteous and thus deserving of a place in the world to come. On the Noahide Commandments, see further Novak, *Image*; for Novak's argument (which differs from Segal's) for differentiating between the rabbinic formulation of the Noahide Commandments and the episode in Jubilees 7, see Novak, *Image*, 17–19.

26. Ezra 9:1–2.

27. Hayes, *Gentile*, 73–91.

28. Himmelfarb, *Kingdom*, 78–84.

29. 4 Ezra 12:32–33, 13:35–38; cf. 2 Baruch 48:40–47 (although 2 Baruch 72 does make an exemption that some gentiles may be saved). For similar examples of gentiles deserving destruction on account of their immorality, see T. Mos. 1.12; 1 Enoch 63.

30. See, for example, the rejection of intermarriage in Jubilees 30:7–17; cf. Himmelfarb, *Kingdom*, chapter 2.

31. See especially Isaiah 60, cited below as the example par excellence for higher and lower levels of salvation.

32. See, for example, Isaiah 56; Psalm 22:27; 1 Enoch 10:21, 91:14; Tobit 13:11, 14: 6–7a; Sib. Or. 3.564–70, 715–23, 757–75. For a broader survey of various types or degrees of gentile respect for and/or conversion to Judaism, see Cohen, "Crossing." For my part, I am more interested in texts relating to the imagined social order and standards of conduct in the eschaton than in "quotidian situations." On this distinction, see further Fredriksen, "Judaism"; and Fredriksen, *Paul*, 73ff.

33. By interpreting these passages and others, like Isaiah 42:6, 49:6 ("a light to the Nations"), as inclusive yet inwardly focused, my argument intersects with the findings of scholars who have challenged the notion that ancient Jews, due in part to their monotheistic beliefs, were active missionaries seeking to convert the world. As opposed to obligating readers to missionary practices, it appears instead that these passages sought to motivate their Jewish audience to be ethical exemplars whose uprightness and conduct should be the

model that all other nations should strive to imitate. There are a number of ancient parallels for such an inwardly focused ethic; perhaps most interesting, because of his surprising similarity, is Plotinus; see Dillon, "Ethic." For scholarly critiques of the representation of ancient (especially Second Temple) Judaism as a "missionary religion," see Fredriksen, "Judaism," 537–43, 545–46; McKnight, *Light*; and Goodman, *Mission*, especially 60–90.

34. Ezekiel's attempt (44:6–7, 9) to reinforce boundaries between Israel and the Nations is discussed below.

35. In contrast, Philo (*Virt.* 20.102–4; *Spec. leg.* 1.52–54) remarks that converted foreigners (τοὺς ἐπηλύτας) should be included among the Jewish community without distinction, but loved as much as "one loves oneself."

36. Himmelfarb, *Kingdom*, 123–24; see CD VI.17–21.

37. On the question and criticism of whether ritual conversion via circumcision could lead to inclusion in the covenantal community of Israel in the Second Temple period, see Thiessen, *Paul*, chapter 3; Thiessen, *Contesting Conversion*, passim, citation from 11–12: "As I will argue, the priestly writer attempts to distinguish between Israelite circumcision (exemplified by Isaac) and non-Israelite circumcision (exemplified by Ishmael) through the timing of circumcision, in order to show that not all who are circumcised belong to the covenant. One is a member of God's covenant with Abraham via proper descent. Eighth-day circumcision, which only the descendants of Isaac practice, protects this genealogical boundary around Abraham's covenantal seed by linking ritual practice as closely as possible to birth. In other words, contrary to many interpretations of Genesis 17, including some early rabbinic ones, circumcision according to the priestly author does not function as an initiatory or conversionistic rite."

Writing recently on these "eschatological gentiles," Paula Fredriksen (*Paul*, 74) commented that "the Kingdom's pagans were a special and purely theoretical category: they were ex-pagan pagans, or (to use the wiggle room afforded by our two English words) ex-pagan gentiles. *Like* god-fearers, these eschatological pagans would retain their native ethnicities; *unlike* god-fearers, these pagans would no longer worship their native gods. *Like* proselytes, these pagans would worship exclusively the god of Israel; *unlike* proselytes, these pagans would preserve their own ethnicities and—another way of saying the same thing—they would not assume the bulk of Jewish ancestral custom (such as, for males, circumcision)."

38. What constitutes "good" is elastic and depends on the point of view of each author; for example, 2 Baruch 72 declares that only those Nations who never knew and thus never oppressed Israel will survive.

39. In addition to Isaiah 60, see the paradigmatic language of Zechariah 14:14b, 16–17.

40. See the excellent article examining this motif of the eschatological worship of the Nations in Enochic literature by Loren Stuckenbruck, "Eschatological Worship."

41. Fredriksen, "Judaism," 547–48.

42. Lévi-Strauss, *Totemism*.

43. Donaldson, *Paul*, 75.

44. Frankfurter, "Jews"; and Marshall, *Parables*.

45. Himmelfarb, *Kingdom*, 137.

46. So far, however, their interpretation has garnered limited acceptance. In addition to Himmelfarb (*Kingdom*, 115–42), see Pagels, "Social History."

47. See, for example, Elisabeth Schüssler Fiorenza (*Revelation*, 67), who on the basis of an incorrect reading of Galatians 6:16 compounds her misreading by (mis)appropriating the

title of Israel for Christians in order to claim that the 144,000 of Revelation 7 refer to the elect, i.e., Christians: "The author of Revelation might utilize Jewish traditions in order to express the conviction that the fate of those Christians experiencing God's judgment day is 'sealed' for salvation. Like 1 Peter 2, Revelation applies Exodus 19:5–6 to the Christian community and thereby stresses its continuity with Israel as the elect 'people of God.' It is likely that in Rev. 7:1–7 the twelve tribes signify the restored Israel of which the church is a significant part . . . the 144,000 probably represent those Christians alive at the 'Day of the Lord' who have no connection with idolatry or the Antichrist."

48. Aune, *Revelation*, 2:443, emphasis in original.

49. See Marshall's criticism (*Parables*, 62) of Schüssler Fiorenza, in which Marshall censures Schüssler Fiorenza with highly polemical language for her overarching argument that Revelation posits a hierarchical dualism between the "poor" (and oppressed) "good Christians" by the "rich" (and oppressive) "bad Jews."

50. Highlighted in 2014 by a series of ten essays in the *Marginalia Review of Books*, *ioudaios* is a hotly contested term. Although the scholars debated whether and in what instances *ioudaios* would be more appropriately translated "Judean" than "Jew," the idea that this term would reference Christians in opposition to Jews was never seriously considered. Thus, John of Patmos would be aberrant and radically innovative if he did utterly transform *ioudaios* into a term for Christian self-designation as well as a source of anti-Jewish polemic. This is unlikely; instead, like "Israel" (e.g., Rev. 7:4), John uses *ioudaios* with Jews/Judeans in mind and not as part of a (later Christian creation of) rejection and replacement theology. See further Richardson, *Israel*.

My own approach here is to translate *ioudaios* as "Jew." John's fierce possessiveness of the term, and its ritual and salvific components are better signified by the term "Jew" than "Judean." On possible pitfalls, as well as letting context help determine how best to translate this term, I am informed by a number of excellent studies, among which are Steve Mason's "Jews" and Daniel Schwartz's "'Judaean.'"

51. Yarbo Collins, *Crisis*, 85.

52. Christian scholars reading the New Testament have often struggled with the problem that their purportedly Christian forefathers use Jewish and not Christian self-designations; see more below. This discomfort is not unique to modern readers but similarly troubled many early Christians; for examples drawn from fourth- to fifth-century authors in particular, see Jacobs, "Jew's Jew."

53. Marshall, *Parables*, 13–16, 133–34; cf. Frankfurter, "Jews." See, in contrast, Steven Friesen ("Sarcasm," 135–36n32), who summarily rejects John Marshall's "referential understanding" of John with his programmatic assertion "We are [not] dealing with referential language here because the general and immediate contexts are full of irony, satire, and sarcasm."

54. Cf. Paul's Judaizing opponents in his Letter to the Galatians, who claim that gentiles must become "righteous gentiles" by embracing specific practices but not the whole of the Torah in order to be included among the descendants of Abraham and God's people. John, similarly, may be addressing a group of gentiles who are, for some reason, claiming Jewish identity without—in John's mind—an authentic right to such a title and its honors (see note 55).

55. Friesen's response ("Sarcasm," 135) to Frankfurter ("Jews") that Pauline churches did not deploy *Ioudaios* or "synagogue" in their self-definitions is an important critique; however, I would quibble with it for two reasons. First, Friesen appears to overlook the range and function of *Ioudaios* throughout Paul's writings, especially in instances when Paul

must lay claim to *Ioudaios* to dispute the claims of rival Jewish missionaries who are preaching incorrect or even "Judaizing" instructions to gentile members of the Jesus movement (e.g., Gal. 2:15ff.; Rom. 2:17–29). And second, although Frankfurter does unnecessarily homogenize John's Letters to the Seven Congregations in order to frame John's opponents in Smyrna and Philadelphia as similar or even analogous to his Neo-Pauline opponents of Pergamum and Thyatira, John, nonetheless, may be writing against a faction who—similarly to some of Paul's opponents in Galatians and Romans—have misappropriated for themselves titles from the Hebrew Bible and contemporary Jewish literature, e.g., the congregation of God. Thus, John may be responding to (or preemptively undercutting) his opponent's illicit appropriation of the language of the "synagogue of the saints" and the "synagogue of the Lord" from Numbers 16:3 LXX. See also Adela Yarbo Collins ("Insiders," 209), who provides a list of similar phrases, e.g., "congregation of God," "assembly of God," and "congregation of Belial," found in the writings of the Qumran community; e.g., the War Scroll 1QM 1:1, 4:9–10; and the Hodayot 1QH 2:22.

56. Paul Duff ("'Synagogue,'" 158–59n48) unintentionally strengthens this reading by noting that the eschatological destiny for the "synagogue of Satan" from Revelation 3:9 is they will be forced to "learn from their mistakes." As Duff notes, a similar eschatological fate appears in Wisdom 5, 1 Enoch 62, and 4 Ezra 7:83–87; what Duff fails to note, however, is that these passages describe the eschatological fate of the gentile Nations who will be forced to endure extreme humiliation (and sometimes torment) for their former oppression of Israel.

57. Cohen, *Beginnings*, 1: "Jews see the world in bipolar terms: Jews versus gentiles, 'us' versus 'them.'"

58. I agree with Himmelfarb (*Kingdom*, 138), *pace* Marshall (*Parables of War*), that John did not posit universal salvation for all of Israel; instead, as we will see, John of Patmos rhetorically privileges certain identities and types of conduct. As Himmelfarb notes, those from the 144,000 who are sealed in Revelation are a *minority* of Israel, just as in Ezekiel 9:4.

59. See Himmelfarb's study of priestly language in Revelation and throughout ancient Judaism generally in her *Kingdom*, in particular 135–42 for her views on Revelation.

60. Cf. Bauckham, *Theology*, 7.

61. Revelation 21:26: καὶ οἴσουσιν τὴν δόξαν καὶ τὴν τιμὴν τῶν ἐθνῶν εἰς αὐτήν.

62. There is an interpretative dispute over how to best render "glory and honor." As we will see below, one of John's major intertexts here is Isaiah 60's expectation of the Nations coming to Jerusalem to pay financial restitution. John, however, has modified this language to highlight the liturgical and cultic resonances of "glory" and "honor" rather than financial reparations; this observation, as we shall see, has important implications.

63. These ethical expectations should not, moreover, be conflated and homogenized with the rabbinic notion of the Noahide Commandments. Although the Noahide Commandments and John's expectations are all genealogically dependent upon *some* of the same biblical passages describing ethical expectations for the Nations/gentiles/sojourners, John differs from the rabbinic context and aim, not the least insofar as he thinks this world is ending, and his ethics reflect this eschatological focus. For a useful introduction and discussion of the conceptual framework and content of the Noahide Commandments, see further Segal, *Paul*, 187–223; Segal, "Universalism."

64. Thus, even in these sections that highlight the participation and worship of God by the Nations, their temporal subordination to Israel is clear. Cf. Kocar, "Hierarchy of Salvation."

65. Fredriksen ("Judaism," 545) emphasizes that these transformed gentiles are not a quotidian reality for ancient Jews; rather, Isaiah expects that if some gentiles do "convert" (whatever this entails), they will do so at some time in the *future*.

66. Himmelfarb, *Kingdom*, 135–42.

67. It is doubtful that John had in mind a prescribed series of ritual practices through which gentiles could "convert" and thus ritually become part of the Jewish people. Although there may be ancient instances of such a notion (e.g., Josephus, *Ant.* 13.257–58, 318, 397), there are also a number of other texts that strongly asserted that Jewish identity could be transferred only through biological descent (e.g., Jubilees 2:19–20). John, however, is occupied here with a different concern altogether. For John, the fact that some gentiles will be chosen by God for a special purpose has very little to do with these gentiles themselves; this is an eschatological promise that confirms God's preeminence and underscores the privilege it is to serve and worship him. See note 37 for references to Matthew Thiessen's analysis of whether circumcision after the eighth day (cf. Gen. 17) could incorporate a gentile into Israel's covenant with God, and Paula Fredriksen's discussion of these "eschatological gentiles."

68. Revelation 5:9–10: "They sing a new song: 'You are worthy to take the scroll and to open its seals, for you were slaughtered and by your blood you have ransomed to God every tribe, tongue, people, and nation (ἐκ πάσης φυλῆς καὶ γλώσσης καὶ λαοῦ καὶ ἔθνους); you have made them a kingdom of priests for our God (καὶ ἐποίησας αὐτοὺς τῷ θεῷ ἡμῶν βασιλείαν καὶ ἱερεῖς).'" Cf. Revelation 7:9ff.

69. On time and space more generally, see Friesen, *Imperial*, chapter 9.

70. *Pace* Michael Labahn ("Resurrection," 338–39), who views Revelation 20:4 as referring to two groups: the beheaded martyrs and "those who had not worshipped the beast or received his mark." See, however, David Aune (*Revelation*, 3:1088), who notes that the καὶ οἵτινες introduces an analeptic relative clause (i.e., a "back reference") and does not refer to a new group of individuals: "The author uses [this back reference] to link this section with the same motifs found earlier in the narrative in Rev 13:4, 8, 12, 15; similar analeptic interpolations occur in 14:11 and 16:2. . . . It is more natural to construe the text as referring to a single group of martyrs, who had been executed for both positive reasons (v 4b: their obedience to the commands of God and their witness to Christ) and negative reasons (v 4c: their refusal to worship the beast or its image and to receive its brand on their foreheads and their right hands)."

71. We will return shortly to the question of what sort of persecution—if any at all—these martyrs and John's own communities experienced.

72. See, for example, his description of the martyr Antipas (Rev. 2:12–13), who is the model for upright conduct, in particular endurance, for the congregation in Pergamum.

73. For an interpretation of this scene that focuses instead on the parody of Roman imperial imagery in play here, see Aune, "Influence."

74. Himmelfarb, *Kingdom*, 135–36.

75. For more on the relationship between Revelation 20:4 and 6:9, see Aune, *Revelation*, 3:1085–88.

76. For a fuller discussion of the relationship between Revelation 21's new earth, new heaven, and new Jerusalem and Isaiah as well as some other biblical and Second Temple authors, see Fekkes, *Isaiah*; Lee, *New Jerusalem*; and Mathewson, *New Heaven*.

77. There is some debate about whether God has renewed creation or whether he has destroyed the old world and has now created a wholly new earth, heaven, and Jerusalem. See Fekkes, *Isaiah*, 228–30, 253–60.

78. See, for example, Gundry, "New Jerusalem."

79. See Beale, *Book*, 1043–44: "The new world that v 1 has portrayed as replacing the old is now called 'the holy city, new Jerusalem.' Not surprisingly, the language comes from another Isaiah passage . . . the commencement of the replacement of the temporary cosmos with the permanent is expressed in the visionary words 'I saw [the city] descending from heaven from God.' This is the consummate irruption of the new creation to replace the old creation."

80. Mathewson, *New Heaven*, chapter 6; Bauckham, *Climax*, chapter 9.

81. See the critical remarks of Robert Royalty on this trend in his *Streets*, 215–18.

82. Beale, *Book,* 1098–99.

83. Cf. the New Jerusalem and the Temple Scroll from Qumran, both of which similarly construct places of elevated sacrality and significance (e.g., the new Jerusalem or the eschatological Temple) and aver that only the right sorts of people can dwell or practice therein. See further Aune, "Qumran."

84. In so doing, John has woven together several biblical passages that portray Jerusalem or Zion as the navel or center of the world (e.g., Ezek. 5:5; Mic. 4:1–5; Pss. 48 and 99).

85. For a compendious treatment of John's allusions to biblical and Near Eastern conceptions of the Temple, see further Briggs, *Jewish*.

86. *Pace* Pilchan Lee (*New Jerusalem*, 278), who concludes that John's elaborate and high walls are exegetical remainders that should not be interpreted as separating two distinct terrains and peoples. John's continued interest in difference may help to explain his emphasis on the "great and high wall" separating the new Jerusalem from the new earth even *after* the second resurrection (Rev. 21:12–14). In light of John's eschatological timeline, it is clear that this wall is not meant to protect and defend Jerusalem from potential attacks from external, evil forces, since only the saved remain; this does not mean, however, that we should abridge and smooth over John's language of spatial hierarchy so that the saved are an undifferentiated mass who enjoy equal salvific honors and access to the new Jerusalem.

87. Furthermore, the imagery and numbers (especially the number 12) signal the impending restoration of the twelve tribes of Israel; see Aune, *Revelation*, 3:1155; Beasley-Murray, *Book*, 320–21.

88. Aune, *Revelation*, 3:1170–71.

89. Bauckham, *Climax*, 278–79: "'To give glory to God' always in Revelation refers positively to giving God the worship which is due to him (4:9; 14:7; 16:9; 19:7). It is used in the Old Testament in this sense, and can be used in connexion with repentance . . . or in contexts which anticipate the universal worship of God. . . . In the Old Testament it occurs almost exclusively in non-Israelite contexts (Gen. 24:7; Ps. 136:26 are the only exceptions). It is used by Jews speaking to non-Jews or non-Jews acknowledging the God of Israel as the universal God."

90. As Zechariah 14:16–19 makes clear, however, financial restitution to Israel and veneration of the God of Israel can coexist in Jewish eschatological speculation.

91. *Pace* Fekkes (*Isaiah*, 272–73), who concludes that John is purposefully ambiguous as to whether "glory" and "honor" should be interpreted as "physical offerings" or "spiritual worship." In contrast, see Royalty (*Streets*, 232–33) and Bauckham (*Climax*, 315–16), who emphatically argue, albeit for different reasons, that John has deliberately signaled liturgical and not monetary offerings.

92. Translated by R. B. Wright in Charlesworth's *Old Testament Pseudepigrapha*, vol. 2.

93. See also Bauckham (*Climax*, 266–73), who examines a comparable spatial hierarchy underlying Revelation 11:1–2's differentiation between the sanctuary and the court outside; Bauckham, however, contends that the "outer court" refers not to the court of the gentiles but rather to the court of the priests. Whatever the correct referent is, it is clear that John has employed a spatial hierarchy of differing levels of sacrality to differentiate among the spaces that gentiles are allowed and denied entry.

94. *Pace* Mathewson (*New Heaven*, 165), who argues that all the saved will reside in the new Jerusalem.

95. Drawing upon the language of encoded and empirical readers (Stowers, *Rereading*, 21–29), it does not appear that John had gentiles in mind for either. For example, he constructed his *encoded* audience such that the gentiles were clearly outsiders (e.g., the tree for the healing of the Nations in Rev. 22:2 treats gentiles as outsiders who must depend upon the encoded audience, Israel, for healing). In terms of an empirical audience, we can only speculate; however, on the basis of the vitriol of Revelation 2:9 and 3:9, it is clear that John expected boundaries between his Jewish insiders and gentile outsiders to be well maintained; consequently, it is unlikely that the first readers of Revelation included many gentiles.

96. Revelation 21:27 also states that "those who are written in book of life" are able to enter as well; we shall return to this verse in much greater depth below.

97. On the importance of martyrdom to John's "ecclesiology," see further Pattemore, *People*, chapter 4.

98. As David Aune (*Revelation*, 1:152–53) suggests, the background to the term νικάω is likely an athletic metaphor wherein someone successfully finishes a race or "wins" a contest.

99. Thompson, *Book*, 78.

100. In addition to entering into the new Jerusalem, both "those who wash their robes" (Rev. 22:14) and "one who conquers" (Rev. 2:7) receive the same salvific honor insofar as both are explicitly said to be able to eat from the tree of life in paradise.

101. For perhaps the most influential study of this sort, see Yarbo Collins, *Crisis*.

102. For a paradigmatic example, see Duff, *Who Rides*.

103. Pagels, *Revelations*.

104. Fredriksen, *Paul*, 92.

105. In terms of a precise date for John's Apocalypse, I follow David Barr's more cautious approach, which maintains that Revelation was likely written over an extended period (perhaps over several decades). Barr, *Tales*, 21.

106. For comparable exhortations toward steadfast endurance in the face of previous violence and widespread deaths, see further 2 Maccabees 7 and 4 Ezra 10–12; both texts guarantee salvific rewards to past martyrs and by extension offer these same rewards to their readers if they can similarly endure and continue to uphold pious, Jewish practices.

107. Bauckham, "Book."

108. Although John never explicitly conflated all three into a single ethical injunction, these three profiles bleed into one another throughout the text. See, for example, Revelation 14:1–13.

109. Although John's description of those dwelling in the new Jerusalem is idealistic (i.e., the best possible and thus an extremely rigorous ethical standard), we should not—

especially in light of John's exclusive language—minimize or soften John's ethical standards. In John's mind, this is what is required for entrance into the new Jerusalem.

110. Aune, *Revelation*, 3:1174.

111. Cf. Revelation 21:8.

112. Aune, "Qumran," 90–92: "Impurity is barred from the city, according to 21:27 . . . [and] at the conclusion of Revelation there is a short list of those who are excluded from the city (22:15): 'outside are the dogs, the sorcerers, the fornicators, murders, and idolaters, and everyone who loves and practices falsehood.' Despite the brevity of these two lists, they exhibit a strikingly common pattern. Both begin with what appears to be a ritual category, which is then followed by a list of moral transgressors. Given the unlikelihood that a Christian author would regard ritual and moral impurity as equally defiling, we are left with two possibilities: 1. The author understands the ritual prescriptions metaphorically in moral terms; or 2. The author incorporates a source in which ritual impurity and moral transgression are equally defiling. It is not easy to choose between these two possibilities, for both may be valid [but] while the generic category of *koinos* might be expected to subsume various other categories of ritual impurity, the author appears to shift gears and provides rather a list of those people who are excluded from the city because of their immoral behavior."

113. Klawans, "Notions"; Klawans, *Impurity*; and Hayes, *Gentile*.

114. Klawans, "Notions," 291–92.

115. Hayes, *Gentile*, 34.

116. Translated by Hayes, *Gentile*, 60.

117. See further Sanders, *Judaism*, 51–76.

118. See Fredriksen, "Judaizing," especially 247–49.

119. As we see elsewhere, the sacrifice of the Lamb has global, salvific implications, even for those who do not belong to John's putative Jesus community; cf. Revelation 5:9, 7:14, and 12:11.

120. It is important to note, however, that even if these gentiles were named in the book of life and offered glory and honor to God, there is no evidence that they *ritually converted* and became Jews; this was a prerequisite, according to John (Rev. 2:9; 3:9), for belonging to his putative community of *Jewish* Jesus followers.

121. As Hayes (*Gentile*, 36) and Klawans ("Notions," 292) show, gentiles are analogous to a deformed priest (Lev. 21:23) who, though not ritually impure, cannot enter into the sacred precincts of the Temple because he is profane.

122. See the contrast between the sanctuary and the courtyard in Revelation 11:1–2.

123. Bickerman, "Warning," 388.

124. *Pace* Bauckham, *Climax*, chapter 9.

125. For a list of examples, see further Bauckham, *Climax*, 278–79.

126. On the "taint" of gold and its association with the destroyed city of Babylon, see Royalty, *Streets*, 232–33.

127. This portrait of gentiles resembles Shaye Cohen's description (*Beginnings*, 150–54) of gentiles who "venerate the God of the Jews and deny or ignore all other Gods."

128. Revelation 15:3–4.

129. In light of this, I would modify slightly Martha Himmelfarb's claim (*Kingdom*, 141) that "all of the redeemed gentiles are priests—just as all of the redeemed Jews are." Those gentiles who are saved qua gentiles, are *not* priests but do *imperfectly* resemble priests insofar

as their actions are incomplete imitations of the venerations of the true priests who dwell within the new Jerusalem.

130. John further articulated the subordination to and possibly even dependence of the Nations on Israel through paradisiacal features of the new Jerusalem; see, for example, Revelation 22:2's tree of life, which represents the restoration of the twelve tribes and the secondary salvation of the Nations—a salvation that depends upon healing, possibly from Israel (cf. Rom. 11): "On either side of the river is the tree of life with its twelve kinds of fruit, producing its fruit each month; and the leaves of the tree are for the healing of the Nations (εἰς θεραπείαν τῶν ἐθνῶν)."

131. *Pace* Aune, "Qumran," 90–92; and Aune, *Revelation* 3:1174–75.

132. Hayes, *Gentile*, 232–33n50: "In fact, grammatical evidence suggests that the phrase "uncircumcised and unclean" is disjunctive and supports a reading of Isa. 52:1 as referring to two distinct types of people. 'Neither the uncircumcised nor the alien shall enter you again.'"

133. For example, see Didache 1.1: "There are two ways, one to life and one to death, but the difference between the two ways is great." Cf. the "two ways" found in other texts, e.g., 1QS 3.18–4.26) and the Letter to Barnabas 18–20. See also McKenna, "Two Ways"; as well as Kurt Niederwimmer's extensive discussion of the existence and transmission of a hypothetical "'two ways' tractate," in his *Didache*, 30–52.

134. Himmelfarb, *Kingdom*, 139.

2. PAUL'S OLIVE TREE

1. I am paraphrasing Romans 11:17–26.

2. The sheer amount of ink that has been spilled over Paul is daunting. Rather than being encyclopedic, my engagement with secondary literature will be confined largely to the branch of Pauline interpretations I find myself closest to, that of the "Radical New Perspective." While I disagree with a number of their conclusions, I begin from some of the same foundational claims about Paul and his Gospel, e.g., Jews stay Jews and gentiles stay gentiles; Paul tailored his letters to their specific audiences, using rhetorical flourishes; and Paul believed the world was about to end and thus eschatological immediacy—not long-term planning—determined his message. For a concise yet helpful overview of "New," "Old," and some Pauls in between, see Thiessen's *Paul*, 4ff. Although I still prefer "Radical New Perspective," many adherents and adjacents now refer to this trend of scholarship as "Paul within Judaism." See, for example, Nanos and Zetterholm's *Paul*.

3. No one scholar is more associated with this "New Perspective" on Paul than E. P. Sanders and his monumental work, *Paul and Palestinian Judaism*; but Sanders was indebted to previous scholars who similarly worked hard to situate Paul in light of various patterns of Judaism, e.g., apocalyptic (Schweitzer) and rabbinic (Davies) Judaism.

4. James Dunn is credited with coining this phrase in his "New Perspective." In recent years there has been a staggering number of developments within, as well as responses to, the New Perspective Paul, with various camps forming around specific interests and emphases. Throughout this chapter, I will engage extensively with a specific subgroup of scholars (e.g., Stendahl, Gaston, Gager, and Stowers) who are perhaps best known (and often criticized) for devising an "ecumenical" interpretive lens for Paul that resists anti-Judaism conclusions, especially rejection-replacement readings. Although I will disagree with these

scholars at various points, I believe that, because of their coherence with one another, distinctiveness from many other approaches, and the overall persuasiveness of their arguments, they provide the most economical orienting point in a field as massive and as diverse as Pauline studies.

5. Stendahl, "Call."

6. Luke (Acts 21:19–26) goes so far as to describe Paul as taking a Nazarite vow, involving sacrifice in the Temple, in order to demonstrate Paul's continued commitment to the Torah and Jewish ritual practices.

7. Jeremiah 1:4–5; cf. Isaiah 49:1.

8. For an analysis of the neologism "Christian" and its later (second-century) development, see Marshall, *Parables*, 68–87; see also Townsend, who argues in her "First Christians" that the term emerges as a gentile (not Jewish) designation for members of the Jesus movement.

9. Thus the language of apostasy and conversion is not appropriate. *Pace* Segal, *Paul*; and Gaston, "Galatians," in Gaston, *Paul*, 76–79.

10. See Romans 9:4–5 for a list of the advantages of the Jews.

11. This is not a new complaint against Paul (cf. 2 Peter 3:15–17); see the excellent overview of these conflicting pro- and anti-Israel sayings found in John Gager's brief but effective *Reinventing*.

12. Galatians 6:15; Romans 3:1.

13. Galatians 3:10–11; Romans 7:7, 12.

14. For a recent and impressively thorough treatment of Paul that nonetheless repeats this contention (albeit in reference to Paul's conflict with Peter at Antioch), see John Barclay's *Paul*, 385, emphasis in original: "The authority of the Torah *has been demolished*: [Paul] has 'died to the Law through the Law in order to live to God' (Galatians 2:19)."

15. For a persuasive source-critical analysis of 2 Corinthians that divides this composite letter into five separate letters and situates them within the larger historical context of the Corinthian correspondences, see Mitchell, "Paul's Letters"; according to Mitchell ("Paul's Letters," 324, 334), 2 Corinthians 3 was part of a Pauline letter dubbed a "self-defense of his ministry."

16. *Pace* Hayes (*Divine Law*, 151–62), who argues that Paul, out of concern for his gentile audience and their genealogical inability to fulfill the Torah, is construing the Mosaic Law as particularist and therefore inferior to a rational, universal law. While I agree with Hayes's assessment of Paul's belief in the superiority of the Torah and the special status of the Jews, the particular dispute here was whether Paul, in the eyes of the Corinthians, was a reliable authority or not. To paraphrase Paul, Why, O Corinthians, should you trust mere interpreters of Moses when I, Paul, am a conduit to God in your very midst, with whom you can actually interact?

17. Lloyd Gaston situates this exegetical project in its polemical context and notes that it was specifically written in opposition to Paul's (so-called Super-apostle) opponents; see Gaston, "2 Corinthians 3," in Gaston, *Paul*, 151–68.

18. Davies, "Paul," 11.

19. For a paradigmatic instance of recent responses to the "New Perspective" that defends the rejection-replacement model as the best interpretative lens for Paul, see Talbert, "Paul." Talbert argues against E. P. Sanders that much of Second Temple (or "Middle") Judaism was in fact "legalistic" and that Paul was attempting to replace this old works-righteousness approach with a new covenant on the basis of Jeremiah 31; although, as Talbert himself notes

("Paul," 19–20), this does make Paul rather anomalous as a first-century Jew and a unique interpreter of this passage in particular. Moreover, Talbert's loaded, theological terminology, especially legalism and grace, do little more than obscure ancient Jewish beliefs and practices. This same critique applies also to Simon Gathercole's *Boasting*, which similarly disputes Sanders's characterization of early Judaism as a religion of grace and election; in contrast, Gathercole argues that "boasting"—a thread he sees throughout early Judaism— requires a notion of merit, according to which "obedience" to the Law entitles one to be eschatologically saved. This argument, despite its caveats and claims to the contrary, still forges too close a link between obedience to the Law and salvation that abridges and obscures the various and diverse aims of the sources themselves. As we shall see, Paul's soteriology does not fit neatly into this artificial and modern dichotomy of grace vs. merit to which so many scholars remain irresistibly drawn. On some of the faulty assumptions underlying these supersessionist constructions of Judaism and Christianity, see Stowers, *Rereading*, 25.

20. Importantly, Paul considers himself called to a special role, and, while urging others to imitate him, he often boasts of his singular calling and gifts, and thus the inability of others in the Jesus movement to be like him (e.g., 1 Cor. 7; 2 Cor. 11—12; Rom. 15). On 1 Corinthians 9 and its reception history, see further Mitchell, "Pauline."

21. For a thorough introduction to the adaptability of a "psychagogue" in philosophical circles (in particular, the Epicureans) in the ancient Mediterranean and similarities found in Paul's approach to moral instruction, see further Glad, *Paul*.

22. Sanders, *Paul, Law, and Jewish People*, 190–92; cf. Fredriksen, "Judaism," 549; and Fredriksen, *Paul*, 82, 165, and 218n48.

23. A number of Pauline studies trace the "discovery" of the "Apocalyptic Paul" to Albert Schweitzer's *Mysticism*. In contrast, see Matlock (*Unveiling*, 47), who dryly points out, although Schweitzer is frequently "claimed" by subsequent proponents of apocalyptic interpretations of Paul, "one finds in Schweitzer's interpretation of Paul almost nothing about 'apocalyptic' as such." In making such a claim, Matlock is seemingly using a tongue-in-cheek definition for apocalyptic that does not include eschatological or cosmic considerations, but refers solely to revelatory practice.

24. See also 1 Corinthians 7:29–31; cf. 1 Corinthians 10:11 and 15:51ff.

25. Thus, history is the arena of God's "mighty acts," and certain pivotal moments determine its overall meaning; see Dodd, *Apostolic Preaching*, 95–96.

26. See the thought-provoking treatment of Paul and especially interpretations of Pauline conception(s) of salvation history by John Marshall in his "Misunderstanding."

27. See, for example, Romans 13:11–12.

28. 1 Corinthians 7:17–20.

29. As Ernst Käsemann (*New Testament*, 102) famously declared, "Apocalyptic was the mother of all Christian theology."

30. In contrast to Paul's *personal opinion* on the marriage of virgins (1 Cor. 7:25ff.), this is a commandment from God and the Lord.

31. In contrast, see Gaston ("Paul," in Gaston, *Paul*, 33) for the suggestion that Paul's message was simply inclusion of the gentiles and not a message that Jesus Christ was the Messiah for all (i.e., also for Jews): "For Paul, Jesus is neither a new Moses or the Messiah, he is not the climax of the history of God's dealing with Israel, but he is the fulfillment of God's promises concerning the Gentiles, and this is what he accused the Jews of not recognizing."

32. In a seminal article, Krister Stendahl persuasively argues—among other brilliant observations—that Romans 9–11 is the climax of the letter. See Stendahl, "Introspective Conscience," in Stendahl, *Paul*.

33. On the use of "Messiah" in Paul, I am informed by Novenson's *Christ*.

34. Gaston, "Retrospective," in Gaston, *Paul*, 7–11; Stowers, *Rereading*, 21–33; Gager, *Reinventing*, 43–46, 78, 107.

35. Gaston, "Paul," in Gaston, *Paul*, 28; cf. Stowers, *Rereading*, 191.

36. In addition to his *Rereading Romans*, see also Stowers, *Diatribe*; and Stowers, *Letter Writing*. In addition to Stowers's work, see Thorsteinsson, *Paul's Interlocutor*.

37. See especially Romans 2:28–29. On the hypocrisy of this Jewish teacher, see Epictetus, who ridicules someone "who is not really a Jew but plays the part" (*Diss.* 2.9.20: οὐκ ἔστιν Ἰουδαῖος, ἀλλ' ὑποκρίνεται; cf. Rev. 2:9 and 3:9). This provocative insult is part of a larger rhetorical argument found throughout the *Discourses* wherein Epictetus is castigating those who lay claim to a name (e.g., Stoic) for its reputation but are undeserving of it in practice (*Diss.* 2.19 and 3.24). See further Stowers, *Rereading Romans*, 144–151 (quote from 151): "[In opposition to this fictive Jewish teacher] Paul's approach was utterly different. Only God can make a person right with him, and he has chosen to justify the gentiles through Jesus Christ in a way analogous to Israel's becoming a righteous people through Abraham's faithfulness. Christ's coming fulfills the expectation that God would gratuitously save the gentile peoples at the end of the age when Israel will be restored."

38. As Gager (*Reinventing*, 147) summarily restates this point: "[Jewish members of the Jesus movement, like Peter,] play no positive role in Paul's thinking."

39. Stowers (*Rereading*, 205–6) delicately evades part of this issue by arguing for separate but interdependent salvific destinies for Israel and the gentiles.

40. Gaston, "Paul," in Gaston, *Paul*, 33; *pace* also Gaston's claim (*Paul*, 114–15, 139) that Paul does not view Jesus as the (Jewish) Messiah; see instead Romans 9:4–5, emphasis added: "They are Israelites, and to them belong the adoption, the glory, the covenants, the giving of the Law, the worship, and the promises; to them belong the patriarchs, and from them, according to the flesh, comes the Messiah, *who is over all*, God blessed forever. Amen." Cf. Romans 1: 1–4.

41. Davies ("People," 24–28) comes close to embracing this position of two covenants, one for Israel and one for the Nations, due to an extremely close and remarkably persuasive reading of Romans 11. Although Davies ultimately rejects this position, he does so in part because he believes faith in the Messiah has replaced the Torah as the sine qua non of inclusion in God's people (i.e., "Israel") and thus salvation ("Paul," 5 and 31). I dispute that Paul ever advocated that *Jews* (i.e., true members of Israel) should abandon the Torah; rather, in addition to Torah observance they must be baptized into Christ. For a critical overview of some of the problems with Gaston's claim, see Donaldson, "Jewish Christianity."

42. Galatians 2:7–9.

43. "Faithfulness" is a complex topic, immersed in a dense historiographic morass; see Pamela Eisenbaum's lucid and economic distillation (*Paul*, 243): "We have already seen . . . the debate over whether the expression *pistis christou* means 'faith in Christ,' as it is typically translated, or 'faith (faithfulness) of Christ.' Following the important work of Sam Williams, Lloyd Gaston, Richard Hays, and others, I argue for the latter interpretation and translate the phrase 'faithfulness of Christ.' This means that the term 'faith' in the phrase 'justification by faith' refers not to the believers' faith, but to Jesus' own faith."

44. My argument on this point is informed by Krister Stendahl (*Final Account*, 7) and Pinchas Lapide (*Paul*, 37–43). I am in full agreement with Stendahl's colorful comment that the salvation of the Jews and gentiles follows, according to Paul, God's preordained "traffic pattern," and with Lapide's pivotal contention that Paul did not preach a zero-sum scheme of salvific replacement, i.e., Christ has replaced the Law as the means to be saved. As Lapide notes, the Torah was never considered the means to be saved. Moreover, neither was the Law a problem for Jewish members of the Jesus movement; rather, Paul assumes its continued validity for Jewish adherents to the Jesus movement.

45. Cullmann, *Christ*, 84.

46. See below for my discussion of all three passages. On reconstructing the views of Paul's addressees or "mirror-reading," see further Barclay, "Mirror-Reading."

47. Despite Paul's situational adaptations, the coherence of many of his overarching themes and convictions remained consistent over his seven authentic letters and is, therefore, largely recoverable. On the dialectic between coherence and contingency, see further Beker, *Paul*.

48. As we see throughout his letters, Paul thought Christ's parousia would happen in his own lifetime; cf. 1 Thessalonians 1:10, 4:15–17; 1 Corinthians 7:26–31, 15:51, 16:22; Romans 13:11; Philippians 4:5.

49. It should be no surprise then that later Christians who saw themselves as world-savers, justified their claims through Pauline exegesis; see further my discussion of this point in Chapter 5; and Kocar, "'Humanity," 213 and 220.

50. Romans 11:29.

51. As Stanley Stowers astutely observes (*Rereading*, 298ff.), Paul repeatedly states that God can save and/or use people however he chooses (e.g., 8:28–30; 9:16–25; 11:25–26). This is God's modus operandi. Attempts to soften Paul's soteriological determinism inevitably shatter the coherence of his thought. Abraham Malherbe's ("Determinism") more subtle approach of unpacking how Paul deployed slogans (and their theoretical baggage) in the service of specific, practical concerns provides a much better way forward.

52. Romans 11:13–16. On this endearing egoism, see Krister Stendahl's colorful description (*Final Account*, 3) of the Apostle to the gentiles: "Paul was arrogant. But he was so blatantly arrogant that one can somehow cope with it. He was always the greatest: the greatest of sinners, the greatest of apostles, the greatest when it came to speaking in tongues, the greatest at having been persecuted. . . . The Messiah, Jesus Christ, chose this apostle for a specific task, and therefore all his writings are expressions of his ministry, and not diaries or journal notes about his inner struggles. . . . Paul was a Jew, hand-picked to be the apostle of Jesus Christ to the Gentiles."

53. See Wagner (*Heralds*, 286–94, citation from 291n225) and his nuanced characterization of this reordering of Isaiah's narrative, calling Paul's gentile "delegates" a "proleptic realization of Isaiah's prophecy in 60:3–9."

54. As E. P. Sanders observed (*Paul, Law, and Jewish People*, 185), Paul would revise biblical history and "rearrange the eschatological sequence so that it accords with the facts." Cf. Fredriksen, "Judaism."

55. This reparation takes the form of the collection for the saints in Jerusalem (Rom. 15; 1 Cor. 16; 2 Cor. 8–9; Gal. 2).

56. Beker, "Faithfulness."

57. As we shall see (e.g., 1 Cor. 7), Paul expected all individuals—whether Jew or gentile—to excel in the state in which they were called.

58. Although Paul's tailored ethic for gentiles is structurally similar to the rabbinic Noahide Commandments insofar as they are guidelines for acceptable gentile conduct, they differ in content as well as purpose; see further below.

59. For an extended treatment of the discourse of ethnicity in Paul's milieu that highlights its apparent malleability, see further Concannon, *Gentiles.*

60. *Contra* N. T. Wright, James D. G. Dunn, Daniel Boyarin, et al., who conclude that because Jews and gentiles are both saved in Christ, Paul has abolished all ethnic difference. As we shall see in my discussion of Pauline soteriology (especially Gal. 3) below, these two, distinct issues ought not to be homogenized. On the continued importance of ethnic categories, even in Christ, see Johnson Hodge, *If Sons.*

61. Meeks and Fitzgerald, *Writings,* 3. See also Meeks, "Social Functions."

62. For an instance of opposition to unpacking Paul's ethical and/or theological convictions in light of the various contexts behind his "occasional letters," see Stowers, "Friends."

63. 1 Thessalonians 4:13–18.

64. As John Gager observed half a century ago, Paul could deploy the same language or concepts (e.g., "end-time language") for various reasons and in support of a multitude of contextual concerns. See Gager, "Functional Diversity."

65. For an exceptionally readable and useful summary of the "Old Paul," see Gager, *Reinventing,* chapter 1; on this section in particular, see Johnson Hodge, *If Sons,* 100–103.

66. Räisänen, "Paul," 180; cf. Terence Donaldson ("Jewish Christianity"), who presents the strongest defense of some traditional elements of the "Old Paul" in response to "radical" new Paul scholars (e.g., Stanley Stowers, John Gager, and Lloyd Gaston).

67. See *Former Jew* by Love L. Sechrest, which attempts to revive and defend, albeit without great success, this traditional view against recent scholarship, especially Johnson Hodge.

68. See, for example, the early claim to supersession in Acts 28:25–28.

69. As a new Jeremiah of sorts, it may be that Jeremiah 31 is motivating Paul here to create these rhetorical binaries. Furthermore, the lack of clarity on Paul's part likely reflects that he did not expect any non-Jesus-following Jews to have read his Letter to the Romans. According to my interpretation, therefore, the "community ethics" section of Romans (chapters 12–15) does not, as some commentators have suggested, assume a mix of gentiles ("strong in faith") and Jews ("weak in faith"), who may or may not be followers of Jesus. Instead, on the basis of parallels with 1 Corinthians, it is far more likely that these two categories were two types of gentiles, where the "weak in faith" are analogous to those gentile believers distressed over members of the community eating meat sacrificed to idols (1 Cor. 8 and 10). *Pace* Nanos, *Mystery,* chapter 3. Cf. William Campbell ("Addressees," 187), who comes to a similar conclusion, albeit for different reasons, i.e., gentiles making accommodations to Jewish dietary and ritual concerns: "This reconstruction [of the 'weak' and 'strong'] leaves us with Paul directly addressing Christ-followers, all of whom are of Gentile origin, but who are severely divided in their attitudes toward Jews and Judaism and who label each other with reference to perceived preferences for and against association with Jewish groups."

70. Romans 11:1–3.

71. Jewett, *Romans,* 701–2.

72. On the importance of recognizing the gentile composition of Paul's audience in Romans, see now Thiessen, *Paul,* chapter 2.

73. Stowers, *Rereading,* 300.

74. Even if this concern was largely rhetorical and aimed to set up the powerful conclusion that God will not reject his people and that all of Israel will be saved (Rom. 11), Paul's grief over his Jewish brethren must have been intelligible to the gentile recipients of his Letter to the Romans who were concerned about the salvation of Israel and the Nations.

75. Gaston, "Israel's Misstep," in Gaston, *Paul*, 146.

76. See Chapter 1 for my criticism of this prevalent interpretation of ancient Judaism as a "missionizing religion."

77. See further Donaldson, "Jewish Christianity," especially 34–35.

78. Stendahl, *Final Account*, 7.

79. What is shared here is the road (soteriological means); how one traverses the road (ethical comportment) is different for Jews and gentiles.

80. Paul has expressed this somewhat contorted logic by means of his famous athletic metaphor of Israel and the Nations running a race; see further Stanley Stowers (*Rereading Romans,* 305), who emphasizes that, according to Paul, the race is fixed: "Paul entirely subverts the logic of his own [athletic] metaphor. Races are about will, effort, achievement, and well-earned rewards. But 9:16 says, 'so it depends not on a person's will or a person's running but on God who shows mercy.' The race is fixed. God has predestined the outcome."

81. Cf. Nanos, *Mystery*, chapter 5.

82. On the meaning of a "full number" of gentiles, see Aus, "Paul's Travel"; cf. Hvalvik, "Sonderweg," especially 100–101.

83. On this instrumentalization, see Stowers, *Rereading,* 300–301.

84. The importance of Israel's *Sonderplatz* cannot be overstated; it permeates all of Paul's thinking about the salvation of Israel and the Nations. Attempts to universalize Paul (erase all ethnic and ethical differences) will inevitably collapse under the stress of these eisegetical readings, because of their inability to account for Paul's tailored messages to Israel and the Nations (1 Cor. 9:19–23), of which, only his messages to the Nations survive.

85. See Esler, "Ancient Oleiculture"; see also Jeremiah 11:16 and Hosea 14:6 for this evocative image of Israel as an olive tree.

86. In his commentary, Origen goes so far as to claim that what Paul has described is impossible (*Comm. Rom.* 8.10); Esler, "Ancient Oleiculture," 115.

87. Esler, "Ancient Oleiculture," 122.

88. Stowers, *Rereading,* chapter 10; Johnson Hodge, *If Sons,* chapter 8.

89. Davies, "Paul," especially 30.

90. See Philip Esler's conclusion ("Ancient Oleiculture," 123–24): "Moreover, by situating this image within its ancient oleicultural context and attending closely to how Paul blatantly subverts the prevailing practice among olive cultivators, we are left with a rather negative picture of the non-Israelite members of the Christ movement. They are attached to the olive tree in a way that is παρὰ φύσιν. Not only do they not contribute to it, since they will not produce fruit, but they are actually parasitic upon its richness."

91. *Pace* A. G. Baxter and J. A. Ziesler ("Paul"), who contend that the engrafting of the wild branches (gentiles) will revive and rejuvenate the withered and sick tree of Israel.

92. Matthew Thiessen argues this claim frequently and to great effect (the following citation is from *Paul*, 68; cf. his more extensive discussion in chapter 3 of the same monograph) by pointing out that a gentile who attempts to become a Torah-observant Jew through circumcision is doomed to failure, since circumcision must occur on the eighth day: "A gentile undergoing circumcision in order to become a Jew fails to keep the law of

circumcision in the very act of being circumcised. He is circumcised and yet becomes a transgressor of the law of circumcision through the letter, *gramma* (understood as the detail or prescription of the law), and through the rite of circumcision." See also Christine Hayes's clear articulation and defense of Paul as a "genealogical exclusivist" (*Divine Law*, 150).

93. See further Caroline Johnson Hodge's excellent treatment (*If Sons*) of the issues of gentile inclusion into the lineage of Abraham through Christ with the result that gentiles can now become "coheirs."

94. Stowers, "Pauline Participation," 359–60; see also Engberg-Pedersen, *Cosmology*.

95. *Pace* Boyarin (*Radical Jew*, 3–4), who states that this passage (Galatians 3:26–28) is his hermeneutical key for all of Paul's letters.

96. As we shall see below, Paul did *not* propose a one-to-one correspondence between soteriology and ethics. Segal (*Paul*, 169, emphasis added) touches upon this important recognition: "Paul thus appears occasionally to approve of the commandments of Judaism and to recommend them as ethical models for Christian behavior, *if the issue is ethical behavior rather than the salvation process.*"

97. See further Nanos (*Mystery*, 179–201), who rightly emphasizes the significance of the Shema (Deut. 6:4: "Hear, O Israel, the Lord our God, the Lord is one") for Paul's soteriology.

98. See W. D. Davies ("Paul," 23), who noted that even in Christ ethnic distinctions will remain.

99. *Pace* Caroline Johnson Hodge (*If Sons,* chapter 7), who argues that gentiles "in" Christ have joined Israel; although her point that people can have more than one identity marker is certainly correct, in this case I see no compelling reason for why a gentile in Christ would also become part of Israel. In short, being a part of Israel is not coterminous with being an heir to Abraham.

100. For an accessible overview of the exceptionally rich historiography on this issue, see further Johnson Hodge, *If Sons*.

101. Sam Williams, "Promise."

102. 2 Cor. 1:21–2. As Stanley Stowers ("Pauline Participation," 356) has rightly emphasized, this *pneuma* or spirit is rarified yet still *physical* "stuff": "Humans participate in Adam because they share bodies consisting of the same stuff as Adam (1 Cor. 15:42–49). Those in Christ participate in him because they share with him the most sublime kind of pneuma, divine pneuma, that he received in being resurrected from the dead."

103. On the issue of "sanctification," wherein profane gentiles are rendered holy, see now Fredriksen, *Paul*, 151–54. See also M. David Litwa (*Transformed*), who considers what it would mean to be "morally and materially" transformed into something Christ-like, that is, something *like* the divine; contrary to Litwa's advocacy, however, I still prefer the language of "participation" to "deification."

104. 1 Corinthians 3:16, 6:19; 2 Corinthians 6:16. In addition to the works by Klawans and Hayes cited in Chapter 1, see also Fredriksen, "Paul," especially 212–13, and Fredriksen, "Judaizing," 244ff.

105. Romans 8: 9–11; Galatians 2:19–20. As Caroline Johnson Hodge suggests (*If Sons*, 73), Ezekiel 36:26–28 is likely an intertext here. Cf. Romans 8:3–4.

106. 1 Corinthians 1:22–24; Galatians 2:15–16; 1 Corinthians 12:12–13.

107. It is unpersuasive to conclude that Christ was, in Paul's eyes, soteriologically effective exclusively for gentiles. Proponents of this view depend upon an argument from silence

in Romans 9–11 as well as rather idiosyncratic readings of a number of other passages; see, for example, John Gager's (*Reinventing*, 84–87) interpretation, which follows Lloyd Gaston, of the inclusive ἄνθρωπος of Galatians 2:15–16 as referring exclusively to gentiles, despite it following Paul's first-person-plural declaration that "we who are Jews by birth . . ." See below for my interpretation of Galatians 2:15–16.

108. Hvalvik, "Sonderweg," 89–91.

109. As we have seen, Paul never rejected Torah practice among Jewish followers of Jesus. Torah was never the means for salvation; what it was and continues to be is a God-given gift entrusted to his special people as a symbol of his enduring promises to their ancestors. See Pinchas Lapide's (*Paul*, 37) discussion of exactly this point: "Even more significant is the contrast of Christ and Torah, in which Christ is said to have replaced the Torah as the way to Salvation, as Paul writes, 'if justification were through the Law, then Christ died for no purpose' (Gal 2:21). Here a faithful Jew can only shake his head in bewilderment. The rabbinate has never even considered the Torah as a way to salvation to God. The Torah is absolutely *not* a means of achieving salvation, for Judaism knows no such means."

110. A number of recent studies that purport to problematize Sanders's contributions and/or seek to move us "beyond the New Perspective" have done little else besides returning to and championing theologically motivated (namely supersessionist) arguments. Two of the more recent examples are Simon Gathercole's' *Boasting* and Francis Watson's *Paul*.

111. *Pace* Pamela Eisenbaum (*Paul*, 251–52, 255), who attempts to sidestep some possible rebuttals to the two-covenant approach by emphasizing the role of grace and appealing to religious pluralism.

112. On the use of the subjective genitive (faithfulness *of* Christ) as opposed to the objective genitive (faith *in* Christ), see further Hays, *Faith*.

113. Nanos, *Mystery*, 183.

114. This, I believe, is the greatest shortcoming of Terence Donaldson's otherwise excellent work, i.e., his failure to recognize that God, in Paul's eyes, has assigned different people to different roles. Instead, Donaldson universalizes the condemnation of the Law in order to argue for a single solution, i.e., gentile conversion to a "redefined" people of Israel. This, however, falsely conflates soteriology with ethics, in particular the gentile negative obligation to not practice a modified form of Torah observance. The Law is not in itself negative; it should, quite simply, not be a consideration in the first place for gentiles seeking to be saved. Thus, Paul's point is that gentiles should not deviate from God's plan by adopting modified Torah practice or even converting. Gentiles should trust God's plan and stay as they are. See further Donaldson, *Paul*, chapters 5 and 8.

115. Christine Hayes (*Divine Law*, 149) presents a fascinating argument that justification through Christ, according to Paul, would enable Jews to practice the Law effortlessly: "Having died to the body with Christ, Jews also are freed from the bodily passions and desires that prevented them from fulfilling the Torah perfectly. . . . Freed of sin (justified) through faith in Christ Jesus, Jews will be able to fulfill the Law effortlessly as intended and envisaged by Jeremiah 31 and Ezekiel 36."

A number of scholars have suggested that Paul believed *missionizing* practices were also expected of *good* Jews, i.e., to "be a light to the world." This is possible, however unlikely. Increasingly the supposed consensus that ancient Judaism was a missionizing religion has been shown to be largely unfounded; instead, texts, such as Isaiah 42:6 and 49:6, were meant to reinforce ethical excellence internally by encouraging one's community to become exemplars for right conduct and behavior for others to imitate. Similarly, Paul expects the majority of his fellow Jews to be moral exemplars, not missionaries; Paul considered his own missionizing practices to be part of his special prophetic call and not an expectation for all Jews. Cf. Fredriksen, "Judaism," 538–39.

116. See, for example, Galatians 5:14 and 1 Corinthians 10:23.

117. 1 Corinthians 7:29–31.

118. Paula Fredriksen (*Paul*, 118) has noted that a number of Paul's dictates to his gentile believers overlap with the Decalogue. Rather than Paul requiring the Ten Commandments as such, however, it is more likely that what we have here is a case of the lowest common denominator in terms of rules for the preservation of social harmony and purity among those gentiles already in Christ.

119. See Longenecker, *Eschatology*, 264.

120. See also Isaiah 45:14; Micah 4:13; and Tobit 13:11.

121. Aus, "Paul's Travel."

122. Romans 11:25: τὸ πλήρωμα τῶν ἐθνῶν; see further Aus, "Paul's," 251–52. "Tarshish" in Isaiah 66:19 should, according to Aus ("Paul's," 242–46) be interpreted as "Tartessos."

123. Aus, "Paul's Travel," 257–60.

124. Paul also subtly exhorted his gentile addressees in Rome to financially support his eschatologically oriented mission to Spain (Rom. 15:24a): "For I do hope to see you on my journey, and to be sent on by you (ὑφ' ὑμῶν προπεμφθῆναι)." See further Jewett, *Romans*, 924–26.

125. Gager, *Reinventing*, 61–62.

126. See further Mitchell, *Paul*; and Martin, *Corinthian Body*.

127. For a useful introduction and discussion of the conceptual framework and content of the Noahide Commandments (e.g., t. Sand. 13.2; t. AZ 8.4), see further Segal, *Paul*, 187–223; Segal, "Universalism"; Novak, *Image*; Nanos, *Mystery*, 50–56 and chapter 4; and Donaldson, *Paul*. See also my discussion of the social situation and aims of the Noahide Commandments and the "Rules of the Sojourner" in Chapter 1, especially notes 25 and 63.

128. Nanos, *Mystery*, 177. According to Nanos (*Mystery*, 168), Luke's Apostolic Decree "stands somewhere between" the biblical Rules for the Sojourner (e.g., Lev. 17–18) and the rabbinic Noahide Commandments.

129. Nanos, *Mystery*, 53; cf. Acts 15:20, 29.

130. In addition to the two reasons I will provide, one might add that Paul never mentioned anything like the Apostolic Decree (*pace* Nanos's [*Mystery*, chapter 4] unpersuasive attempts to find such an allusion, e.g., Romans 6:17–19: "obedience to *that* form of teaching"). Generally speaking, Luke's later versions of events tell us much less about the historical Paul than they do about Luke and his historical situation. Consequently, we should exercise much greater caution in reading Luke back into Paul.

131. Stowers, *Rereading*, 151. Recently, Matthew Thiessen (*Paul*, 43ff.) has persuasively argued that Paul's opponent in Romans 2 is a Judaizing gentile; cf. my discussion of Revelation 2:9 and 3:9 in Chapter 1, especially notes 52–55. Whoever Paul's opponent is, it is clear that, according to Paul, a gentile cannot be made righteous through Torah observance.

132. *Pace* Donaldson (*Paul*, chapter 8), who argues for a much more *formal* and causal link between the conduct of a righteous gentile and justification or inclusion within his "reconfigured Israel."

133. À la Carl Sagan, Matthew Thiessen (*Paul,* 150) construes this point more poetically, connecting *pneuma* to star stuff: "Enabled by Christ's *pneuma* to participate in the pattern of Christ's life, Paul's gentiles can live a moral life that is comparable to the unblemished life of the stars."

134. Mark Nanos has argued extensively that Paul preached the Apostolic Decree in order for Jews and gentiles to eat and worship together; while it is certainly true that Paul would have expected gentile accommodation so that both could dine together, there is no evidence that Paul systematically included the Apostolic Decree as his baseline for normative gentile behavior. Instead, he urged ethical solidarity and claimed that care for others should determine one's actions; see 1 Corinthians 10:31–33.

135. See further Segal, *Paul,* 236ff.

136. As we shall see in Part II, the danger of apostasy and postbaptismal sin was a significant social and theoretical problem among subsequent generations of Jesus followers.

137. Caird, "Review," 542–43; cf. Watson, *Paul,* 7.

138. This divide is, of course, an outdated cliché to some but still gospel truth to others. For an excellent deconstruction of the creation of Christianity as a "universalist" religion, see further Denise Kimber Buell ("Race"; *New Race*), who demonstrates that Christianity's invention of a "universal *genos*" was not the abolition of categories but a historically situated invention meant to argue for the superiority of the Christian *genos*.

3. IN HEAVEN AS IT IS ON EARTH

1. The textual coherence of the *Shepherd of Hermas* is disputed. Although *Hermas* contains three smaller collections (5 *Visions,* 12 *Mandates,* and 10 *Similitudes*), I am persuaded that (with the possible exception of *Similitude* 10; see below for my analysis) the *Shepherd* was composed over time but still as a unity before it was divided into the smaller subcollections that characterize its later circulation. For surviving instances and discussions of these subcollections, see further Osiek, *Shepherd,* 1–10.

2. The standard edition of all four manuscripts is Waldstein and Wisse's *Apocryphon.*

3. I do not want to be mistaken for claiming that John or Paul were unconcerned with practical matters (e.g., Rev. 2–3; Rom. 12–15); rather, I want to signal that my emphases will be different in how I introduce and discuss both texts.

4. See Chapter 4.

5. See Christine Trevett's pellucid overview of repentance in the second century, "'I Have Heard.'" See also Dallen, *Reconciling.*

6. Hebrews 6:4–6; cf. 10:26–31; 12:17.

7. *De pud.* 20. Tertullian even cites Hebrews 6. Compare, however, Tertullian's earlier views (*De paen.* 12.1), in which he allowed limited repentance.

8. Polycarp, *Philippians,* 6; cf. Dionysius of Corinth, who, as reported by Eusebius (*Hist. eccl.* 4.23.6), advocates total forgiveness of all penitent sinners.

9. Cf. Ignatius, *Trallians* 1–3; for a similar consolidation of authority into the hands of the presbyters, see 1 Clement 57; and Polycarp, *Philadelphians* 6.

10. See the studies by Allen Brent (*Hippolytus*), Peter Lampe (*Paul*), and Harry Maier (*Social*). Cf. Hermas, *Vis.* 3.9.7–10; *Sim.* 8.7.4–6 and 9.31.

11. See, for example, Matthew 7:21 and the *Gospel of Truth* (33.1–32), which reduce ethical obligation to obedience to the "will of the Father."

12. Often sin is represented or discussed through metaphors of what it is like and/or entails in legalistic (breach of contract or debt) or ritual (pollution) language. For a general introduction, see Fredriksen, *Sin*.

13. Clement (*Stromata* 2) and Origen (*Peri archon* 3) are noteworthy members of the latter camp. For a lengthier discussion of these differences, see further my discussion of competing notions of moral responsibility in Chapter 5.

14. Bauckham, "Apocalypse"; and Himmelfarb, *Tours*. Although there are a number of issues with the manuscript tradition, Clement of Alexandria (*Ecl.* 41, 48) quotes from the text, thereby providing an *ante quem* of the late second/early third century; it is possible that Theophilus of Antioch (*Ad Autolycum* II, 19) alludes to a passage preserved in the Akhmimic recension (Schneemelcher, *NTA*, 2:634), which would place the *ante quem* at ca. 180 CE.

15. See Himmelfarb, *Tours*, 68–105.

16. Schneemelcher, *NTA*, 2:628 (Akhmimic recension, 22).

17. Schneemelcher, *NTA*, 2:629 (Akhmimic recension, 24).

18. Schneemelcher, *NTA*, 2:629 (Ethiopic recension, 7).

19. For an outsider's perspective on these practices, see further *Contra Celsum* 6.15; cf. 1 Clement 51, 57; 2 Clement 16.

20. To the best of my knowledge, no one has previously written on the theoretical and social impact of *Hermas*'s higher and lower levels of salvation, argued that the *Ap. John*'s two tiers of salvation address the communal problem of ethical variance, or compared and contrasted the forms and implications of *Hermas* and the *Ap. John*'s higher and lower levels of salvation.

21. Cf. Didache 6.2: "For if you can bear the whole yoke of the Lord (τὸν ζυγὸν τοῦ κυρίου), you will be perfect (τέλειος). But if you cannot, do as much as you are able."

22. Michael Williams, "Life," 20.

23. I borrow the term "auto-Orientalizing" from Dylan Burns's *Alien God*.

24. A (and possibly *the most*) prevalent instance of this is scholars who look to Greco-Roman philosophical parallels to explain the *system*—thereby imbibing Irenaeus's heresiological rhetoric (*Haer.* 1)—of so-called heretical thought. As Mark Edwards (*Origen*, 8) observed with respect to Origen, however, this mistakes the education of a writer for his or her commitments and aims. For an example of the differing questions available and outcomes possible when using *comparanda* from biblical and philosophical sources in the study of so-called heretical texts, see further Kocar, "'Humanity.'"

25. See Morton Smith's seminal article ("History") pointing out the different and inexplicable ways in which the term *gnostikos* is used by modern scholars when describing so-called heretics, as opposed to how it is used in studies on Clement of Alexandria, who self-identifies as a "gnostic." In actuality, the practice of separating orthodox and heterodox texts has no historical utility but rather serves to buttress modern theological and apologetic concerns. See further Karen King, *Gnosticism*, 218; cf. Koester, "*GNOMAI*," 115–17.

26. I am also provisionally setting aside labels such as "Sethian" (which I support) and "Gnostic" (which I reject) for the *Apocryphon of John* in the interest of avoiding additional categorical distinctions. Despite the important contributions of Michael Williams (*Rethinking*) and Karen King (*Gnosticism*), the dominant practice among scholars is to continue using "gnostic" and other terms that reinscribe modern categories of normative vs. marginal; what has changed is that scholars recognize the fraught and tenuous nature of Gnosticism itself and signal this with scare quotes (i.e., "Gnosticism").

27. On the connection between gentiles (non-Jews) and the very term *Christian*, see further Townsend, "First Christians."

28. For example, as the events of Christ's life and death became increasingly distant, the fervor for his imminent parousia began to cool for many as well. An earlier and better-known instance of precisely this sort of growing pain is the dilemma faced by the author of 2 Thessalonians, who must confront the listlessness and ethical laxness that sets in as the community adapts to a lengthier wait for the parousia; see, for example, 2 Thess. 3.11–13. On the phrase "ex-pagan pagans," see Fredriksen, *Paul*, 34.

29. On this use of *rhetorical exempla* for ethical paraenesis, see Philip Tite's overview (*Valentinian*, 147–64) of the use of moral *exempla* in the Greco-Roman world.

30. *Sim.* 8. Importantly, all are *saved* in the same way as well, i.e., only by accepting "the name of God's Son" (*Sim.* 9.12.4).

31. *Metanoia* is a difficult term to properly render; some scholars prefer conversion over repentance. Repentance, however, captures both the change in social and mental disposition and the recurrent idea of returning to the proper moral code that will be a focus of mine here (*Man.* 4.3); though recurrent, this motif of turning back is not always present or emphasized (cf. *Vis.* 2.2.4). For a discussion of difficulties in translating *metanoia*, see further Osiek, *Shepherd*, 28–30; and Lipsett, *Desiring Conversion*, 19–20.

32. *Metanoia* may, therefore, retain its two different meanings here: repentance *and* conversion.

33. As of the 2007, Eldon Epp ("New Testament," 319n1) counted ten papyri and one parchment copy of the Gospel of John and thirteen papyri and two parchment copies of the Gospel of Matthew. In 2018, Brent Nongbri (*God's Library*, 231) put those numbers at still fifteen total copies of Matthew but now fourteen total copies of John.

34. The ten previously known Greek fragments of the *Shepherd of Hermas* from Oxyrhynchus are *P.Oxy.* 404, 1172+3526, 1599, 1783, 1828, 3527, 3528, 4705, 4706, and 4707. A fourth- or fifth-century Coptic fragment has recently been edited by Geoffrey S. Smith ("*Shepherd*"). On the late antique circulation and consumption of the *Shepherd of Hermas* based on manuscript evidence from Egypt, see Malcolm Choat and Rachel Yuen-Collingridge's "Egyptian Hermas."

35. It is also included in the list attached to Codex Claromontanus (Osiek, *Shepherd*, 6). For an up-to-date survey, with relevant bibliography, on the topic of the *Shepherd of Hermas* and its relationship with the New Testament canon, see Batovici, "Shepherd."

36. For a deft and thorough overview of some of the major scholarly debates, see Gamble, "New Testament."

37. See David Brakke ("Scriptural Practices"), who considers the creation and diverse use of subcollections in order to shift the scholarly debate away from exclusive preoccupation with the teleological questions of when and in what context the canon was "closed."

38. See further Osiek (*Shepherd*, 4–7), who discusses, for example, how both Clement and Irenaeus refer to *Hermas* as scripture.

39. See Lipsett (*Desiring Conversion*, 27): "Hermas is neither epistle, nor tractate, nor manual, nor homily, but story . . . with minimal plot—little action, but much talk. Long passages are given to description as Hermas relates the visions he is given."

40. The problem is not—despite how *Hermas* describes it—that the church has become schismatic and rivalrous; rather *Hermas* is attempting to unify and reform the church by rhetorically retrojecting its utopian ideals into the past. Thus, *Hermas*'s appeal to church

unity was not a reflection of an attenuated past reality, but rather it is a pioneering voice attempting to address the theological and social difficulties faced by fourth- or fifth-generation followers of Jesus. A central concern for *Hermas* was the proper use of wealth and the disastrous consequences if it was ill used: *Vis.* 1:1.8–9; 3:3.5–6; 3:9.2–10; *Man.* 6.2.5; 8:3, 10; 10.1.4; 10:4.2–3; 12:2.1–2; *Sim.* 1:1–11; 2:1–10; 5:2.9–11; 5:3.7–8; 9:19:3; 9:30.4–5; 9:31.2; 10:4.2; see further Osiek, *Rich and Poor.*

41. Osiek (*Shepherd*, 18) adds also that the "description of vines grown on elm trees in *Similitude* 2 is characteristic of central Italy."

42. See J. Christian Wilson (*Reassessment*, 60–61), who, in part due to this link with Romans, dates *Hermas* to approximately 80–100 CE.

43. The author of 1 Clement, who is conventionally dated to the last two decades of the first century; see Lampe, *Paul,* 206–17.

44. Osiek, *Shepherd,* 18–19.

45. Irenaeus's reference (*Haer.* 4.20.2) to *Man.* 1, where he cites it as "Scripture," provides an *ante quem* of approximately 180 CE.

46. Fox, *Pagans,* 381: "Yet [*Hermas's*] author is the early Christian whom we know best after St. Paul."

47. Lampe, *Paul,* 218–20; cf. Osiek, *Shepherd,* 23–28.

48. Osiek, *Shepherd,* 18–19.

49. *Vis.* 2.4.3: "And so, you will write two little books, sending one to Clement and the other to Grapte. Clement will send his to the foreign cities, for that is his commission." I have consulted the Greek and the English found in Ehrman's *Apostolic Fathers;* my translations, however, will often differ in order to call attention to and clarify certain terms and for stylistic reasons.

50. Koester, *Introduction,* 2:12. On the anachronisms apparent in the Muratorian Canon, especially of a monarchial episcopacy, see now Brent, *Hippolytus,* chapter 7.

51. Translated by Osiek, *Shepherd,* 18–19n141.

52. Some scholars have appealed to other factors in addition to the three pegs; for example, Hermas's lack of monarchial episcopacy (*Vis.* 2.4.3; 3.1.8; see Maier, *Social,* 55ff.). This, however, does not provide a secure date.

53. Osiek, *Shepherd,* 23–24.

54. Emblematic of this negative view is B. H. Streeter's characterization of Hermas as the "White Rabbit" from among the apostolic fathers: "He was timid and fussy, a 'kindly, incompetent middle-aged freedman, delightfully naïve,' whose writing, said Streeter, showed his 'pottering mediocrity.'" Trevett, "I Have Heard," 9, citing B. H. Streeter, *The Primitive Church* (London, 1929), 203. For a general overview of past scholarship on *Hermas*, see Osiek's useful summary (*Shepherd,* 8–10).

55. Osiek, *Shepherd,* 8ff. Further strengthening the argument for a single author and weakening the hypothesis that subcollections of *Hermas* first circulated independently is the fact that early Christians, such as Clement of Alexandria and Origen, treat *Hermas* as a unity and already quote from all three parts (*Visions, Mandates,* and *Similitudes*). Citing *Hermas's* overall linguistic, theological, and conceptual consistency, J. Christian Wilson (*Reassessment,* 22–23) affirms the hypothesis of a single author and suggests the useful parallel of Luke-Acts for understanding *Hermas* insofar as both are the work of a single author over an extended period.

56. Osiek, *Shepherd,* 12–16; and Osiek, "Oral World."

57. Osiek, *Shepherd,* 15–16.

58. I have some reservations that *Similitude* 10, due to its uneven manuscript transmission—surviving almost exclusively in Latin (for the exception, see *P.Oxy.* 404, which preserves Greek fragments of *Sim.* 10.3 and 10.4)—and clearly appended nature, comes from the same author as the rest of *Hermas*. My approach throughout this book is to treat texts as unities unless it is absolutely necessary to engage in source criticism; nonetheless, I will exercise some caution with respect to *Similitude* 10. For a helpful, general summary of the manuscripts, see Osiek, *Shepherd*, 1–4; see also Ehrman's list (*Apostolic Fathers*, 2:170–71) of the contents of the various surviving manuscripts.

59. See the survey of scholarship in Osiek, "Genre"; and Osiek, *Shepherd*, 10–11.

60. In fact, *Hermas* contains more of such elements than the average "Christian apocalypse"; see Osiek ("Genre," 115): "For those impressed by statistics, of the 28 elements suggested as constitutive of apocalyptic form, *Hermas* possesses 16 of them, in a list of Christian apocalypses whose average number is 13.3."

61. Osiek (*Shepherd*, 11) lists those scholars who advocate that *Hermas* should *not* be classified as an apocalypse.

62. Vielhauer and Strecker, "Apocalyptic," 599.

63. Osiek, *Shepherd*, 11.

64. Clement, *Strom.* 1.29.181.1; cf. *Strom.* 2.1.3.5. For other, modern modifiers, see David Aune (*Prophecy*, 299–310), who characterizes different segments of *Hermas* as "Salvation-Judgment Oracles" (*Visions* 1–4); "Oracles of Assurance" (*Mandates*); and "Parenetic Salvation-Judgment Oracles" (*Similitudes*).

65. As Carolyn Osiek observed ("Genre"), this function (e.g., providing divine sanction and authority for its ethical paraenesis) is unfortunately overlooked when scholars are concerned only about specific genre traits such as historical speculation or concrete crises. In short, I agree with Adela Yarbo Collins's pithy conclusion ("Early Christian," 74–75) that "there is no good reason to exclude [*Hermas*] from the genre of apocalypse."

66. For the apt description of Hermas's language as "folksy," see Lampe, *Paul*, 233; Lipsett (*Desiring Conversion*, 39) dryly refers to Hermas's repetitive style as its "principle of copiousness."

67. Miller, *Dreams*, 138: "In Hermas' text, there is a metonymous movement from the literary consciousness of Hermas as author to the oneiric consciousness of Hermas as dreamer and on to the interpretative consciousness of the individual reader and the communal assembly of readers for whom the text operates as a mirror."

68. See the list of scholars ridiculing *Hermas* and the acumen of its author in Wilson, *Reassessment*, 2.

69. In addition to these, see the vices listed in *Mandate* 8.

70. William Wilson, "Career," 35, cited in Trevett, "I Have Heard," 10–11n27: "If men such as Hermas had become the real leaders of Christianity, if such books as his had made up the New Testament, the church could hardly have survived."

71. Meeks, *Origins*, 126.

72. Miller, *Dreams*, 142.

73. For additional discussion on the eroticized scenes of *Hermas*, see the excellent chapter by Lipsett, *Desiring Conversion*, 19–53.

74. Lipsett, *Desiring Conversion*, 20.

75. *Hermas* makes these claims in *Vis.* 3.10 (and more elaborately in *Vis.* 3.11–13); yet, as Osiek (*Shepherd*, 84–85) observes, the "rejuvenation" of both Hermas and Lady Church is introduced for the first time here and not in prior appearances of Lady Church.

76. Miller, *Dreams*, 145.

77. Miller, *Dreams*, 147.

78. We will return to this theme in the following chapter.

79. Peter Brown (*Body*, 69) attributes much of *Hermas*'s literary success to its realistic and relatable portrait of Hermas's internal conflict.

80. Already by the third century images from *Hermas* had been translated into art; for example, the Catacomb of San Gennaro at Naples preserves an image that resembles the idealized tower from *Similitude* 9. See further the bibliography provided by Osiek, *Shepherd*, 7.

81. Miller, "All the Words," 332.

82. As we will see when I return to this issue in Chapter 4, the goal of this externalizing process is ethical self-reflection; see further Miller, *Dreams*, 145. On the interaction between imagined and social space and its role in constructing communal ethics, see the recent article by Maier, "Material Place," 144–45.

83. *Sim.* 2.3–6.

84. Cf. Paul's similar use of the body of Christ; see further Mitchell, *Paul*; and Martin, *Corinthian Body*.

85. Lipsett, *Desiring Conversion*, 37.

86. See further Candida Moss (*Other Christs*), who explores the various, higher salvific honors martyrs were said to enjoy, e.g., immediate entry into heaven bypassing the general resurrection, priority seating, as well as thrones and crowns; cf. Karen King, Secret *Revelation*, 143.

87. This hierarchy between saints (specifically martyrs) and normal or the majority of Christians is another instance of higher and lower levels of salvation. It is important to note, however, that unlike *Hermas* or the *Ap. John* Tertullian is not deploying salvific difference to address the problem of sin or to advocate repentance.

88. See Thomassen, "Orthodoxy and Heresy."

89. In this characterization, I am influenced by Michael Williams's work (*"Life of Antony"*) on the domestication of charismatic authority.

90. For the full context, see further *Sim.* 8.7.3–8.3.

91. Osiek, *Shepherd*, 206; cf. 2 Clement 7.6, 8.6.

92. See further Chapter 4.

93. Cf. 2 Clement 8–9, which rhetorically highlights the limited time available for repentance for similar purposes.

94. Karen King, *Secret Revelation*, vii.

95. Michael Williams, *Rethinking*, 247–55.

96. Karen King, *Secret Revelation*, 215–24, 235–38; Rasimus, *Paradise Reconsidered*, 243–79, esp. 267–68; and John Turner, "Johannine Legacy."

97. Pleše, *Poetics*, 1: "A fair number of scribal errors (e.g., *saut du même au même*, haplography) in the four witnesses leave no doubt that each was copied from a Coptic exemplar."

98. Some scholars speculate it may be earlier, while others would prefer a later date. Often these debates revolve around reconstructing the various sources and uncovering/dating the editorial process that culminated with the final forms of the two recensions. I will take the mean of these scholarly arguments and provisionally accept a ca. second-century date. For some of the most recent and best instances of studies on relative chronology, see Turner, *Sethian Gnosticism*; and Turner, "Sethian Gnosticism. For a fascinating, alternative

approach, see Tuomas Rasimus (*Paradise Reconsidered*), who instead charts and categorizes mythic themes and elements.

99. For an excursus on some of the philological issues present in Porphyry's *Life of Plotinus* 16, see Burns, *Alien God,* 161–63.

100. See the conjectural stemma provided (albeit with the heavy caveat that it is an oversimplification) in Karen King, "Approaching the Variants," 125.

101. Karen King, "Approaching the Variants," 123.

102. Barc and Painchaud, "Réécriture."

103. Karen King ("Approaching the Variants," 126–37) is certainly right to caution against facilely assuming that *the* original text of the *Ap. John* is recoverable due to an allegedly straightforward and linear progression from the shorter to the longer recension. Nonetheless, as the work of Barc and Painchaud demonstrates, we can plausibly recover a rationale for some scribal modifications through close synoptic study; see also Michael Williams, "Response to Papers."

104. David Frankfurter connects the *Ap. John* specifically to 4 Ezra in his "Legacy," 159–60. On this relationship more generally, see Attridge, "Valentinian"; and Burns, *Alien God,* chapters 3–6.

105. See the helpful list provided by Dylan Burns (*Alien God,* 54n43) of the numerous instances of this trope in Jewish apocalyptic literature.

106. See Karen King, *Secret Revelation*, 184; Pleše, *Poetics*, 17–19.

107. As the titular colophon makes clear, the *Apocryphon of John* is a hidden (*Apocryphon*) dialogue; by signaling both its dialogue format and its esoteric content, the *Apocryphon of John* enhances its appeal and authority. Karen King, *Secret Revelation*, 155; see further Thomassen, "Revelation as Book."

108. Although it has been argued that the *Ap. John* is Christian in form only (due to its frame narrative), see now David Brakke's (*Gnostics*, 85) and Zlatko Pleše's (*Poetics*, 13–19) persuasive rebuttals.

109. NHC II, 1.1–2.25; BG 19.6–23.16. Whether Arimanios (NHC II) or Arimanias (BG and NHC III), the name likely relates to the malicious Zoroastrian deity Ahriman.

110. This alludes to the Gospel of John (8:42, 14:3).

111. Abandoning the Temple Mount is not inconsequential. This supports an overarching narrative aimed at rejecting Ialdabaoth, who is portrayed as a parody of the Jewish God Yahweh; cf. Elaine Pagels (*Johannine Gospel*), who similarly examined the symbolic register of varying characters and places in Valentinian exegesis.

112. On "your fellow spirits," see NHC II, 2.23: [ⲛⲉⲕϢⲂⲢⲠ]ⲚⲀ; BG 22.13–14: [ⲛⲉⲕⲢⲟ]ⲘⲟⲡⲚⲀ). See also Dylan Burns (*Alien God,* 53n37) for a list of comparable commands toward missionizing activities, found at the conclusion of the contemporaneous Jewish apocalyptic texts (e.g., 2 En. 39; 4 Ezra 14:13–18, 27–26; 2 Bar. 31, 44–45; 76:4–77:1).

113. Michael Williams, "Negative Theologies, 280–83; Karen King, *Secret Revelation*, 86.

114. Pleše, *Poetics,* 88–91; yet, as Michael Williams argues ("Negative Theologies," 277), this does not entail then that the *Ap. John* is somehow anti-intellectual or shows "a despair and abandonment of rationality."

115. Pleše, *Poetics,* 88: "God transcends discursive reasoning and univocal definitions. 'Positive epithets,' even when applied to God, say nothing about his essence, but simply emphasize God's absolute transcendence and ontological priority. For example, God is not essentially good, but only bestows good, is not being but is beyond being (*ousiotes*), and is self-perfect in the sense of being non-deficient etc."

116. Kenney, "Ancient Apophatic."

117. I have streamlined the complex mytho-poetic account of the *Apocryphon of John* here. For a fuller account of some of the hypostatic and personified divine predicates mentioned in the theogonic section, see the helpful chart in Karen King, *Secret Revelation*, 87.

118. Pleše, *Poetics*, 140.

119. Reconstructed from ⲦⲢⲒⲆⲈⲀ in NHC III, 12.11.

120. Michael Williams, *Rethinking*, 154–56.

121. See further Michael Williams, "Life Full."

122. Karen King, *Secret Revelation*, 90.

123. Michael Williams, *Rethinking* 10–11.

124. I use the word "inferior" to denote the relative value of the created world vis-à-vis the perfect, aeonic realms; see below, note 126, for my discussion of the perils in labeling the temporal world "evil" in the *Ap. John*.

125. *NHC* II, 12.33–13.5.

126. There has been a lot of ink spilled over whether and to what degree the temporal world is either good or evil in the *Ap. John*. In a recent study of this issue, Michael Williams ("Life Full") rightly emphasizes that Ialdabaoth created the world "according to the divine image"; thus, it is misleading and a gross oversimplification to characterize the world as simply evil. On how best to describe the temporal world, I am persuaded by an excellent, unpublished paper by Benjamin Nickodemus. Nickodemus ("Temporal World") argues that the binary of either a good or an evil world is something inherited from polemical sources and should thus be jettisoned from discussions; instead, Nickodemus argues, it is better to construe the temporal world as in flux or a "process" insofar as it is the site for the redemptive story that unfolds.

127. BG (45.1) even retains the Greek ⲈⲠⲒⲪⲈⲢ[Ⲉ] of the LXX.

128. BG 46.13–15; NHC II, 13.36–14.1; BG (45.12–13) states that it was Ialdabaoth's apostasy that led to Sophia's repentance (ⲘⲈⲦⲀⲚⲞⲈⲒ).

129. BG 46.18: ⲚⲈⲤⲚⲎⲨ (brothers); *NHC* II, 14.3–4: ⲠⲈⲠⲖⲎⲢⲰⲘⲀ ⲦⲎⲢϤ (the whole Pleroma).

130. It is probable that the *Ap. John* expected this ethical ideal of lending assistance to repenting community members to be replicated on the level of human interactions.

131. An interesting and provocative difference between the shorter and longer recensions is the different characters who intercede over the course of salvation history. For example, BG (50.9) states that it is Autogenes and the four lights who trick Ialdabaoth into breathing into the lifeless body of Adam, whereas NHC II (19.19) does not mention Autogenes and instead has five luminaries.

132. Karen King, *Secret Revelation*, 97; cf. Michael Williams, *Immovable Race*, 122–26.

133. On ancient context for the (demonic) construction of the "psychic" body of Adam, see van den Broek, "Creation."

134. See further note 155 below.

135. These passages are notoriously difficult and thus invite a great deal of exegetical creativity; see further Michael Williams's (*Rethinking*, 54–79) excellent classification and discussion of them as "scriptural chestnuts."

136. *Pace* Karen King ("Body and Society," 96), who focuses too much on the anthropological limitations of humanity and therefore significantly underestimates the importance of moral effort in the *Ap. John*: "Hence the *Apocryphon of John* speaks less of ethics than Philo,

not because it countenances a greater acceptance of moral evil, but because ethics imply a purposefulness and power to human action that the *Apocryphon of John* does not experience."

137. See further Chapter 4.

138. Jenott, "Emissaries."

139. NHC II, 27.17–21; cf. BG 70.3–8. Whether this (likely ritual) infusion of the Living Spirit resembled the baptism of the five seals is unclear; on the five seals, see further Sevrin, *Dossier*; Turner, "Ritual in Gnosticism"; and Turner, "Sethian Baptismal Rite," 941–92. For a different approach making use of additional sources and categories, see also Rasimus, *Paradise Reconsidered*, 255–79.

140. Building on exegesis of Genesis, the *Ap. John*'s hierarchy of humanity is articulated genealogically, i.e., on the priority of one's proximity to the divine spark of the perfect human: so Adam, Seth (Adam's third son), seed of Seth, and the rest of humanity.

141. Turner, *Sethian Gnosticism*, 599.

142. Brakke, *Gnostics*, 57.

143. Although it should be noted that Brakke's interpretation of the *Holy Book* is not without difficulties, namely pushing for a very literal reading of "children of Seth" to mean Seth's biological offspring as opposed to a ritual or social category. Furthermore, the *Holy Book*'s schema differs from the *Ap. John* in multiple ways, such as including Jesus in the second luminary and having an additional *fifth* station, Yoel, below Eleleth.

144. See the excellent discussion and cautious approach to diversity among Sethian texts in Lance Jenott's *Gospel of Judas*, 70–101.

145. The Berlin Codex (as reported by Waldstein and Wisse) reads ΠΤΗΡϤ; lacking an object marker (cf. NHC III, 35.3: ЄΠΤΗΡϤ), the supralinear stroke may serve this function.

146. Waldstein and Wisse (*Apocryphon*, 144) translate ΠЄϹΠЄΡΜⲀ (BG 64.5) as "*her* seed," though this would require an additional sigma, which may have fallen out; however, all the other manuscripts (III, 32.16; II, 25.10; IV, 39.8) report only the single sigma.

147. ΜЄΤⲀΝΟΙⲀ (and its cognates) appears six times in the Berlin Codex: three times describing Sophia's repentance (45.13; 46.13, 16), twice describing those who will dwell in Eleleth who delay before repenting (36.10, 12), and once describing the fate of apostates for whom there is no repentance (70.15).

148. It is essential to differentiate between this use of universalism (in scope) and other resonances of the term, most notably that universalism connotes the total erasure of all difference. This second meaning has been employed as part of strategies meant to create and popularize a single, uniform model for humanity and ethical responsibility.

149. Michael Williams, *Rethinking,* 196–98; Karen King, *Gnosticism,* 200; Karen King, *Secret Revelation,* 143.

150. See most recently Williams's argument in "Life Full" (49–52), which makes use of the sociological categories of first- and second-order believers.

151. Michael Williams, *Rethinking,* 195–98; Karen King, *Secret Revelation,* 210.

152. Karen King, *Gnosticism,* 200; cf. Michael Williams, *Rethinking,* 196. The polemical charge that a rival moral framework or ideal is elitist does not end with these early heresiologists. An interesting and illuminating parallel is Stanley Cavell's defense of Emersonian perfectionism against Rawls's analogous criticism that it is ultimately elitist. See Cavell, *Conditions Handsome.*

153. For a Sethian text that presents a binary of salvation/damnation, see the *Gospel of Judas* (Jenott, *Gospel of Judas*, 88), which affirms that only the holy race will be saved.

154. BG 65.11–66.1; NHC II, 25.29–26.1. On the life of the Stoic sage, see Brennan, *Stoic Life*; and Graver, *Stoicism*.

155. The *Ap. John* has elaborate cosmogonic and demonological explanations for why some persons become perfect while others are possessed by the Counterfeit Spirit; central to this discussion is the function and construction of the body as the location for redeeming others and oneself. Especially problematic are apostates, whose existence should be impossible, since baptism ought to transform a person utterly and render them unable to sin again (NHC II, 25.23–26.7). Seemingly recognizing this theoretical difficulty, the longer recension has a much more elaborate demonological discussion. Thus, not only does the longer recension discuss the virtues of true baptism (*Pronoia* hymn), but it also contains an elaborate and lengthy section in which 365 demons construct the human anatomy. The demonological construction of body not only explains why those in the body might still sin even after baptism, but it also provides the pragmatic solution to this problem: if you know the demon's name who is upsetting or targeting a specific passion zone or part of your body, you can abjure and command him to cease his activities. See further Michael Williams, *Immovable Race*, 127–29; Michael Williams, *Rethinking*, 132–38; Valantasis, "Adam's Body"; Brakke, "Body"; Karen King, "Approaching the Variants," 112–14; and Karen King, *Secret Revelation*, 110–14, 148–55.

156. A cliché when it comes to the body that is still remarkably popular despite Michael Williams's (*Rethinking*, 116–62) thorough dismantling of it; cf. Williams's catalogue ("Life Full," 48n86) of scholars who still choose to promulgate it.

4. DIAGNOSING SIN AND SAVING SINNERS

Note to epigraph: Although Ephesians was likely written at least a generation or two before the *Shepherd of Hermas* or *Apocryphon of John*, its concern over about the physical presence and influence of demonic powers further attests to the prominence of this view and its influence on moral psychology.

1. This chapter also circumvents a poorly argued yet persistent cliché among scholars, namely that groups later designated as heretics did not (and *could* not) have had the same kinds of social organizations (i.e., churches) as those retrospectively called orthodox. Once we remove this anachronistic binary (heresy vs. orthodoxy) as an orienting tool, however, we find that there is no sound reason internal to *Hermas* or the *Ap. John* to assign these texts to radically different social settings. Instead, as we will see, the constructions of human sinfulness promulgated by both *Hermas* and the *Ap. John* come from texts that were both deeply concerned about the stability of their communities and the intimate danger of their sinning members. Consequently, both *Hermas* and the *Ap. John*'s discussion of human wrongdoing makes the best sense within the setting of close-knit, urban house-churches of the late first and early second centuries.

2. To be clear, I do not presuppose a genealogical relationship between these Jewish texts describing demonic sources of sin and *Hermas* or the *Ap. John*; rather, this comparison

is meant to be heuristic. Thus, I am comparing Jewish sources and *Hermas/Ap. John* with respect to their common feature of a demonic source for human sinfulness. See further J. Z. Smith's explanation (*Drudgery Divine*, 51) of this comparativst approach. My thinking on comparison has also been influenced by the important criticisms and caveats voiced by Samuel Sandmel ("Parallelomania") and Peter Schäfer ("New Testament"). Finally, my contention that similar narratives may reflect similar social and/or ethical aims is bolstered by the work of Bruce Lincoln (*Apples*, especially 113–21).

3. Although Rosen-Zvi never mentions the *Ap. John*, it is, as we will see, an even better *comparandum*, especially for his claim (*Demonic Desires*, 57) that a *single* yetzer was "the more prevalent model in rabbinic literature."

4. *Man.* 6.2.1–4.

5. Rosen-Zvi, *Demonic Desires*, 55–56.

6. Rosen-Zvi lists (*Demonic Desires*, 136–37nn15–16, 18) Jonathan Schofer, Michael Satlow, and Daniel Boyarin as noteworthy representatives of this trend.

7. Rosen-Zvi, *Demonic Desires*, 5–6, emphasis added.

8. Rosen-Zvi, *Demonic Desires*, 6–7.

9. See, for example, the extensive work by Christopher Gill, especially his *Structured Self*; see also Part III for a discussion of divided selves.

10. For an overview of Plato's influential rendering of a divided soul in the *Republic*, see Ferrari, "Three-Part Soul."

11. Rosen-Zvi, *Demonic Desires*, 7.

12. In addition to *Hermas*, *dipsychia* and its cognates appear in James 1:8, 4:8; Didache 4.4; Barnabas 19.5; 1 Clement 11.2, 23.2–3; 2 Clement 11.2, 23.5, 19.2 (Osiek, *Shepherd*, 30 n232).

13. In arguing against psychologizing demons (rightly so), Rosen-Zvi, nonetheless argues (seemingly exclusively so) against a Platonic conception of psychology that distinguishes between physical and mental/psychological phenomena, thereby importing a material vs. immaterial divide. This was just one view of psychology in antiquity, and though it is what many modern readers may intuitively assume, it was not the most prevalent view among the ancients prior to late antiquity. For an alternative, materialistic (or monistic) conception of the whole person ("psychophysical holism") that differs significantly from this Platonic dualism and its divided soul, see Christopher Gill's survey in *Structured Self*; see also Inwood, *Ethics*, chapter 2.

14. Rosen-Zvi, *Demonic Desires*, 7; cf. 56–57; Rosen-Zvi is paraphrasing Peter Brown's oft-cited passage (*Late Antiquity*, 68) responding to E. R. Dodds, wherein Brown claims "the multiplicity of self" was a key inheritance from Greece. As we shall see below, however, I do not find the explanation of "multiple selves" to be the best or most economical way of clarifying what *Hermas* means by the idea of *dipsychia*.

15. Fundamentally, Rosen-Zvi's heuristic divide between natural (psychology) and unnatural or foreign (demonology) is illuminating, though, see note 13 above and my discussion below for important caveats; his use of "self," however, is less clear. Rosen-Zvi provides a lengthy endnote to his "Afterword" (*Demonic Desires*, 212n5)—citing inter alia Marcel Mauss, Bernard Williams, and Charles Taylor—that describes the self as roughly equivalent to self-reflective consciousness that is distinct from a Platonic "inner self" or the Foucauldian idea of "self-fashioning" i.e., "becoming what you are not yet." A further "self" we should add to this list is a *symbolic space* that can be filled, emptied, or even fought over by competing powers (e.g., angels and demons).

Hermas and the *Ap. John* are literary texts with rhetorical agendas; thus, there is no single conception of a "self" found throughout either text. My focus, however, will be on the final conception of a "self," i.e., the self as symbolic space. Nonetheless, since the term "self" has so many possible meanings, I will avoid this ambiguity by not using the term "self," preferring instead "person" or "people." An added resonance that I wish to make clear, however, is that for both *Hermas* and the *Ap. John* people, psychologies, emotions, etc. are portrayed as physical stuff; see further the "physicalism" and "materialism" of ancient conceptions of the mind, emotions, and agency expertly described by Julia Annas in her *Hellenistic Philosophy*.

16. In this way, I agree with Rosen-Zvi's claim (*Demonic Desires*, 41) that this struggle against demonic influence is fundamentally a moral struggle.

17. Cf. Evagrius Ponticus, who practiced personalized demonological discernment; see David Brakke's excellent chapter on Evagrius in his *Demons*, 48–77.

18. See Lipsett's similar characterization (*Desiring Conversion*, 52).

19. On the Jewish background for the idea of wicked angels, see the following section.

20. See Carolyn Osiek's discussion (*Shepherd*, 124) of the Christian associations for this term and its connection with Stoic ethical theory.

21. Didache 1.1. A number of scholars have claimed that various Jewish (e.g., 1QS's Treatise on the Two Spirits, the supposedly Jewish Testament of Asher et al.) and Christian texts (e.g., the Didache, Barnabas, Didascalia, Canons of the Apostles, et al.) transmit a version of an early "two ways" source; moreover, these scholars have attempted to trace the historical development of this source to uncover its origins. Emblematic of this genealogical approach is John Kloppenborg ("Transformation"), who offers a stemma outlining the literary relationships of various *Christian* texts to this putative source on the basis of doctrinal differences. An alternative approach (and better one, I think) is to use the "two ways" as a typological grouping of texts, comprised of individual or subgroups of texts that may (and in some cases certainly do) have historical interrelationships; all, however, share a typologically similar rhetorical technology—a radical, all-encompassing divide—that is meant to encourage its audience to abide by a certain ethical standard. In this characterization, I draw upon but also disagree with Suggs's article "Christian Two Ways."

22. Neither, in fact, does another text, 1QS 3:13–4:26, often included among the "two ways tradition," have this sense of total freedom of choice; see, in contrast, Test. Ash. 1.3–8.

23. In contrast, this idea is near-axiomatic for many ancient philosophers, especially the Stoics, for whom free or autonomous choice is not incompatible with the idea that our choices are still causally determined by who we are, i.e., our experiences, current mental states, and moral formation or character. In other words, the Stoics, like most ancient thinkers, did not ascribe to a person a completely free will that could in identical circumstances choose either to cross the street or to remain where he or she is from sheer capriciousness. See further Bobzien, "Inadvertent Conception"; Bobzien, "Epicurus"; Salles, *Stoics*; and Michael Frede, *Free Will*.

24. For the permeability of people, see further Martin, *Corinthian Body*, especially part 2, "Pollution."

25. This materiality/physicality of both angels and humans (see below) bypasses an ancient philosophical puzzle—often subsumed within the dualistic (Platonic) soul/mind vs. body problem—of how something immaterial could control or affect something material.

For a concise overview of this problem, see further Dillon, "Soul Direct." *Hermas*'s physical assumptions appear to closely align with Stoic arguments that both mind and body are material, even if one (mind) is more rarified; cf. Annas, *Hellenistic Philosophy*, chapter 2.

26. At this point, it is anachronistic and misleading to refer to the concept of a free will, which imports additional ideas and concepts not yet invented or popularized. See below for my discussion of the difficulties of this idea.

27. See the Testament of the Twelve Patriarchs (Test. Ash. 1; cf. Test. Jud. 20), which describes the moral struggle of a person to overcome wicked impulses as a battle against opposing dispositions or spirits in one's own heart; moreover, a person's "conscience" is between (e.g., Test. Jud. 20:2: καὶ μέσον ἐστὶ τὸτῆς συνέσεως τοῦ νοός) and able to select between the two.

28. Cf. Rosen-Zvi, *Demonic Desires*, 180, 184.

29. See especially *Stromata* 2.20.110.1 and 2.20.111.4.

30. By "habituated," I mean that these practices are repeated until they become internalized as ethical dispositions; see further Dihle, *Theory of Will*, 56.

31. The superiority of Torah practice and its ability to grant complete freedom is not paralleled by *Hermas* or the *Ap. John*; both express concern that certain behaviors are slippery slopes toward sinfulness and demonic influence.

32. Sifre Deut 45, translated by Rosen-Zvi (*Demonic Desires,* 21, emphasis in original).

33. For a summary of Stoic ideas of assent and its internal (as opposed to external) role in moral responsibility, see further Kocar, "Humanity"; and Kocar, "Ethics."

34. "Irascibility" (ὀξυχολία) was also a danger, according to *Hermas*; it was, however, less so than grief (*Man.* 10.1).

35. Remarkably, *Hermas* (*Man.* 10.2.6) describes the Spirit of God as entering into the flesh (εἰς τὴν σάρκα). In its description here, *Hermas* may be making use of or alluding to Stoic ideas of blending/mixing vs. juxtaposition. Although sharing space within a person, both grief and the Holy Spirit retain their original properties but also clearly remain distinct entities; thus they do not blend or form a "new stuff." See Julia Annas's helpful summary (*Hellenistic Philosophy*, 47–48) distinguishing among juxtaposition, fusion, and blending. See also the passages gathered together by Long and Sedley in their *Hellenistic Philosophers*, 1:48.

36. Although the body is frequently described as the container for the soul by a number of ancient thinkers, this differs from *Hermas*, which contends that the container is the whole person, who can then be invaded and filled with good or evil impulses. For the more standard position of the body as a container to be filled with various psychic (demonic, mental, etc.) forces, see Algra, "Stoics on Souls."

37. Osiek, *Shepherd*, 30: "*Dipsychia* ('double-soulness' or 'doublemindedness') and its related verb and adjective occur 55 times in *Hermas* . . . as contrasted to a total of 10 times in all other early Christian literature up to this time"; see note 12 above.

38. *Pace* Reiling (*Hermas*, 32–33), who reduces *dipsychos* to simply the opposite of wholeminded/hearted faith without attention to social contexts and implications. See, in contrast, Miller, *Dreams*, 143–45.

39. Long, *Hellenistic Philosophy*, 153. According to materialist philosophers, all of existence is comprised of physical phenomena; see Julia Annas (*Hellenistic Philosophy*, 3–4), who contrasts Hellenistic physicalism with the marginal and "far from dominant" view of Platonic dualism, which differentiates between physical things and mental or psychological

phenomena and assumes that each (physical vs. mental) requires a different method of inquiry.

40. In contrast, the Stoics, for example, were (in)famous for conceiving of emotions as erroneous belief or uncontrolled impulses, i.e., mental events generated through a misfiring of a person's reasoning faculties (cf. Long and Sedley, *Hellenistic Philosophers*, vol. 1, 65A: Stobaeus 2.88.8–90.6). Accordingly, they developed strategies for scrutinizing and rejecting such impressions and corresponding beliefs that required a person to inculcate the right beliefs and fortify his or her character to resist assenting to these emotional impulses. *Hermas*, on the other hand, portrays emotions as demons; and demons, according to *Hermas*, are not mental events and thus cannot be refuted by withholding assent. As we saw above, demons are invasive forces that can easily overpower even the good person, if there is space available in his or her heart. Thus, different strategies are required.

41. There are several questions left unresolved; perhaps most perplexing: Are demons the source for all sin or simply the specific cases that *Hermas* discusses?

42. Certainly, Ialdabaoth and the archons are also demonic, but my emphasis will be specifically upon the Counterfeit Spirit; I will briefly consider the archons vis-à-vis their role in the construction of Adam's body at the end of this section.

43. *Pace* Pleše ("Evil," 118), who cites the *Ap. John's* account of the creation of Adam as evidence that the body is a major source for evil. In contrast, it is better to construe the body as setting practical limits on conduct, analogous to other natural laws. In this way, though the body may limit absolute freedom and it can be dangerous, it is not evil. Moreover, this demarcation of human capacity is pragmatic. It does not remove the possibility for "purposefulness" in action, but rather it addresses why people are in the state they are in, what their practical limitations are, and what they are still expected to do (*pace* Karen King, "Body and Society," 96).

44. This characterization parallels Rosen-Zvi's description (*Demonic Desires*, 6) of the *yetzer* as "antinomian," i.e., interested in sin for sin's sake.

45. Michael Williams, *Rethinking*, 11–13, 67–79.

46. Adam has an active role in NHC II, 22.15–18 as opposed to BG 58.8–10's terse rendering:

BG 58.8–10	NHC II, 22.15–18
	And he [Adam] was disobedient to him
And he [the Chief Ruler] knew that she	[the Chief Ruler] because of the light of
(ЄΠЄΙΝΟⲀ) would not obey him because	ЄΠЄΙΝΟⲀ who is in him, which set
she was wiser than him.	straight his thought (ΠЄϤΜЄЄΥЄ) above
	that of the Chief Ruler (ΠϢΟΡΠ ⲚⲀΡΧⲰΝ).

47. Understanding the limits of human freedom was a major topic in ancient philosophy. See, for example, the excellent discussion of autonomy of decision vs. freedom of action (i.e., deciding to cross a street v. actually crossing a street) found in Michael Frede's *Free Will*, chapter 3. See also Bobzien, "Stoic Conceptions."

48. Miller, "Dreaming the Body, 281–82.

49. Cf. Seneca (*Ep.* 65) and Epictetus (*Diss.* 1.9), both of whom, drawing on Plato's *Phaedo*, portray the body as a prison from which the soul will be released. So too with these Stoics (e.g., Epictetus, *Diss.* 1.3), however, the *Ap. John's* devaluing of the body reinforces its

relative hierarchy and proper orientation. Thus, this anti-body language was meant to curtail and warn against attachments and inculcate indifference to the body and its passions.
Consequently, as A. A. Long clarifies (*Epictetus*, 159–60), this does not entail extreme asceticism or body mortification; rather, it requires proper treatment of the body as an instrument
in the service of our proper aims.

50. The *Ap. John* engages directly and offers its own correction to Genesis here,
claiming that this trance, "unlike what Moses said" (BG 58.16–18; NHC, II 22.22–24),
was not sleep but the deprivation of Adam's perception (ⲁⲓⲥⲑⲏⲥⲓⲥ; BG 58.19; NHC II,
22.25).

51. ⲉⲡⲉⲓⲛⲟⲓⲁ: ⲉⲡⲉⲓⲛⲟⲓⲁ ⲙ̄ⲡⲟⲩⲟⲉⲓⲛ.

52. This is a point on which the shorter and longer recensions have important differences. The Berlin Codex emphasizes their essential/substantial similarities insofar as Eve
possesses Adam's ⲟⲩⲥⲓⲁ (BG 60.4). In contrast, NHC II states that Eve is based on the likeness of the reflection (NHC II, 22.35–36: ⲕⲁⲧⲁ ⲡⲓⲛⲉ ⲛ̄ⲧⲉⲡⲓⲛⲟⲓⲁ) and was Adam's likeness
(NHC II, 23.9: ⲡⲉϥⲉⲓⲛⲉ) rather than his essence/substance. This shift, as elsewhere (BG
63.13, 19; NHC II, 24.35, 25.4) where BG and NHC II render ⲟⲩⲥⲓⲁ and ⲉⲓⲛⲉ, respectively,
may reflect a discomfort on the part of the longer recension with connecting the core identify of a person with materialist language like ⲟⲩⲥⲓⲁ, especially when it is through the
body/flesh that the Counterfeit Spirit was transmitted.

53. On the diversity of opinions in early Christianity on marriage and sexuality, see
Clement of Alexandria, *Stromata* 3.

54. BG 63.1–64.12; NHC II, 24.26–25.16. Both BG (54.11–55.13) and NHC II (20.23–
21.13) present this Counterfeit (ⲁⲛⲧⲓⲙⲓⲙⲟⲛ) or Contrary (ⲁⲛⲧⲓⲕⲉⲓⲙⲉⲛⲟⲛ) Spirit as an integral part in the archontic construction of Adam's body or "prison." BG (56.14–17) further
states that the Counterfeit Spirit was created in order to "lead him astray." BG (55.8–9) does
contain a singular reading of ⲁⲛⲧⲓⲕⲉⲓⲙⲉⲛⲟⲛ (cf. NHC III, 26.19: ⲁⲛⲧⲓⲙⲓⲙⲟⲛ). Deciding
whether this indicates corruption in the manuscript tradition or that BG simply used another title or characteristic for the Counterfeit at 55.8–9 does not concern me here. It appears
that both ⲁⲛⲧⲓⲙⲓⲙⲟⲛ and ⲁⲛⲧⲓⲕⲉⲓⲙⲉⲛⲟⲛ reference what, for the sake of convenience, I
call the Counterfeit Spirit; see especially BG's continuation of the same thread and its use of
ⲁⲛⲧⲓⲙⲓⲙⲟⲛ at 56.14.

55. See Stuckenbruck, "'Angels' and 'Giants'"; and Reed, *Fallen Angels*; see also the recent piece by Bull, "Women."

56. See Karen King (*Secret Revelation*, 109, 157–73), who offers an interpretation of this
passage that emphasizes the deception of the angels as part of her argument that the *Ap.
John* is best understood not as an overtly political text but as a subversive, anti-Roman imperial text. Although I agree with King's claims that the *Ap. John* is utopian, I do not agree
with her implications that this counsels disengagement or disinterest in practical (i.e., everyday) ethical concerns or that the *Ap. John* ought to be understood as a prototype for
postcolonial theory and empire criticism. On this latter point, see Michael Williams, *Rethinking*, chapter 5.

57. The longer version, likely recognizing the repetition and incompatibility of *two* accounts for the creation of the Counterfeit Spirit, refers here (e.g., NHC II, 29.24, 30.11; cf.
26.27, 36) to this demonic entity as the Despicable or Bitter Spirit (ⲡ̄ⲛ̄ⲁ ⲉⲧϣ̄ⲏⲥ).

58. This may provide evidence of the spliced and diverse textual traditions underlying
the uneven transmission history of the *Ap. John*; see also the difference between the insider

terminologies of the immovable race (BG 65.2–3; NHC II, 25.23) as opposed to the seed of Seth (BG 36.2–7; NHC II, 9.14–17).

59. See, for example, Rosen-Zvi's description (*Demonic Desires*, 54) of Philo's suppression of demonic responsibility in favor of ascribing blame to the individual (e.g., *De spec. leg.* 1.89).

60. Cf. Reed's discussion ("Trickery of Fallen," 151) of the *Book of the Watchers'* comparable claim.

61. Justin differentiates between the fallen angels of Genesis 6 and the souls of the dead Nephilim, which he calls demons. See Reed, "Trickery of Fallen," 153; cf. Himmelfarb, *Ascent to Heaven*, 74.

62. In contrast, Justin's *Dialogue with Trypho* does place responsibility for human sinfulness on the individual, in particular Jewish persons, as part of its polemical attack on Judaism; see further Annette Yoshiko Reed ("Trickery of Fallen," 155, and passim), who lays out precisely how Justin fashions his conceptions of sin in order to suit his polemical targets.

63. Translation from *ANF*, 1.190, modified.

64. As Annette Yoshiko Reed argues ("Trickery of the Fallen," 159), Justin connects this angelic etiology of sin and suffering with illicit religious practices as part of his broader rhetorical strategy of refuting paganism.

65. Thus, as in *Hermas*, there should not be space available for the entry of the Counterfeit Spirit; this, however, does seem to reflect the *lived experience* of the *Ap. John*'s community, as we shall see below.

66. The Counterfeit Spirit is an inferior variation of the True Spirit; in an interesting parallel, NHC II consistently (e.g., 21.9) refers to the Counterfeit Spirit as ΠΕΥΠΝΑ ΕΤϢΒΒΙΑΕΙΤ, which is the same term it uses to differentiate between Sophia and Ialdabaoth at 10.4: ΑΥϢ ΕϤϢΒΒΙΑΕΙΤ ΑΠΕϹϹΜΟΤ.

67. On the theoretical and social tension in the *Treatise of the Two Spirits*, see Rosen-Zvi, *Demonic Desires*, 50.

68. BG 70.10: ΑΥΚΟΤΟΥ ΕΒΟΛ; NHC II, 27.23: ΑΥ2ΝΤΟΥ ΕΒΟΛ.

69. See further Miryam Brand's discussion (*Evil Within*, 59–73) of the physicality of sin and its link to "unrighteous flesh" in both the Thanksgiving Scroll (Hodayot) and the Hymn of Praise from the end of the Community Rule (1QS 10.9–11.22).

70. BG 68.17–69.5; NHC II, 26.36–27.4.

71. See, in contrast, BG 65.11–66.1; NHC II, 25.29–26.1 for the *Ap. John*'s ethic of living free from the passions.

72. For an argument that this infusion of the Spirit coincided with the ritual of baptism, see Karen King, *Secret Revelation*, 148–49.

73. For the whole list, see NHC II, 15.29–19.10.

74. See further NHC II, 18.14–31 for the interrelationships and functions of these demonic passions.

75. *Contra Celsum* 1.6, 24; 8.58; cf. Plotinus, *Ennead* 2.9.14–15; Dillon, "Magical Power." See further Michael Williams, *Immovable Race*, 127–29; Michael Williams, *Rethinking*, 132–38; Valantasis, "Adam's Body"; Brakke, "Body"; Karen King, "Approaching the Variants," 112–14; and Karen King, *Secret Revelation*, 110–14, 148–55.

76. Commenting on comparable lists of *voces magicae* and ritual incantations, Wayne Meeks (*Origins*, 112–14) reduces these "magical" texts to expressions of power and technical efficacy, apart from any moral framework.

77. Perhaps a list of names and ritual commands could be classified as "amoral," just as a list of statistics or empirical observations could be (although there may be very real concerns here); however, once such lists or statistics are embedded within and provide motivational content as well as encourage certain behaviors they cease being amoral.

78. For an example of something closer to this sort of freedom in choice, see Clement, *Stromata* 4.24.153.1.

79. Both texts lack, for example, the capacity "to have done otherwise" or to be able to exercise volition freely apart from any preceding causes, including one's very own character. On the former issue, see Bobzien, "Inadvertent Conception"; on the latter, see Bobzien, "Epicurus"; Boys-Stones, "'Middle' Platonists"; and Boys-Stones, "Human Autonomy."

80. *Pace* Michael Williams, *Rethinking*, 205; and Karen King, *Secret Revelation*, 147.

81. For bibliography on the history of a "free will," see notes 70 and 71 in the Introduction.

82. This is structurally similar to the fragment of Valentinus (fragment 2) preserved by Clement of Alexandria (*Stromata* 2.114:3–6), in which Valentinus represents the human heart as an inn filled with unruly and demonic occupants.

83. This phrase is a Socratic maxim (see, for example, *Protagoras* 358c: ἐπί γε τὰ κακὰ οὐδεὶς ἑκὼν ἔρχεται οὐδὲ ἐπὶ ἃ οἴεται κακὰ εἶναι"). This concept has been central to some reconstructions of the development a free will (e.g., Dihle, *Theory of Will*, 39ff.). See Michael Williams, *Rethinking*, 205 for this contention regarding free will and apostasy; Williams's objection, I should note, points to an important but understudied theoretical issue—i.e., the problem of apostasy is an enormous lacuna that is unaccounted for in Dihle's and many others' accounts.

84. I do not mean to import an absolute dichotomy between the two; however, this shift toward external, bodily practices and concerns may help explain the longer recension's extensive *melothesia* section. This section could have been added during the transmission history of the text to provide a diagnostic tool and pragmatic solution for sinners in their midst.

85. Brown, *Late Antiquity*, 4.

86. Interestingly, there is a provocative parallel here with the community at Qumran. Discussing a diachronic shift within the Qumran community, Rosen-Zvi (*Demonic Desires*, 53) observed that when faced with the problem of sinners among the elect they too devised demonic explanations to account for this. The theoretical difficulty of ethical variance among the elect may have also contributed to the shift away from egalitarian communal structures toward the reintroduction of hierarchical subgroups on the basis of "merit." On this second point, see Himmelfarb, *Kingdom*, 124–28.

87. This insider/outsider divide was elaborated in a number of ways through demonology. Especially interesting was Origen's "patronage" system; see Martin, *Inventing Superstition*, 182ff.

88. While *Hermas* and the *Ap. John* accommodate sinfulness within their communities, both agree that apostates will surely be damned. This implies at the very least a communal identity that expected solidarity and boundary maintenance. The very idea of apostasy, however, is at odds with the presuppositions of both texts, e.g., their ideas of angelic/demonic influence. Both texts ascribe a great deal of influence to external compulsion; so if someone has already obtained the support of the Holy Spirit, how could that person become so corrupted and utterly turned around as to deserve the damnation of an apostate? This theoretical tension can best be explained if both texts had to deal with the problem of actual apostasy.

89. Even early Christians who fashioned themselves as philosophers and teachers, such as Justin Martyr, apparently met in domestic spaces where they practiced rituals, such as liturgies (*1 Apol.* 61–67); cf. Brent, *Hippolytus*, 401–5. In his article examining the relationship between Justin Martyr's social and spatial context in second-century Rome and his writings, H. Gregory Snyder ("Baths of Myrtinus") expertly draws readers into the close, "noisy, smelly, and crowded" confines of second-century Christian meeting places throughout this crowded metropolis. The *Acts of Justin* reports that at his trial Justin located his residence, which also served as his place of instruction, above "the baths of Myrtinus." Extrapolating from this, Snyder provides a textured and rich description of the physical and social features of such a domicile, citing a wide range of literary and material evidence.

90. For examples of other approaches, see the beginning of Chapter 3, "The Problem of Suitable Deserts." In drawing on the language of experimentation, I am influenced by a number of scholars who have argued for employing the metaphor of a laboratory to capture the innovativeness of the second century; see especially Löhr, "Modelling"; and Lieu, "Modelling."

91. Thomassen, "Orthodoxy and Heresy."

92. Thomassen, "Orthodoxy and Heresy," 242–43.

93. For more on Justin and his heresiological project, see the recent studies by Geoffrey Smith, *Guilt*, chapter 2, and Lieu, *Marcion*, chapter 2.

94. Notably, Lampe's *Paul*.

95. Lampe, *Paul*, 369: "In the first two centuries, there was no real estate which was owned collectively and centrally administered by the church community. On the contrary, all property used by the church was de jure individual private property (owned or rented), that one fraternally placed at the disposal of the community." Such shops and living quarters for early Christians likely would have been compact and ill-suited for large groups (e.g., *tabernae* and *insulae*); see the summary of literature in Trevett's "'I Have Heard,'" 11n29.

96. Meeks (*First Urban*, 107–10) already makes note of the idea of a worldwide church in Paul.

97. Thomassen, "Orthodoxy and Heresy," 248.

98. Strangely, Justin has dropped out of Thomassen's discussion at this point ("Orthodoxy and Heresy," 251ff.). I include him here because (1) he fits well into Thomassen's paradigm of centralizing/decentralizing forces and (2) he is a much more potent and destabilizing person to pair with Marcion than Valentinus or Hermas.

99. See, for example, BG 64.14–65.16 and *Vis.* 3.5. Alasdair MacIntyre (*After Virtue*, 220ff.) has argued persuasively that the modern invention of "individualism" has sacrificed important elements of social identity that are essential for living ethically sound lives.

100. Jackson, *Politics*, 26–27.

101. Both display concern about the integrity and cohesion of their small, intimate social groups meeting, most likely, in house-churches. Nonetheless, we must continue to revise and clarify what we know of ancient house-churches, e.g., How small (or large) were these communities? How committed did a member have to be? How would a member express commitment? How did networks of communication with other house-churches work to exert centripetal and/or centrifugal force on the ideas and practices of these communities? For a promising new study that considers many of these very questions, see Pheme Perkins's recent "Valentinians and the Christian Canon."

5. MAPPING THE HEAVENS

1. Translations of Irenaeus, albeit with some modifications, are from the *ANF*.

2. Stendahl, "Call"; cf. my discussion in Chapter 2.

3. Desjardins, *Sin*, 116.

4. For the Coptic text and translation of the *Gospel of Truth*, I rely upon Attridge and Pagels, *Nag Hammadi*, vol. 1.

5. Desjardins, *Sin*, 78.

6. For example, see Elaine Pagels's influential article "Conflicting Versions."

7. This portrait of Valentinian authors accommodating their minority views to the taste of the majority church appears to underlie Harold Attridge's influential article on the *Gospel of Truth* as a gateway text as well as his and Pagels's commentary on the *Tripartite Tractate*. See Attridge, "Gospel of Truth"; Attridge and Pagels, *Nag Hammadi*, 2:217–497.

8. See, for example, Hans Jonas's heated response to Rowan Greer's "Dog," in Layton, *Rediscovery of Gnosticism*, 1:173–74.

9. Heracleon presents a less cosmologically and more genealogically oriented view of the threefold division of humanity. Moreover, in what survives, he does not describe higher and lower salvific rewards. We will consider to what degree Heracleon might have been engaged in intra-Valentinian debate, and to what degree his divergent views were a product of genre and social circumstances. Regardless, Heracleon agrees with both the *Excerpts of Theodotus* and the *Tripartite Tractate* about what constitutes good ethical conduct: the more advanced (pneumatics) are obligated to lend assistance and imitate the saving actions of the Savior toward less advanced, but likely receptive individuals (psychics).

10. For paradigmatic instances of these two views, see the competing 2013 articles by Einar Thomassen ("Saved") and Ismo Dunderberg ("Valentinian Theories").

11. Both camps, however, especially the recent work of Thomassen and Dunderberg, can often come very close to agreeing with each other in terms of a final portrait of Valentinians, despite privileging very different *comparanda* (Thomassen: Neo-Pythagorean metaphysics; Dunderberg: Hellenistic, especially Stoic, study circles) in their discussions.

12. Kocar, "Humanity."

13. Causal responsibility is often associated with ancient Stoics and their interest in preserving the autonomy of an agent in spite of universal causation and the overriding power of Fate. See especially Bobzien, *Determinism;* and Bobzien, "Inadvertent Conception."

14. I focus especially on the third major section of the *Excerpts of Theodotus* (43.2–65), since it has been at the center of the debate surrounding Valentinian soteriology. I will not discuss Heracleon's *Commentary on John* in this chapter because it does not explicitly describe soteriological ends, and its commentarial genre requires additional considerations. On the constraints and impact of the commentarial genre on Heracleon's anthropology, see further Pagels, *Johannine Gospel*; Trumbower, *Born from Above*; Wucherpfennig, *Heracleon Philologus*; and Thomassen, "Heracleon."

15. The two manuscripts are Florence, Biblioteca Laurenziana, Laur. V.3 (eleventh century) and Paris, Bibliotheque Nationale, Suppl. graec. 250 (sixteenth century). See the introduction by Robert Casey to his *Excerpta*.

16. Hippolytus 7.35 and 7.36 likely do not refer to this Theodotus; see further Sagnard, *Clément*, 5–6.

17. The division into two schools (Eastern and Western) is based upon various alleged doctrinal differences (e.g., Is the Savior's body pneumatic or psychic?). It is unclear whether and to what degree this division reflects internal and self-reflexively acknowledged Valentinian diversity or external and heresiologically designed polemics. The most clear and succinct overview, synthesis, and critical evaluation of the model of two schools and their essential characteristics is Dubois, "Sotériologie Valentinienne."

18. Sagnard, *Clément.* Jean-Daniel Dubois ("Remarques") has recently revisited Sagnard's work in order to demonstrate the importance of the *Excerpts of Theodotus* for the study of the Valentinians.

19. Casey, *Excerpta,* 5.

20. See especially Kovacs, "Clement of Alexandria"; and Kovacs, "Language of Grace."

21. See the helpful summary of various opinions by Kovacs, "Clement of Alexandria," 188–89.

22. First observed by Otto Dibelius, "Studien."

23. In *Excerpts of Theodotus* 56 and following, neuter and masculine forms of the three classes of pneumatic, psychic, and hylic are used in complex and interrelated ways. Though it has been suggested that the three neuter terms were salvifically autonomous from their eponymous classes of people, this, as I will show below, misconstrues the overall meaning of the text. As I understand these terms, *pneumatika,* for example, refers not only to the distinctive part of a person (a *pneumatikos*) but also corporately to a class of persons (the *pneumatikoi*). See below for my discussion of the exegetical justification of this interpretation.

24. For the Coptic text of the *Tripartite Tractate,* I rely on two critical editions: Attridge and Pagels, *Nag Hammadi,* vol. 1; and Thomassen, *Traité tripartite.* My English translations are often guided by Thomassen's exceptionally lucid translation in Meyer's *Nag Hammadi Scriptures.*

25. *Tri. Trac.* 107.20–108.12.

26. Even the passion-filled fall of the Sophia-like figure, the Logos, was providential, according to the *Tripartite Tractate,* insofar as it was in accordance with the will of the Father and his divine *oikonomia* or salvific ordering of the cosmos; cf. *Tri. Trac.* 76.23–30.

27. Thomassen and Painchaud, *Traité tripartite,* 18–20.

28. See further Irenaeus (*Haer.* 1.8.3), who observes that the Valentinian anthropology merged 1 Cor. 2:14–15 ("Those who are psychic do not receive the gifts of God's spirit . . . because they are spiritually (*pneumatically*) discerned. Those who are pneumatic discern all things") with 1 Cor. 15:48 ("As was the man of earth, so are those who are earthly").

29. For Pauline exegesis in the *Excerpts of Theodotus,* see further Pagels, "Valentinian Claim"; Kovacs, "Echoes"; Kovacs, "Clement of Alexandria"; and Kovacs, "Language of Grace." For a possibly parallel use of Romans 9–11 in the *Tripartite Tractate,* see Kocar, "Humanity," 212–16.

30. Cf. *Excerpts of Theodotus* 56.5, which continues to identify pneumatics with Israel: "But Israel allegorizes the pneumatic (ὁ πνευματικός), the one who sees God, the son of faithful Abraham, true-born of a free-woman."

31. Thomassen, *Spiritual Seed,* 182–86; Kocar, "Humanity," 212–16.

32. While some scholars suggest that psychics are included in the "members" of the ecclesial body that require a school (*Tri. Trac.* 123.12), this interpretation is not certain. The interpretative dispute regarding this passage is over the identity of the "perfect man" and the "members" of the Savior mentioned in *Tri. Trac.* 123.3–12. According to Attridge and Pagels

(*Nag Hammadi*, 2:460–64), the perfect man refers to the pneumatic portion of the "Man of the Church" (*Tri. Trac.* 122.30), and so the "members" are the psychics who still require instruction after the pneumatic portion of the community "immediately received knowledge and returned to its unity" (*Tri. Trac.* 123.4–7). In support of identifying the perfect man with the pneumatic component of the community, Attridge and Pagels note that his "immediate" response is characteristic of pneumatics. Furthermore, the fact that the "members" need instruction demonstrates, according to Attridge and Pagels, that pneumatics—who "receive gnosis immediately"—cannot be these "members" who require instruction. In contrast, Einar Thomassen argues that the perfect man is the Savior (*Spiritual Seed*, 55; cf. *Traité tripartite*, 436–37); in addition, Thomassen ("Valentinian Ideas") provides instances in which pneumatics need and/or receive instruction. Moreover, the following section of the *Tripartite Tractate*, which focuses on the link between the restoration of the church and the aeons, sets the members of the community in opposition to the dominion of those on the left *and* right, i.e., psychics (*Tri. Trac.* 123.23–124.25), thereby suggesting that the church community and its "members" are most easily identified as pneumatics. In contrast, see *Exc.* 58.1, which states the church consists of both the pneumatic elect and the psychic called.

33. *Tri. Trac.* 123.23–124.3.

34. For a clear discussion of the likely corruption of ⲦⲞⲨⲰ to †ⲒⲰ, see Attridge and Pagels, *Nag Hammadi*, 2:468.

35. Pagels, "Conflicting Versions"; McCue, "Conflicting Versions."

36. Pagels, "Conflicting Versions," 44–45.

37. McCue, "Conflicting Versions," 404.

38. McCue, "Conflicting Versions," 415.

39. Pagels, "Conflicting Versions," 44–53, see especially 50–51.

40. McCue, "Conflicting Versions," 413, referring to *Exc.* 54–58.

41. McCue, "Conflicting Versions," 415.

42. Einar Thomassen similarly argues that salvation is a physical reaction enacted through "consubstantiality" (like responding to like) and "*syngeneia*" ("Saved," 135, 138).

43. Martin, *Corinthian Body*.

44. *Stromata* 7.2.9; cf. *Stromata* 4.18.114; 6.13.107; and 6.14.111, 114.

45. *Haer.* 5. 36.

46. Pagels, "Conflicting Versions," 46; James McCue ("Conflicting Versions," 405–7) disputed Pagels's claim that this twofold emission of the pneumatic seed was available to both the pneumatics and the psychics who were attending the eschatological celebration (*Exc.* 63–65) by observing that Pagels had homogenized earlier sections of the *Excerpts of Theodotus* (*Exc.* 21 and 39) with 43.2–65; most scholars, McCue noted, consider these passages to come from different and at times incompatible sources.

47. Pagels, "Conflicting Versions," 44–46; Dunderberg, *Beyond Gnosticism*, 139–40.

48. On the rhetorical and thus ethical importance of corporate salvation, see the section "On Earth as It Is in Heavens" in Chapter 4.

49. Dunderberg, *Beyond Gnosticism*, 139.

50. "This is the human being then, 'psychic' in 'earthly,' not part by part, but as a whole united altogether by God's ineffable power. . . . This is the meaning of 'this is now bone of my bones.' (Gen. 2:23): it hints at the divine soul which is hidden in the flesh, solid, impassive, and very powerful.' And 'flesh from my flesh' [hints] at the material soul (τὴν ὑλικὴν ψυχὴν) which is a body for the divine soul" (*Exc.* 51.1–2).

51. "Thus Wisdom first put forth a pneumatic seed into Adam in order that it should be 'the bone' (Gen. 2:23), the logical and heavenly soul, not empty but full of pneumatic marrow" (*Exc.* 53.5).

52. Dunderberg, *Beyond Gnosticism,* 139; cf. Pagels, "Conflicting Versions," 46.

53. As I will show in the second half of this chapter, it also overlooks how Valentinians deployed a single, naturalistic discourse to explain all physical, ethical, and eschatological difference. See further Brad Inwood's article ("Moral Causes") on the rhetorical appeal of naturalistic explanations.

54. Harmonizing Paul's language in 1 Cor. 2–3 with Luke 2:40, the *Excerpts of Theodotus* 61 differentiates between psychics and pneumatic by claiming pneumatics need wisdom, whereas psychics, as children, require growth. Judith Kovacs has convincingly shown that Clement of Alexandria went to great lengths to respond to precisely this sort of Valentinian exegesis of 1 Corinthians 2–3; see especially Clement's extended and complex exegetical argument at *1 Paed.* 6. See Kovacs, *Clement of Alexandria;* and Kovacs, "Echoes."

55. *Exc.* 55.2, emphasis added: "Therefore, Adam sows neither *from* (ἀπὸ) the pneumatic nor *from* (ἀπὸ) 'that which was breathed into [him]' (Gen. 2:7). For both are divine and both sprout *through* him (δι' αὐτοῦ) but not by him (ὑπ' αὐτοῦ)." Interestingly, according to Origen (*Comm. Jo.* 2.14.102), Heracleon, in his interpretation of John 1:3 ("All things came to be through him, and without him not one thing came into being"), makes use of similar prepositional distinctions to describe the relationship of the Logos/Savior to the creation of the world: "The one who provided the demiurge with the cause for the genesis of the world, that is the Logos, is not the one 'from whom,' (ἀφ' οὗ) or 'by whom,' (ὑφ' οὗ), but the one 'through whom' (δι' οὗ)." For a meticulous discussion of this passage and its different modes of agency, see further Wucherpfennig, *Heracleon Philologus,* 139–51; for analogous language in the *Tripartite Tractate,* see further Attridge, "Greek Equivalents."

56. For this two-sided dynamic of fixity and fluidity, see further Buell, *New Race,* 6–7.

57. Cf. Aristotle (*NE* 10.9, 1179b20–30), who similarly uses the imagery of seeds and growth to note that the fortunate "through some divine causes" (διά τινας θείας αἰτίας) have superior natures and are thus better suited for virtue.

58. For an overview of Aristotle's (in particular *Metaphysics* 6) discussion of cause, explanation, and necessitation, see Sorabji, *Necessity.*

59. See further Kovacs ("Clement of Alexandria"), who outlines how Clement and the Valentinians deployed the compelling Pauline imagery of the church as the body of Christ.

60. Thomassen, *Spiritual Seed,* 66: "This notion rests . . . on a logic of mutual participation between the Saviour and the *salvandi.* The Saviour submits himself to the condition from which he saves."

61. David Aune ("Pauline Models") makes note of similar analogical reasoning in Paul and some of Paul's near contemporaries.

62. *Pace* Pagels, "Conflicting Versions," 46–51.

63. This passage is unclear, but "souls" likely has multiple referents, i.e., both a part of a person (which a pneumatic, like a psychic, possesses) and the class of persons who are "faithful souls" (*Exc.* 63.1), which, based on the μέν and δέ contrast with *pneumatika,* likely refers to the *psychika.* It is important to note, however, that there is no explicit reference to psychic salvation after 61.8, at which point the *Excerpts of Theodotus* states simply that psychics enjoy an inferior salvation to that of the pneumatics. See also Einar Thomassen

("Saved," 140), who similarly points to the ambiguity and likely overlap of meanings between "soul" and "psychic."

64. *Excerpts of Theodotus* 56.5 also allegorically characterizes the pneumatic as "Israel . . . the one who *sees* God."

65. I follow Sagnard's division of the *Excerpts of Theodotus* into four main sections/sources: (1) 1–28; (2) 29–43.1; (3) 43.2–65; (4) 66–86.

66. Thomassen, *Spiritual Seed*, 377–83.

67. *Exc.* 36.2: "Since we had been divided, Jesus was baptized on account of this, so that the undivided [our angels] be divided until he should unite us in the Pleroma in order that we, the many, having become one, should all be united with the one who was divided for us."

68. To put as fine point on this as possible: in some Valentinian texts, pneumatics can save others through the ritual of baptism; in contrast, psychics are either saved by others or can save themselves, but they never save others. See further Kocar, "Humanity," 213 and 220 for my suggestion that Pauline exegesis fuels the contention that pneumatic baptism hastens the Pleromatic restoration in the *Tripartite Tractate*.

69. *Pace* Dunderberg (*Beyond Gnosticism*, 140), who states that there is a strict binary between the saved and the damned with no gradients of salvation.

70. Einar Thomassen ("Saved," 144) argues that some markers of salvific difference are abrogated at the eschatological finale, e.g., the rewards of the bridal chamber are made available to saved psychics. Thomassen's interpretation, however, is uncertain, since it depends entirely on a reconstruction of the text: "And the Church will remember them as good friends and faithful servants once it has been redeemed, and [it will give them] (ⲉ[ⲥⲛⲁϯ] ⲛ[ⲛⲉⲩ ⲛ̄) the rewards consisting of the joy that reigns in the bridal [chamber] (*Tri. Trac.* 135.25–31). In contrast, Attridge and Pagels render this passage differently: "The Church will remember them as good friends and faithful servants, once she has received the redemption [from the one who gives] (ⲁ[ⲃⲁⲗ ϩ]ⲛ [ⲡⲉⲧϫⲓ]) requital. Then the [grace] which is in the bridal [chamber] . . ." In either case, what follows this passage (*Tri. Trac.* 136.11–28) maintains a hierarchy of deserts and honors among the saved, tailoring salvific rewards to the relative praiseworthiness of different soteriological roles. Consequently, as Attridge and Pagels observed, the pneumatic church mirrors the saving power of the Savior such that "just as the revelation of the Savior provided exaltation to the spiritual Church (124.3–25), [so too does] the spiritual Church provide some form of salvation to the beings who serve her" (Attridge and Pagels, *Nag Hammadi*, 2:496).

71. For other instances of salvific hierarchy in the *Tripartite Tractate*, see 119.20–120.14; 121.25–38; 125.24–127.25; 131.14–133.15.

72. See further the excellent summary of this enduring cliché provided by Michael Williams in *Rethinking*, 189–212.

73. Bobzien, "Inadvertent Conception," 135.

74. For moral praise and blame and their conditions, see especially Bobzien, "Choice."

75. See the section "Free Will vs. Determinism" in the Introduction.

76. In the following three paragraphs, I am simplifying and synthesizing Bobzien's "Inadvertent Conception," *Determinism*, and "Epicurus" to create for heuristic purposes a clear dichotomy between causal and "two-sided," (i.e., could do otherwise) models for moral responsibility.

77. Chrysippus explains the difference between internal and external causes by analogy to the spinning of a cylinder or a top: an external cause provides the force necessary to spin the

objects, but it is internal cause (i.e., the nature of the cylinder or top) that determines the manner and duration of their spinning (Cicero, *De fato* 42–43; cf. Gellius, *NA* 7.2 [*SVF* 2.1000]).

78. For an illustration of just how pervasive and ultimately influential the internally divided conception of the self has been, see further Krister Stendahl's seminal article against the "introspective" Paul, in Stendahl, *Paul*, 78–96.

79. "It is clear even in itself that 'what depends on us' is applied to those things over which we have the power of also choosing the opposite things" (Alexander of Aphrodisias, *De fato* 181.5, translated by Sharples, *Alexander*.

80. Importantly, actions or choices that result from our own character and dispositions are still said to have originated in us because our internal quality (character and disposition) is never *external* to ourselves. See Salles, *Stoics*, 47.

81. In addition to the Bobzien works listed above, especially "Epicurus," 290–92, see also Gill, *Structured Self*.

82. Recall the example from the Introduction of the praiseworthy hero who, based on experience and/or disposition, runs headlong into danger to save others.

83. See the discussions of embedded or situated rationality in Stout, *Flight*, 149–76, and MacIntyre, *Whose Reason*.

84. Löhr, "Gnostic Determinism."

85. Clark, *Clement's Use*.

86. *Stromata* 4.24.153.1; cf. 2.6.27.4; 2.12.55.1–2; 5.1.3; 5.13.86; 6.17.156.2; and 7.15.91.

87. Scholars often question Eusebius's (*Hist. eccl.* 6.6.1) claim that Clement was the head of the Alexandrian catechetical school; thus, a debate continues over whether Clement might have been a private household teacher, as opposed to Eusebius's propagandist portrait of him as a successive link in the chain of instructors at the Alexandrian catechetical school. See further Le Boulluec, "École d'Alexandrie"; Le Boulluec, "Aux origines"; van den Broek, "Christian 'School'"; van den Hoek, "'Catechetical' School"; Dawson, *Allegorical Readers*, 219–22; and Grafton and Williams, *Christianity*, 70–78.

88. In recognizing the significance of the social and ideological context for ancient thinkers, I am indebted to the insightful article by Brent Shaw ("Divine Economy"), wherein he examined Stoicism as an ideology that was dynamic and interconnected with the social and political situations in which its "propagators" lived.

89. This translation for αὐτεξούσιον avoids the problem of importing the ideological foreign language of a "will." Cf. Epictetus's use of αὐτεξούσιον in his "On Freedom" (*Diss.* 4.1).

90. Cf. *Tri. Trac.* 119.20–24: "The psychic race, however, since it is in the middle by virtue of the way it was brought forth as well as by virtue of its creation, is double according to its assignment to good as well as to evil."

91. For a more thorough discussion of the contemporary philosophical debates relating to Romans 7 and its formulation of an internal, psychological conflict, see further Wasserman's *Death of the Soul*.

92. Cf. *Tri. Trac.* 121.25–38: "For those on the right [good psychics] who will be saved, the road to eternal rest leads from humility to salvation. After they confessed the Lord, the thought as to what is good for the Church, and the song of the humble with the Church, they will, for all the good they have been able to do for it, sharing its afflictions and sufferings like people who have consideration for what is good for the Church, they will share her hope."

93. For a fuller treatment of the parallels between Stoic moral psychology and the *Tripartite Tractate*, see further Kocar, "Humanity."

94. Alexander of Aphrodisias preserves a similarly naturalistic account of conduct: "And the things that are brought about by each thing come about in accordance with its nature—those of a stone in accordance with that of a stone, those by fire in accordance with that of fire and those by a living creature in accordance with that of a living creature . . . for it is not possible for a stone, if it is released by some height, not to be carried downwards, if nothing hinders. Because it has weight in itself, and this is the natural cause of such a motion, whenever the external causes which contribute to the natural movement of the stone are also present, of necessity the stone is moved in which it is its nature to be moved . . . and as it is in the case of inanimate things, so it is also the case for living creatures" (Alexander of Aphrodisias, *De fato* 181.18–182.6, translated by Sharples, *Alexander*).

95. See further Gill, *Structured Self*, 29–66; and Bobzien, "Epicurus."

96. See Thomassen's list ("Saved," 130) of the three different contexts for the threefold classes: "First it has a place in the etiological myth that is a fundamental feature of the Valentinian system and which explains the origins of the substances (*ousiai*) of matter, soul, and spirit. Second, the theme also appears in the context of descriptions of how the Saviour's revelation of saving *gnosis* was differently received among humankind. A third context is eschatology: the accounts of the ultimate fates reserved for each of the three human kinds."

97. According to at least one school of thought among the ancient debates over moral responsibility, this would be enough for assigning moral praise or blame, because "what happens through us according to our nature depends upon us," since we are responsible for such conduct when it comes about through our nature as persons, which is rational (see Nemesius, *On the Nature of Man* 106.3–4). Attributing this claim to the late Stoic Philopator, Bobzien (*Determinism,* 386) explicates that the linchpin for moral accountability for Philopator was that an action "come about through us," where the "us" is rational; cf. Salles, *Stoics*, 52–54.

98. Gill, *Structured Self,* 33–34.

99. Translated by Long and Sedley, *Hellenistic Philosophers*, vol. 1, 53G; cf. 53H, K–M.

100. As modern readers, we might question whether a pneumatic is truly morally responsible without an account justifying how an agent is causally responsible for his or her own internal dispositions; the *Excerpts of Theodotus*, however, does not appear to address itself to this issue. Instead, the *Excerpts of Theodotus*, like the *Tripartite Tractate*, contains a totalizing and teleological narrative of salvation history, wherein past, present, and future events are all told through the lens of knowing precisely how everything will eventually turn out. Consequently, though there are very real theoretical difficulties, e.g., internal determinism, that arise from this narrative of salvation history and its predetermined types of persons and soteriological ends, this does not mean that the *Excerpts of Theodotus* or the *Tripartite Tractate* advocated internal determinism; rather, this was likely an unintended (and likely unrecognized) outcome of their choice of literary genre and their preceding ideological commitments. For more on "internal determinism," see further Bobzien, "Epicurus."

101. For example, see Aristotle (*NE* 3.5), who argues that it is not necessary for a virtuous person to be able to have done vicious actions for him or her to be morally responsible for his or her virtuous acts.

102. This is, however, only in theory and based upon the logic internal to the *Tripartite Tractate* and the *Excerpts of Theodotus*. In practice, there was likely a great deal of fluidity and uncertainty.

103. See Michel Desjardins's seminal *Sin*. See also the twofold ethical imperatives in the *Gospel of Truth* (33.1–32). These ethical imperatives could not only encourage missionary actions, e.g., "Make firm the feet of those who stumbled and stretch out your hands to those

who are ill. Feed those who are hungry and give repose to those who are weary," but they also could simultaneously reinforce ethical ideals among community members so that adherents would not revert to previous sins, e.g., "Do not return to what you have vomited." For an analysis of the *Gospel of Truth* that highlights the paraenetic function of these ethical imperatives, see further Tite, *Valentinian Ethics*.

104. This compassionate concern and care for others, especially those who are less advanced, is a major, motivating concern throughout the *Tripartite Tractate*. In this way, the *Tripartite Tractate* programmatically portrays advanced persons and aeons as lending assistance to others in order to guide them toward perfection/unity. For example, see *Tri. Trac.* 85.33–86.18: "For the aeons of the Father of the All, who had not suffered, took upon themselves the fall that had happened as if it were their own, with concern, goodness, and great sweetness. . . . They gathered together and prayed to the Father with a useful mind that help might come from above, from the hand of the Father, for his glory."

105. Cf. the missionary practices contained in Heracleon's *Commentary on John* (e.g., fragment 27) in which pneumatics, represented by the Samaritan woman, are expected to engage in missionary work by proclaiming the advent of the Savior.

106. See Thomassen, *Spiritual Seed*, 333–41 for a discussion of initiatory rites present in the *Excerpts of Theodotus* 66–86.

107. Ferguson, *Baptism*, 284; see also Thomassen, *Spiritual Seed*, 353–55.

6. THE THREEFOLD DIVISION AND EXEGESIS

1. Michael Kaler and Marie-Pierre Bussières ("Heracleon") recently argued that scholars are mistaken in calling Heracleon a Valentinian. Their argument, however, as demonstrated by Einar Thomassen ("Heracleon," 173), is unconvincing and makes errors of both omission (overlooking *testimonia*) and philological interpretation (interpreting Origen's phrase at *Comm. Jo.* 2.14.100 τὸν Οὐαλεντίνου λεγόμενον εἶναι γνώριμον Ἡρακλέωνα as Origen distancing himself from the claim that Heracleon was a Valentinian, as opposed to its more likely meaning, i.e., emphasizing that "Heracleon was said to be personally a pupil of Valentinus").

2. See the bibliography of both sides supplied by Einar Thomassen, "Heracleon," 182nn36–39.

3. This absence of higher and lower levels of salvation is not evidence that Heracleon has rejected this soteriology; rather, among the surviving fragments there simply is no mention of what salvation will resemble. Thus, we should adopt a much more agnostic approach; i.e., the absence of reference to higher and lower levels of salvation is not evidence that Heracleon has rejected this belief. As a cautionary example, see fragment 36, which implies that salvation may be tailored to specific tasks.

4. *Pace* Pier Franco Beatrice ("Greek Philosophy"), who concludes via an argument from silence that—since Origen preserves only forty-eight fragments—Heracleon wrote only forty-eight fragmentary opinions on the Gospel of John; consequently, according to Beatrice, Heracleon did not in fact compose an actual and whole commentary. Instead, Beatrice avers (195–96), Heracleon composed a "gnostic" and noncommentarial treatise that "eisegetically," "arbitrarily," and "violently" distorted the meaning of scripture in order to support his own theological beliefs. Origen then extracted all passages referring to parts of the Gospel of John from this "violently eisegetical" work and placed them into his own *Com-

mentary on John, thereby creating the illusion that Heracleon had never composed a *Commentary on John* himself. While there are several points at which Beatrice's argument fails to convince, I will single out only three: (1) Beatrice's argument from silence overlooks the fragmentary state and haphazard transmission of Origen's own *Commentary*; to put it quite simply, we cannot know how many passages from Heracleon Origen ultimately knew or cited because not all of Origen survives; (2) Origen himself was writing a *Commentary on John*; nowhere does he say his aim in so doing was to preserve every line of Heracleon's opus; (3) Beatrice's survey of the term *upomnemata* demonstrated the diversity of the term, but not its incompatibility with the genre of a Gospel commentary; see further Ansgar Wucherpfennig, *Heracleon Philologus*.

5. Pettipiece, "Nature," 377.

6. In addition to his *Commentary,* there is an additional fragment or better "remark" from Heracleon preserved by Photius on John 1:17, and Clement (*Ecl.* 25.1; *Strom.* 4.9.71–72) preserves two additional fragments of Heracleon, neither of which appears to be from his commentary on the Gospel of John.

7. See the helpful table found in Thomassen, "Heracleon," 176.

8. See Dunderberg, *Beyond Gnosticism*, 144; Thomassen is more reticent in making this claim, and so a tension emerges where he both claims that there is no logic of transformation ("Heracleon," 183) and notes the psychics cannot be saved qua psychics ("Heracleon," 190).

9. In either case, Heracleon's *Commentary on John* complicates as well as supports some of the conclusions we arrived at in the preceding chapter, and it also provides additional insights into the diversity of this early Christian missionizing movement. Tertullian attacked Valentinian teachers for precisely this apparent diversity of opinions and their constant invention of new beliefs and practices (*Against the Valentinians* 4)

10. Beatrice, "Greek Philosophy," 191–97; Wucherpfennig, *Heracleon Philologus*, 32–38; Thomassen, *Spiritual Seed*, 13–14n11. See now Larsen's thorough examination (*Gospels*, chapter 2) of these ancient sources and his reframing of them as "unfinished and less authored texts."

11. Origen (*Comm. Jo.*13.34.225) points out that Heracleon did *not* write anything about a particular line of John (4:32). Pagels (*Johannine Gospel*, 47) suggests that Heracleon wrote a commentary focused on cosmic concerns and thus omitted verses, like John 1:1–2, that occurred *prior* to the cosmos.

12. Though speculative, the likeliest social context for Heracleon's exegetical and ethically minded *Commentary on John* is his own study circle/house-church community. White's article ("Moral Pathology") on the social context for Clement of Alexandria's homily "Who Is the Rich Man That Will Be Saved?" may provide a model for further study that aims to link Heracleon to the physical and social contexts in which he wrote. While likely not as formal as Epictetus's classroom with its four stages of reading, exegesis, analysis, and argument (*Diss.* 4.4.14; cf. Snyder, *Teachers and Texts*, 22–30), Heracleon's role as a teacher likely affected his compositional process. It may be fruitful, therefore, to reconsider his *Commentary* in light of possible audience questions and interactions. Such an approach would also emphasize the "unfinishedness" and elastic nature of ancient ὑπομνήματα; on this, see further Larsen, *Gospels*.

13. Wucherpfennig, *Heracleon Philologus*.

14. Origen's *Commentary on John* consisted of at least thirty-two books, of which only nine now survive: 1, 2, 6, 10, 13, 19, 20, 28, 32. See further Heine, "Catena Fragments."

15. See Wucherpfennig, *Heracleon Philologus*, 52n.21 for an explanation of the corruption of τῷ νάῳ to τῶν ἄνω, which is the manuscript reading.

16. Thomassen ("Heracleon," 184–85) outlines the spatial dynamics of the temple in the following way: "*Hieron* designates the whole temple and not just the inner sanctuary, the *naos*. It includes the forecourt (*pronaos*), where the Levites go, as well as the Holy of Holies, where only the high priest may enter."

17. Wucherpfennig, *Heracleon Philologus*, 52, 67–72.

18. Thomassen, "Heracleon," 185n50.

19. Interpreters of Heracleon's social circumstances have sometimes been led astray by his commentarial genre (*pace* Dunderberg, *Beyond Gnosticism*, 141; and Pettipiece, "Nature," 391). Heracleon expresses social and ideological distance through characters mined from his exegetical commentary; however, it does not seem likely that he is drawing the same boundary lines or targeting the same opponents as, for example, the Gospel of John was, i.e., unbelieving (especially Pharisaic and priestly) Jews. Consequently, we must be cautious and avoid importing ethnic or historical opponents, e.g., Pharisaic Jews, when upon closer analysis Heracleon uses these characters as rhetorical *exempla*. See further Tite, *Valentinian Ethics*, 147–64; and Pagels, *Johannine Exegesis*, 67–68.

20. Thomassen, "Heracleon," 198–99. *Pace* Wucherpfennig, *Heracleon Philologus*, 333–53; and Dunderberg, *Beyond Gnosticism*, 141–44.

21. Moreover, this may be an insertion from Origen; see Thomassen, "Heracleon," 191–92n74.

22. Thomassen, "Heracleon," 188–90.

23. Tertullian (*Adv. Val.* 1) similarly remarks that Valentinians persuade men before instructing them.

24. Thomassen, "Heracleon," 189–90; see also Pagels, *Johannine Exegesis*, 85.

25. On this issue generally, see Dunderberg, *Beyond Gnosticism*, pt. 2.

26. Cf. 1 Corinthians 2–3. Whether we imagine the pneumatics as wandering charismatics, à la Gerd Theissen, or local scribal elites, à la William Arnal, this dichotomy between these specialized individuals (preachers or scribes) and the general community helpfully illustrates what the social and theoretical hierarchy among these communities *may* have resembled. See further Tite, *Valentinian Ethics*, chapter 7; cf. Theissen, *Sociology*; and Arnal, *Jesus*.

27. There is a tremendous amount of excellent scholarship on the social context of instruction and study in the broader Greco-Roman world; for a sampling, see the following: Gamble, *Books*; Snyder, *Teachers*; Watts, *City and School*; and Eshleman, *Social World*.

28. Provocatively, Ansgar Wucherpfennig (*Heracleon Philologus*, 332–57) questions whether we should import the three classes (hylic/choic, psychic, and pneumatic) for the three characters of the Samaritan woman, the petty king, and the hostile Jews. Most persuasive of his three criticisms is his reluctance to call those who are the children of the devil "choics," since the term appears only in fragment 46 and was most likely inserted by Origen as a gloss. Though Wucherpfennig is rightfully critical of importing foreign labels into Heracleon (especially where they are not explicitly claimed!), he nonetheless goes too far by first making arguments from absence (e.g., there are no concrete allusions to the myth of the fall of Sophia) into positive claims (e.g., Heracleon does not abide by or endorse a Valentinian system). This sort of argumentation disregards the fragmentary and irregular preservation of Heracleon's fragments, and also assumes that Heracleon's *Commentary* would have been amenable to such theoretical discussions (thus their exclusion was deliberate). Further-

more, Wucherpfennig treats these labels (choic/hylic, psychic, and pneumatic) as fossilized and fixed typological categories, each with a *single form*; thus, because Heracleon's use of the threefold division of humanity differs from the typological construction of these categories (which Wucherpfennig assembled from other Valentinian accounts), Wucherpfennig concludes that Heracleon did not endorse *the Valentinian* threefold division of humanity. It is better, however, to avoid such homogenizing typologies, and instead we should conclude that Heracleon was a member of a diverse and adaptive tradition based around Pauline exegesis, and that he deployed a threefold division of humanity tailored for and informed by ongoing missionizing practices. In this way, Heracleon emphasized what was most important: there are three types of conduct, epitomized by three different reactions to the Savior.

29. Cf. *Tri. Trac.* 118.29–19.13.

30. Though obscured by Origen's comments, it is important to note that Heracleon only mentions substance as regards those who are the children of the devil; whatever the difference is between psychics and pneumatics, it is not, according to what survives from Heracleon, a difference of substance.

31. For example, Heracleon, at least in what survives, does not explain all material, moral, and cosmological difference by analogue to the hierarchical relationship among three natures/substances.

32. See further Trumbower, *Born from Above*, 22–30.

33. As we will see, Heracleon uses the term nature (*physis*) nineteen times: frags. 17, 19, 24, 37, 40 (four times), 44, 46 (six times), and 47 (four times); in contrast, he uses the term substance (*ousia*) only four times: frags. 43, 44, 45, and 46). Heracleon's use of *ousia* is confined to riffing off a singular line of the Gospel of John: "'You are from your devil the father' means 'you are from the substance of the Devil'" (ὑμεῖς ἐκ τοῦ πατρὸς τοῦ διαβόλου ἐστέ ἀντὶ τοῦ 'ἐκ τῆς οὐσίας τοῦ διαβόλου) appears in fragments 44 and 46; cf. *Comm. Jo.* 20.20.168. The use of *ousia* in fragments 43 and 45, if authentic to Heracleon, is an allusion to this same line from John.

34. In my dissertation, I followed the minority position of Robert Grant (*Gnosticism*, 199) in translating κατάλληλον as "alien" or "contrary"; at the time, I thought this made good sense and I wanted an against-the-grain approach. I am grateful, however, to Dylan Burns for his recommendation against that translation. I have revised my argument accordingly.

35. Both the literal "from above" and "anew" are given as possible meanings for ἄνωθεν; in fact, ἄνωθεν is treated as meaning "anew" in John 3:3 and 3:7, and "from above" just a few verses later in 3:31, in Danker's *Greek-English Lexicon* (92). I am not interested in resolving what the Gospel of John means by ἄνωθεν; my interest here is that Heracleon appears to capitalize on the polyvalence of this term.

36. On the language of ethnic descent and kinship, see Johnson Hodge's exceptional *If Sons*.

37. Heracleon's claim (e.g., frag. 8; *Comm. Jo.* 6.39) that John the Baptist represents the Demiurge and was thus a psychic rather than pneumatic has puzzled some scholars; see, for example, Thomassen's discussion on this issue ("Heracleon," 183): "To conclude . . . it seems that the ambiguity of [John the Baptist] arises from the fact that he, as a prophet, is essentially part of the old dispensation, and in that sense psychic, like the demiurge, although he is necessarily psychic in the sense of not being spiritual. In fact, his being more than a prophet and having a superior inner 'self,' which is able to perceive the true nature of the Saviour, suggests that the Baptist is a spiritual person as well. Thus, because the category of

the psychic has a double meaning, and because the Baptist stands at the very point between the old and new dispensation, Heracleon seems to have been able to conceive of him, exceptionally, as being both psychic and spiritual at once." Heracleon's link between John the Baptist and the Demiurge, thereby labeling John a psychic, is likely a result of his commentarial genre and fastidious commitment to John's text. In John 3:27–30, for example, John the Baptist clearly subordinates himself to the Messiah (and by extension pneumatics). John the Baptist's implicit exclusion from the bridal chamber most likely contributed to Heracleon labeling him a psychic; on the significance of the bridal chamber as a ritual in Valentinianism, see further Thomassen, *Spiritual Seed*.

38. How best to render the *ioudaioi* of the Gospel of John is a contentious topic; cf. Attridge ("Heracleon and John," 205n34), who lists much of the relevant scholarship. Out of concern for consistency across this book, I will translate this term as "Jew" with the obvious caveat that John is polemically constructing a proximate other with whom he deeply disagrees; for his part, Heracleon is drawing upon and repurposing this polemical framework.

39. As we will see, *physis* appears to have a similar rhetorical range (theoretical fixity and sociological fluidity), one that Denise Kimber Buell (*New Race*) attributes to "race."

40. In addition to fragment 27 (see more below), see also fragments 37 and 39 for other instances of this missionizing ethic.

41. Frag. 17; *Comm. Jo.* 13.10.59–60.

42. Frag. 18 (*Comm. Jo.* 13.11) continues to emphasize the difference between an old life mired in sin and a new, heavenly life: in this passage, the Samaritan woman receives a new husband (her aeonic syzygy) and leaves behind her old life with her six inferior and evil husbands who abused her. See also fragment 19 (*Comm. Jo.* 13.15), which details specifically that the Samaritan woman, prior to her rebirth, had lived immorally and could not escape from her misconduct without the Savior. *Pace* Pagels (*Johannine Gospel*, 86–92) insofar as more than revelation and realization is needed by the Samaritan woman here; she requires a rebirth.

43. For an alternate view to Heracleon's conception of the tripartite division of humanity, see *Tri. Trac.* 116, 118–22. For our purposes, an important distinction between the two, as we will see, is that the fixed origins of Heracleon are of kinship and descent; whereas in *Tri. Trac.* they correspond to a much larger cosmological drama and hierarchy of existence, thereby connecting with clearly articulated (and fixed) ends.

44. *Physis* and its cognates appear eleven times in the New Testament, e.g., Romans 1:26 (two times); 1:27; 11:21; 11:24 (three times); 1 Corinthians 11:14; James 3:7; 2 Peter 2:12; Jude 10.

45. Plotinus, *Enn.* 3.1.6.1–3 (Armstrong); cf. Thiessen, *Paul*, 110.

46. Johnson Hodge, *If Sons*, 80.

47. Frag. 2; *Comm. Jo.* 2.21.237. It may be that Heracleon had passages like Romans 8:29 and Colossians 1:15–20 in mind here as well. Cf. Johnson-Hodge, *If Sons*, chapter 6.

48. See, for example, Romans 9:7 for "in Isaac," and Galatians 3:14, 26–29 for "in Christ."

49. For the argument that Paul's use of "in" refers to patrilineal descent, see Johnson-Hodge, *If Sons*, chapter 5.

50. The pneumatics generate more pneumatics by means of Spirit and as part of (or under: ὑπὸ τοῦ πνεύματος) the continued activity of the Spirit.

51. On the rhetorical function of kinship language to create fixity in discourse and expected practice, see Buell, *New Race*, 40: "What is crucial is the *function* that genealogical

claims play: namely, they imbue ethnoracial identities with a sense of stability, essence, and longevity."

52. Recall the importance of shared history and identity; see the section "On Earth as It Is in Heavens" in Chapter 4.

53. In other words, Heracleon's emphasis on three genealogical classes is very different from the Stoic conception of universal and individual natures; see, for example, Diogenes Laertius 7.87–89 (*SVF* 3.1): "Further, living in accordance with virtue is equivalent to living in accordance with experience of what happens by nature, as Chrysippus says in *On ends* book 1: for our own natures are parts of the nature of the whole" (Long and Sedley, *Hellenistic Philosophers*, vol. 1, 63C).

54. Much more, however, is implicit with Heracleon, and so we do not know for sure how he constructs agency and the sense of self, i.e., who/what is in charge of giving or withholding assent.

55. If fragment 2 is connected with Romans 8:29 (see note 47 above), however, then pneumatics were foreknown, even if not yet reborn.

56. In this way, natures as corporate categories are consistent and not "manifested" (*pace* Wucherpfennig, *Heracleon Philologus*, 347); also *pace* Trumbower (*Born from Above*, 25), who says that the complete threefold division existed prior to the advent of the Savior; and *pace* Attridge ("Heracleon and John," 203–5), who characterizes the reaction of humanity to the advent of the Savior as an "actualization" of a "potentiality"; while I think that is the right way of looking at the response of humanity to the Savior in the *Tripartite Tractate*, it does not encompass the language of rebirth and generation that I think is central to Heracleon's exegesis. I am mostly in agreement with Einar Thomassen's claim ("Heracleon," 182) that pneumatics did not exist prior to the advent of the Savior; although I do wonder if Heracleon would have considered the Savior to be a savior (thus of the pneumatic *physis*) prior to his saving advent.

57. Cf. the language of radical transformation following baptism preserved in the *Excerpts of Theodotus* 78.1: "Until baptism Fate is real, but after it the astrologers are no longer right." See also Tatian, *Oratio* 9.2.

58. *Pace* Thomassen ("Heracleon," 191–92), who rejects the idea that psychics could be the children of the devil; however, when we consider the disputed passage, its description is well suited to describe the psychological profile of bad psychics who choose to do the desires of the devil and become his children by adoption (frag. 46; *Comm. Jo.* 20.24.211–13). Thus, although the devil may not be able to produce children himself, people can become his children via inclination or merit (psychic and hylic, respectively?). Thus, when these damned psychics have the same nature (i.e., a distinctive sort of conduct and transmittable traits) as the devil (frag. 47; *Comm. Jo.* 20.28.252), which is error and ignorance (ἐκ πλάνης καὶ ἀγνοία), the responsibility is their own. Like the pneumatics, the means of their entry into this specific kinship (error and ignorance for the children of the devil) is also the means by which *they* can generate more like themselves as well.

59. Interestingly, *ousia* appears only twice in the New Testament (Luke 15:12, 13), and there it refers to the "property" or "possessions" of Luke's prodigal son; cf. *Gospel of Truth* 20.16, where ΟΥСΙΔ has a similar meaning.

60. It is difficult to tell for certain. Origen's predeterminist polemics specifically target the notion of substance; though certainly polemically Origen's rebukes would make little sense if Heracleon did not also use the term *ousia*. This does not mean, however, that Heracleon used *ousia* in a determinist manner, which is Origen's accusation. Therefore, although

who wrote *ousia* may be ultimately uncertain, I think a more conservative approach is warranted, and thus without textual confusion we should not attribute this ambiguous section to Origen's pen (*pace* Wucherpfennig, *Heracleon Philologus*, 347–49).

61. John 8:44: "You are from your father the devil, and you choose to do your father's desires (καὶ τὰς ἐπιθυμίας τοῦ πατρὸς ὑμῶν θέλετε ποιεῖν). He was a murderer from the beginning and does not stand in the truth, because there is no truth in him. When he lies, he speaks according to his own property (ἐκ τῶν ἰδίων λαλεῖ), for he is a liar and the father of lies."

62. *Comm. Jo.* 20.20.168: ὑμεῖς ἐκ τοῦ πατρὸς τοῦ διαβόλου ἐστέ ἀντὶ τοῦ 'ἐκ τῆς οὐσίας τοῦ διαβόλου; cf. *Comm. Jo.* 20.23.198: "You are from the substance of the devil" (ἐκ τῆς οὐσίας τοῦ διαβόλου ἦσαν).

63. See Wucherpfennig, *Heracleon Philologus*, 342ff. See note 60 above, however, as I have some reservations about this claim.

64. In contrast, see the *Tri. Trac.* 118ff.; cf. Kocar, "'Humanity."

65. On the mechanics of Pauline participation, especially the materiality of the *pneuma*, see further Chapter 2. A possible intertext here for Heracleon may be John 3:21, in which those who come to the light do their works in God: "but the one who does what it is true comes to the light so that it may clearly be seen that his deeds have been done in God (αὐτοῦ τὰ ἔργα ὅτι ἐν θεῷ ἐστιν εἰργασμένα)."

66. *Comm. Jo.* 20.23.199; cf. Thomassen, "Heracleon," 181–83 for bibliography on differing scholarly opinions of Heracleon's view of the tripartite division of humanity.

67. An illuminating parallel is Romans 1:18–32; in this passage, Paul claims that sexual immorality was the penalty for the disobedience of the Nations, not the cause of their disobedience.

68. Frag. 46; *Comm. Jo.* 20.24.215–18.

69. Frag. 47; *Comm. Jo.* 20.28.252–53.

70. On the fall of Sophia and its role in Valentinian protology and cosmology, see especially Thomassen, *Spiritual Seed*, chapters 21 and 23; for Valentinian texts in which *pathos* and desire are synonymous, see Thomassen, 289n59; on the connection between desire and the Platonist-Pythagorean tradition of the Dyad (see: plurality from unity), see Thomassen, 291.

71. Thomassen, *Spiritual Seed*, 254.

72. Kocar, "Humanity," 200–207, especially 204–5; on the interpretation of these effluences as part of a Valentinian therapy of the passions, see further Dunderberg, *Beyond Gnosticism*, chapter 6.

73. Thomassen, *Spiritual Seed*, 257–58.

74. See Ismo Dunderberg's helpful chart (*Beyond Gnosticism*, 112), in which desire is listed as one of the classic passions among both the Sethians and the Stoics.

75. Thomassen, "Saved," 145; cf. Thomassen, "Heracleon," 190.

76. See also Dunderberg, *Beyond Gnosticism*, 144.

77. Wasserman, *Death of the Soul*, 60–76.

78. Wasserman, *Death of the Soul*, 62.

79. Cf. fragment 13 (*Comm. Jo.* 10.33.213), discussed above, which depicts the saving actions of the Savior as the cleansing of the temple, in which the whip symbolizes the "power and energy of the Holy Spirit" that remove the wicked.

80. Again, there is a lot that is simply unknown: it is possible that Heracleon *chose* not to include fixed endings; it is also possible, however, that Heracleon did connect these three types of humanity to different soteriological fates.

81. Bell, *Ritual Theory*, 98.

82. Karen King, *Gnosticism*.

83. While it could be said that Heracleon's ethic resembles that of Clement's insofar as they both privilege the moral decision to give or withhold assent to the advent of the Savior (cf. *Strom.* 4.24.153.1; cf. 2.6.27.4; 2.12.55.1–2; 5.1.3; 5.13.86; 6.17.156.2; and 7.15.91), moral responsibility for Heracleon was ineluctably linked with being part of the right lineage, determined by the right sort of rebirth and the proper generation of others like you. He does not construct moral advancement as a singular path of progress through a specific curriculum of natures; in this way, he differs from Clement and others. On this curriculum or stages of moral progress in Clement, see especially Kovacs, "Clement of Alexandria and the Valentinian Gnostics."

CONCLUSION

1. On Cicero's use of divinizing language in his political maneuverings, see further Spencer Cole's *Cicero and the Rise of Deification at Rome* (Cambridge: Cambridge University Press, 2013).

2. Cicero, *Tusculan Disputations* 1.12.27 (trans. J. E. King; LCL).

3. In addition to Cole's *Cicero*, see also Luck ("Studia Divina"), who notes the influence of various Hellenistic schools on Cicero here.

4. Pelagius, *Letter to Demetrias* 17, translated by J. P. Burns in his *Theological Anthropology*, 54.

5. See further Peter Brown's excellent study *The Ransom of the Soul*.

6. Brown, *Ransom of the Soul*, 108.

7. "It is agreed that the statement 'x resembles y' is logically incomplete, for what is being asserted is not a question of the classification of species x and y as instances of a common genus, but rather a suppressed multi-term statement of analogy and difference capable of being properly expressed in formulations such as: 'x resembles y more than z with respect to . . .' or, "x resembles y more than w resembles z with respect to . . ." (J. Z. Smith, *Drudgery Divine*, 51).

8. F. J. P. Poole, "Metaphors and Maps: Towards Comparison in the Anthropology of Religion," *Journal of the American Academy of Religion* 54 (1986): 414 - 15 in J. Z. Smith, *Drudgery Divine*, 53.

9. J. Z. Smith, *Drudgery Divine*, 52.

10. The role of Jesus in the book of Revelation requires further clarification, and I plan to return to this in a subsequent paper.

11. MacIntyre, *After Virtue*, 219.

12. J. Z. Smith, "Map Is Not Territory," in *Map*, 308.

13. I believe I have shown, however, that there are sound historical rationales for grouping these authors and texts together, even if such groupings are rather rare (John and Paul) or to the best of my knowledge unprecedented (*Hermas* and the *Ap. John*).

14. This is not to say that this is a wholly original book, or that I have not at every step benefited from excellent scholarly conversation partners; rather, I am attempting to explain why the reader might unconsciously have heard John Cleese's voice announcing at the start of every new section: "And now for something completely different."

15. I am especially indebted to J. Z. Smith's reworking and application of Paul Ricoeur's famous phrase; see, for example, Smith, "Pearl"; Smith, *To Take Place*; and Smith, "Map Is Not Territory" in *Map*.

16. Meeks, *Origins of Christian Morality*.

17. Observing a cognate potential for novels in the academic study of philosophy, Martha Nussbaum (*Love's Knowledge*, 46) similarly has sought to reframe and expand the canon of morally edifying literature to include novels.

Bibliography

Algra, Keimpe. "Stoics on Souls and Demons: Reconstructing Stoic Demonology," in *Body and Soul in Ancient Philosophy* (ed. Dorothea Frede and Burkhand Reis; Berlin: Walter de Gruyter, 2009), 359–87.

Annas, Julia. *Hellenistic Philosophy of the Mind* (Berkeley: University of California Press, 1992).

Armstrong, A. H. *Plotinus: Ennead III* (Loeb Classical Library; Cambridge, MA: Harvard University Press, 1967).

Arnal, William. *Jesus and the Village Scribes: Galilean Conflicts and the Setting of Q* (Minneapolis: Fortress Press, 2001).

Attridge, Harold W. "Greek Equivalents of Two Coptic Phrases: CG I, 5.65.9–10 and CG II, 2.34.26," *Bulletin of the American Society of Papyrologists* 18 (1981): 27–32.

Attridge, Harold W. "The Gospel of Truth as an Exoteric Text," in *Nag Hammadi, Gnosticism, and Early Christianity* (ed. C. W. Hedrick and R. Hodgson; Peabody, MA: Hendrickson, 1986), 239–55.

Attridge, Harold W. "Valentinian and Sethian Apocalyptic Traditions," *Journal of Early Christian Studies* 8.2 (2000): 173–211.

Attridge, Harold W. "Heracleon and John: Reassessment of an Early Christian Hermeneutical Debate," in *Essays on John and Hebrews* (Grand Rapids, MI: Baker Academic, 2012), 193–207.

Attridge, Harold W., and Elaine Pagels. *Nag Hammadi Codex I: The Jung Codex* (2 vols.; Leiden: Brill, 1985).

Aune, David E. *Prophecy in Early Christianity and the Ancient Mediterranean World* (Grand Rapids, MI: Eerdmans, 1983).

Aune, David E. "Two Pauline Models of the Person," in *The Whole and Divided Self* (ed. David Aune and John McCarthy; New York: Cross Road, 1997), 89–114.

Aune, David E. *Revelation* (3 vols.; WBC 52; Nashville: Thomas Nelson, 1997–98).

Aune, David E. "Following the Lamb: Discipleship in the Apocalypse," in *Apocalypticism, Prophecy, and Magic in Early Christianity* (Grand Rapids, MI: Baker Academic, 2008), 66–78.

Aune, David E. "Qumran and the Book of Revelation," in *Apocalypticism, Prophecy, and Magic in Early Christianity* (Grand Rapids, MI: Baker Academic, 2006; 2008), 79–98.

Aune, David E. "The Influence of Roman Imperial Court Ceremonial on the Apocalypse of John," in *Apocalypticism, Prophecy, and Magic in Early Christianity* (Grand Rapids, MI: Baker Academic, 2006; 2008), 99–119.

Aus, Roger. "Paul's Travel Plans to Spain and the 'Full Number of the Gentiles' of Romans 11:25," *Novum Testamentum* 21.3 (1979): 232–62.

Barc, Bernard, and Louis Painchaud. "La réécriture de l'*Apocryphon de Jean* à la lumière de l'hymne final de la version longue," *Le Muséon* 112 (1999): 317–33.

Barclay, John M. G. "Mirror-Reading a Polemical Letter: Galatians as a Test Case," *Journal for the Study of the New Testament* 31 (1987): 73–93.

Barclay, John M. G. *Paul and the Gift* (Grand Rapids MI: Eerdmans, 2015).

Barr, David. *Tales of the End: A Narrative Commentary on the Book of Revelation* (Santa Rosa, CA: Polebridge Press, 1998).

Batovici, Dan. "The *Shepherd of Hermas* in Recent Scholarship on the Canon: A Review Article," *Annali di storia dell'esegesi* 34.1 (2017): 89–105.

Bauckham, Richard. "The Book of Revelation as a Christian War Scroll," *Neotestamentica* 22.1 (1988): 17–40.

Bauckham, Richard. *The Climax of Prophecy: Studies on the Book of Revelation* (Edinburgh: T&T Clark, 1993).

Bauckham, Richard. *The Theology of the Book of Revelation* (Cambridge: Cambridge University Press, 1993).

Bauckham, Richard. "The Apocalypse of Peter: A Jewish-Christian Apocalypse from the Time of Bar Kokhba," in *The Fate of the Dead: Studies on Jewish and Christian Apocalypses* (Atlanta: Society of Biblical Literature, 1998), 160–258.

Baxter, A. G., and J. A. Ziesler. "Paul and Arboriculture: Romans 11.17–24," *Journal for the Study of the New Testament* 24 (1985): 25–32.

Beale, G. K. *The Book of Revelation: A Commentary on the Greek Text* (Grand Rapids, MI: Eerdmans, 1999).

Beasley-Murray, George. *The Book of Revelation: Based on the Revised Standard Version* (Grand Rapids, MI: Eerdmans, 1981).

Beatrice, Pier Franco. "Greek Philosophy and Gnostic Soteriology in Heracleon's 'Upomnemata,'" *Early Christianity* 3.2 (2012): 188–214.

Beker, J. C. *Paul the Apostle: The Triumph of God in Life and Thought* (Philadelphia: Fortress Press, 1980).

Beker, J. C. "The Faithfulness of God and the Priority of Israel in Paul's Letter to the Romans," in *Christians Among Jews and Gentiles: Essays in Honor of Krister Stendahl on His Sixty-Fifth Birthday* (ed. George W. E. Nickelsburg and George W. MacRae; Philadelphia: Fortress Press, 1986), 10–16.

Bell, Catherine. *Ritual Theory, Ritual Practice* (New York: Oxford University Press, 1992).

Bickerman, Elias. "The Warning Inscriptions of Herod's Temple," *Jewish Quarterly Review* 37.4 (1947): 387–405.

Bobzien, Susanne. "Stoic Conceptions of Freedom and Their Relation to Ethics," in *Aristotle and After* (ed. Richard Sorabji; London: Institute of Classical Studies, School of Advanced Study, University of London, 1997), 71–89.

Bobzien, Susanne. "The Inadvertent Conception and Late Birth of the Free-Will Problem," *Phronesis* 43.2 (1998): 133–75.

Bobzien, Susanne. *Determinism and Freedom in Stoic Philosophy* (Oxford: Oxford University Press, 1998).

Bobzien, Susanne. "Did Epicurus Discover the Free Will Problem?," in *Oxford Studies in Ancient Philosophy*, vol. 19 (ed. David Sedley; Oxford: Oxford University Press, 2000), 287–337.

Bobzien, Susanne. "Choice and Moral Responsibility in *Nicomachean Ethics* iii, 1–5," in *The Cambridge Companion to Aristotle's "Nicomachean Ethics"* (ed. Ronald Polansky; Cambridge: Cambridge University Press, 2014), 81–109.

Boustan, Ra'anan S. "Augustine as Revolutionary? Reflections on Continuity and Rupture in Jewish-Christian Relations in Paula Fredriksen's *Augustine and the Jews*," *Jewish Quarterly Review* 99.1 (2009): 74–87.

Boyarin, Daniel. *A Radical Jew: Paul and the Politics of Identity* (Berkeley: University of California, 1994).

Boyarin, Daniel. *Borderlines: The Partition of Judaeo-Christianity* (Philadelphia: University of Pennsylvania, 2004).

Boys-Stones, George. "Human Autonomy and Divine Revelation in Origen," in *Severan Culture* (ed. Simon Swain et al.; Cambridge: Cambridge University Press, 2007), 489–99.

Boys-Stones, George. "'Middle' Platonists on Fate and Human Autonomy," in *Greek and Roman Philosophy, 100 BC–200 AD*, vol. 2 (ed. Richard Sorabji and Robert W. Sharples; London: Institute of Classical Studies, 2007), 431–47.

Brakke, David. "The Body in Early Eastern Christian Sources," *Bulletin of the American Society of Papyrologists* 37 (2000): 119–34.

Brakke, David. *Demons and the Making of the Monk: Spiritual Combat in Early Christianity* (Cambridge, MA: Harvard University Press, 2006).

Brakke, David. *The Gnostics: Myth, Ritual, and Diversity in Early Christianity* (Cambridge, MA: Harvard University Press, 2010).

Brakke, David. "Scriptural Practices in Early Christianity: Towards a New History of the New Testament Canon," in *Invention, Writing, and Usurpation: Discursive Fights over Religious Traditions in Antiquity* (ed. Jörg Ulrich et al.; Frankfurt: Peter Lang, 2012), 263–80.

Brand, Miryam. *Evil Within and Without: The Source of Sin and Its Nature as Portrayed in Second Temple Literature* (Göttingen: Vandenhoeck & Ruprecht, 2013).

Brennan, Tad. *The Stoic Life: Emotions, Duties, and Fate* (Oxford: Oxford University Press, 2005).

Brent, Allen. *Hippolytus and the Roman Church in the Third Century: Communities in Tension Before the Emergence of a Monarch-Bishop* (Leiden: Brill, 1995).

Briggs, Robert A. *Jewish Temple Imagery in the Book of Revelation* (New York: Peter Lang, 1999).

Brown, Peter. *The Making of Late Antiquity* (Cambridge, MA: Harvard University Press, 1978).

Brown, Peter. *Body and Society: Men, Women, and Sexual Renunciation in Early Christianity* (New York: Columbia University Press, 1988).

Brown, Peter. "Alms and the Afterlife: A Manichaean View of Early Christian Practice," in *East and West: Papers in Ancient History Presented to Glen Bowersock* (ed. T. Corey Brennan and Harriet I. Flower; Cambridge, MA: Harvard University Press, 2008), 145–58.

Brown, Peter. *The Ransom of the Soul: Afterlife and Wealth in Western Christianity* (Cambridge, MA: Harvard University Press, 2015).

Buell, Denise Kimber. "Race and Universalism in Early Christianity," *Journal of Early Christian Studies* 10.4 (2002): 429–68.

Buell, Denise Kimber. *Why This New Race? Ethnic Reasoning in Early Christianity* (New York: Columbia University Press, 2005).

Bull, Christian H. "Women, Angels, and Dangerous Knowledge: The Myth of the Watchers in the *Apocryphon of John* and Its Monastic Manuscript-Context," in *Women and Knowledge in Early Christianity* (ed. Ulla Tervahauta et al.; Leiden: Brill, 2017), 75–107.

Burns, Dylan. *Apocalypse of the Alien God: Platonism and the Exile of Sethian Gnosticism* (Philadelphia: University of Pennsylvania Press, 2014).

Burns, J. Patout. *Theological Anthropology* (Philadelphia: Fortress Press, 1981).

Caird, George. "Review of E. P. Sanders, *Paul and Palestinian Judaism: A Comparison of Patterns of Religion*," *Journal of Theological Studies* 29.2 (1978): 538–43.

Campbell, William S. "The Addressees of Paul's Letter to the Romans: Assemblies of God in House Churches or Synagogues?," in *Between Gospel and Election: Explorations in the Interpretation of Romans 9–11* (ed. Florian Wilk and J. Ross Wagner; Tübingen: Mohr Siebeck, 2010), 171–95.

Caputo, John D., and Linda Martin Alcoff, eds. *St. Paul Among the Philosophers* (Bloomington: Indiana University Press, 2009).

Casey, Robert. *Excerpta ex Theodoto of Clement of Alexandria* (London: Christophers, 1934).

Cavell, Stanley. *Conditions Handsome and Unhandsome: The Conditions of Emersonian Perfectionism* (Chicago: University of Chicago Press, 1990).

Charlesworth, James, ed. *The Old Testament Pseudepigrapha* (2 vols.; New York: Doubleday, 1985).

Choat, Malcolm, and Rachel Yuen-Collingridge. "The Egyptian Hermas: The Shepherd in Egypt Before Constantine," in *Early Christian Manuscripts: Examples of Applied Method and Approach* (ed. Thomas J. Kraus and Tobias Nicklas; Leiden: Brill, 2010), 191–212.

Clark, Elizabeth. *Clement's Use of Aristotle: The Aristotelian Contribution to Clement of Alexandria's Refutation of Gnosticism* (New York: Edwin Mellon Press, 1977).

Cohen, Shaye J. D. "Crossing the Boundary and Becoming a Jew," *Harvard Theological Review* 82.1 (1989): 13–33.

Cohen, Shaye J. D. *The Beginnings of Jewishness: Boundaries, Varieties, Uncertainties* (Berkeley: University of California Press, 1999).

Cole, Spencer. *Cicero and the Rise of Deification at Rome* (Cambridge: Cambridge University Press, 2013).

Collins, John J. *The Apocalyptic Imagination: An Introduction to Jewish Apocalyptic Literature* (2nd ed.; Grand Rapids, MI: Eerdmans, 1998).

Concannon, Cavan W. *"When You Were Gentiles": Specters of Ethnicity in Roman Corinth and Paul's Corinthian Correspondence* (New Haven, CT: Yale University Press, 2014).

Cribiore, Raffaella. *Gymnastics of the Mind: Greek Education in Hellenistic and Roman Egypt* (Princeton, NJ: Princeton University Press, 2001).

Cullmann, Oscar. *On Christ and Time: The Primitive Christian Conception of Time and History* (trans. F. V. Filson; 2nd ed.; London: SCM Press, 1962).

Dallen, James. *The Reconciling Community: The Rite of Penance* (New York: Pueblo, 1986).

Danker, Frederick William, ed. *A Greek-English Lexicon of the New Testament and Other Early Christian Literature* (3rd ed.; Chicago: University of Chicago Press, 2000).

Davies, W. D. "Paul and the People of Israel," *New Testament Studies* 24 (1977): 4–39.

Dawson, David. *Allegorical Readers and Cultural Revision in Ancient Alexandria* (Berkeley: University of California Press, 1992).

Desjardins, Michel. "The Sources for Valentinian Gnosticism: A Question of Methodology," *Vigiliae Christianae* 40 (1986): 342–47.

Desjardins, Michel. *Sin in Valentinianism* (Atlanta: Scholars Press, 1990).

Dibelius, Otto. "Studien zur Geschichte der Valentinianer," *Zeitschrift für die neutestamentliche Wissenschaft* 9 (1908): 230–47.

Dihle, Albrecht. *The Theory of Will in Classical Antiquity* (Berkeley: University of California Press, 1982).

Dillon, John. "The Magical Power of Names in Origen and Later Platonism," in *Origeniana tertia* (ed. Richard Hanson and Henri Crouzel; Rome: Edizioni dell'Ateneo, 1985), 203–16.

Dillon, John. "An Ethic for the Late Antique Sage," in *The Cambridge Companion to Plotinus* (ed. Lloyd P. Gerson; Cambridge: Cambridge University Press, 1996), 315–35.

Dillon, John. "How Does the Soul Direct the Body, After All? Traces of a Dispute on Mind-Body Relations in the Old Academy," in *Body and Soul in Ancient Philosophy* (ed. Dorothea Frede and Burkhard Reis; Berlin: Walter de Gruyter, 2009), 349–56.

Dodd, C. H. *The Apostolic Preaching and Its Development* (London: Hodder &Stoughton, 1936; reset 1944).

Donaldson, Terence. *Paul and the Gentiles: Remapping the Apostle's Convictional World* (Minneapolis: Fortress Press, 1997).

Donaldson, Terence. "Jewish Christianity, Israel's Stumbling, and the *Sonderweg* Reading of Paul," *Journal for the Study of the New Testament* 29.1 (2006): 27–54.

Donaldson, Terence. *Judaism and the Gentiles: Jewish Patterns of Universalism to 135 CE* (Waco. TX: Baylor University Press, 2007).

Dubois, Jean-Daniel. "La sotériologie Valentinienne du Traité Tripartite (NH I,5)," in *Les textes de Nag Hammadi et la problème de leur classification* (ed. Louis Painchaud and Anne Pasquier; Québec: Les Presses de l'Université Laval, 1995), 221–32.

Dubois, Jean-Daniel. "Remarques sur la cohérence des extraits de Théodote," in *Gnosticism, Platonism, and the Late Ancient World* (ed. Kevin Corrigan et al.; Leiden: Brill, 2013), 209–23.

Duff, Paul. *Who Rides the Beast? Prophetic Rivalry and the Rhetoric of Crisis in the Churches of the Apocalypse* (Oxford: Oxford University Press, 2001).

Duff, Paul. "The 'Synagogue of Satan': Crisis Mongering and the Apocalypse of John," in *The Reality of the Apocalypse: Rhetoric and Politics in the Book of Revelation* (ed. David Barr; Leiden: Brill, 2006), 147–68.

Dunderberg, Ismo. "The School of Valentinus," in *A Companion to Second-Century Christian "Heretics"* (ed. Antti Marjanen and Petri Luomanen; Leiden: Brill, 2005), 64–99.

Dunderberg, Ismo. *Beyond Gnosticism: Myth, Lifestyle, and Society in the School of Valentinus* (New York: Columbia University Press, 2008).

Dunderberg, Ismo. "Stoic Traditions in the School of Valentinus," in *Stoicism in Early Christianity* (ed. Tuomas Rasimus, Troels Engberg-Pedersen, and Ismo Dunderberg; Grand Rapids, MI: Baker Academic, 2010), 220–38.

Dunderberg, Ismo. "Valentinian Theories on Classes of Humankind," in *Zugänge zur Gnosis*: *Akten zur Tagung der Patristischen Arbeitsgemeinschaft vom 02.–05.01.2011 in Berlin-Spandau* (ed. Christoph Markschies and Johannes van Oort; Leuven: Peeters, 2013), 113–28.

Dunn, James D. G. "The New Perspective on Paul and the Law," *Bulletin of the John Rylands University Library of Manchester* 65 (1983): 95–122.

Dunn, James D. G. "Works of the Law and the Curse of the Law (Galatians 3:10–14)," *New Testament Studies* 31 (1985): 523–42.

Dunn, James D. G. *The Christ and the Spirit: Collected Essays* (Grand Rapids, MI: Eerdmans, 1998).

Edwards, Mark. *Origen Against Plato* (Burlington, VT: Ashgate, 2002).

Ehrman, Bart. *The Apostolic Fathers*, vol. 2 (Loeb Classical Library; Cambridge, MA: Harvard University Press, 2003).

Eisenbaum, Pamela. *Paul Was Not a Christian: The Original Message of a Misunderstood Apostle* (New York: HarperOne, 2009).

Engberg-Pedersen, Troels. *Cosmology and Self in the Apostle Paul: The Material Spirit* (Oxford: Oxford University Press, 2010).

Epp, Eldon. "New Testament Papyri and the Transmission of the New Testament," in *Oxyrhynchus: A City and Its Texts* (ed. A. K. Bowman et al; Graeco-Roman Memoirs, 93; London: The Egypt Exploration Society's Arts and Humanities Research Council, 2007), 315–31.

Eshleman, Kendra. *The Social World of Intellectuals in the Roman Empire: Sophists, Philosophers, and Christians* (Cambridge: Cambridge University Press, 2012).

Esler, Philp F. "Ancient Oleiculture and Ethnic Differentiation: The Meaning of the Olive Tree in Romans 11," *Journal for the Study of the New Testament* 26.1 (2003): 103–24.

Fekkes, Jan, III. *Isaiah and the Prophetic Traditions in the Book of Revelation: Visionary Antecedents and Their Development* (Sheffield: Sheffield Academic Press, 1994).

Ferguson, Everett. *Baptism in the Early Church: History, Theology, and Liturgy in the First Five Centuries* (Grand Rapids, MI: Eerdmans, 2009).

Ferrari, G. R. F. "The Three-Part Soul," in *The Cambridge Companion to Plato's Republic* (ed. G. R. F. Ferrari; Cambridge: Cambridge University Press, 2007), 165–201.

Fishbane, Michael. *Biblical Interpretation in Ancient Israel* (Oxford: Oxford University Press, 1985).

Flemming, Dean. "'On Earth as It Is in Heaven': Holiness and the People of God in Revelation," in *Holiness and Ecclesiology in the New Testament* (ed. Kent Brower and Andy Johnson; Grand Rapids, MI: Eerdmans, 2007), 343–62.

Fox, Robin Lane. *Pagans and Christians* (New York: Alfred A. Knopf, 1987).

Frankfurter, David. "The Legacy of Jewish Apocalypses in Early Christianity: Regional Trajectories," in *The Jewish Apocalyptic Heritage in Early Christianity* (ed. James C. VanderKam and William Adler; Minneapolis: Fortress Press, 1996), 129–200.

Frankfurter, David. "Jews or Not? Reconstructing the 'Other' in Rev 2:9 and 3:9," *Harvard Theological Review* 94 (2001): 403–25.

Frankfurter, David. "Beyond 'Jewish Christianity': Continuing Religious Sub-Cultures of the Second and Third Centuries and Their Documents," in *The Ways That Never Parted: Jews and Christians in Late Antiquity and the Early Middle Ages* (ed. Adam Becker and Annette Yoshiko Reed; Tübingen: Mohr Siebeck, 2003), 131–43.

Frede, Dorothea. "Stoic Determinism," in *The Cambridge Companion to the Stoics* (ed. Bran Inwood; Cambridge: Cambridge University Press, 2003), 179–205.

Frede, Michael. *A Free Will: Origins of a Notion in Ancient Thought* (ed. A. A. Long; Berkeley: University of California Press, 2011).

Fredriksen, Paula. "Judaism, the Circumcision of Gentiles, and Apocalyptic Hope: Another Look at Galatians 1 and 2," *Journal of Theological Studies* 42.2 (1991): 532–64.

Fredriksen, Paula. "Paul, Purity, and the *Ekklesia* of the Gentiles," in *The Beginnings of Christianity* (ed. Jack Pastor and Menachem Mor; Jerusalem: Yad Ben-Zvi Press, 2005), 205–17.

Fredriksen, Paula. "Historical Integrity, Interpretative Freedom: The Philosopher's Paul and the Problem of Anachronism," in *St. Paul Among the Philosophers* (ed. John D. Caputo and Linda Martin Alcoff; Bloomington: Indiana University Press, 2009), 61–73.

Fredriksen, Paula. "Judaizing the Nations: The Ritual Demands of Paul's Gospel," *New Testament Studies* 56 (2010): 232–52.

Fredriksen, Paula. *Sin: The Early History of an Idea* (Princeton, NJ: Princeton University Press, 2012).

Fredriksen, Paula. *Paul: The Pagans' Apostle* (New Haven, CT: Yale University Press, 2017).

Fredriksen, Paula. "How Jewish Is God? Divine Ethnicity in Paul's Theology," *Journal of Biblical Literature* 137.1 (2018): 193–212.

Friesen, Steven J. *Imperial Cults and the Apocalypse of John* (Oxford: Oxford University Press, 2001).

Friesen, Steven J. "Sarcasm in Revelation 2–3: Churches, Christians, True Jews, and Satanic Synagogues," in *The Reality of the Apocalypse: Rhetoric and Politics in the Book of Revelation* (ed. David Barr; Leiden: Brill, 2006), 127–44.

Gager, John. "Functional Diversity in Paul's Use of End-Time Language," *Journal of Biblical Literature* 89.3 (1970): 325–37.

Gager, John. *Reinventing Paul* (Oxford: Oxford University Press, 2000).

Gamble, Harry. *Books and Readers in the Early Church: A History of Early Christian Texts* (New Haven, CT: Yale University Press, 1995).

Gamble, Harry. "The New Testament Canon: Recent Research and the *Status Quaestionis*," in *The Canon Debate* (ed. Lee Martin McDonald and James A. Sanders; Peabody, MA: Hendrickson, 2002), 267–94.

Gaston, Lloyd. *Paul and the Torah* (Eugene, OR: Wipf and Stock, 1987).

Gathercole, Simon. *Where Is Boasting? Early Jewish Soteriology and Paul's Response in Romans 1–5* (Grand Rapids, MI: Eerdmans, 2002).

Gill, Christopher. *The Structured Self in Hellenistic and Roman Thought* (Oxford: Oxford University Press, 2006).

Glad, Clarence E. *Paul and Philodemus: Adaptability in Epicurean and Early Christian Psychagogy* (Leiden: Brill, 1995).

Goodman, Martin. *Mission and Conversion: Proselytizing in the Religious History of the Roman Empire* (Oxford: Clarendon Press, 1994).

Grafton, Anthony, and Megan Williams. *Christianity and the Transformation of the Book: Origen, Eusebius, and the Library of Caesarea* (Cambridge, MA: Belknap Press of Harvard University Press, 2006).

Grant, Robert M. *Gnosticism: A Sourcebook of Heretical Writings from the Early Christian Period* (New York: Harper & Brothers, 1961).

Graver, Margaret. *Stoicism and Emotion* (Chicago: University of Chicago Press, 2007).

Greer, Rowan. "The Dog and the Mushrooms: Irenaeus' View of the Valentinians Assessed," in *The Rediscovery of Gnosticism*, vol. 1, *The School of Valentinus* (ed. Bentley Layton; Leiden: Brill, 1980), 146–75.

Gundry, Robert H. "The New Jerusalem People as Place, Not Place for People," *Novum Testamentum* 29 (1987): 254–64.

Haines-Eitzen, Kim. *Guardians of Letters: Literacy, Power, and the Transmitters of Early Christian Literature* (Oxford: Oxford University Press, 2000).

Harvey, Graham. *The True Israel: Uses of the Names Jew, Hebrew, and Israel in Ancient Jewish and Early Christian Literature* (Leiden: Brill, 1996).

Hauerwas, Stanley. *The Peaceable Kingdom: A Primer in Christian Ethics* (Notre Dame: University of Notre Dame Press, 1983).

Hayes, Christine. *Gentile Impurities and Jewish Identities: Intermarriage and Conversion from the Bible to the Talmud* (Oxford: Oxford University Press, 2002).

Hayes, Christine. *What's Divine About Divine Law?* (Princeton, NJ: Princeton University Press, 2015).

Hays, Richard. *The Faith of Jesus Christ: An Investigation of the Narrative Structure of Galatians 3:1–4:11* (Chico, CA: Scholars Press, 1983).

Hays, Richard B. *Echoes of Scripture in the Letters of Paul* (New Haven, CT: Yale University Press, 1989).

Heine, Ronald E. "Can the Catena Fragments of Origen's *Commentary on John* Be Trusted?," *Vigiliae Christianae* 40.2 (1986): 118–34.

Himmelfarb, Martha. *Tours of Hell: An Apocalyptic Form in Jewish and Christian Literature* (Philadelphia: Fortress Press, 1983).

Himmelfarb, Martha. *Ascent to Heaven in Jewish and Christian Apocalypses* (New York: Oxford University Press, 1993).

Himmelfarb, Martha. "Review of Daniel Boyarin's *A Radical Jew: Paul and the Politics of Identity* (Berkeley: University of California Press, 1994)." *Association for Jewish Studies* 21 (1996): 148–51.

Himmelfarb, Martha. *A Kingdom of Priests: Ancestry and Merit in Ancient Judaism* (Philadelphia: University of Pennsylvania Press, 2006).

Himmelfarb, Martha. "Judaism and Hellenism in 2 Maccabees," in *Between Temple and Torah: Essays on Priests, Scribes, and Visionaries in the Second Temple Period and Beyond* (Tübingen: Mohr Siebeck, 2013), 191–210.

Hvalvik, Reidar. "A Sonderweg for Israel: A Critical Examination of a Current Interpretation of Romans 11:25–27," *Journal for the Study of the New Testament* 38 (1990): 87–107.

Inwood, Brad. *Ethics and Human Action in Ancient Stoicism* (Oxford: Clarendon Press, 1985).

Inwood, Brad. "Moral Causes: The Role of Physical Explanation in Ancient Ethics," in *Thinking About Causes: From Greek Philosophy to Modern Physics* (ed. Peter Machamer and Gereon Woltes; Pittsburgh: University of Pittsburgh Press, 2007), 14–36.

Jackson, Michael. *The Politics of Storytelling: Variations on a Theme by Hannah Arendt* (2nd ed.; Copenhagen: Museum Tusculanum Press, 2013).

Jacobs, Andrew. "A Jew's Jew: Paul and the Early Christian Problem of Jewish Origins," *Journal of Religion* 86 (2006): 258–86.

Jenott, Lance. *The Gospel of Judas: Coptic Text, Translation, and Historical Interpretation of 'the Betrayer's Gospel'* (Tübingen: Mohr Siebeck, 2011).

Jenott, Lance. "Emissaries of Truth and Justice: The Seed of Seth as Agents of Divine Providence," in *Gnosticism, Platonism, and the Late Ancient World: Essays in Honor of John Turner* (ed. Kevin Corrigan, Tuomas Rasimus, et al.; Leiden: Brill, 2013), 43–62.

Jewett, Robert. *Romans: A Commentary* (Minneapolis: Fortress Press, 2007).

Johnson, William. "Toward a Sociology of Reading in Classical Antiquity," *American Journal of Philology* 121.4 (2001): 593–627.

Johnson, William. *Readers and Reading Culture in the High Roman Empire: A Study of Elite Communities* (Oxford: Oxford University Press, 2010).

Johnson Hodge, Caroline. *If Sons, Then Heirs: A Study of Kinship and Ethnicity in the Letters of Paul* (Oxford: Oxford University Press, 2007).

Kahn, Charles H. "Discovering the Will: From Aristotle to Augustine," in *The Question of 'Eclecticism': Studies in Later Greek Philosophy* (ed. John Dillon and A. A. Long; Berkeley: University of California Press, 1988), 234–59.

Kaler, Michael, and Marie-Pierre Bussières. "Was Heracleon a Valentinian: New Look at Old Sources," *Harvard Theological Review* 99.3 (2006): 275–89.

Käsemann, Ernst. *New Testament Questions of Today* (trans. W. J. Montague; London: SCM Press, 1969).

Kenney, John Peter. "Ancient Apophatic Theology," in *Gnosticism and Later Platonism: Themes, Figures, and Texts* (ed. John Turner and Ruth Majercik; Atlanta: Society of Biblical Literature, 2000), 259–75.

King, J. E. *Cicero: Tusculan Disputations* (Loeb Classical Library; Cambridge, MA: Harvard University Press, 1945).

King, Karen. "The Body and Society in the *Apocryphon of John*," in *The School of Moses: Studies in Philo and Hellenistic Religion* (ed. Peter John Kenney; Atlanta: Scholars Press, 1995), 82–97.

King, Karen. "Approaching the Variants of the *Apocryphon of John*," in *The Nag Hammadi Library After Fifty Years: Proceedings of the 1995 Society of Biblical Literature Commemoration* (ed. John Turner and Anne McGuire; Leiden: Brill, 1997), 105–37.

King, Karen. *What Is Gnosticism?* (Cambridge, MA: Harvard University Press, 2003).

King, Karen. *Secret Revelation of John* (Cambridge, MA: Harvard University Press, 2006).

King, Karen. "Which Early Christianity?," in *The Oxford Handbook of Early Christian Studies* (ed. Susan Ashbrook Harvey and David G. Hunter; Oxford: Oxford University Press, 2008), 66–84.

Klawans, Jonathan. "Notions of Gentile Impurity in Ancient Judaism," *Association for Jewish Studies* 20.2 (1995): 285–312.

Klawans, Jonathan. *Impurity and Sin in Ancient Judaism* (Oxford: Oxford University Press, 2000).

Kloppenborg, John S. "The Transformation of Moral Exhortation in *Didache* 1–5," in *The Didache in Context: Essays on Its Text, History, and Transmission* (ed. Clayton Jefford; Leiden: Brill, 1995), 88–109.

Knibb, M. A. "Christian Adoption and Transmission of Jewish Pseudepigrapha: The Case of 1 Enoch," *Journal for the Study of Judaism in the Persian, Hellenistic, and Roman Periods* 32 (2001): 396–415.

Kocar, Alexander. "'Humanity Came to Be According to Three Essential Types': Ethical Responsibility and Practice in the Valentinian Anthropogony of the *Tripartite Tractate* (NHC I, 5)," in *Jewish and Christian Cosmogony in Late Antiquity* (ed. Lance Jenott and Sarit Kattan Gribetz; Tübingen: Mohr Siebeck, 2013), 193–221.

Kocar, Alexander. "A Hierarchy of Salvation in the Book of Revelation: Different Peoples, Dwellings, and Tasks in the End Times," in *Placing Ancient Texts: The Ritual and Rhetorical Use of Space* (ed. Mika Ahuvia and Alexander Kocar; Tübingen: Mohr Siebeck, 2018), 101–30.

Kocar, Alexander. "The Ethics of Higher and Lower Levels of Salvation in the *Excerpts of Theodotus* and the *Tripartite Tractate*," in *Valentinianism: New Studies* (ed. Christoph Markschies and Einar Thomassen; Leiden: Brill, 2019), 205–38.

Koester, Helmut. "*GNOMAI DIAPHORAI*: The Origin and Nature of Diversification in the History of Early Christianity," in *Trajectories Through Early Christianity* (Eugene, OR: Wipf and Stock, 1971), 114–57.

Koester, Helmut. *Introduction to the New Testament* (2 vols.; New York: Walter de Gruyter, 1995, 2000).

Kovacs, Judith. "Clement of Alexandria and the Valentinian Gnostics" (PhD diss., Columbia University, 1978).

Kovacs, Judith. "Echoes of Valentinian Exegesis in Clement of Alexandria and Origen: The Interpretation of I Cor. 3:1–3," in *Origeniana Octava* (ed. L. Perrone; Leuven: Peeters, 2003), 317–29.

Kovacs, Judith. "Clement of Alexandria and Valentinian Exegesis in the *Excerpts of Theodotus*," *Studia Patristica* 41 (2006): 187–200.

Kovacs, Judith. "The Language of Grace: Valentinian Reflection on New Testament Imagery," in *Radical Christian Voices and Practice: Essays in Honour of Christopher Rowland* (ed. Zoë Bennett and David B. Gowler; Oxford: Oxford University Press, 2012), 69–85.

Kraft, Robert A. "In Search of 'Jewish Christianity' and Its 'Theology': Problems of Definition and Methodology," *Recherches de science religieuse* 60 (1972): 81–96.

Kraft, Robert A. "The Multiform Jewish Heritage of Early Christianity," in *Christianity, Judaism, and Other Greco-Roman Cults: Studies for Morton Smith* (ed. J. Neusner; Leiden: Brill, 1975), 3:174–99.

Kraft, Robert A. "The Pseudepigrapha in Christianity," in *Tracing the Threads: Studies in the Vitality of Jewish Pseudepigrapha* (ed. J. C. Reeves; Atlanta: Scholars Press, 1994), 55–86.

Kraft, Robert A. "Setting the Stage and Framing Some Central Questions," *Journal for the Study of Judaism in the Persian, Hellenistic, and Roman Periods* 32 (2001): 371–95.

Labahn, Michael. "The Resurrection of the Followers of the Lamb: Between Heavenly 'Reality' and the Hope for the Future," in *Resurrection of the Dead: Biblical Traditions in Dialogue* (ed. Geert Van Oyen and Tom Shepherd; Leuven: Peeters, 2012), 319–42.

Lampe, Peter. *From Paul to Valentinus: Christians at Rome in the First Two Centuries* (Minneapolis: Fortress Press, 2003).

Lapide, Pinchas. *Paul: Rabbi and Apostle* (trans. Lawrence Denef; Minneapolis: Augsburg, 1984).

Larsen, Matthew D. C. *Gospels Before the Book* (New York: Oxford University Press, 2018).

Le Boulluec, Alain. *Le notion d'hérésie dans la literature grecque IIe–IIIe siècles* (Paris: Études augustiniennes, 1985).

Le Boulluec, Alain. "L'école d'Alexandrie: De quelques aventures d'un concept historiographique," in *Alexandrina: Hellénisme, judaïsme et christianisme à Alexandrie; Mélanges offerts à Claude Mondésert* (Paris: Cerf, 1987), 402–17.

Le Boulluec, Alain. "Aux origines, encore, de l'école d'Alexandrie," *Adamantius* 5 (1999): 7–36.

Lee, Pilchan. *The New Jerusalem in the Book of Revelation: A Study of Revelation 21–22 in the Light of Its Background in Jewish Tradition* (Tübingen: Mohr Siebeck, 2001).

Lévi-Strauss, Claude. *Totemism* (trans. Rodney Needham; Boston: Beacon Press, 1971).

Lieu, Judith. "'The Parting of the Ways': Theological Construct or Historical Reality?," *Journal for the Study of the New Testament* 56 (1994): 101–19.

Lieu, Judith. "Accusations of Jewish Persecution in Early Christian Sources, with Particular Reference to Justin Martyr and the *Martyrdom of Polycarp*," in *Tolerance and Intolerance in Early Judaism and Christianity* (ed. Graham Stanton and Guy Stroumsa; Cambridge: Cambridge University Press, 1998), 279–95.

Lieu, Judith. *Christian Identity in the Jewish and Graeco-Roman World* (Oxford: Oxford University Press, 2004).

Lieu, Judith. *Marcion and the Making of a Heretic: God and Scripture in the Second Century* (Cambridge: Cambridge University Press, 2015).

Lieu, Judith. "Modelling the Second Century as the Age of the Laboratory," in *Christianity in the Second Century: Themes and Developments* (ed. James Carleton Paget and Judith Lieu; Cambridge: Cambridge University Press, 2017), 294–308.

Lincoln, Bruce. *Apples and Oranges: Explorations In, On, and With Comparison* (Chicago: University of Chicago Press, 2018).

Lipsett, B. Diane. *Desiring Conversion: Hermas, Thecla, Aseneth* (Oxford: Oxford University Press, 2011).

Litwa, M. David. *We Are Being Transformed: Deification in Paul's Soteriology* (Berlin: Walter de Gruyter, 2012).

Löhr, Winrich. "Gnostic Determinism Reconsidered," *Vigiliae Christianae* 46 (1992): 381–90.

Löhr, Winrich. "Modelling Second-Century Christian Theology as *Philosophia*," in *Christianity in the Second Century: Themes and Developments* (ed. James Carleton Paget and Judith Lieu; Cambridge: Cambridge University Press, 2017), 151–68.

Long, A. A. "Freedom and Determinism in the Stoic Theory of Human Action," in *Problems in Stoicism* (ed. A. A. Long; London: Athlone Press, 1971), 173–99.

Long, A. A. *Hellenistic Philosophy: Stoics, Epicureans, Sceptics* (New York: Charles Scribner's Sons, 1974).

Long, A. A. *Epictetus: A Stoic and Socratic Guide to Life* (Oxford: Clarendon Press, 2002).

Long, A. A., and D. N. Sedley. *The Hellenistic Philosophers* (2 vols.; Cambridge: Cambridge University Press, 1987).

Longenecker, Bruce W. *Eschatology and the Covenant: A Comparison of 4 Ezra and Romans 1–11* (Sheffield: Sheffield Academic, 1991).

Luck, Georg. "Studia Divina in Vita Humana: On Cicero's 'Dream of Scipio' and Its Place in Graeco-Roman Philosophy," *Harvard Theological Review* 49.4 (1956): 207–18.

MacIntyre, Alasdair. *After Virtue: A Study in Moral Theory* (Notre Dame: University of Notre Dame Press, 1981).

MacIntyre, Alasdair. *Whose Reason? Which Rationality?* (Notre Dame: University of Notre Dame Press, 1988).

Maier, Harry. *The Social Setting of the Ministry as Reflected in the Writings of Hermas, Clement, and Ignatius* (Waterloo, ON: Wilfried Lauer University Press, 1991).

Maier, Harry. "From Material Place to Imagined Space: Emergent Christian Community as Thirdspace in the *Shepherd of Hermas*," in *Early Christian Communities Between Ideal and Reality* (ed. Mark Grundeken and Joseph Verheyden; Tübingen: Mohr Siebeck, 2015), 143–60.

Malherbe, Abraham. "Determinism and Freedom in Paul: The Argument of 1 Corinthians 8 and 9," in *Paul and His Hellenistic Context* (ed. Troels Engberg-Pedersen; Minneapolis: Fortress Press, 1994), 231–55.

Markschies, Christoph. *Valentinus Gnosticus? Untersuchungen zur valentinianischen Gnosis mit einem Kommentar zu den Fragmentem Valentins* (Tübingen: Mohr Siebeck, 1992).

Marshall, John. *Parables of War: Reading John's Jewish Apocalypse* (Waterloo, ON: Wilfrid Laurier University Press, 2001).

Marshall, John. "John's Jewish (Christian?) Apocalypse," in *Jewish Christianity Reconsidered: Rethinking Texts and Groups* (ed. Matt Jackson-McCabe; Minneapolis: Fortress Press, 2007), 233–56.

Marshall, John. "Misunderstanding the New Paul: Marcion's Transformation of the *Sonderzeit* Paul," *Journal of Early Christian Studies* 20.1 (2012): 1–29.

Martin, Dale. *The Corinthian Body* (New Haven, CT: Yale University Press, 1995).

Martin, Dale. "Paul and the Judaism/Hellenism Dichotomy: Toward a Social History of the Question," in *Paul Beyond the Judaism/Hellenism Divide* (ed. Troels Engberg-Pedersen; Louisville: Westminster John Knox Press, 2001), 29–61.

Martin, Dale. *Inventing Superstition: From the Hippocratics to the Christians* (Cambridge, MA: Harvard University Press, 2004).

Martin, Dale. "The Promise of Teleology, the Constraints of Epistemology, and Universal Vision in Paul," in *St. Paul Among the Philosophers* (ed. John D. Caputo and Linda Martin Alcoff; Bloomington: Indiana University Press, 2009), 91–108.

Mason, Steve. "Jews, Judaeans, Judaizing, Judaism: Problems of Categorization in Ancient History," *Journal for the Study of Judaism in the Persian, Hellenistic, and Roman Periods* 38 (2007): 457–512.

Mathewson, David. *A New Heaven and a New Earth: The Meaning and Function of the Old Testament in Revelation 21.1–22.5* (London: Sheffield Academic Press, 2003).

Matlock, R. Barry. *Unveiling the Apocalyptic Paul: Paul's Interpreters and the Rhetoric of Criticism* (Sheffield: Sheffield Academic Press, 1996).

McCue, James. "Conflicting Versions of Valentinianism? Irenaeus and the *Excerpta ex Theodoto*," in *The Rediscovery of Gnosticism*, vol. 1, *The School of Valentinus* (ed. Bentley Layton; Leiden: Brill, 1980), 404–16.

McKenna, Margaret Mary. "'The Two Ways' in Jewish and Christian Writings of the Greco-Roman Period: A Study of the Form of Repentance Parenesis" (PhD diss., University of Pennsylvania, 1981).

McKnight, Scot. *A Light Among the Gentiles: Jewish Missionary Activity in the Second Temple Period* (Minneapolis: Fortress Press, 1991).

Meeks, Wayne. *The Moral World of the First Christians* (Philadelphia: Westminster Press, 1986).

Meeks, Wayne. "Social Functions of Apocalyptic Language in Pauline Christianity," in *Apocalypticism in the Mediterranean World and the Near East: Proceedings of the International Colloquium on Apocalypticism in Uppsala, August 12–17, 1979* (ed. David Hellholm; 2nd ed.; Tübingen: J.C.B. Mohr (Paul Siebeck), 1989), 687–705.

Meeks, Wayne. *The Origins of Christian Morality: The First Two Centuries* (New Haven, CT: Yale University Press, 1993).

Meeks, Wayne. *The First Urban Christians: The Social World of the Apostle Paul* (2nd ed.; New Haven, CT: Yale University Press, 2003).

Meeks, Wayne, and John T. Fitzgerald, eds. *The Writings of Saint Paul: A Norton Critical Edition* (2nd ed.; New York: W. W. Norton, 2007).

Meyer, Marvin, ed. *The Nag Hammadi Scriptures* (New York: HarperOne, 2007).

Miller, Patricia Cox. "'All the Words Were Frightful': Salvation by Dreams in the *Shepherd of Hermas*," *Vigiliae Christianae* 44.4 (1988): 327–38.

Miller, Patricia Cox. *Dreams in Late Antiquity: Studies in the Imagination of a Culture* (Princeton, NJ: Princeton University Press, 1994).

Miller, Patricia Cox. "Dreaming the Body: An Aesthetics of Asceticism," in *Asceticism* (ed. Vincent Wimbush and Richard Valantasis; New York: Oxford University Press, 1995), 281–300.

Mitchell, Margaret M. *Paul and the Rhetoric of Reconciliation: An Exegetical Investigation into the Language and Composition of 1 Corinthians* (Tübingen: Mohr Siebeck, 1991).

Mitchell, Margaret M. "Pauline Accommodation and 'Condescension' (*sugkatabasis*): 1 Cor. 9:19–23 and the History of Influence," in *Paul Beyond the Judaism/Hellenism Divide* (ed. Troels Engberg-Pedersen; Louisville: Westminster John Knox Press, 2001), 197–214.

Mitchell, Margaret M. "Paul's Letters to Corinth: The Interpretative Intertwining of Literary and Historical Reconstruction," in *Urban Religion in Roman Corinth: Interdisciplinary Approaches* (ed. Daniel N. Schowalter and Steven Friesen; Cambridge, MA: Harvard University Press, 2005), 305–38.

Moss, Candida. *The Other Christs: Imitating Jesus in Ancient Christian Ideologies of Martyrdom* (Oxford: Oxford University Press, 2010).

Moss, Candida. *The Myth of Persecution: How Early Christians Invented a Story of Martyrdom* (New York: Harper Collins, 2013).

Nanos, Mark. *The Mystery of Romans: The Jewish Context of Paul's Letters* (Minneapolis: Fortress Press, 1996).

Nanos, Mark, and Magnus Zetterholm, eds. *Paul Within Judaism: Restoring the First-Century Context to the Apostle* (Minneapolis: Fortress Press, 2015).

Nickelsburg, George. *Jewish Literature Between the Bible and the Mishnah* (2nd ed.; Minneapolis: Fortress Press, 2005).

Nickelsburg, George, and James VanderKam. *1 Enoch: A New Translation* (Minneapolis: Fortress Press, 2004).

Nickodemus, Benjamin. "The Temporal World as Process in the *Apocryphon of John* and Origen of Alexandria" (unpublished paper).

Niederwimmer, Kurt. *The Didache: A Commentary* (trans. Linda Maloney; Minneapolis: Fortress Press, 1998).

Nongbri, Brent. *Before Religion: A History of a Modern Concept* (New Haven, CT: Yale University Press, 2013).

Nongbri, Brent. *God's Library: The Archeology of the Earliest Christian Manuscripts* (New Haven, CT: Yale University Press, 2018).

Novak, David. *The Image of the Non-Jew in Judaism: The Idea of the Noahide Law* (ed. Matthew Lagrone; 2nd ed.; Oxford: Littman Library of Jewish Civilization, 2011).

Novenson, Matthew. *Christ Among the Messiahs: Christ Language in Paul and Messiah Language in Ancient Judaism* (Oxford: Oxford University Press, 2012).

Novenson, Matthew. "Paul's Former Occupation in *Ioudaismos*," in *Galatians and Christian Theology: Justification, the Gospel, and Ethics in Paul's Letter* (ed. Mark W. Elliott et al.; Grand Rapids, MI: Baker Academic, 2014), 24–39.

Nussbaum, Martha. *Love's Knowledge: Essays on Philosophy and Literature* (New York: Oxford University Press, 1990).

Olson, Daniel C. *A New Rereading of the Animal Apocalypse of 1 Enoch: "All the Nations Shall Be Blessed"* (Leiden: Brill, 2013).

Osiek, Carolyn. *Rich and Poor in the Shepherd of Hermas: An Exegetical-Social Investigation* (Washington, DC: Catholic Biblical Association of America, 1983).

Osiek, Carolyn. "The Genre and Function of the *Shepherd of Hermas*," in *Early Christian Apocalypticism: Genre and Social Setting* (ed. Adela Yarbo Collins; Decatur, GA: Scholars Press, 1986), 113–21.

Osiek, Carolyn. "The Oral World of Early Christianity in Rome: The Case of Hermas," in *Judaism and Christianity in First-Century Rome* (ed. K. Donfried and P. Richardson; Grand Rapids, MI: Eerdmans, 1998), 151–72.

Osiek, Carolyn. *The Shepherd of Hermas: A Commentary* (Minneapolis: Fortress Press, 1999).

Pagels, Elaine. "The Valentinian Claim to Esoteric Exegesis of Romans as the Basis for Anthropological Theory," *Vigiliae Christianae* 26.4 (1972): 241–58.

Pagels, Elaine. *The Johannine Gospel in Gnostic Exegesis: Heracleon's Commentary on John* (SBLMS 17; Nashville: Abingdon Press, 1973).

Pagels, Elaine. "Conflicting Versions of Valentinian Eschatology: Irenaeus' *Treatise* vs. the *Excerpts from Theodotus*," *Harvard Theological Review* 67 (1974): 35–53.

Pagels, Elaine. "The Social History of Satan III: John of Patmos and Ignatius of Antioch—Contrasting Visions of 'God's People,'" in *Heresy and Identity in Late Antiquity* (ed. Eduard Iricinschi and Holger Zellentin; Tübingen: Mohr Siebeck, 2008), 231–52.

Pagels, Elaine. *Revelations: Visions, Prophecy, and Politics in the Book of Revelation* (New York: Viking, 2012).

Paget, James Carleton, and Judith Lieu, eds. *Christianity in the Second Century: Themes and Developments* (Cambridge: Cambridge University Press, 2017).

Pattemore, Stephen. *The People of God in the Apocalypse: Discourse, Structure, and Exegesis* (Cambridge: Cambridge University Press, 2004).

Perkins, Pheme. "Valentinians and the Christian Canon," in *Valentinianism: New Studies* (ed. Christoph Markschies and Einar Thomassen; Leiden: Brill, 2019), 371–99.

Pettipiece, Timothy. "The Nature of 'True Worship': Anti-Jewish and Anti-Gentile Polemic in Heracleon (Fragments 20–24)," in *L'Évangile selon Thomas et les textes de Nag Hammadi* (ed. Louis Painchaud and Paul-Hubert Poirier; Québec: Les Presses de l'Université Laval, 2007), 377–93.

Pleše, Zlatko. *Poetics of the Gnostic Universe: Narrative and Cosmology in the Apocryphon of John* (Leiden: Brill, 2006).

Pleše, Zlatko. "Evil and Its Sources in Gnostic Traditions," in *Die Wurzel allen Übels: Vorstellungen über die Herkunft des Bösen und Schlechten in der Philosophie und Religiondes 1.–4. Jahrhunderts* (Tübingen: Mohr Siebeck, 2014), 101–32.

Plotinus. *Ennead III* (trans. A. H. Armstrong; Loeb Classical Library; Cambridge, MA: Harvard University Press, 1967).

Räisänen, Heiki. "Paul, God, Israel: Romans 9–11 in Recent Scholarship," in *The Social World of Formative Christianity* (ed. J. Neusner et al.; Philadelphia: Fortress Press, 1988), 178–206.

Rasimus, Tuomas. *Paradise Reconsidered in Gnostic Mythmaking: Rethinking Sethianism in Light of the Ophite Evidence* (Leiden: Brill, 2009).

Reed, Annette Yoshiko. "The Trickery of the Fallen Angels and the Demonic Mimesis of the Divine: Aetiology, Demonology, and Polemics in the Writings of Justin Martyr," *Journal of Early Christian Studies* 12.2 (2004): 141–71.

Reed, Annette Yoshiko. *Fallen Angels and the History of Judaism and Christianity: The Reception of Enochic Literature* (Cambridge: Cambridge University Press, 2005).

Reiling, J. *Hermas and Christian Prophecy: A Study of the Eleventh Mandate* (Leiden: Brill, 1973).

Richardson, Peter. *Israel in the Apostolic Church* (Cambridge: Cambridge University Press, 1969).

Ricoeur, Paul. *Time and Narrative*. Vols. 1–3 (trans. Kathleen Blarney and David Pellauer; Chicago: University of Chicago Press, 1984–88).

Roberts, Alexander, and James Donaldson. *The Ante-Nicene Fathers*, vol. 1 (Peabody, MA: Hendrickson, 2004).

Rosen-Zvi, Ishay. *Demonic Desires: Yetzer Hara and the Problem of Evil in Late Antiquity* (Philadelphia: University of Pennsylvania Press, 2011).

Rosen-Zvi, Ishay, and Adi Ophir. "Paul and the Invention of the Gentiles," *Jewish Quarterly Review* 105.1 (2015): 1–41.

Rousseau, Philip. *Pachomius: The Making of a Community in Fourth-Century Egypt* (Berkeley: University of California Press, 1985).

Royalty, Robert. *The Streets of Heaven: The Ideology of Wealth in the Apocalypse of John* (Macon, GA: Mercer University Press, 1997).

Sagnard, François. *Clément d'Alexandrie: Extraits de Théodote* (1st ed., 1948; Paris, 1970).

Salles, Ricardo. *The Stoics on Determinism and Compatibilism* (Burlington, VT: Ashgate, 2005).

Sanders, E. P. *Paul and Palestinian Judaism: A Comparison of Patterns of Religion* (Minneapolis: Fortress Press, 1977).

Sanders, E. P. *Paul, the Law, and the Jewish People* (Philadelphia: Fortress Press, 1983).

Sanders, E. P. *Jesus and Judaism* (Philadelphia: Fortress Press, 1985).

Sanders, E. P. *Judaism: Practice and Belief, 63 BCE–66 CE* (London: SCM Press, 1992).

Sandmel, Samuel. "Parallelomania," *Journal of Biblical Literature* 81 (1962): 1–13.

Schäfer, Peter. "New Testament and Hekhalot Literature: The Journey into Heaven in Paul and in Merkavah Mysticism," in *Hekhalot-Studien* (Tübingen: Mohr Siebeck, 1988), 234–49.

Schäfer, Peter. *The Origins of Jewish Mysticism* (Princeton, NJ: Princeton University Press, 2011).

Schenke, Hans-Martin. "Das sethianische System nach Nag-Hammadi-Handschriften," in *Studia Coptica* (ed. Peter Nagel; Berlin: Akademie-Verlag, 1974), 165–73.

Schenke, Hans-Martin. "The Phenomenon and Significance of Gnostic Sethianism," in *The Rediscovery of Gnosticism*, vol. 2, *Sethian Gnosticism* (ed. Bentley Layton; Leiden: Brill, 1981), 588–616.

Schneemelcher, Wilhelm, ed. *New Testament Apocrypha (NTA)* (trans. R. McL. Wilson; 2 vols.; Louisville: Westminster John Knox Press, 2003).

Schüssler Fiorenza, Elisabeth. *Revelation: Vision for a Just World* (Minneapolis: Fortress Press, 1991).

Schüssler Fiorenza, Elisabeth. *The Book of Revelation: Justice and Judgment* (2nd ed.; Minneapolis: Augsburg Press, 1998).

Schwartz, Daniel R. "'Judaean' or 'Jew'? How Should We Translate IOUDAIOS in Josephus?," in *Jewish Identity in the Greco-Roman World/Jüdische Identität in der griechisch-römischen Welt* (ed. Jörg Frey, Daniel R. Schwartz, and Stephanie Gripentrog; Leiden: Brill, 2007), 3–27.

Schwartz, Seth. *Imperialism and Jewish Society: 200 B.C.E. to 640 C.E.* (Princeton, NJ: Princeton University Press, 2001).

Schweitzer, Albert. *The Mysticism of Paul the Apostle* (trans. W. Montgomery; 2nd ed.; London: A. & C. Black, 1953).

Scott, Alan B. "Churches or Books? Sethian Social Organization," *Journal of Early Christian Studies* 3.2 (1995): 109–22.

Sechrest, Love L. *A Former Jew: Paul and the Dialectics of Race* (London: T & T Clark, 2009).

Segal, Alan. *Paul the Convert: The Apostolate and Apostasy of Saul the Pharisee* (New Haven, CT: Yale University Press, 1990).

Segal, Alan. "Universalism in Judaism and Christianity," in *Paul in His Hellenistic Context* (ed. Troels Engberg-Pedersen; Edinburgh: T & T Clark, 1994), 1–29.

Sevrin, Jean-Marie. *Le dossier baptismal séthien: Études sur la sacramentaire gnostique* (Québec: Les Presses de l'Université Laval, 1986).

Sharples, R. W. *Alexander of Aphrodisias on Fate* (London: Duckworth, 1983).

Shaw, Brent. "The Divine Economy: Stoicism as Ideology," *Latomus* 64 (1985): 16–54.

Smith, Geoffrey. *Guilt by Association: Heresy Catalogues in Early Christianity* (Oxford: Oxford University Press, 2015).

Smith, Geoffrey. "The *Shepherd of Hermas, Mandates* V.2–VI.I," in *The Oxyrhynchus Papyri* (forthcoming).

Smith, Jonathan Z. "A Pearl of Great Price and a Cargo of Yams: A Study in Situational Incongruity," in *Imagining Religion: From Babylon to Jamestown* (Chicago: University of Chicago Press, 1982), 90–101.

Smith, Jonathan Z. *To Take Place: Toward a Theory in Ritual* (Chicago: University of Chicago Press, 1987).

Smith, Jonathan Z. *Drudgery Divine: On the Comparison of Early Christianities and the Religions of Late Antiquity* (Chicago: University of Chicago Press, 1990).

Smith, Jonathan Z. *Map Is Not Territory: Studies in the History of Religion* (Chicago: University of Chicago Press, 1993).

Smith, Morton. "History of the Term *Gnostikos*," in *The Rediscovery of Gnosticism*, vol. 2, *Sethian Gnosticism* (ed. Bentley Layton; Leiden: Brill, 1981), 796–807.

Snyder, H. Gregory. *Teachers and Texts in the Ancient World: Philosophers, Jews, and Christians* (London: Routledge, 2000).

Snyder, H. Gregory. "'Above the Baths of Myrtinus': Justin Martyr's 'School' in the City of Rome," *Harvard Theological Review* 100.3 (2007): 335–62.

Sorabji, Richard. *Necessity, Cause, and Blame: Perspectives on Aristotle's Theory* (Chicago: University of Chicago University Press, 1980).

Stark, Rodney, and William Sims Bainbridge. *The Future of Religion: Secularization, Revival, and Cult Formation* (Berkeley: University of California Press, 1985).

Starr, R. J. "The Circulation of Literary Texts in the Roman World," *Classical Quarterly* 37.1 (1987): 213–23.

Stendahl, Krister. "Call Rather Than Conversion," in *Paul Among Jews and Gentiles* (Minneapolis: Fortress Press, 1976), 7–23.

Stendahl, Krister. *Paul Among Jews and Gentiles* (Minneapolis: Fortress Press, 1976).

Stendahl, Krister. *Final Account: Paul's Letter to the Romans* (Minneapolis: Fortress Press, 1995).

Stock, Brian. *Listening for the Text: On the Uses of the Past* (Baltimore: John Hopkins University Press, 1990).

Stone, Michael Edward. *Fourth Ezra: A Commentary* (Minneapolis: Fortress Press, 1990).

Stough, Charlotte. "Stoic Determinism and Moral Responsibility," in *The Stoics* (ed. John Rist; Berkeley: University of California Press, 1978), 203–31.

Stout, Jeffrey. *The Flight from Authority: Religion, Morality, and the Quest for Autonomy* (Notre Dame: University of Notre Dame Press, 1981).

Stowers, Stanley. *The Diatribe and Paul's Letter to the Romans* (Chico, CA: Scholar's Press, 1981).

Stowers, Stanley. *Letter Writing in Greco-Roman Antiquity* (Philadelphia: Westminster, 1986).

Stowers, Stanley. "Friends and Enemies in the Politics of Heaven: Reading Theology in Philippians," in *Pauline Theology*, vol. 1, *Thessalonians, Philippians, Galatians, Philemon* (ed. Jouette Bassler; Minneapolis: Fortress Press, 1991), 105–22.

Stowers, Stanley. *A Rereading of Romans: Justice, Jews, and Gentiles* (New Haven, CT: Yale University Press, 1994).

Stowers, Stanley. "What Is Pauline Participation in Christ?," in *Redefining First-Century Jewish and Christian Identities: Essays in Honor of Ed Parish Sanders* (ed. Fabian E. Udoh; Notre Dame: University of Notre Dame Press, 2008), 352–71.

Stowers, Stanley. "The Concept of 'Community' and the History of Early Christianity," *Method and Theory in the Study of Religion* 23.3/4 (2011): 238–56.

Stuckenbruck, Loren. *Angel Veneration and Christology: A Study in Early Judaism and in the Christology of the Apocalypse of John* (Tübingen: Mohr Siebeck, 1995).

Stuckenbruck, Loren. "The 'Angels' and 'Giants' of Genesis 6:1–4 in Second- and Third-Century BCE Jewish Interpretation: Reflections on the Posture of Early Apocalyptic Traditions," *Dead Sea Discoveries* 7.3 (2000): 354–77.

Stuckenbruck, Loren. "The Eschatological Worship of God by the Nations: An Inquiry into the Early Enoch Tradition," in *With Wisdom as a Robe: Qumran and Other Jewish Studies in Honour of Ida Fröhlich* (ed. Károly Dániel Dobos and Miklós Köszeghy; Sheffield: Phoenix Press, 2009), 189–206.

Suggs, M. Jack. "The Christian Two Ways Tradition: Its Antiquity, Form, and Function," in *Studies in New Testament and Early Christian Literature: Essays in Honor of Allen P. Wikgren* (ed. David Edward Aune; Leiden: Brill, 1972), 60–74.

Talbert, Charles H. "Paul, Judaism, and the Revisionists," *Catholic Bible Quarterly* 63 (2001): 1–22.

Taylor, Joan. "The Phenomenon of Early Jewish Christianity: Reality or Scholarly Invention?," *Vigiliae Christianae* 44 (1990): 313–34.

Theissen, Gerd. *Sociology of Early Palestinian Christianity* (trans. John Bowden; Philadelphia: Fortress Press, 1978).

Thiessen, Matthew. *Contesting Conversion: Genealogy, Circumcision, and Identity in Ancient Judaism and Christianity* (Oxford: Oxford University Press, 2011).

Thiessen, Matthew. *Paul and the Gentile Problem* (New York: Oxford University Press, 2016).

Thiessen, Matthew. "Paul, the Animal Apocalypse, and Abraham's Gentile Seed," in *The Ways That Often Parted: Essays in Honor of Joel Marcus* (ed. Lori Baron et al.; Atlanta: SBL Press, 2018), 65–78.

Thomassen, Einar. *Le traité tripartite (NH I, 5): Texte établi, introduit et commenté par Einar Thomassen; traduit par Louis Painchaud et Einar Thomassen* (Québec: Les Presses de l'Université Laval, 1989).

Thomassen, Einar. "Notes pour la délimitation d'un corpus valentinien à Nag Hammadi," in *Les textes de Nag Hammadi et la problème de leur classification* (ed. Louis Painchaud and Anne Pasquier; Québec: Les Presses de l'Université Laval, 1995), 243–59.

Thomassen, Einar. "Revelation as Book and Book as Revelation: Reflections on the *Gospel of Truth*," in *The Nag Hammadi Texts in the History of Religions* (ed. S. Giversen et al.; Copenhagen: C.A. Reitzel, 2002), 35–45.

Thomassen, Einar. "Orthodoxy and Heresy in Second-Century Rome," *Harvard Theological Review* 97.3 (2004): 241–56.

Thomassen, Einar. *Spiritual Seed: The Church of the "Valentinians"* (Leiden: Brill, 2008).

Thomassen, Einar. "Valentinian Ideas About Salvation as Transformation," in *Metamorphoses: Resurrection, Body, and Transformative Practices in Early Christianity* (ed. Turid Karlsen Seim and Jorunn Økland; Berlin: Walter de Gruyter, 2009), 169–87.

Thomassen, Einar. "Heracleon," in *The Legacy of John: Second-Century Reception of the Fourth Gospel* (ed. Tuomas Rasimus; Leiden: Brill, 2010), 173–210.

Thomassen, Einar. "Saved by Nature? The Question of Human Races and Soteriological Determinism in Valentinianism," in *Zugänge zur Gnosis: Akten zur Tagung der Patristischen Arbeitsgemeinschaft vom 02.–05.01.2011 in Berlin-Spandau* (ed. Christoph Markschies and Johannes van Oort; Leuven: Peeters, 2013), 129–49.

Thomassen, Einar. "The Valentinian Materials in *James* (NHC V, 3 and CT, 2)," in *Beyond the Gnostic Gospels: Studies Building on the Work of Elaine Pagels* (ed. Nicola Denzey et al.; Tübingen: Mohr Siebeck, 2013), 79–90.

Thompson, Leonard L. *The Book of Revelation: Apocalypse and Empire* (Oxford: Oxford University Press, 1990).

Thorsteinsson, Runar M. *Paul's Interlocutor in Romans 2: Function and Identity in the Context of Ancient Epistolography* (Stockholm: Almqvist and Wiksell, 2003).

Tite, Philip. *Valentinian Ethics and Paraenetic Discourse: Determining the Social Function of Moral Exhortation in Valentinian Christianity* (Leiden: Brill, 2009).

Townsend, Philippa. "Who Were the First Christians? Jews, Gentiles, and the *Christianoi*," in *Heresy and Identity in Late Antiquity* (ed. Eduard Iricinschi and Holger Zellentin; Tübingen: Mohr Siebeck, 2008), 212–30.

Townsend, Philippa. "Another Race? Ethnicity, Universalism, and the Emergence of Christianity" (PhD diss., Princeton University, 2009).

Trevett, Christine. "'I Have Heard from Some Teachers': The Second-Century Struggle for Forgiveness and Reconciliation," in *Retribution, Repentance, and Reconciliation* (ed. Kate Cooper and Jeremy Gregory; Woodbridge: The Boydell Press, 2004), 5–28.

Trumbower, Jeffrey. *Born from Above: The Anthropology of the Gospel of John* (Tübingen: Mohr Siebeck, 1992).

Turner, John. "Ritual in Gnosticism," in *Gnosticism and Later Platonism: Themes, Figures, and Texts* (ed. John Turner and Ruth Majercik; Atlanta: Society of Biblical Literature, 2000), 83–139.

Turner, John. *Sethian Gnosticism and the Platonic Tradition* (Québec: Les Presses de l'Université Laval, 2001).

Turner, John. "The Sethian Baptismal Rite," in *Coptic, Gnosica, Manichaica: Mélanges offerts à Wolf-Peter Funk* (ed. Louis Painchaud and Paul-Hubert Poirer; Québec: Les Presses de l'Université Laval, 2006), 941–92.

Turner, John. "Sethian Gnosticism: A Revised Literary History," in *Actes du huitième congrès international d'études coptes, Paris, 28 juin–3 juillet 2004*, vol. 2 (ed. N. Bosson and A. Boud'hors; Leuven: Peeters, 2007), 899–908.

Turner, John. "The Sethian School of Gnostic Thought," in *The Nag Hammadi Scriptures* (ed. Marvin Meyer; New York: HarperCollins, 2007), 784–89.

Turner, John. "Johannine Legacy: The Gospel and Apocryphon of John," in *The Legacy of John: Second-Century Reception of the Fourth Gospel* (ed. Tuomas Rasimus; Leiden: Brill, 2010), 105–44.

Valantasis, Richard. "Adam's Body: Uncovering Esoteric Traditions in the *Apocryphon of John* and Origen's *Dialogue with Heraclides*," *Second Century* 7 (1989–90): 150–62.

van den Broek, Roelof. "The Creation of Adam's Psychic Body in the *Apocryphon of John*," in *Studies in Gnosticism and Hellenistic Religions Presented to Gilles Quispel on the Occasion of His Sixty-Fifth Birthday* (Leiden: Brill, 1981), 38–57.

van den Broek, Roelof. "The Christian 'School' of Alexandria in the Second and Third Centuries," in *Studies in Gnosticism and Alexandrian Christianity* (ed. Roelof van den Broek; Leiden: Brill, 1996), 197–205.

van den Hoek, Annewies. "The 'Catechetical' School of Early Christian Alexandria and Its Philonic Heritage," *Harvard Theological Review* 90.1 (1997): 59–87.

Vielhauer, Philipp, and Georg Strecker. "Apocalyptic in Early Christianity," in *New Testament Apocrypha (NTA)* (ed. Wilhelm Schneemelcher; trans. R. McL. Wilson; 2 vols.; Louisville: Westminster John Knox Press, 2003), 592–602.

Völker, Walther. *Quellen zur Geschichte der christlichen Gnosis* (Sammlung ausgewählter kirchen und dogmengeschichtlicher Quellenschriften, Neue Folge 5; Tübingen: Mohr-Siebeck, 1932).

Vonnegut, Kurt. *Slaughterhouse-Five or the Children's Crusade* (New York: Random House, 1969).

Vonnegut, Kurt. *Timequake* (New York: Penguin, 1997).

Wagner, J. Ross. *Heralds of the Good News: Isaiah and Paul in Concert in the Letter to the Romans* (Leiden: Brill, 2003).

Waldstein, Michael, and Frederik Wisse. *The Apocryphon of John: Synopsis of NHC II,1; III,1; and IV, 1 with BG 8502, 2* (Leiden: Brill, 1995).

Wasserman, Emma. *The Death of the Soul in Romans 7: Sin, Death, and the Law in Light of Hellenistic Moral Psychology* (Tübingen: Mohr Siebeck, 2008).

Watson, Francis. *Paul, Judaism, and the Gentiles: Beyond the New Perspective*: Grand Rapids, MI: Eerdmans, 2007).

Watts, Edward J. *City and School in Late Antique Athens and Alexandria* (Berkeley: University of California Press, 2006.

White, L. Michael. "Moral Pathology: Passions, Progress, and Protreptic in Clement of Alexandria," in *Passions and Moral Progress in Greco-Roman Thought* (ed. John T. Fitzgerald; London: Routledge, 2008), 284–321.

Williams, Michael. "The *Life of Antony* and the Domestication of Charismatic Wisdom," in *Charisma and Sacred Biography* (ed. Michael Williams; Chambersburg, PA: American Academy of Religion, 1982), 23–45.

Williams, Michael. *The Immovable Race: A Gnostic Designation and the Theme of Stability in Late Antiquity* (Leiden: Brill, 1985).

Williams, Michael. *Rethinking Gnosticism: An Argument for Dismantling a Dubious Category* (Princeton, NJ: Princeton University Press, 1996).

Williams, Michael. "Response to Papers of Karen King, Frederik Wisse, Michael Waldstein, and Sergio La Porta," in *The Nag Hammadi Library After Fifty Years: Proceedings of the 1995 Society of Biblical Literature Commemoration* (ed. John Turner and Anne McGuire; Leiden: Brill, 1997), 208–213.

Williams, Michael. "Negative Theologies and Demiurgical Myths in Late Antiquity," in *Gnosticism and Later Platonism: Themes, Figures, and Texts* (ed. John Turner and Ruth Majercik; Atlanta: Society of Biblical Literature, 2000), 277–302.

Williams, Michael. "Sethianism," in *A Companion to Second-Century Christian "Heretics"* (ed. Antti Marjanen and Petri Luomanen; Leiden: Brill, 2008), 32–63.

Williams, Michael. "Did Plotinus' 'Friends' Still Go to Church? Communal Rituals and Ascent Apocalypses," in *Gnosticism, Platonism, and the Late Ancient World* (ed. Kevin Corrigan and Tuomas Rasimus; Leiden: Brill, 2013), 495–522.

Williams, Michael. "A Life Full of Meaning and Purpose: Demiurgical Myths and Social Implications," in *Beyond the Gnostic Gospels: Studies Building on the Work of Elaine Pagels* (ed. Eduard Iricinschi et al.; Tübingen: Mohr Siebeck, 2013), 19–59.

Williams, Sam K. "Promise in Galatians: Paul's Reading of Scripture," *Journal of Biblical Literature* 107.4 (1988): 709–20.

Wilson, J. Christian. *Toward a Reassessment of the Shepherd of Hermas: Its Date and Pneumatology* (Lewiston, NY: Edwin Mellon Press, 1993).

Wilson, William Jerome. "The Career of the Prophet Hermas," *Harvard Theological Review* 20 (1927): 21–62.

Wisse, Fredrik. "Stalking Those Elusive Sethians," in *The Rediscovery of Gnosticism,* vol. 2, *Sethian Gnosticism* (ed. Bentley Layton; Leiden: Brill, 1981), 565–76.

Wisse, Fredrik. "Prolegomena to the Study of the New Testament and Gnosis," in *The New Testament and Gnosis: Essays in Honour of Robert McL. Wilson* (ed. A. H. B. Logan et al.; Edinburgh: T & T Clark, 1983), 138–45.

Wucherpfennig, Ansgar. *Heracleon Philologus: Gnostische Johannesexegese im zweiten Jahrhundert* (WUNT 142; Tübingen: Mohr Siebeck, 2002).

Yarbo Collins, Adela. "The Early Christian Apocalypses," in *Semeia 14: Apocalypse; A Morphology of a Genre* (ed. John J. Collins; Atlanta: Society of Biblical Literature, 1979), 61–121.

Yarbo Collins, Adela. *Crisis and Catharsis: The Power of the Apocalypse* (Philadelphia: Westminster Press, 1984).

Yarbo Collins, Adela. "Insiders and Outsiders in the Book of Revelation and Its Social Context," in *"To See Ourselves as Others See Us": Christians, Jews, "Others" in Late Antiquity* (ed. Jacob Neusner and Ernest S. Frerichs; Chico, CA: Scholars Press, 1985), 187–218.

Yarbo Collins, Adela. "Vilification and Self-Definition in the Book of Revelation," *Harvard Theological Review* 79.1 (1986): 308–20.

Yuval, Israel. *Two Nations in Your Womb: Perceptions of Jews and Christians in the Middle Ages* (Berkeley: University of California Press, 2003).

Zetterholm, Magnus. *Approaches to Paul: A Student's Guide to Recent Scholarship* (Minneapolis: Fortress Press, 2009).

Index

Acknowledgments

It is a pleasure to acknowledge and thank the many people who have contributed to this project. I would like to thank my doctoral supervisor, Elaine Pagels, for striving to make me a better writer and clearer thinker. I thank Martha Himmelfarb for her incomparable instruction on Second Temple Judaism, for saving me from many embarrassing errors, and for all her encouragement over the years. I owe a great debt to Christian Wildberg for allowing me to join the Princeton Hermetic Lodge and also for asking me one of (if not *the*) best question I received in graduate school. I am also deeply grateful to AnneMarie Luijendijk, who took the time to read through the Pauline corpus with me during my first year; many of the arguments that I went on to make started to percolate during this reading group. Although I only ever had the opportunity to take the one class from him, Jeff Stout changed my way of thinking about a number of important issues. Naphtali Meshel provided great insights into Revelation and Isaiah. John Gager's comments and criticisms helped me to clarify my discussion of Paul. I also have had the pleasure of studying with a number of my scholarly heroes, from whom I learned a great deal while at Princeton, including Peter Brown, Harriet Flower, Kathleen McVey, Peter Schäfer, and Brent Shaw.

While at the University of Washington, I had the very great privilege of studying with Michael Williams. It was incredibly fortuitous that I studied with Mike—he has been a constant source of timely criticisms and warm support for a decade. Ruby Blondell, Martin Jaffee, Joel Walker, and Jim Wellman have all taught me much and provided me with great advice. Furthermore, I thank my many wonderful professors at the University of Minnesota who tempted me away from being a math major with their infectious love of their subject matter. Most especially, I thank Melissa Sellew and Oliver Nicholson, who patiently tolerated my incessant questions and debates for years. Thank you also to Calvin Roetzel who was the faculty sponsor for my UROP (undergraduate research opportunity) project on the Apostle Paul in the Second-Century.

I have been truly blessed to have wonderful colleagues over the years. I learned an incalculable amount from Lance Jenott and Geoff Smith. Ben Nickodemus has been and continues to be a challenging and highly entertaining conversation partner. Christian Bull has guided me through the streets of Paris, Rome, and Oslo, charitably argued over Hermetica, and provided a lot of unexpected entertainment. Mika Ahuvia, Simon Oswald, and Jamey Walters were wonderful classmates and friends. I am also grateful for the participants in the Religion of Mediterranean Antiquity group, namely Aryeh Amihay, A. J. Berkovitz, Sarit Kattan-Gribetz, David Grossberg, and David Jorgensen. Although they passed through the program well ahead of me, Adam Becker, Derek Krueger, and Moulie Vidas were all kind enough to offer me excellent advice whenever I spoke with them.

I am indebted to a number of additional mentors and colleagues that I have met over the years. John Turner and his wife, Elizabeth, hosted me for "Coptic Camp" in the summer of 2009; and although I could not eat any Nebraskan corn on the cob because of my broken jaw, the Turners were so warm and welcoming they only *slightly* held this against me during my month-long stay with them. I also thank the many Nag Hammadi friends and colleagues who have sharpened and shaped my thinking over the years, especially Dylan Burns, Jean-Daniel Dubois, Ismo Dunderberg, Greg Given, Tilde Bak Halvgaard, Judith Kovacs, Hugo Lundhaug, Jörgen Magnusson, Christoph Markschies, Nanna Liv Olsen, Tuomas Rasimus, and Einar Thomassen. I owe a special and lasting debt to Einar; he has read and improved a number of my papers as well as invited me to participate in conferences and workshops all over the world. Similarly, Ismo has been a willing, insightful, but also patient interlocutor who has prompted me to refine my views on a number of Valentinian authors.

Part of Chapter 1 was previously published as "A Hierarchy of Salvation in the Book of Revelation: Different Peoples, Dwellings, and Tasks in the End Times," in *Placing Ancient Texts: The Ritual and Rhetorical Use of Space* (ed. Mika Ahuvia and Alexander Kocar; Tübingen: Mohr Siebeck, 2018), 101–30. Part of chapter 5 was published as "The Ethics of Higher and Lower Levels of Salvation in the *Excerpts of Theodotus* and the *Tripartite Tractate*," in *Valentinianism: New Studies* (ed. Christoph Markschies and Einar Thomassen; Leiden: Brill, 2019), 205–38.

I thank the editors and staff at UPenn, especially Jerry Singerman and Zoe Kovacs, for all their guidance. I must single out Derek Krueger again for his beyond generous willingness to read drafts and offer terrific feedback on them. Thank you also to the anonymous reviewers for their fruitful comments and questions.

Finally, I thank my family and friends. Thank you Joe, Matt, and John for insisting I take a break and come camping. Thank you, Sam, for all the cappuccinos. Thank you to my mom, Vanessa, and Ian for your love and support. Most of all, thank you to Meghan, Gwen, Heidi, and Iggy. Words simply cannot express how thankful I am for Meghan, so I will not even try. I love you, Meghan. You are kind and intelligent beyond measure, and I dedicate this book to you.

CPSIA information can be obtained
at www.ICGtesting.com
Printed in the USA
JSHW021056010621
15419JS00002B/2

9 780812 253269